To Nancy

Make Life an Adventure!

All the Best,

Michael Modzelewski

ANGELES CREST

ALSO BY MICHAEL MODZELEWSKI

Inside Passage: Living With Killer Whales,
Bald Eagles and Kwakiutl Indians

ANGELES CREST

A MEMOIR

Michael Modzelewski

ADVENTURES UNLIMITED
alaska • wyoming • florida • chile

Published by ADVENTURES UNLIMITED
Jackson Hole, Wyoming
www.pride-net.com/adventures

Library of Congress Catalog Card Number: 99-63270
ISBN 0-9660625-9-0

Book Design by Karen Wheeler
kwheeler@alltel.net

Grateful acknowledgment is made to the following for permission to reprint previously published material: *DOVER PUBLICATIONS*: Excerpt from *MAGIC AND MYSTERY IN TIBET by Alexandra David-Neel, Copyright © 1932. WEIDENFELD AND NICHOLSON PRESS*: Excerpt from *WHERE THE GODS ARE MOUNTAINS: THREE YEARS AMONG THE PEOPLES OF THE HIMALAYAS* by Rene von Nebesky-Wojkowitz, Copyright © 1956. *THAMES & HUDSON LTD. LONDON*: Excerpt from *KUNDALINI: THE AROUSAL OF THE INNER ENERGY* by Ajit Mookerjee, Copyright © 1982.

Portions of this book previously appeared in different form in *Sports Illustrated, Sierra Heritage, Wine Country* and *Master Chef* magazines, and *The Los Angeles Times, Napa Valley Times* and *Palm Beach Post* newspapers.

Manufactured in the United States of America

First Edition

For Scott

"*The camera's eye*
Does not lie,
But it cannot show
The life within,
The life of a runner"
—W. H. Auden, "Runner"

"*Men go forth to wonder at the heights of mountains, the huge waves of the sea,*
the broad flow of the rivers, the vast compass of the ocean, the courses of the stars;
and they pass by themselves without wondering."
—St. Augustine, *Confessions*

"*Great ideas originate in the muscles.*"
—Thomas Edison

"*There's no sensation to compare with this*
Suspended animation, a state of bliss
Can't keep my mind from the circling sky
Tongue-tied & twisted just an earthbound misfit, I."
—Pink Floyd, "Learning To Fly"

Author's Note

In an effort to safeguard the privacy of certain individuals, their names have been changed, along with identifying details. As for the book's structure, the large type describes The Angeles Crest 100 Mile Endurance Run in the present tense; and the passages in smaller type are memories and reflections. There are no dividing chapters. Like life, itself, the book is all one flow, with mile markers atop pages for orientation. Although our lives seem to proceed in a linear fashion, as I learned, time doesn't really exist and memory is elliptical, rolling back and forth—flinging up experiences like fragments in a mosaic.

I am honored by your presence. Thank you, reader, for your participation!

There is no sleeping the night before you run 100 miles. If it's your first ultra marathon, you are kept awake by the fear of the unknown, wondering if you really have it in you to go a distance far-beyond what you have ever run before. If you have finished one or more ultras, raw fear has abated, but with the previous memory seared indelibly throughout your being, you're now in a state of hyper-arousal with mind and body marshaling their forces, readying all systems on "Full-Alert" for the immense challenge only a few hours away.

I lay restless on a futon on the floor of a small, rented ski chalet in Wrightwood, California, awaiting the start of The Angeles Crest 100 Mile Endurance Run. My brother, Scott, is temporarily dozing in the bed above, and family (our support crew) are sleeping in the other rooms. Lying there wide-awake in the darkness, I think of my younger brother and how far he has come to be here. I think of Ed "Big Mo" Modzelewski, football great and loving father—now listening to the ebb-and-flow of his snoring just as I used to for so many years; and on that sonorous rhythm my mind drifts back home to suburban Cleveland, Ohio where we were raised. It is comforting now to go there, to dwell a bit in the secure past, taking my mind away from what's ahead. Of all the rooms in our Cleveland home, I thought most of the basement; how I would go down there as if entering church, spending hours alone in awe of my father. On the knotty pine walls, Dad displayed his all-American college trophies, plaques, awards and NFL action photos. He was a first round draft-choice of the Pittsburgh Steelers in 1952 (after defeating Tennessee in the Sugar Bowl for the collegiate championship by single-handedly, as a fullback, gaining more yardage than the entire UT offense combined). He entered the NFL when it was still a game and not yet taken-over by greed and rampant commercialism. A number one pick today would be guaranteed millions, but Dad was paid the grand total of $10,000 plus a signing bonus check for $2,000 that the kid from the impoverished Polish coal-mining town of West Natrona, PA, gratefully took out of his shirt pocket at every red light on the way home to make sure a few of the zeroes hadn't fallen off. He couldn't believe they were actually paying him to play a game!

With five sleepless hours to pass before the start of the race, I thought back to how when I was a child my father worried me. Every Sunday during the fall he would come home physically battered. His arms were swollen and contused, and his right shoulder usually drooped lower than his left. Once he came in with 12 stitches in his bottom lip and another time his thumb had been yanked so far out of its socket that for months Dad had to shake hands with only four fingers. Always his fingers were sprained and scraped raw.

Dad, where do you go every Sunday? You can tell me, I won't tell Mom. Who does this to you, huh? Tell me and I'll help you fight 'em! Nobody pushes my dad around. But Dad . . . Why? Why do you do it?

One Sunday evening after he had collapsed in his big chair, I walked over to him, carefully climbed up on his knee and demanded an explanation. He hugged me tight against his chest and whispered in my ear, "Mickey, I do this so you and your mother can have plenty to eat and nice clothes to wear."

That's all?

I questioned my mother when Dad was gone: "Where does he go every Sunday and why does he come home looking like that?" She told me that he went to work. Well, my buddies all had dads who went to work, but none of them came home pounded out of shape like mine.

One Friday, Mother and I went to the airport to wave good-bye to Dad. We watched as he boarded the plane with a crowd of men who all resembled one another; everyone had short hair and big shoulders. Mom said that Dad was going to Los Angeles in California.

That Sunday after church I went upstairs to my room. Mom was busy in the basement. I was quietly looking at a book when suddenly I heard yelling downstairs. I raced down and found Mom alone, sitting on the couch watching the TV set. I walked over to her and put my hand on her shoulder, but she didn't seem to see me or feel me. She kept staring at the TV, biting her nails and jiggling her legs up and down. I glanced at the television and saw something very peculiar—a man wearing a numbered costume and a strange hat was running with a ball and everyone was trying to slam him to the ground. I sat down next to Mom on the couch, put my arm around her and watched the fighting in amazement.

"Oh Mickey, that's your father! Do you see him? There he is . . . No. 36. That's Daddy!"

"What?"

Sure enough, the TV announcer kept repeating Dad's name. *So those are the guys who beat him up.*

"But Mom, it's not fair, all of those guys picking on Dad at once!" Mother then finally explained my father's job.

He arrived home late that Sunday from the West Coast. This time his other shoulder drooped and one of his eyes was swollen shut, but he wore a wide grin on his face. My dad picked me up, tucked me tightly under his arm like the football I had seen him carrying and started pacing around the dining-room table telling Mom all about the game. Suddenly our house was filled with people. Everyone kissed Mom, and the men shook hands with Dad and playfully slapped him on his bad shoulder.

Mr. Jordan kept following Dad around the house, slapping his shoulder and calling him a "champ." Mr. Jordan lived across the street and he never uttered a basic seven-word sentence without using three or four cuss words. Champ wasn't in my vocabulary then, so knowing Mr. Jordan, I thought it was a profanity directed toward my father. I watched Dad closely to see how he would react. He kept smiling. I overheard Mrs. Krupinsky whisper to Mom, "Whatever are you and Ed going to do with all of the championship money?" The next morning before I left for school, I asked Mom what champ and championship meant. She said that it meant that Dad's team was the best. "So that means Daddy is the best player in the whole wide world, right, Mom?" She chuckled and I think she nodded her head.

The next season my neighborhood buddies and I started watching football on TV and every Sunday we went through the same ritual. We would all gather in my basement to see the Browns play. At half-time we would rush into the street, pick teams, throw the ball around and then rush back down to the basement to view the second half. At the crack of the final gun, we all raced back outside to begin the game of imitating our heroes.

To transform a pot holed street into a gridiron requires a bit of creative vision. Two telephone poles were chosen as goal posts. Approximately halfway between them was a fireplug that, if passed, was an automatic first down. The outer edges of the sidewalks served as sidelines. Trees and parked cars were extra blockers. For two hours late on Sunday afternoons we put our own identities aside and became Renfro, Graham, Groza, Gibron, Lavelli or Modzelewski. We each took one of our T shirts and brown paint and put our alter ego's number on the front and back. Once after I darted from the fireplug all the way to the telephone pole, Gordon, the fat kid who was the permanent center, whispered to me as we huddled for the extra point. "Geez, Mick, you run just like your dad!"

The season finished in December with Cleveland on top and we clobbered the guys from two streets over. Summer came quickly and Dad said good-bye. He left in early July to go to training camp. We shook hands firmly and I promised to take good care of Mom. I didn't see him again until one day in late August when Mom and I drove out for a visit.

For a youngster, the Browns training camp was a comfortable place. Dad moaned about camp, curfews, not seeing Mom and the double practices. I couldn't sympathize with him. Cows and horses were all around, and you could run through acres of green fields without any telephone poles in the way.

After practice we walked over to a large shady tree and sat down. I couldn't keep still, so I ran down to the practice fields and charged at the tackling bag as I had seen the big guys do. I kept calling to Dad to watch me, but he ignored my pleas and I ran back toward the tree to attract his attention. When I got close, I could hear that he and Mom were conversing in low voices. That meant that I should be silent and not interrupt. I sat on the grass to listen. Dad kept repeating two phrases over and over, "The handwriting's on the wall," and "I feel like the guy who played behind Babe Ruth." I knew who Babe Ruth was and I couldn't figure out what he had to do with football and my father. I didn't understand what he was talking about, but I knew Mom did because she was dabbing her eyes with a tissue.

When the season started, something was terribly wrong—my father didn't play. Someone else was the fullback, someone I had never seen before. I was accustomed to seeing 36 out there, but now suddenly it was 32.

Dad was talking on the phone one night early in the season with my Uncle Dick, a defensive tackle with the New York Giants: "Yes . . . yes, he's everything they said. Paul figured it would take him a year or two to pick up the system, but he's coming fast . . . yes . . . Dick, mark my words, he's going to be a great one, even better than Motley. He's a natural back with fluid power . . . . What? . . . Yes . . . well, I have a feeling that I may be traded to this new expansion club out in Dallas . . . I don't know. I may go ahead with the restaurant. As long as Jimmy Brown is in Cleveland, the Browns will be a threat . . . . Dick, mark my words, this guy can carry a team . . . . "

About that time, Dad started taking me to practice with him every Saturday morning. I sat on his dressing stool and looked over this new man Brown. I refused to believe that my father could ever have his job taken away by anyone human, but after studying Mr. Brown I had to make an exception. Watching him move, whether it was in the locker room or out on the football field, was a lesson in kinesiology. He was like Nat Cole's music: smooth and deliberate with absolutely no wasted motion. When he walked naked around the locker room, it seemed that while a few of his leg muscles flexed, all the others were resting, in a peculiar way that left them relaxed, but still poised.

One Saturday, Mr. Brown came over to borrow a jockstrap. He looked down at me as he spoke with Dad and my cheeks became flushed. He smiled an easy grin and put out his hand for me to shake. It was huge and covered with red nicks just like Dad's. I put my hand in his and closed my eyes thinking that he would squeeze it hard, but as soon as my fingers touched his, he was gone.

I also started going to the Browns home games at Municipal Stadium. Those Sundays were special to me. I never felt as alive as I did sitting with 80,000 other people cheering for Dad's team. My spine tingled every time Cleveland scored, and I always broke out in pre-game goose bumps during the player introductions. The public-address announcer would boom out 11 names and after each we would roar our approval. Brown was always the last one out. For all I know, the announcer never said his name; all I ever heard was, "And at fullback . . . . " Then the crowd would scream as 32 jogged slowly under the goal post with the bright orange helmet in his hand.

For the next 2 1/2 hours, the stadium would resound with cheers and thunderous applause for Brown. A wall of tacklers would surround him, but 32 would either find a slight crack—or make one—and slip through. He humiliated linebackers and defensive backs one-on-one in the open field. He allowed them to make preparations. They would plant their feet and position themselves at the proper angle with their heads up, tails down and eyes on his belt buckle. Then once they committed themselves and flung their bodies at his, Brown would dip a hip or stick out a well-timed stiff arm and leave them sprawling.

Brown always seemed to save a special move for late in the game when Cleveland needed a big play. After being gang-tackled, he would slowly get up from the bottom of the pile and drag himself back to the huddle. He gave the appearance of being utterly exhausted, of being unable to run another step. It was a psychological ploy he used over and over. He coaxed the defense into thinking it had sapped him of his strength. He made them relax and feel confident that they had finally gotten to him. Then on the next play he would dash past them with a burst of fresh speed.

I practiced this technique in my own games. I called it the "J.B. Shuffle." After being tackled, something that happened pretty often in our rough brand of touch football, I would wobble, limp, stagger, drag my feet and barely make it back to the huddle. On the next play, all the defense would see were my heels as I sprinted past the fireplug on my way to the telephone pole. In our street games I had become someone new and I had another T shirt with 32 painted on it.

Soon Dad retired from football to go into the restaurant business. The Browns held an Old-timer's Day before one of the home games and during the ceremonies they presented him with his jersey. He gave it to me, but I was No.

32 then and couldn't change. After all, Jimmy Brown was the best running back in the NFL and I was the leading rusher in the neighborhood.

When the restaurant opened, I worked there as a busboy. Visiting teams would come in the night before their games with the Browns to eat steaks and gulp down a few beers. I always looked forward to seeing the Giants because my uncle would introduce me to the players. I would collect all of their autographs and then pass them out to my friends. At that time New York had the best defense in football and the tacklers would sit up on the terrace, talking about how they were going to stop Jim Brown. Sam Huff usually talked the loudest.

In the restaurant I got a view of the professional football player that was far different from what I saw from my seat in the upper deck of Municipal Stadium. During those long Saturday nights, I learned that football players were people. A sure-handed end who could catch any ball he got a finger on was constantly dropping ketchup all over himself or knocking his drink into someone's lap. Once a halfback leaned too far back in his chair and ended up flat on his back in the middle of the floor with his legs waving in the air. I began to realize that football players aren't immortal. Quite a few of those burly linemen got cramps and spasms in their backs just getting up from the table. They had to walk out bent over like old men.

As I poured water or cleared away plates, I heard some of the men talk about retiring. Whey they talked about women, food or Brown, they always spoke in loud voices, but when they talked about retiring they whispered and glanced around before they spoke. One night I overheard a bald old quarterback mumble, "The mark of a real pro is that on the way out he leaves some of himself, some of his experiences, behind with a rookie."

Those words disturbed me. They lingered in my mind for a long time because I didn't understand what they really meant. I thought that if someone deliberately took your job away, you should resent him and never speak to him. You should bear an eternal grudge. I was wrong and years later Jim Brown, himself explained it all to me in his book, *Off My Chest*.

"In a way Ed Modzelewski was much bigger than I or, for that matter, Babe Ruth. The son of Polish immigrants, he had come out of the Pennsylvania coal fields and made a good life for himself in football. Yet even while his friends were trying to prevent me from eating his lunch, as the saying goes, Big Mo was going out of his way to help me. In practice whenever I couldn't remember my assignment, Mo would whisper it to me with no coach the wiser."

One day, in the basement I found Dad's Brown's jersey in the bottom of a trunk. As I unfolded it and saw the big brown square 36 stitched on the white cloth, I felt proud, very proud, of the way he wore it. And the way he took it off.

All those memories of a great player and wonderful father were there for me—preserved in the basement. But the shrine was invaded, a few years later, by a small army showing little respect for the 'old man' as my younger teen-age brothers, Scott, Bruce and their suburban gang of innocents claimed the basement as their base of operations: a combination of iron-pumping cave, beer pub and make-out pad if they were lucky enough to actually lure a female down into that den of iniquity stained by sweat, hops and a raging flood of testosterone.

Dad's marble-and-gold trophies were soon broken into pieces by roughhouse play; the highlight pictures replaced by black light posters of heavy metal bands like Megadeth, Def Leppard, and the "The Motor City Madman": Ted Nugent, whose screeds "Wango-Tango" and "Cat Scratch Fever" spun full-blast on the turntable for weeks-at-a-time.

With Dad and Mom divorced, and Dad gone, having moved out west, it was now up to "Mother Mary" to attempt to reign over the leather-clad legions in the darkness below. She usually kept the kitchen door closed, sealed-off to the thundering din . . . opening it every few hours to send down into the hungry maw platters of meaty hamburgers or sheet-after-sheet of homemade pizzas. She worried only when she detected smoke wafting up into the house proper—of if she didn't hear any noise at all. That's when she employed her secret weapon—the laundry chute, a wide open, 'tin-ear' that picked-up the sound of every serious smooch or zipper being undone from any floor she was on. And she had a spy who worked undercover—her toy Yorkshire terrier, Chippy, who bolted back up the basement stairs; scratching frantically at the door whenever Scott and Tina filled the air with pheromones of passion. (Once the dog actually dashed away with "irrefutable proof"—Tina's jettisoned panties in its mouth, but luckily a fully outstretched Scott nabbed a furry back foot on the last top stair, recovering the silky evidence with Mom none the wiser.)

Just when I was leaving Cleveland for good, after college, my brothers and their buddies had graduated to The Doors. It was a bit incongruous hearing out of that staid Midwest cellar the racy "L.A. Woman" with at least a half-dozen, deep-voiced giants shaking the house walls, chorusing: "MIS—TER MO—JO RI—SIN . . . . GOT TO KEEP ON RISIN!!! RISIN RISIN!!!!!!"

Now even inquisitive Chippy refused to set foot down there.

Then the small basement couldn't hold them. Playing-out the rite-of-passage for most teenage males, they tested their all-consuming Toughness on the outside world.

Arriving at family gatherings, we all held our breath—afraid of what we'd see: Scott exhibiting a horribly contused eye; next time his proud grin was nearly as wide as the knife slash across his back; then he unfurled an indelible marking on his right deltoid, the tattoo of a screaming eagle. Scott and his gang of suburban ruffians roamed The Flats, then, (prior to Cleveland's Renaissance) a series of blues bars and shabby waterfront dives down along the Cuyahoga River, where motorcycle gangs ruled and alcohol-fueled fights erupted with one errant glance.

Dad called me one day. "Michael, Scott really looks-up to you. He's a great kid, but I'm afraid we're losing him. Is there anything you can think of to help pull him out of this?"

There *was* something. I wrote to Scott, asking if he would help crew for my second Western States 100 Mile Ultra Marathon. The first year I had to dropout at Mile 87 with a tendon injury. I could see the lights of the town of Auburn, the finish; and hours ahead of buckle-pace, I could have walked it in, but just could not press down an inch further on my foot. It was either summon the courage to quit or risk permanent damage . . . . All the next year I trained like a man possessed. Like Jason in quest of The Golden Fleece—I prepared myself around-the-clock to be worthy of that silver belt buckle (the award for finishing under 24 hours).

When Dad heard about my attempts to run 100 miles, he thought I was insane. The farthest he had ever loped was a 63 yard touchdown against the Chicago Bears—but if it kept me in shape and could help Scott—he was all for it.

At Western States II, something wonderful occurred. With his own eyes, Scott saw "Toughness" totally redefined. And it had nothing to do with boasting, macho bravura or size. What changed his mind were seeing silent loners— spare, whipcord lean men, and especially the women, such as 4'11," 98 pound Kathy D'Onofrio (who's diminutive stride required her to run nearly double the distance) and a grandmother, Helen Klein, who at 78 years young (with the lithe legs of a teenager)—all finished the race by, literally, moving mountains. The next day, at the Award's Banquet, I sent Scott up on the stage to accept the buckle that money can't buy. As he handed it to me back in the audience, his often-battered eyes were now shining as clear and bright as the silver, itself.

An alarm clock goes off like a sudden explosion. Dad pokes his head into our room: "Burn'n Daylight!" I smile at the familiar command he often uses to arouse his slumbering boys to action. "It's gonna be A GREAT DAY!!" he booms.

Just before 5:00 a.m., in downtown Wrightwood, Scott and I stand in the center of a pack of runners. There's last minute stretching; plenty of leg and arm jiggling in place. Everyone has a wide, vacant-eyed look—what combat soldiers call the 'thousand-yard stare': the inner spirit leaving the surface, gathering forces deep within, here creating a trance that helps insulate you against the demands of running 100 miles, with 19,100 feet of cumulative uphills and 24,230 feet down, through the Angeles National Forest to finish at the Rose Bowl stadium in a very distant Pasadena. We look over at family standing off to the side and nod. Just as I swallow hard, the gun sounds and we're off—running through darkness up toward the solid bulk of mountains ahead.

"*Trail!*" many runners call as they blitz by, passing us and we fight back the urge to go out with them. From past ultras, we know that if we start out calm and even, there will be satisfaction later in the day, as we reel-in many of the adrenaline-fueled, hopped-up "rabbits" now blowing lickety-split by us. Wild whoops and hollers cut the cool autumn air. It doesn't take long for the bunched field of 160 runners to spread-out through the twilight.

We run through strengthening light. Deep-down, I now agree with Dad: *This will be a great day!* I know a race of this magnitude is not won or lost now, but during the hundreds of hours of prior training; and we had trained religiously—making it the center of our lives. As we move away from Wrightwood, I thought back on the weekly ritual of leaving work in Berkeley, California late-Friday afternoons to drive up alone to Lake Tahoe, with the 15-speed Cannondale bike, tent and sleeping bag stowed behind me in the Honda hatchback. Five hours later, alongside the remote north shore of the lake, with the stars blazing crystal clear at eight thousand feet, I setup camp in the cool pine air and felt the balm of the mountains comfort me. I drank-in the mountain air in great drafts, like a sweet elixir. In the high country, I never arose groggy like in the city, but clear-headed and instantly energized—without the slightest need for caffeine. Each Saturday I then pedaled the bike for 72 hilly miles around the lake, and the next day ran 30-35 miles out-and-back on grueling Sierra Mountain trails. In training to run 100 miles, I learned it's not the immense quantity of miles per week you compile (often leading to injuries and over-training), but the quality of your mileage. And quality in ultra running equates directly with hills, which 'double' your investment. That's why Flatlanders: runners living in states like Florida have so much trouble in the ultras out west. One Floridian who buckled at Western States said at the banquet afterwards that he owed his success to endlessly running up-and-down the stairwell inside Miami's tallest skyscraper . . . .

I thought of how I went up to Tahoe ten weekends in succession, after putting in 50 miles Monday through Friday. But those city runs were mostly half-efforts, squeezed in around work and a social life. Up in the mountains, I was alone and undistracted: picking up right where I left-off the weekend before, building a clear, cohesive strength. I knew I was ready for Angeles Crest when the last weekend before the race, on Saturday I pedaled two successive 'laps' around the lake; then the next day loped 50 miles over the toughest section of the Western States course.

Lean and trim, carved-down to a vital essence by the rigorous training there was no slack, all systems were now unified and tuned to peak performance. Then "tapering"—not training at all during the last week leading up to the race, stored-up an immense bank of energy while simultaneously building a hunger. At the previous day's check-in, all the runners buzzed around like honeybees about to hit the clover.

Feeling great, I pass Scott and lead up the steep inclines into a pine forest. *Uphill is my country!* I love the feeling of ascension—shortening the stride, pumping the arms in synch with legs and lungs, and then topping a rise, eagle-eyeing the vast wilderness below and feeling so full, so satisfied knowing that with every stride you're earning the privilege of moving through the high-country under your own power—by "non-mechanized means." Up on the wild ridges, I feel the very forest and mountains; the cool wind fueling my being with "Hi-test."

Scott gives a loud *WAA-HOO!* as if reading my mind. Far-removed from any signs of man, alone together up in the mountains, we are now witness to the dawning of a new day. Up at 9,000 feet, near the summit of Mt. Baden-Powell (named in honor of Lord Baden-Powell, founder of The Boy Scouts), we float through pure, golden light and are caressed by gossamer webs, silken strands, spider-spun between the trees—stretching taut—then breaking against our cheekbones. We are kids again, laughing for no other reason than the sheer joy of being alive! How freeing the simplicity feels: only having to place one foot in front of the other for as long as we can—attempting to reach a destination somewhere unseen out in the distance, a day away.

A woman once asked me, "I get tired just *counting* to a hundred. How on earth do you ever run that many consecutive miles?"

Some runners try to convince the mind that it's only ten 10 mile runs; others look only at their watches, never mile-markers. I do neither—any numerical measurements seem out of place here in the wilderness, including finishing rankings. Although I hope to come-in under 24 hours, and place high in the standings, race day, I always run "watch-less"—with bare wrists and competing against nothing or no one. The only way I will be successful today is if I am *with*, not against: pliable, like the Zen reed or willow—losing none of the precious energy that running 'against' the clock, mileage, mountains, fellow man consumes.

The worst thing I had ever witnessed as a runner took place during my first Western States 100. After climbing almost 3,000 feet in the first three miles, from Squaw Valley to the top of the 9,000 foot Emigrant Pass, a veteran runner who prides himself on always finishing in the top five, turned to a very talented, but winded rookie atop the Pass, and in a drawn-out voice stated: "Well, three down . . . only *niiiiiiiinnnnnnnnnteeeeee——sevvvvveennnn* more miles to go!" The newcomer was finished then and there.

At the summit, we pause to run our hands over the gnarled, marble-smooth Limber Pines, close to being the oldest living things in the world, growing here during the time of Christ. One of the ancient, exposed roots spirals inward— reminding us to keep a lookout for Big Horn sheep: Herds are often spotted in the San Gabriel high country.

Moving downhill through the forest, suddenly, we are bouncing over a soft, pine-needle "trampoline." The vertical movements shake loose the sensation of being doubled, halved—the release of the *doppleganger* who sometimes shows-up out of the blue, especially at altitude (the first 30 miles are above 7,000 feet). I feel I am now both running and watching, active and passive in a real dreamlike state.

In the state of "Flow," the miles effortlessly roll by. I have long been a student of psychology professor and author Mihaly Csikszentmihalyi. His books on "flow experiences"—stretches of intense living; optimum performance, when body, mind and soul are engaged fully—produces an effortless transcendence. By losing ourselves in something far greater than self, we feel and function at our best. Athletes most easily enter "The Flow Zone," when the doer seems to disappear, erased by the activity itself or as W.B. Yeats wrote: "How can we know the dancer from the dance?" Man is meant for motion, movement—it brings forth the very best in us.

I think of how running cleanses all anger and hatred out of the system.

So many times I start a run feeling frazzled, stressed at the end of the day; bogged-down under a draining mishmash of negative thoughts, but after a few minutes on the trails, or even on pavement I feel rejuvenated, as if the rhythmic, flowing motion, itself, restores me to my best self. If I go into a run disliking anyone, planning "revenge"—it's then impossible to expand on those pernicious feelings after just a quarter-mile of running, and after completing a run of at least a half-hour, I return to challenges with a totally clean-slate. I wonder . . . that if Hitler and Pol Pot had been runners, maybe the Holocausts in Germany and Cambodia would not have been possible?

Nothing new—the ancient Greeks and Romans, with their gymnasiums, spas, arena sports, Olympic games laid the foundation with their often practiced: *Men Sana in Corpore Sano*—"A sound mind in a sound body."

We see horse tracks embedded in the trail: a series of evenly spaced U-U-U-U—the earth stamped with that one alphabetic letter from steel-shoed equines. "Incredible!" I say to Scott, "how we're always running where only horses go!"

I thought back to our family farm and the privilege of having horses: a pinto, a palomino, a roan Tennessee Walker and how Uncle Dick had bought a beautiful buckskin quarter horse to add to the stable—that proved, at first, too wild for anyone to ride. Everyone in the Modzelewski clan tried, but soon after someone mounted him, the big gelding reared high up on his back legs like Trigger; then when he dropped, front hooves hitting the ground, he immediately shifted that momentum into reverse: back through his body in a corkscrew motion that loosened you and then with a final mighty back-kick—bucked us off. . . . With Uncle Dick about to return the horse for a refund, I went into the barn late one night, a young teenager. "Buck" was sleeping, not standing on his feet with one leg flexed, hoof-up, as most horses do, but was lying down, full-out on his side inside a stall on a bed of fresh straw. I was afraid of him, but for some reason—not that night. In one motion I went over the stall wall, and pressed his head back down as he abruptly started up. He was also a biter, but I caught him off guard. He went back to the straw with startled eyes as my own legs scissored down with his. I never took my hand off his forehead and never stopped talking: No precise "horse whispering" here—I just babbled on and on, telling him unless he allowed us to ride him he was going back where he came from, which probably wasn't a place he liked very much from the way he acted; and that he should give us a chance to love him, which we did very much! I talked and talked and then must have fallen asleep, for when I woke up there was the big, unpredictable brute standing over me. It was early morning. I clipped a lead onto his halter, led Buck out of the barn and tied him to the hitching post. I saddled him; made the sign-of-the-cross—and hopped on. I reined him tightly, cautiously out into the clover field; clutching the saddle horn, bracing myself at any moment to go flying off. . . . Out in the wide open field, he snapped his head forward; the reins snaking through my fingers and he took off—bolting into a full, flat-out gallop all the way across the field; the faster he ran, the smoother his gait: like dropping into a deep rocking chair. And run he did: putting the hammer down—accelerating faster and faster until the only way I could breathe was to whoop and holler through the wind tearing my eyes—as if finally deciding to allow someone to see what he was made of; what he was really all about.

After that morning, still in control, he allowed only one rider. Uncle Dick didn't return him, but was a bit miffed, understandably so, that he and others couldn't ride him for any length of time before the horse lived-up to his name. I tried and tried to expand his ridership, but despite leading him by the reins and talking in his ear until I was blue in the face—no go. At the first appearance of another rider, he'd bare his teeth and flatten his ears back like: *Don't even think about it!* Even though he had to be his own Master, Buck had a heart bigger than the barn. On a long oval racetrack Dad mowed into the clover field, he whipped all neighboring horses in races of a quarter mile by simply refusing to lose. Now secure with his surroundings he went on a self-improvement kick. He began stretching himself—trying to expand his repertoire: play against being 'typecast.' He turned into a jumper, finessing his squat, muscular bulk up over a long broom stick held-up by milk cans and cinder blocks. He would jump and jump until his shins were bruised; until that bar reached four feet! He took his jockey far over trails in the back-forty woods and deep within myself. As Buck galloped flat-out, which he loved to do more than anything else, I took off the cumbersome western saddle and rode him bareback—absorbing his energy surging directly into my coltish, growing legs; and later, after brushing him down; feeding and watering him—I would go run down the country roads, hoping someday I could move like that horse.

Other horses who taught me about running were Breezy, whom I only rode once in Colorado: another buckskin, that matched the autumn-gold aspen leaves. He was a muscled athlete and in peak condition, even faster than Buck—a pure sprinter with bursts of speed that blurred the world. When I went to Spain I rode Amador, a coal-black stallion who thundered through the surf along the Costa del Sol. Then there was—Ginger, the prettiest long-haired palomino mare in Canada, with five gaits, each so fine and smooth. If I was a horse, I would have asked sweet Ginger to "marry" me! (Hey, we've all read about how girls love their horses, why can't a guy?)

However, the best of them all was Rowdy. While living in northern California, I was the caretaker of a small horse ranch. Rowdy was a colossus, standing 17 hands high and weighing over 1500 pounds. He was a mixture of Arabian, Thoroughbred, and American Saddle breeds. He was a true bay: brown with a black mane and tail, and his lower legs were burnished black up to the knees.

Rowdy emanated strength, from the tip of his Roman nose, throughout a deep chest to hindquarters, where in-between thick muscles and thin hide, small veins spread-out like a filigree of lace. He was, in the bodybuilder's vernacular: "a piece of work."

Beyond his physical power, the horse had charisma: a special spark, a pride in himself that everyone felt upon meeting him. "Rowdy has to always be first," Bill Dodd the owner of the ranch said the first day while showing me around. "That's just his way, to be boss of the herd. That's why I had to buy another horse, Jesse—so I could actually talk alongside people on trail rides!"

Rowdy deserved his name. One day, I was in his stall, bent over with my back to him, spreading hay into the feeder when suddenly I was lifted and held-off the ground—Rowdy's teeth clamped around my leather belt.

"Hey—*Down!*" He dropped me; I swung around to face him. He tossed his head back, but stood firm. I started reprimanding him further, but then smiled. His flopped ears and slack lower lip showed that he was 'laughing' inside.

During our first ride, Rowdy tried the usual tricks: attempting to bang my knee against a mailbox; whisk me through the trees. It was a David and Goliath contest: he had the brute strength but I was quicker, anticipating his moves (prepped by Buck), and reining him short.

Seeing that I could handle Rowdy, Dodd and I saddled-up one day, and he showed me the trail up Mount George. Bill Dodd is a double for John Wayne with the same big-boned physique and gruff, authoritative voice—even the conservative crewcut under his cowboy hat! He was like a second father to me. Many times we sat astride the horses atop the mountain, passing the "snakebite medicine"—a brandy flask back and forth as we looked over all the Napa Valley and talked of past adventures and future dreams.

The first time I went solo up Mount George on Rowdy, I got us into trouble—took a wrong turn and hit a dead end. The trail dissolved out on the exposed edge of a cliff: No room to turn around or back up all that way. I then made another mistake—looking down over my boot, into the chasm below. Panic climbed my spine, and Rowdy sensed it. He then took it upon himself to remove us from danger. As he shifted his weight back over his hind feet, I loosened the reins, giving him plenty of slack.

He reared and pivoted, out into midair—a dizzying flash of the drop off— then his front hooves touched down. My heart was slamming in my ears, but we were planted firmly in place, facing the opposite direction. Rowdy whinnied, and trotted, freeing his (and my) adrenaline over the false trail.

After that experience, our rapport ascended to a higher level. During our many rides, I placed complete trust in Rowdy and he felt free to unleash all that was within him. We went up that mountain at least a hundred times. Like one athlete teaching another, he showed me how to move over challenging trails.

Rowdy was such a good sport. During an exceptionally hot California drought summer, the green pasture in Rowdy's corral dried to dust, and every time he urinated (leaning forward so as not to splash his legs), the disturbed powder atop the hardpan 'smoked' up and, unfortunately, stuck to his lengthy penis, so that after urination, when he repeatedly retracted his phalange—dust, pulled back into the sheath all summer, eventually compacted into stones and a nasty infection ensued.

Treatment required swabbing with rubbing alcohol, the full length of Rowdy's painful penis—then reaching in and removing the coagulated grit from the purse-like pouch where his penis retracted into; and then top it all off by thoroughly applying an antibiotic cream to all affected areas.

The procedure took three men. With the arrival of the veterinarian, Bill Dodd led the horse out onto the driveway. As smart as Rowdy was, there's no way to even begin explaining to him: "O.K., here's the drill: We need to grab hold of your penis—stretch it all the way out and then, for starters, pour burning alcohol all over it!" To distract the *ahem* 'Big Guy' from the task at hand, as the vet gloved-up, Dodd put a twitch (small rope loop you could slowly tighten) on the tip of Rowdy's nose, while to add another, further point of diversion, I stood up on a step ladder and nibbled on the point of one of Rowdy's ears . . . .

Just then, with three grown men manning their battle stations, a UPS truck zoomed up the driveway: A squeal of brakes and the driver then refused to get out of the truck, yelling: "YOU WHITE FOLKS—ARE *CRAZY!*"

After Rowdy forgave me, and I was about to move-on, we rode up Mt. George for one last time. It was what the mountain men used to call a "shining day": high-pressure weather, in autumn, with a blue dome sky full of clarity and reach. We could look into San Francisco and gaze out to sea. The north wind swept up the canyons, shaking the chaparral; infusing us with energy.

After reaching the summit, "Last time, Rowdy: It's all yours!" I said, dropping the knot-end of the reins over the saddle horn. His ears perked and he went up on his "toes," charging down the mountain. By surrendering control, I gained the best ride of my life.

He matched the mountain perfectly: trotting footloose downhill; walking the slick-rock; sprinting the flats; jumping logs—my arms out for balance, for flying along.

Rowdy accelerated down into the trail curves: like riding a roller coaster with gravity increasing our momentum. I ducked the low trees but then allowed bay laurel leaves to smash their pungent scent against my face. The child that rode over clover fields returned: *Heee-Yah!* I shouted, releasing the wild power of the mountain that Rowdy heaved into me.

As we poured out of the woods, I reluctantly took-up the reins. On pavement, passing cars in suburbia—it all seemed so tame and out of place.

Inside the barn, I took off the saddle and brushed Rowdy down in his stall. As I walked away, he whinnied. Thinking he was hungry, I went back. His head was out over the gate. Rowdy lowered his nose; and for a long moment puffed his sweet breath against my cheek—as if he knew I was leaving.

Last time I checked, Rowdy was 21 years old. At an age when most horses are already in the glue factory, Rowdy is building a legend, still showing that all-out spirit. He continues as "point" horse on long trail rides and, a year ago, when he damaged a front knee, he changed his running style to a less-taxing Peruvian Paso "side-stroke," to stay in action—lead the charge up mountains, and into the hearts and minds of all who ride him.

Horses were really responsible for Scott and me now running; for Angeles Crest and all mountain ultra marathons: Horses and, one day, the lack thereof . . . Previous to 1974, in the U.S., the 26 mile marathon was considered the ultimate test of human endurance; then there were 50 milers and multi-day, stage races but all run on flat land. In 1973, a young man named Gordon Ainsleigh was entered in The Tevis Horse Endurance Race (begun in 1955 by Wendell Robie), covering 100 miles from Squaw Valley to Auburn, California. That year, Gordy's horse pulled up lame on the mountainous course 35 miles in. While later confiding his troubles to Wendell Robie's secretary, Drusilla Barner, she then told him: "You always hop off your horse downhill and hold onto its tail uphill—so why not just run the thing all by yourself?"

The more the 200 pound athlete thought about it, and then asked long-distance runners their opinions (the unanimous consensus was that no way could a human being do it in 24 hours), the more Gordy considered it. Then the more runners that said "No!" the more Gordy thought "Yes!!"

In its wide-open, untamed nature the American West calls certain men to greatness, men who resonate with the heaving mountains, rip-roaring rivers, white schooner clouds. Gordy Ainsleigh is a throwback to the pathfinders like Kit Carson, Jim Bridger, Hugh Glass—misfits in the city, but giants out in the wilds.

After six weeks of intense training, Gordy arrived in Squaw Valley the night before the race, sleeping in an empty horse trailer. At the starting line of the 1974 Tevis Horse Endurance Run there was a herd of entrants with four legs and just one, with two: Gordy Ainsleigh. "I was veted (checked by veterinarians) through just like the horses and was given a 10 minute head-start," Gordy told me one day during a training run. At first, his adrenaline got the best of him, racing the horses to the top of the 8,750 foot Emigrant Pass, but then with 97 more miles to go, he wised-up and slowed down. Thirty-five miles in, at Robinson Flat (where his horse had pulled-up lame the year before) Gordy felt pretty good. "But then the stretch from Deep Canyon to Last Chance hit me hard. It was very hot that year—110 degrees or more and I couldn't focus on where I was going . . . but somehow managed to keep putting one foot in front of the other . . . . "Then, at the American River, Gordy saw a rider wade his horse into the water and the horse collapsed. "That made me wonder—what am I doing out here on foot?"

Up at Devil's Thumb, a bit more than halfway through, Gordy felt done-in, totally bonked. Then various friends helped pace him along, including a horse riding friend, "But the horse kept looking at me like 'what the heck are you doing here?'"

At No Hands Bridge (that normally looks as wide as a highway when you're fresh, but after running 90+ miles it narrows to a tightrope), Gordy was staggering around and almost ran off the edge. With the last big obstacle behind him, he started up the hill to Robie Point. Hearing hoof beats behind him—spurred him on. "I was determined that no horse would pass me on that last climb . . . ." None did. Gordy Ainsleigh, "First Man," crossed the finish line in 23 hours and 42 minutes—starting hundreds of wild mountain ultra marathons by stomping one more human limitation into the dust.

As we run on, we feel a linkage even farther back, past horses—to ancestral man, following the deep instinct to run free in wild places. Trail running is an ancient sport and many flatland runners I know, feeling burned-out and beat-up after city marathons and training on concrete streets, feel totally renewed out on the trails. "We all lived on softer and more irregular surfaces until a few hundred years ago," wrote Peter Severance, publisher of "Running Wild" magazine. "An irregular surface requires a sophisticated musculature and suspension. Part of the thrill of trail running is waking up all those parts of the body again." Unlike running on pavement, every step on the trails is different as you dodge rocks or tree roots; move up or down hills and switchbacks. It becomes a dance as you rhythmically power over and around things. A podiatrist and runner friend said that trail running may have helped to create adaptability in the human body and possibly why we have 26 bones in each foot—to shift and flex and dance along the varied paths.

We swerve around rocks and roots; hop over fallen trees or sudden puddles. And the tangos aren't solo, for the obstructions are "partners" leading the dance, stirring the rhythm that travels up your legs and into the soul. We run on—WAA-HOOO!—with full-body smiles.

It feels so freeing and joyous to be away—out of the boxes that enclose us throughout the day as we trade one small cubical for another: going apartment to car to office to car to apartment again. We've become prisoners, our free-romping-range now shrunk to limited encasements as we sit in front of computers; sit in front of televisions: cubes within the boxes of "progressive" modern life that is shutting us down with an epidemic of motion-deprivation diseases. I'm convinced that the wellsprings of human life are motion and movement. In some cities, school boards have done away with recess, giving kids 'more productive' things to do—yet passing out Ritalin and Prozac as if it were candy. Children need long stretches of unstructured play; adults the same. Motion should join Water, Food and Sleep as the basic daily requirements for sustaining human life. Many of our chronic diseases: obesity, heart disease, diabetes, cancer, migraine headaches and joint replacements stem from the simple lack of movement that pervades our society. The cliché of "Use-it or Lose-it" is loaded with truth, as is the peasant (who long-outlived the pampered gentry) expression: "I have two doctors: my right leg and my left." And it's not just physical. A friend who works downtown for a major corporation once told me: "When you sit in a tiny office for eight hours a day under artificial light with the windows sealed-shut, you just want to SCREAM!"

There is such primal joy in movement, especially fresh and new: "out of the box(es)." I slap the sheen of sweat lightly oiling our legs now. It feels like a tonic that soothes the soul.

As we move through the pristine forest, feeling so at home, I think of how it was *out here*—in nature where we progressed as a species. If you believe in evolution, man has been on Earth for at least one million years. During that vast time frame we moved into cities during the past "ten seconds." The rest of the time, out in the natural world, is where we developed our finest human qualities of empathy; an aesthetic appreciation of beauty; a sense of wonder; community; and love. That's why many of us spend our weekends or vacations in national parks, wild places or merely an hour in a sun-drenched or tree-filled backyard, where we feel rejuvenation and a sense of returning "Home."

Dad and Joanne are waiting at the checkpoints. It is their very first time crewing, and they try to conceal their excitement under calm demeanors, but Dad, especially, wears his heart on his sleeve and keeps an eye glued to the clock. He's extremely goal-oriented, which was the key to his success on the gridiron and later in the business world; and he wants that buckle as much, if not more than we do. Feeling "wide-open"—in some sort of extrasensory state, I experience his desire and energy directly: He's like a force of nature, a veritable tornado of white light whirls within him, and uncontainable, swirls out—zip-zapping us as he struggles to contain himself, so proud, supportive of his own flesh-and-blood. Dad fills us with far more than bananas and water. We leave the checkpoints prancing out at least two miles on the life-force we have absorbed from him. I think of Walt Whitman's line: "I sing the Body electric!" If "Big Mo" was plugged into a voltage generator this day, he'd empower the entire city of Los Angeles!

Buckle pace, to finish 100 miles under 24 hours, is 15 minutes a mile, or approximately 4 mph—certainly slow enough to talk, which we do, keeping our minds off the overwhelming distance. To intelligently race 100 miles is to physically relearn that wizened, old Aesop Fable, "The Turtle and The Hare." An ultra marathon definitely favors tortoise-like consistency. Sure, the winner usually breaks the tape in an amazing 16 hours, but eventually many of the turtles actually step-over the lickety-split, front-running rabbits in the later stages, for they've "blown-up"—collapsed right on the trail from relentlessly pushing the pace. The mentality of most of the winners is to do just that: go all-out for every mile or see "DNF" (Did Not Finish) next to their name in the subsequent Results. If your goal is to buckle, then just average 15 minute miles—but do it up and down steep mountain ranges; across unmarked snow fields; through stifling heat in dead-air canyons; while fording icy rivers; through 30 or so miles of bone-weary, brain-dead darkness . . . .

"My first year at Western States," I say to Scott, "I was running with the pioneer, Gordy Ainsleigh up near Cougar Rock, about 20 miles in—and there, sticking out like a sore thumb in all that wilderness was a flaming red can of Coke, empty, that a runner dropped against the base of the rock. Gordy pointed to that need for an early boost, saying: 'He'll never make it.'"

"Who I really admire," Scott says, "are the ones who never buckle, but finish—stay the course for 30+ hours! They're the real heroes. Imagine being out here so long that you see the sun come up twice!!"

As the day progresses, a brother I previously knew little about, becomes very familiar. We are covering more ground in a day than we had in previous decades. As with most males, we find it easier to open-up and talk "indirectly": while engaging in physical activity; a shared goal. Deep in the mountains, we speak from the heart about our hopes and dreams. I tell Scott how proud I am of him; and how very far he has come in just a few years.

The day after crewing at Western States, Scott stopped drinking and started running. He moved from Cleveland to Phoenix and introduced himself daily to the desert via its long hilly trails. He was soon running mountain marathons, then 50 milers, and winning his young age-group and placing high over-all—unusual, for the ultra-distances usually favor the middle-aged, who in the later stages of races call upon more familiar inner resources. But Scott proved to be a natural runner and had no fear of pain. He further conditioned himself by working construction during the summer's blast-furnace days; then went to night school, studying to be a massage therapist: devouring books on nutrition, kinesiology, holistic healing—applying everything he learned, first to himself, then to a burgeoning practice. He stopped dating bar girls, with whom he often had to pull a "Coyote." ("When the next morning you wake-up in bed, and have to 'chew' your arm off to slip away from someone you'd rather not face over the breakfast table.") In the bright light of day, while hiking-up the popular Squaw Peak, he met the knockout Karey, his total soul-mate, whom he soon married. Movie-star handsome, he started modeling, appearing in national television commercials, print-ads, and on the covers of "Outside" and "Men's Health" magazines. A son, Lance, and daughter, Jennifer were born. They were the "picture perfect" family—shining with health and happiness. Even Scott's 'soundtrack' changed with the helter-skelter clangings of heavy metal now replaced by soulful Country: his new anthem, Clint Black's resolute "I'm Leav'n Here A Better Man."

"Did a 360 with my life," Scott says as he leads up a steep switchback. "Had to—going nowhere fast. Running turned me around—gave me goals; got me hooked on feeling healthy. Got so bad I used to drink first thing in the mornings to hold the buzz—no hangovers that way. Now I get up and already have ten miles in when before I was just getting to bed . . . . Look what we're doing!" he said, extending his arms out, as if to embrace the very mountains, rocks and trees. "Look what the body can do with a balanced spirit. You showed me this world, bro. You're my hero. You saved my life!"

"No, Scott—it wasn't me. All you needed was a challenge, a place big enough to pour all that energy."

"Guess we found it, huh! And I have it now for life. No drug can touch this. This is the greatest high in the world!"

We prance on through the wilderness with that full-body smile intact, for we're in a transcendental state—as if we don't end at our skin, but continue on into everything. The sky is the deepest blue; the clouds pure white; the forest air a pungent "pine wine"; shafts of sunlight taste like vitamins; even the rocks have heartbeats. And our very atoms mingle indivisibly with it all. I recall the advice of a Zen monk: "Breath in the World; Breath out the Self." High in the San Gabriel Mountains, we are nearing nirvana.

Hours pass blissfully, but eventually an incremental measurement cuts into the vast spell. Arriving at the next checkpoint, Scott and Dad argue about our time. Not having "synchronized watches" at the start, Dad's trusty Hamilton Classic shows we are 14 minutes behind buckle pace; Scott's digital flashes that we're down only five. Scott is shouting his is right; Dad insists we have to pick it up if we want to buckle. It feels ugly; so discordant to what had just been. *Only at the halfway point, 50 miles, and already 14 minutes down?!* Having a goal (the buckle), a manifestation of Ego, interferes with the state I crave most: transcendence. Carrying a goal/ego is a constant agitation, as we have to worry over every minute, apply time to distance; divided by ourselves. I feel ambivalent. A part of me wants the buckle but I want more to enjoy the crossing, itself—the freedom of soaring through wild country with no demarcations, without a finish line holding us hostage all day long.

After gobbling a Power Bar; a few bites of banana; and with Joanne topping-up our boda-belts with water and Exceed (electrolyte drink)—we look over a course map. Next up is a long, steep drop on fire roads descending into a river canyon, then regaining it all again up another mountain. With Scott and Dad still arguing over whose ticker is right I take off. Trying to buy time, I open it up—surging downhill, punching the pace. We fly, swooping past other runners, their heads swiveling as we blow-by . . . but now they prudently stay back, ignoring the pull from the Mad Hares . . . continuing to wisely "turtle" along the sloping gravel road.

In ultra running there's a reverse twist on a common cliché: What goes down must come up—and up and up some more. After blitzing the downhill, it then takes a Sisyphean effort to reach the next checkpoint atop an endless ascent . . . . Just when you think: *finally, the summit in sight!* your spirit plunges as you top a rise only to see the trail climbing higher still, with no end to it. I struggle to silence my brain, switch-off energy-draining anticipation, so as to live "mindless" in the present . . . blending moment into moment . . . breath-into-breath until the summit appears surprisingly, (rather than *about time!*) of its own accord. Ultra running is all about fueling effort with patience—perfect Zen practice, in that you are actively "doing" but with detachment.

Joshu Sasaki Roshi asked: "Where do you dwell when you are running?" I try to reside in the present moment, for even though running is such a simple mechanical motion, if the mind wanders forward, I'm tripped-up immediately by a protruding stone or root—like the cane of the *zazen* meditation master cracking down: *"Pay Attention!"* Or as Ram Dass said, "Be Here Now" (for by mindfully living each-and-every moment, the future unfolds effortlessly upon a perfected present foundation).

Of the trio of Dimensions: past, present and future, the best this runner can manage is moving through two of the three "time zones" at once: the present, of course, and the past, which doesn't seem to interfere since it has already been experienced. Memory is, therefore, permitted: a comforting "gum" to chew while running at the same time. It's when I literally 'get-ahead-of-myself' that I'm sent sprawling: when the Mind abandons the harmonious present or comforting past for the worrisome future, as if trying to inhabit the unknown short-circuits the system, flips-up "Stop Signs"; and sure enough I stumble or if I really wander/ worry—pole axed to the ground!

It's not a random occurrence: It happens every time! I can be running on a path as flat and smooth as a pool table, but start to think ahead and up pops a rock; *stub!* goes the toes and I'm wrenched forward like a flailing dervish and once finally righted, now have foot or back pain to deal with as "payment" for leaving the present. It's as if there's a direct correlation between thoughts and objects; a tangible cause-and-effect. More than once, I would have bet my life upon first striding out that there wasn't the slightest obstruction on an unruffled path; that I could allow myself the liberty of thinking ahead. *But Nooooooo*—start making plans and down you go. Running proves, as the Lankavatara Sutra states:

"Everything in the world comes from the mind, like objects appearing from the sleeve of a magician."

I recalled reading about the marathon monks of Mount Hei in Japan. They use long-distance running as "moving meditation": their ultimate goal not to cross a finish-line, but to reach a far more difficult goal—inner enlightenment. During a 100-day stretch, in handmade straw sandals, they cover 52.5 mountain miles *every day*! "Learn through the eyes, practice with the feet," is the main tenant of Tendai Buddhism.

Then there are the *lung-gom-pa* runners of old Tibet. Many explorers to Tibet encountered these running monks, who appeared to bound across the high steppes in a trance, traveling nonstop for forty-eight hours, covering over 200 miles per day. The famed French explorer, Alexandra David-Neel wrote of her eyewitness meeting with a *lung-gom-pa* in *Magic and Mystery in Tibet*: "Towards the end of the afternoon, Yongden, our servants and I were riding leisurely across a wide tableland, when I noticed, far away in front of us, a moving black spot which my field-glasses showed to be a man. I felt astonished. Meetings are not frequent in that region, for the last ten days we had not seen a human being. Moreover, men on foot and alone do not, as a rule, wander in these immense solitudes. Who could the strange traveler be?

" . . . As I continued to observe him through the glasses, I noticed that the man proceeded at an unusual gait and, especially, with an extraordinary swiftness. Though, with the naked eyes, my men could hardly see anything but a black speck moving over the grassy ground, they too were not long in remarking the quickness of its advance. I handed them the glasses and one of them, having observed the traveler for a while, muttered: '*Lama lung-gom-pa chig da.*' (It looks like a lama *lung-gom-pa* . . . .)

"The man continued to advance towards us and his curious speed became more and more evident. What was to be done if he really was a *lung-gom-pa*? I wanted to observe him at close quarters, I also wished to have a talk with him, to put him some questions, to photograph him . . . . I wanted many things. But at the very first words I said about it, the man who had recognized him as a lama *lung-gom-pa* exclaimed:

"'Your Reverence will not stop the lama, nor speak to him. This would certainly kill him. These lamas when traveling must not break their meditation. The god who is in them escapes if they cease to repeat the *ngags*, and when thus leaving them before the proper time, he shakes them so hard that they die.' . . .

"By that time he had nearly reached us; I could clearly see his perfectly calm impassive face and wide-open eyes with their gaze fixed on some invisible far-distant object situated somewhere high up in space. The man did not run.

He seemed to lift himself from the ground, proceeding by leaps. It looked as if he had been endowed with the elasticity of a ball and rebounded each time his feet touched the ground. His steps had the regularity of a pendulum. He wore the usual monastic robe and toga, both rather ragged. His left hand gripped a fold of the toga and was half-hidden under the cloth. The right held a *phurba* (magic dagger). His right arm moved slightly at each step as if leaning on a stick, just as though the *phurba*, whose pointed extremity was far above the ground, had touched it and were actually a support.

"My servants dismounted and bowed their heads to the ground as the lama passed before us, but he went his way apparently unaware of our presence . . . .

"We followed him for about two miles and then he left the track, climbed a steep slope and disappeared in the mountain range that edged the steppe. Riders could not follow that way and our observation came to an end . . . . "

David-Neel goes on to explain that to qualify as a *long-gom-pa* runner a fledgling first had to master seated meditation. Breath control and visualization were the first steps: good breath control and imagining one's body to be as light as a feather. Then a novice practiced at night by fixing his gaze intently on a single star as he ran and harmonizing his pace with a secret *mantra* given by his teacher. The key was to keep your eyes fixed on the star and never allow yourself to be distracted. The master *lung-gom-pa* runner could then glide along through the air in a state of moving meditation.

Providing another glimpse into similar secret training techniques, in *Where The Gods Are Mountains: Three Years Among The People of The Himalayas*, Rene von Nebesky-Wojkowitz wrote: " . . . I had heard a great deal about a kind of mystic marathon held in the Land of Snow every twelve years. The reports of some travelers in Tibet contained references, echoing Tibetan descriptions of mysterious runners who are said to cross the country running for days on end without a pause in a kind of ecstasy. There was also talk of a Tibetan yogi alleged to have covered the distance between the capital and a group of monasteries in Central Tibet, for some special purpose, in an incredibly short time. The West received these meager and often very confused accounts with understandable skepticism. But my conversations with Tibetans convinced me that these fantastic-sounding stories contained a hard core of truth. Priest and laymen, officials and merchants assured me that every 12 years one of the Snow Land's two most important yogis, accompanied by two of his pupils, passed through Lhasa on a cross-country run. They called this mysterious personage Mahaketongwa, the 'Great Caller.'

" . . . All three wear large shell earrings. Their long hair hangs loose on their shoulders, apart from the fact that a few of the Mahaketongwa's locks are bound, on the crown of his head, into a knot from which a thunderbolt protrudes. On their brows they wear magical blinkers, whose long black fringes of bear's hair hang down as far as the nose and obscure the eyes. The Great Caller's pupils are armed with long staves; he himself holds in his right hand a trident decorated with silk ribbons, and in his left a bone trumpet. In addition, a rosary is hung round his neck and he carries in his belt a *phurbu*, a magic dagger for fighting demons.

"Many Tibetans believe that the three yogis do the run in a semi-trance, or that they know magic formulas which give them 'fleetness of foot.' Most of those whom I questioned, however, had a simpler explanation. In their opinion the fabulous performance of the Great Caller and his pupils is due primarily to perfect bodily control, acquired by years of strenuous exercise, and the development of certain powers that are actually latent in everyone."

You don't have to go to the far east to find running's spiritual disciples. In Boulder, Colorado, the favored high-altitude (and attitude) area for American distance runners, there's "Divine Madness": a metaphysical running club, 100 members strong. No 'loneliness' for these long-distance runners, for they train in groups, live communally and practice meditation, holistic healing methods and open sexual relationships. Mainstream runners and former members describe the group as a cult, but if so, there hasn't been a destructive downside (mass-suicide while wearing their Nikes to board a spaceship). Even though gentle souls, they're not afraid to transform inner-strength into outward competition. Divine Madness member Steve Peterson won the extremely challenging Leadville Trail 100, "The Run In The Sky," through the heart of the Rocky Mountains, with the course elevation averaging 10,152 feet.

As I run on, it's as if thought creates tangible matter. I can feel the shimmering souls of the Shinto monks, the *lung-gom-pa*, and Divine Madness members swirling around in the air: "Brothers in Legs," offering-up a supportive bank of energy.

Then the pleasant shock of emerging from a long stretch of isolated wilderness, turning a corner—into walls of applause as you speed through a tunnel of spectators to a remote cull-du-sac in the woods, filled for this one day with a couple hundred people—individual runner's crews and generous checkpoint volunteers there for the common good. It's barely controlled chaos as fatigued runners, arriving ahead of predicted pace, search frantically for their much-needed support.

The crews have carved-out small encampments for their runner's temporary comfort, closer to the main trail the better, with water coolers, lawn chairs, a vast assortment of foods and liquids, first-aid, fresh clothes all laid-out at the ready. From past experience, crews know that the one thing they've casually left behind in the car is the very thing desperately needed, so everything, including the kitchen sink is, front and center, poised for use. In many ways it is much harder to *crew* than run for 100 miles. A crack, ultra crew member must be equal parts chef, chemist, psychiatrist, meteorologist, masseuse, insomniac and mechanic, with the path finding skills of both Lewis and Clark. Finding the checkpoints on mimeographed, topographical maps is like trying to orienteer to the very points of needles amidst vast haystacks: requiring the transverse of perilous mountain "roads" that you disbelieve are actually leading anywhere; and if only you could stop to get your bearings without the sheer fear of rolling backward into that canyon 4,000 feet below or see your way clear past yet another hairpin turn or through the clouds of dust that infiltrate all orifices regularly. And no one trains to stay up for 24-30 hours straight, let alone be able to read the mind of a brain-dead runner, but it's the efficiency and stamina of the crews, especially in the later stages that is often the difference between a runner attaining the silver buckle or ultimately buckling to fatigue. The hardest part is the waiting . . . sometimes hour-upon-hour at checkpoints without being lulled into lethargy, for just when you start nodding-off—your runner then bursts upon the scene with more needs than a newborn.

As Scott and I swing into Chantry Flats we see a mandatory Medical checkpoint, with three things happening at once: while standing on the scale for a weigh-in, your blood-pressure is read, and so are your eyes. If your brain is still tracking, the tell-all eyeballs are straight ahead, relaxed and micro-focusing. If you are down more than five percent of your starting weight, or if your eyes are floundering uncontrollably out to the sides, you are either permanently pulled from the race or asked to sit it out for awhile.

"Keep drinking," a nurse prescribes. "Other than that, you guys are in good shape!"

Dad waits at the perimeter, smiling. "You *really* picked it up!"

"Yeah," Scott says, putting his arms around Dad and Joanne. "Like slalom skiing down that hill a ways back. Mike led the way. We were pick'n off runners left and right."

"Well, you made-up time and really jumped in the standings. Top twenty now!!"

For the first time, after running for more than half-a-day—we sit down. "Saw some hunters on the way in," Dad continues, as we re-hydrate and eat. "Deer season opened today! They asked what all the commotion was about. When we told them about the race, how far you're running—at first, they refused to believe us. Then they asked how much you were getting paid. Told 'em zero; and that you had to pay $150 bucks to get in. 'Well, any free beer then?' No. 'Then they gotta be outta their minds!'"

"Great," Scott moans. "Just what we need out there—trigger happy, beer-swillin' hunters!"

Out of the corner of my eye I watch the runner next to us. Anal-retention even infiltrates ultra marathons. Every one of his bottles is color-coded; the contents of fluid bottles differentiated by size; and his food baggies for the day are all consecutively numbered in waterproof ink. Having overheard what Dad said about the hunters he hands over to me a packet of strange tissues.

"Toilet paper, camouflage pattern," he says matter-of-factly. "Recommend using it for pit-stops. Two hunters were shot dead last year when they stopped to take a dump in the woods. The flash of white T. P. did 'em in. Other gunners, a bit overeager, thought they had themselves a white-tail buck dead-to-center."

Instead of laughing, I thank him profusely while stuffing the camo T. P. into a cargo pouch. We stand-up, stiff-legged—now regretting having sat down. This is the last check point for crews. The wilderness is too rugged for them to reach us during the remaining miles. We won't see them now until the finish—one of the reasons Angeles Crest is so tough: a runner is "crew-less" when he or she needs them the most. Joanne hands us flashlights, which we slip into the cargo pouches on our boda-belts.

"GO GET 'EM MICHAEL; SCOTT! LOVE YOU GUYS!! *WAA—HOOOO!!*"

Big Ed's voice carries down the trail, filling our spirits like wind in a sail.

Then the woods and silence quickly closes around us. As we run-on, limber again I then feel trouble brewing—inside my shoes. The 'seeds' of blisters, hot-spots, are developing on the bottoms of my feet—sparked by the full-throttle friction on the downhill gravel. Saying nothing to Scott, I try to run light-footed; and with mental-imaging convert each breath into a tonic that I send down through my solar plexus and legs, flooding the roots of the blisters with a cool balm. It had worked before . . . . Many times, during training runs or races, knee pain or that stabbing stitch in the side was erased with breath, *prana* or life-force, by directing each intake of oxygen to the unbalanced area—picturing it as a healing 'broom' whisking the pain away. For added medicine, I recall a powerful saying from the Ojibway Indians: "Now and then I go about pitying myself and all the while my soul is being blown by great winds across the sky."

As we move on, I ride those winds around the world: running in CHINA with a group of American athletes and coaches. After a long 13 hour flight, we awoke the first morning in Shanghai and inside the walled hotel courtyard, we stretched for our first run by learning *tai chi*, led by Mr. Chou, 74 years young. *Tai Chi* is a Chinese martial art dating back to about 1200 AD. The slow, flowing movements, based originally on animal movements, gently enlivened our muscles like no herky-jerky calisthenics ever could. Following Mr. Chou's rhythmic movements and deep breathing felt like being underwater on land. We then formed three groups of 12 and eagerly ran out the hotel gate for our first glimpse of China. At first, it wasn't much different than home: in the thick of morning rush hour, but the modes of transport were much simpler: an endless stream of one-speed Flying Pigeon bicycles, with thousands of slender riders moving perfectly synchronized wheel to wheel. We were there just before Modernization, and modesty still ruled. The only skin Chinese women showed was a one inch strip of wrists and ankles under their shapeless Mao uniforms. But no one informed our gals of the conservative dress-code. On that warm spring morning, three extremely leggy blondes from southern California were running in high-cut, nylon, short-shorts down the main street in Shaghai and wrecking absolute havoc. With each stride of their bare, elongated legs—male Chinese commuters shifted attention away from the tire in front and that one frozen stare was enough to cause massive pileups and entanglements of wheels and men. Our ladies felt terrible (well, somewhat flattered too) but in deference to the country's rules and traffic patterns, never again ventured forth without wearing baggy sweat pants over their gorgeous gams.

For ten days we moved around China, with Mr. Chou emerging as our favorite coach. Each morning, as he stepped out in front of us, we all bowed with gratitude and reverence as his *tai chi* sessions really loosened and centered us before our training runs. There was an oceanic dimension to the crowds in the streets, with one in five people on Earth being Chinese. To curtail the runaway population, the "One Child" rule had been in effect for a decade and I wondered if they were raising a generation of spoiled brats, for in the evenings and especially on Sundays, the proud parents paraded their little dolls and soldiers around the boulevards with great aplomb.

In Jinan, we ran a 10-K with 700 Chinese runners. Road racing was a relatively new sport in China; and winning wasn't yet "Everything." When a speedster or fast group came up alongside you, they purposely slowed to run with you, bowing all the while. I'd wave them on, especially toward the end but they refused to go—so that when each American crossed the finish line we were escorted by a squadron of smiling Chinese.

After the race, we and the Chinese spontaneously exchanged the T-shirts off our backs and posed for pictures with arms wrapped around one another: Communists and Capitalists, all runners, smiling together and sharing the athletic camaraderie that transcends differences.

So taken with the exchange of T-shirts after the 10-K, back at the hotel after a shower, I proudly put the soggy shirt back on and hiked over to Thousand Buddha Mountain—aptly named for on every flat surface; in every cave and hollow was a carved stone Mr. B. Hit it just at the right time, for monks with shaved heads and saffron robes were arriving on a long distance pilgrimage. They cleansed their sins by burning juniper incense and leaving offerings of food on the recessed altars beneath the ancient Buddhas. Our hotel was near the mountainside temples. All night we heard chanting; saw the flicker of incense sticks. The mountain, itself, seemed to be a living entity: pulsating with sound and light.

The culmination of our journey came when the tour bus dropped us off five kilometers from The Great Wall. We ran uphill, each step lifting us closer to what we had previously anticipated for years. Around a final bend—there was the legendary Wall—topping the high mountain ridges like a writhing dragon.

Striding up on the ancient blockade, I felt palpable vibrations—an ancient past rush into me. The Wall was built in the year 3 B.C. and extends for 4,000 miles. No photograph prepares you for the steepness. Struggling up irregularly shaped stone steps, I finally reached the top watchtower. Shimmering in the distance was the Gobi Desert and Mongolia. Like a hawk in the wind, I let out a piercing scream: carried back through time by The Great Wall and empowered by its monumental tenacity.

Covering the event, the Beijing Evening News reported: "In the spring The Great Wall is beautiful. The wind is mild and the sun is bright. The tourists ran in groups that were like clouds floating by. Besides running, they think they can enjoy tourism inside China, meet Chinese people, and make friends. That is to hit two birds with one stone."

Before leaving, I wanted to see the Temple of Heaven in Beijing. The official name for the People's Republic of China is *Zhongguo*—the Middle Kingdom. I walked toward an exquisite, blue-tiled building adorned with dragons, the upturned eaves of the roof making the massive pagoda appear weightless. Inside, a marble altar signified the center of the world: a place only the Emperor was allowed to approach in order to commune with Heaven; and all other peoples away from the middle—out on the distant edges were considered barbarians.

Outside, the late-afternoon air was cooling. I put on a "Team U.S.A." jacket and paced slowly around the Temple of Heaven, savoring its magnificence. A Chinese man with an adorable young son dressed in a miniature Red Army uniform approached. The man held up a camera. I smiled and nodded, reaching for the camera—but instead the man picked-up his son and handed him over to me. He stepped backwards, squinting through the viewfinder . . . .

Clearly, outsiders are now accepted into the inner sanctum.

I thought of running in the SOVIET UNION, participating in the first "Soviet Super Marathon": 10 marathons in 10 consecutive days, nicknamed

"The Golden Circle" for we would run from town to town with gold, onion-shaped domed churches. Before leaving, rather than contact my usual product sponsors: Nike and Powerbar, I wrote instead to Avon and Victoria's Secret. With the Cold War still frosting U.S.—Soviet relations, I thought a way to break the ice with the Nikitas and Katarinas I might meet along the way would be to gift them with rare, heartwarming commodities: lipstick and lingerie. To my surprise both Avon and Victoria's Secret kicked-in product (a Vic Secret marketing guy saying on the phone, when I called to thank him, that they were "glad to have a U.S. 'Agent' start sowing a few product samples in lieu of our future expansion through the Soviet Bloc . . . .") The times they were a changin': The Berlin Wall had just come down and Gorbachev's thunderclap proclamations of *perestroika* (restructuring) and *glasnost* (openness) were the first signs that communism was being questioned; with the unthinkable: capitalism, quite possibly the ultimate answer.

While packing my suitcase—deep inside the toe-box of running shoes and under T-shirts and shorts I tucked-in tubes of "Ruby Red" lipstick and that gorgeous frilly lingerie. Arriving in Moscow, I held my breath as we approached Customs: *If my bag's inspected, I'm done. 'Cross-Dressers' are probably shot on sight or at least shipped off to Siberia to be a bad man's boyfriend!* But our group of American runners was waved right on through, due to the earthy charm of our Russian-speaking leader, Joe "Mighty" Oakes.

Pushing 60, the man had the strength and life force of two 30 year olds. Joe had run innumerable marathons, finished the Iron man Triathlon and completed a non-mechanized circumnavigation of the earth, including a swim across the Bering Sea! His letterhead was a top view of black and white arms embracing the globe with "HUG YOUR MAMA" underneath, and the tag-line: "A not-for-profit organization teaching a close, personal love for the earth and a harmony among its inhabitants."

We were 14 North American runners; 30 Soviets; 9 French; 1 Dutch; 1 Czech and the memories were many: an American accidentally shot in the side the very first morning by the starter's pistol . . . running past massive wooden buildings made with only ax, chisel, plane . . . the old Russian general who iron-willed himself through severe back pain to finish every stage . . . hanging with the young hipster, 'Nail,' a speedy Soviet strider who raced very successfully in the U.S. . . . running alongside wild, mystic birch forests, the Russians' true home as they picked wild mushrooms; ate picnics in the sun . . . a toothless peasant couple who set up a makeshift aid station with fresh strawberries sweeter than candy . . . lace curtains afloat in walls of rough wood . . . gold, onion-dome churches chiming welcoming bells . . . statues of Lenin being toppled . . . Tom

Z., a venture capitalist from California assaulted in a park by a Soviet hard-liner . . . a Russian couple who came along for all 262 miles to Uglich on bicycles . . . the Mayor of each town hosting lengthy banquets, each statement deconstructed four times into that many languages, his final vodka toast: "Hup yu kuum to ur tuwn wit pleesur an leaf wit regreet!!" We did, traveling non-stop on both emotions.

There was little time or opportunity to meet Nikitas or Katarinas, but I did give away nearly all my stash of lipstick and lingerie—to soldiers, who tore the medals and buttons off their uniforms in exchange for a pair of silk stockings or tube of lipstick that when given to a wife or sweetheart would make him "Czar for The Year." I collected so much military hardware that I could have opened a Soviet Army-Navy store back home!

Each new day was an increasingly hard march and by Day/Marathon 6 the attrition rate was climbing. Fewer and fewer runners toed the Starting Line. The fun of running was now all work. What kept us moving toward each new town was knowing there was immediate relief waiting. When Jim Ryan, the great U.S. miler was asked why he ran so much, replied: "Because it feels good when I stop." In Russia, doubly so, for never far from the day's finish line; gloriously rewarding all your hard labor was a sauna. Not the Americanized small, wooden hot box—*nyet*, the Russian *banya* was an entire building, built pre-revolution and still with czaristic "Land of The Fire Bird" elements: a combination social club, cafe, temple of philosophy and hydro spa—frothed-up with a touch of mild S/M. You limped or crawled in—and an hour later bounded out almost ready to run another marathon.

There was a dry heat room; the more popular steam chamber; whirlpools that really whirled; ice-cold plunging tanks; and everywhere heaps of fresh-cut birch branches thick with leaves that you used on yourself, or better yet—had a comrade thrash you from head-to-toe. Marvelous to see all the nationalistic boundaries disappear with our clothes as Soviets whipped Americans; France switched Germany—good-naturedly bringing the blood to the surface, whisking up all the body's impurities, released then through copious amounts of sweat. In the muslin-thick clouds of steam you couldn't see for beans, but heard the whips come down and smelled pungent crushed leaves. Then as red as a Russian beet, you'd shiver your 'Timber' plunging into an icy water barrel; then emerge a new man, ready for tea.

Off to the side was a wood-panelled room divided by a long table with an enormous silver samovar topped with a double-eagle as the centerpiece. Totally relaxed, with a cup of mint tea and a garden-fresh cucumber sandwich, you were ready to wax philosophical and often did, solving the world's problems together in close, mellow tones.

Each *banya* came equipped with an attendant nearly as old as the place itself, usually a *babushka*, an elderly lady (fully clothed) in charge of the towels and tea. This I didn't expect, with 50 naked men gamboling around. The first time I saw Granny—*Whoooah!* I grabbed-up a towel and covered myself. Joe Oakes, seeing my reaction, belly-laughed. "Relax, Mojo—she's seen more penises than a porn star!"

In Kostroma, one of the last towns, again, there were complications. Gannady, one of the Russian organizers, announced: "Thee 29 buks of Lenin culd knot explan all prublems we have meet. Nuw—dere is knot enouf ruum at Hotil . . . . Su suree. We haff ohder ludging, at lest minut—Yung Piuneer Camp where chillren ar instruuktid to be Communist. Anee voluntears, puleeze?"

I jumped at the chance. So far, we were so given over to running that other than the *banya* we hadn't experienced what it was like to actually live in Russia. Seven of us hobbled onto a bus and we rolled out into the lap of Mother Russia—that wild, dreamy countryside. I read from the *Insight Guide*: "The name 'Russian' has a feminine gender in the Russian language and according to Russian tradition the country itself has a feminine soul. The myth of 'mother Russia,' deriving from the divinity of 'mother earth' is central to the history of Russian culture . . . . This is reflected in Russian fairy tales, folklore, art and social structures.

"Although the concept of motherhood was and still is very important in Russian culture, there are other images of feminine strength, such as *Russalki*, virgin mermaids with powers of witchcraft and self-transformation, and *Baba Yaga*, an unmarried old witch with a wooden leg, and *Vassilisa Premudraya* (Vassilisa the Wisest), a woman who is far wiser and cleverer than any of the men in pagan myths and fairy tales."

We then turned down a long dirt road, finally stopping amidst an isolated ring of rustic cabins. Waiting to greet us was the Headmaster. The man was a monolith—at least 6,' 6" and 300 rock-solid pounds, with a beard that started just below his eyes, the hairs like steel wool: Rasputin on steroids.

His greeting was so warm (and bone-crunching) as he bear-hugged each of us down from the bus. Then he bellowed a loud command over his shoulder. There was a momentary lull, then at least one hundred wide-eyed children engulfed us, applauding wildly and jumping up and down as if we were the Beatles! They had never met the "enemy" before and getting with the program of *perestroika* Americans were now most welcome. Two angelic blonde girls, in red felt dresses trimmed in handmade lace ceremoniously presented us a round loaf of bread and salt. Everyone sang a Russian welcome song that made your heart swell as we broke bread together.

The Headmaster gave us a quick tour. The cabins were dorms and classrooms, but in the back, in extreme contrast to the primitive buildings, was an Olympic-sized swimming pond and a manicured quarter mile track. Gymnastic and weight lifting equipment filled the infield. It was in the Young Pioneer Camps that the future Soviet Olympic Champions were first discovered and cultivated.

After a tasty meal of sausages, black bread and borscht, the burly Headmaster, with bits of beets impaled on his beard then slammed a fist that made the Last Supper-sized table jump. "NUU VEE GU TU DEEZ-KU!"

Our group followed him out the door, whispering: "Did he say 'Disco?'" "No, couldn't be, not way out here . . . ." Our Russian interpreter just shrugged.

Sure enough, marching through the dew-wet grass, we heard a beat from the past over cut by a trio of familiar falsettos—the Bee-Gees: *"Stayin' Alive! Stayin' Alive!!"* inside a cabin in the back 'o beyond crammed full of dancing Communists. Climbing the steps, the walls and floor were shaking.

I leaned back against the vibrating wall, suddenly feeling totally done-in, as if all the marathons were now cumulatively extracting their toll. I couldn't dance if my life depended on it: had a blown left quad, a right Achilles tendon ratcheted-down tighter than a vise, and a blister the size of a silver dollar on my heel. Then just as I was shutting down—a ravishing young woman swayed before me: thick chestnut hair cascading over her shoulders and eyes like two burning coals. She took my hand and led me out onto the dance floor.

"I, *ah* can't move very well," I protested, dragging my heels.

In open space, she spun around and with a devilish gleam in those eyes, asked: "Du yu knuu tha Luum-baada?"

The 'Forbidden Dance' HERE? "No, I —"

"Den I vill teech yu!"

She did and it was nearly an out-of-body experience: A weary, broken-down marathoner, under Olga's life-giving touch, suddenly became Gene Kelley, Fred Astaire and Rudy Nureyev rolled into one!

After 'Deez-ku' we all poured out of the building into the fresh air. In the center of a meadow was a blazing bonfire. All hundred of us held hands in a giant circle and danced around the flames, ring-around-the-rosey style. An elderly, wispy bearded man appeared playing a violin—the strings attached directly to our feet. The sun was setting, the white birch forest breathing . . . . We were deep in Zhivago Country and while two-stepping back and forth, to-and-fro, hands lifting, my head swiveled: searching for Olga. She was three down. Over the heads of the children, we locked eyes and in the depths of her gaze, the width of her smile, and the heat of the flames—I fell hopelessly in love.

After the dancing, with everyone walking toward the dormitory cabins, we had time to talk. Olga told me she was the Russian Literature teacher. I told her I was a journalist and was writing my first book. She asked what it was about and after I described it: "Et sunds lik yu ar veree muuch lik my favurit Ameeriken autur, Jeek Luunden!" We then tossed the titles of all his books and short stories back-and-forth and then she said he was almost as popular in Russia as Tolstoy! Olga then stopped, rocking back and forth on her feet, in front of a large cabin all the girls were pouring into.

Not wanting to let go of her, desperate, I asked if we could just walk together for a few minutes more? And that I had gifts for her! "Yeez, budt, I hahv—dunt nu huw tu sah wurd in Ingleesh . . . . "

"Ah, *curfew*!" O.K. I understand, but please! wait here, just for a few seconds—I'll be right back!!"

I sprinted all-out, tore through my duffel bag, and dashed back to Olga. But now we had company—the Headmaster, looming on the porch of the main cabin like a Dostoevskian priest. Under his glaring iconic gaze, I handed Olga tubes of lipstick and silk stockings and a Victoria Secret bra that I had the foresight to stuff inside a copy of Jack London's *Call of The Wild*, but one of the lavender cups bulged out of the book. Olga was incredulous. Her brown eyes, enormous to begin with, swelled as large as walnuts. "Ih dunt knuw vat tu sey . . . . " A tear slid down her cheek; she squeezed my hand for a long moment, then head down—hurried away. When I turned around, the Headmaster was gone.

Early the next morning, back on the bus, with our Russian interpreter counting heads and the driver starting up the engine, I felt sad, so conflicted. For the very first time in my life I wanted to stop the constant traveling, the incessant movement and stay: expand those magical moments last night into the rest of my life. I gave serious thought to jumping ship and somehow staying at the Pioneer Camp: "FIRST AMERICAN DEFECTS TO THE SOVIET UNION!" *I could teach English here, yes, why couldn't I? Hell—I just can't bear to leave her!!* Just then, at the very last moment before the bus pulled away a young woman came dashing out from the compound, the scarf concealing her face sent sailing by the speed of her legs. It was Olga, her outstretched arms encircling a massive bouquet of wildflowers: vibrant crimson, gold, lavender blooms that she stepped up onto the bus with and poured into my lap while burning her eyes into my soul. Olga ran off, doubling her speed—a "pre-emptive strike" at the stern Headmaster: daring the unforgivable by doing the unthinkable.

As the bus rolled forward, I kept my head down, pretending to take long sniffs of the flowers, but I was really 'watering' them—hiding my tears from further teasing from the guys and loopy in love with Olga Pobendimskaya . . . .

One last (gasp) marathon and we all then cruised up the Volga River for a day and night on a boat. What should have been a relaxing float turned stormy as the French team threatened to mutiny over the lousy food and exposed sleeping conditions (on the outer decks, rain or shine; and rain it did, incessantly). At one point, with the scow in a river-lock, Francois led his men ashore and they marched away across a levee into the mists—before contrite concessions were finally shouted across the water.

Now in Moscow, with the 10 consecutive marathons completed, we had a few days of total R & R before flying home. Joe Oakes gathered us together in front of Red Square. "O.K., listen-up. Rather than stay in another hotel, after sightseeing, we're going to divide up to stay with local Russians so you can get the flavor of what's it's really like here. Unfortunately, there are big shortages now. These people have very little, barely the basics, but what they do have they will gladly share with you. Keep in mind you're not only representing yourselves, but the United States, as well. The people who have invited you to stay with them have rarely, if ever, met Americans."

Joe then read off who was staying with whom. "And finally, the two young 'uns, Ed and Mojo—you're with Nail."

After playing tourists, later that afternoon we went underground, riding that immaculate subway: the stations like museums built from the finest marbles and showing historic statues and frescoes, instead of grit and graffiti on the walls. We rode and rode—Moscow, away from the monuments, a huge, hodgepodge of city; then another long bus ride past mile after mile of the same drab concrete apartment buildings. Finally, we jumped off—entered one of the cement edifices and followed Nail up a long staircase. Ed and I looked at each other and nodded: *Like Joe said, we're appreciative of anything they might offer* . . . . Nail knocked sharply. Instead of what we expected (middle-age to elderly couple with maps of lifetime suffering on their faces), standing before us was a fresh-faced, drop-dead gorgeous young woman with impossibly high cheekbones, stylish black hair and, again, those smoldering eyes! We followed Katarina into the apartment. Our preconceptions were now totally shattered. No shabby, cabbage-scented, tiny one-room apartment crammed full with three generations of family. No, Katarina lived *alone* in four opulently appointed rooms! Nail swung open the refrigerator (stuffed full) and grabbed up three Heinekens. Katarina laid out a platter of meats and cheeses. MTV (Soviet-style) played on a Sony Trinitron. In broken English, her rounded Slavic vowels making her even more alluring she asked if we wanted to "tak shuuwer or batt?" Yes! I still had birch leaf bits embedded in places God or Lenin never intended . . . . Seeing us settled-in, Nail said good-bye; that he would stop by tomorrow. Ed sat down with Katarina; I went first into the bathroom. As the tub thundered with hot water, I felt totally disoriented: *This Moscow—or Paris?* The shelves above the sink were stocked with Chanel perfumes, Lancome cosmetics, expensive scented soaps. The towels were large and full and bearing "Hotel Ritz" logos. *What's the Story here?* the writer in me wondered. *Only Royalty lives this well in Russia!*

Then with Ed in the bathroom, I sipped beer, picked at the spread and learned that Katarina was originally from Siberia, the frontier town of Irkutz on the shores of the largest freshwater body in the world, Lake Baikal. I was dying to ask what she did for a living, but, rather than risk being impolite, instead I inquired about Siberia, snowstorms, wolves and the Baikal seals, the only freshwater pinnipeds.

We then went out for a walk, past a small neighborhood center of stores, each with an unbelievably long line tailing out of it. Picture around-the-corner lines in the U.S. for a blockbuster movie, but in Russia people go to the same lengths, not for light entertainment, but for the very basics of life: meat, bread, vodka, cigarettes. Then for most, after a three hour wait, when they finally step into the store the shelves are totally bare. In a land of constant shortages and suffering, hope continues to "spring eternal." Many Russians, not able to see the distant store, itself, will join a line simply because it exists.

Katarina strode past all the Sisyphean strugglers, leading us down a shabby side street. She approached a bare, nondescript door and rapped a deliberate knocking pattern. The door swung open and we stepped into a miniature supermarket to rival any in America. It was comparable to a condensed version of Zabar's Deli in New York City, a cornucopia overflowing with anything and everything edible on Earth. Katarina knew exactly what she wanted and where it was: sun dried tomatoes, oranges, a whole salmon, *bing-bing-boom.* She paid from a roll of dollars that could have choked Luca Brasi.

Walking back to her apartment we discussed Communism. Her English was broken and my Russian nearly nonexistent but I quickly learned that yes, despite Gorbachev's *perestroika,* communism was still in effect for the masses—*nothing* now to share equally, but for the elite, riches existed behind doors if you knew how to knock and had dollars, not worthless rubles, to pay the freight. I told her of running past all that rich black soil in the countryside outside Moscow; all the bountiful gardens and farms. She said that there was no infrastructure, no dependable delivery system to get those goods into the cities; and if products did arrive, they were undermined by corruption. Both the "vig" and most of the pot went to the Soviet upper-class, with very little trickling down to the hoi-polloi. The have-nots could easily have much more than the basics, but it would never be, unless the peasants, once again, rebelled . . . but then the cycle would repeat all over again: the 'crem(lin)' would rise to skim from the common 'milk' all over again.

"Vladamir Lenin must be rolling over in his grave!" I said. "Over how his pure communistic principles are now being violated."

"Hav yu seen uld Vlad latlee? Leenen's Tumb makz mur munee fur Pulutburu than anytheng elz. Gud tu haf waxen Gudz—day leev furevahr!"

It was killing me inside not asking exactly how Katarina was connected: *by birth? occupation?* but I kept biting my tongue, sensing better not to push it . . . that the answers would come in time.

Later that evening, with all of us cleaned-up and Katarina in a lethal, full-length red silk dress, slit high up both thighs, we stepped out into the street. A cab appeared out of nowhere. Ten minutes later, arms-linked-three-across, Eddie and I snapped our heads back behind "The Kat" (as we called her), rolling eyes as we walked up a red carpet into a frosted-cake building: a casino. *Gambling? One of the Evils of Capitalism—in the Soviet Union?!* The Kat greased an obtrusive bouncer's palm with a knot of dollars and he looked away from our stevedore appearances (blue jeans and wrinkled warm-up jackets—hey, we never expected *this!*)

With an insouciant swing of her hips (and alternate flashes of creamy thighs) Katarina walked in as if she owned the place. In the main room it was early "Goldfinger," with Chinese, Japanese, bald monocled Germans wearing Saville Row suits, clicking chips and tossing back vodka shooters. The air was thick with the aroma of Cuban cigars deftly cut now by "Poison," Katarina's scent. As I watched her beauty totally disrupt the room, I thought of how a young woman's sexuality is *THE* most powerful force on Earth. As she leaned to murmur something into the ear of a lucky man—all the gamblers seemed to list that way. The scene made me recall an old proverb: "The whisper of a pretty girl can be heard farther than the roar of a lion."

Ed played blackjack and won enough up front so as to ease the inevitable pain of losing more later. Out of the corner of my eye I watched as, throughout the evening, at least half of the international players in the room nodded to Katarina as if they knew her; and she exchanged business cards with the rest.

We then linked-up again at the tiny bar, tossed back a few nightcaps, and Katarina asked if during the Super Marathon we had met any Russian "garls?" I nearly burst into tears there on the spot! Requiring only the slightest nudge, my heart erupted with a lengthy love sonnet extolling the virtues of Olga Pobendimskaya that would have made the great poet Yevtushenko smile. All the while Katarina kept shaking her head and rolling her onyx eyes. She whipped a Cross pen out of her clutch purse and scribbled down the name and town of the Pioneer Camp on a bar napkin. We then headed home.

The next day, after sleeping in, rain pounded down and Nail came by with a half-case of fresh stock. It was the first opportunity we had to totally relax and let-go. We started drinking vodka midday, rerunning and toasting each of the marathons we had completed. Feeling left out, Katarina cut into our male bravura by pulling out her photo albums. Drop-dead in teeny bikinis, there she was in many of Europe's hot spots with men old enough to be her father.

When Kat padded into the kitchen, Nail announced: "She es furst-clazz call garl. Garlfrand of beeg-shot KGB, and alsu frand tu yur pulyticens whu cumes heer to Musscuw."

Ed nonchalantly shrugged his shoulders. (In the Guinness Book of World Records for running coast-to-coast across the United States *three times!* nothing much rattled him.) I said, "More power to her!" Nail disclosed this information only because we hadn't asked for it. Now he was appreciative that we didn't judge her negatively. Another solid clink of shot glasses and he said: "In Amarika, I saw men tak garl tu deener, muvee, buy her manny expinsieve thengz—den wunt sex. Su, wut the diffarance ef they geve munee to garl, op frunt—direklee?"

Ed nodded, "Many times, that's what the garls would rather have."

Michael (ever the romantic): "Yes, but as long as it doesn't keep her from someday finding love."

Katarina entered the room with more food and Nail talked to her in Russian for a long minute. She answered back, looking both relieved and gesturing animatedly.

Nail translated: "She say Luv es fur Fuls. Munee, Capitlizm rulz!" Another ringing toast and then we all sang along with Paula Abdul on MTV: *"Ahme Furevar Yur Garl!"*

Katarina said that her dream was to marry an American; come to the U.S., then make really big money 'working' Loz Veegaz! She had already met her husband: another runner named Jeff who came through on a previous tour. He was now saving money to send for her and she was trying to (carefully) get out with a passport and visa on the black market.

Although Gorbachev was exploring other options to Communism with *perestroika*, the Russians still remained cautious and suspicious. They were afraid that if they really pushed against the confines of the Iron Curtain, they would be hit with the "Chinese Solution"—the recent massacre in Tiananmen Square, so subterfuge and secrets were still the *modus operandus* for most.

At some point in the rising tide of vodka, Katarina scribbled down Jeff's phone number and handed it to me. "Yes, I promise to call the lucky bastard when I get home," I said standing at attention with my hand over my heart, "and tell him I met the faire, the beautiful, the incomparable Katarina!"

Later that night, completely pickled in alcohol; and passed out in the spare bedroom, I then kept hearing an alarm: *ring-ringg-ringgging* and then my name being called—Katarina's voice: "MISHA, QUEEKLEE! IT TIZ YUR ULGA!"

I pulled on a pair of jeans and burst out the door. "Wha—?! *WHERE?*"

"KUUM HEER!"

I followed her voice into a new room where she held out a telephone. In the split-second it took to lift the horn to my ear, I saw that I was in the Soviet call girl's love nest, and Katarina was sitting crossed-legged on the middle of the bed, totally naked, with a blue curl of cigarette smoke rising above her. I blubbered away into the phone, pouring my heart out to Olga over the sputtering connection and she returned much of the same. After two failed attempts to write down her mailing address correctly, Katarina snatched the phone away and in an exchange of rapid-fire Russian scribbled down all the numbers. She tossed the paper my way; shot me a laser-beam look; and in English said into the phone: "Yu arr awhl thees mun talkz abutt!" More slobbering from me and then Olga was gone.

"*Spasiba*, Katarina. Such a nice thing you did!" I said clumsily extending my hand across the bed to shake her's.

The Kat hissed and flung a pillow at my head.

Returning home to California, I wrote letter after letter to Olga, enclosing pictures, spare dollars, department store perfume samples, heady dreams, Jack London paperbacks, the Victoria's Secret catalog . . . . Few missives got through (intercepted by the Dostoevskian Headmaster?) Then all my latest communiqués were sent back, stamped with that Elvis lament, 'Return To Sender.'

Evidently the Cold War had yet to thoroughly thaw or Olga had moved on. Eventually, I did the same. And I did call Jeff . . . . He lived in nearby Oakland and we met for drinks—shots of Stoly (what else?) at the Jack London Pub (where else!). Yes, he fell head-over-Nikes in love with Katarina, but unlike me, decided ultimately not to pursue it. "Some things are best left alone, framed forever in that time and place. As much as those 'garls' want to come over, their souls are and always will be attached to Mother Russia. They wouldn't be happy here in the long run. But hey—" he said clinking shot glasses, "how can we ever forget those smoldering eyes?!"

Then, as if punctuating the entire experience, like a birch branch out of the blue, a scroll arrived one day in the mail with the official "Soviet Super Marathon" logo, bearing these words (Russian sentimentality best read with vuudka in raised hand):

THIS HEREBY CONFIRMS
THAT *MISHA MODZELEWSKI*
TROD THE LAND OF "THE GOLDEN RING
OF RUSSIA" AND SAVED IN THE HEART
ITS CHARMS AND WONDERS FOR LIKE
THE SUN GENEROUSLY SHEDS ITS
LIGHT AND WARMTH, SO DOTH OUR
LAND SHARE ITS BEAUTY WITH
BENEVOLENT TRAVELERS, THAT BECOME
WISER AND THE EYES OF THE WISE
ALWAYS WISH
WELL
WRITTEN.

My attention zips back to the present as we close-in on a pack of other runners: their colorful day-glo clothes and flex patterns in their legs leap anew to my eyes, after following in Scott's shadow most of the day. I feel a keen sense of unreality, running together now with other human beings miles from nowhere, deep in the woods. It feels good to be with other runners: two men and a woman, whom we don't know—drafting a bit behind them. They gladly take us in. There is no defensive wall of competition. Not at this stage, when you boost anyone for being out here at all and encourage everyone still moving to finish.

Talking comes in short staccato bursts, on the exhales: "Great day huh?" Scott says, as we lope up behind them.

"Hey! Yah!!"

"Guys look great!"

"You all too!!" I say.

"YA EAT AN ELEPHANT ONE BITE AT A TIME!" one of the men announces his strategy while bounding along. After bathing in their bright energy, and discharging a bit of our own, Scott and I slowly pull away.

Over the smooth trail—time expands out again like taffy, pulling memory along.

I thought of *not* running in AFRICA. The second morning of a three week safari in Kenya, I got up early; laced up a new pair of Nikes and was doing a few *tai chi* stretches under a big baobab tree that had just finished "playing" music. Before heading out to run, in my journal I wrote: *"It's dark and you're inside a tent in the depths of Africa. It's dark, yet your ears awaken you again. Last time it was the lion that roared from across the river. Now it's in the trees above you—the same primordial force, but in multiple voices. The dawn chorus has begun. The trees are pulsating in a wild rhythm—a crosshatch of calls from bush babies, birds, barking baboons, screeching insects—all rising to a crescendo for the sun, then fading as the light increases, leaving one instrument: the atonal 'gong' of the Tropical Boubou . . . . ."*

With a few metallic notes still chiming, I finished my stretches and joyfully stepped through the tall grass to the dirt trail unfolding out to the horizon—"Go ahead . . . if you want to be bloody breakfast for a lion or leopard!" said Robert Carr-Hartley, our safari guide, lifting a cup of coffee to his lips. "What are you thinking? You're not in Kansas anymore, Bub."

What *was* I thinking? Force of habit: seeing a trail rolled-out in the new morn . . . but take three steps and get taken down by a 500 pound lioness out to feed her pride! Since I was 12 years old I had never gone more than a couple days without running and now was looking at 3 solid weeks of being camp and Range Rover bound. I never run fast enough to miss time to serious injuries; and I'm blessed with sound motion mechanics. (Best indicators are the bottoms of your running shoes: If the heels wear evenly across you'll run forever, but if they wear-down at a slant to either side, you're pronating: stressing an out-of-alignment hip, knee, ankle—or all of above.) Turning my back on the trail, panic stabbed my spine. I feared if I had to quit cold-turkey, withdrawing from endorphins: the brain/mood chemicals responsible for the "runner's high," I would turn surly and skitzo like injured, addicted runner friends knocked off their feet by knee surgery or stress fractures for weeks. But there was no withdrawal from any high in Africa, when you were constantly pumped by seeing a dazzling animal or landscape, and besides, you got a solid 8 hour aerobic and anabolic workout every day bouncing all around the interior of the Range Rover, as we moved over the pitted and corrugated "roads."

Robert, not only saved my life, but absolutely made the trip! The history of the Carr-Hartley family spans the entire British colonial era in Kenya. Robert's great-grandfather, a veterinarian, administered to the domestic stock that helped build the railroad from Nairobi to Mombasa in the late 1880s. His grandfather was Kenya's first official "Elephant Controller," trying to keep the pachyderms out of the pioneers' crops. The Carr-Hartley clan evicted elephants by banging pots and pans and firing shots into the air; then running for their lives—grandmother chucking her boys into the bushes and sprinting flat-out amid the stampeding, trumpeting herd.

With such a family history, desk jobs would be death sentences. The current Carr-Hartleys make their living guiding safaris and live-trapping and transporting big game for Kenya's national parks. The road fronting the family ranch used to be the runway where Denys Finch-Hatton parked his plane when visiting Karen

Blixen (*Out of Africa* author Isak Dineson) at her nearby estate. When not leading Monaco's royal family or trapping lions, Robert lives on a small house on the ranch, with servants providing him the free time to paint lavish wildlife murals on his walls.

He earned his fixed wing and helicopter pilot licenses (graduating from the Bell Ranger Helicopter School in Florida in record time). In his late-twenties, he drove his own Range Rover and spoke fluent Swahili, which he learned before English from a native nanny.

"My family is always surprising me," Carr-Hartley said. "I was looking through a scrapbook the other day and saw snapshots of Clark Gable and Ava Gardner. They filmed most of *"Mogambo"* at the ranch.

When asked about his most unusual safari clients, Robert told about a certain Hollywood producer and his wife. "When I met them at the airport in Nairobi—I couldn't believe it. His wife was in high heels, a satin jump suit and rhinestones—looking like never in her life had she stepped off concrete.

"But the first night out in the bush they got me good. The went to bed ahead of me. All of a sudden the producer lets out an almighty scream. He comes running out across the camp—a short, tubby guy—toupee falling off to the side, holding up a big snake by the neck. 'Oh my God!' I thought, 'I'm going to lose a client.' The snake turned out to be rubber—a prop from one of his movies. Every day we played some sort of gag with it.

"Then there were the five women: the wife of a famous Las Vegas casino owner and four of her friends. I had to wake them up at 4:00 a.m. for the first game drive because it took 'em two hours to get ready. I said, 'The wildebeest won't care what makeup you have on.'

"One of the women bought a batik tablecloth in a market along the way. I told her to wash it in salt water so the colors wouldn't run."

"You do it," she said.

"No way," I said. "I've never washed anything in my life. At the end, Elaine thought I was 'It'—Tarzan or something. She still writes to me, wants me to come to Las Vegas. No bloody way!"

Like the great white hunters before him, Carr-Hartley didn't want us to think he suffers fools gladly. Tongue-in-cheek, he told us that "Whenever a guide has a difficult client he'll shoot a zebra and at night, tie the carcass to the client's bed. Straightens him right out—when a lion takes hold of the meat!"

Modern-day Africa is full of conundrums. Robert is a "watch doctor" to a tribe of Samburu. "They love our watches. They'll trade a sacred cow for a digital watch. But it's not keeping time that interests them; it's the way the designs: the numbers and symbols pulse on the screens that they love. When I visit them every few months back in the bush—I bring them fresh batteries . . . ." We were there for one of his watch doctor runs, breaking the planned itinerary by unanimous consent to make an arduous journey out to see the Samburu. Finally after an all-day carom, fending ourselves off the Range Rover's walls like pebbles in a gourd (and Robert announcing more than once that he was "quite bloody lost!")—out in an open spot we were suddenly 'attacked' by a group of Samburu warriors. They charged from all sides, shrieking fierce ululations at the top of their voices and shaking their spears as they surrounded the vehicle— fighting for position in front of the SUV's wing mirrors . . . to readjust their facial make-up and ochre-caked hairdos! Just as the male bird is a riot of primary colors and often fluffs and displays to attract attention from females, so, too, do aboriginal males. Despite their lithe frames and interest in cosmetics, there wasn't the slightest thing "pouf" about them. A Samburu man can drop a 500 pound lion with nothing more than a spear dipped in courage.

The smiling warriors then led us into the village, hugging the Watch Doctor and allowing us to photograph their entire tribe. They were absolutely astonished by my Polaroid Camera . . . huddled together, watching, like magic, as the camera spat out a small square that slowly turned into *them*! (Our expensive Nikon systems they deemed worthless, for after the click of the shutter—no picture emerged.)

As we moved across Kenya, at promptly 4:00 p.m. every afternoon, no matter where we'd be, our caravan of vehicles would screech to a halt and the camp workers would set up a table, snap out a white tablecloth and boil water for tea. It was absolutely surreal to be sitting smack in the middle of a dry river bed, sipping Earl Grey from the original Carr-Hartley solid-silver tea set, a family heirloom spanning three centuries. As you lifted a bone china cup and saucer to your chest, an inquisitive giraffe swung its head above the treetops or a herd of yoke-horned Cape Buffalo crossed with a thick-flanked swagger a few yards away.

Whenever things went right, which was nearly all the time for this safari, Robert, in his clipped British accent declared: "Well done!" We then all drove that oft-repeated pronouncement into the ground, echoing *"Whal dun!"* at every possible opportunity, not to mock Robert, but because it made you feel so prim-and-proper saying it—momentarily abandoning barbaric American for the lofty ramparts of The Queen's English! Robert often uttered another word, uniquely British, that is quite simply the best adjective in the world. I first heard it in London while doing an interview on BBC Radio about my first book. I just happened to be very talky that day and afterwards the producer came on in my headphones saying: "Michael, that was absolutely *smashing!*"

Now Robert was using the same superlative on a near hourly basis. We Yanks followed suit—gleefully mimicking "Bwana's" favorite words, with them popping out at the most surprising moments. After sex one night with my wife, without thinking I punctuated the act with: *"Whal dun!"*

"Yes quite!" she chortled back, and for added measure: *"Smashing!"*

The last few days of the safari we entered the Maasai Mara, the northern edge of the fabled Serengeti Plains. Instead of having to stay strictly on the dirt roads as in all the other game parks, the Serengeti was open range and you could drive anywhere. Immediately, on the way in we followed a pack of Wild Dogs—clipping along at speeds of 40 mph—taking down an impala right in front of the Rover! The sky in the Serengeti stretched forever, the grass was emerald green; and millions of grazing animals dotted the landscape.

We camped in a bend of the Mara River, where we were warned to keep our cameras close, not only for great shots, but a previous safarist had placed his expensive Nikon down for a moment and a baboon had made off with it! It was a great spot. Besides a pack of *paparazzi* baboons, the trees were adorned with "flying jewels," like the Golden-Winged Sun Bird and the Lilac Breasted Roller. When we could tear our eyes away from the birds—we watched colossal hippos blimp-up to the surface of the river and yawn, displaying four sword-length incisors. (Which of the "Big Five": lion, leopard, elephant, rhino, cape buffalo kills the most people every year in Africa? Neither, it's the huffy, territorial hippopotamus, often smashing up through a native's flimsy raft and then biting the poor bloke in half with those wicked teeth.) The first night in the Mara, while enjoying our evening ritual of sitting in canvas chairs around a cracking fire sipping a cold libation, we were joined by two local Maasai natives who stepped into the firelight right "Out of Africa." The legendary men, nearly as tall and thin as their towering spears, stayed with us for the remainder of the safari as guards and resident "naturalists." Robert spoke their language and we peppered him with a thousand questions for them. What an honor to be in the presence of such men! Innately regal in bearing, they were truly "Masters of the Universe"—without even trying.

One night, after a lion chuffed from across the river and a full moon cleared the treetops I finally fell asleep, only to awaken a few hours later—wide-awake. I felt edgy. Something was off, amiss. The air was still, too still. I knew that absence of sound from wilderness living in British Columbia, Canada—the lull before a sudden storm—or animal attack? I sat up in bed and looked at the moonlit canvas walls of the tent. All I saw were the tall dark shadows of surrounding tree trunks. Then—the tree trunks began to move! *What tha?!?* I got out of bed, uncorded the tent flap and peered out—into a living dream: a herd of wild elephants moving silently, absolutely without a sound through our camp as their towering legs sauntered by a few feet from my eyes; their tusks aglow in the moonlight: "Jumanji"—for real!

At breakfast, I asked Robert and, via him, the Maasai if they had seen the elephants last night? I was surprised when they said no, especially our Maasai guard/warriors. "Were they *pink?*" Robert teased. I then described what I saw and how silently they moved.

"Yes," Robert said, "Amazing how when they eat you can hear them strip a bush or shatter a tree from miles away, but when they're on the move they can be like phantoms—you won't hear a twig snap. As much as they weigh, there's pad-like cushioning in their feet."

Then proof surfaced . . . . I had placed my running shoes that I wore all day outside the tent before going to bed that night. Not a good move, as Robert had advised us, with sneaky hyenas rapidly evolving a taste for expensive athletic shoes ('Reeboks'— a new species of African game!) from the many safarists coming though—but the shoes were just too muddy to bring into our homey abode. Now, looking around the tent for elephant tracks with the Maasai, I found only one shoe. The youngest of the Maasai found the other nearby, calling out excitedly in his native "Maa" language. We went over to him. He had found the mate— flattened. With the tip of his spear, he flicked the shoe out of the earth. I gave a low whistle. It looked like it had been steam rolled, but the "Air Max" bubble sac, sealed in at the heel, was still intact! (Should have sent it to Nike headquarters in Oregon with a note: "Your Air Max stands up to everything—including a herd of elephants.)

I thought of how some of my most memorable runs took place on cruise ships plying ALASKAN WATERS. Hired in the summers as a ship's Naturalist, I lectured and pointed-out wildlife to the passengers. The remainder of the time I wrote, read and ran. All the ships have jogging tracks looping around the top deck, wide open to the sky and sea. Living at home, I tried to avoid boredom by rotating runs in different places throughout the week. However, the scenery of those places remains much the same, but go 10 miles around a platform continuously moving through narrow fjords, under towering mountains, alongside calving glaciers and no run is ever the same lap-after-lap on any given day! Fourteen stories up in that freshest of air, cutting tight into the turns and sprinting the straight-aways out along the teak rail—you're striding through the sky and having a "swell time" as the long roller waves out in the Gulf of Alaska pitch the track beneath you. The ocean is a living, capricious presence, constantly commanding your attention on both sides—out to far horizons. One morning, just I was kicking in the last lap of an 8-miler, a 40 ton Humpback whale stopped me in my tracks—as it broke through the surface, breaching high into the air: laying-out a full barrel roll while twirling long flippers; then smashing down in a white-walled explosion! Another day, with the sea like glass, a vast multitude of pacific white-sided dolphins suddenly danced along both sides of the ship, surfing the bow wave and a few bursting upwards to eyeball stunned passengers . . . . Then, one afternoon coming out of Glacier Bay, the ship slowed for a very unusual sight: two bull moose swimming for the far shore, their antler racks swinging like rocking chairs—when a pod of killer whales materialized out of nowhere: after a few minutes all that was left of the 1,500 pound moose were two blood slicks on the surface . . . . In late-May, with winter refusing to relinquish its hold on the land: the pine mountains dusted white down to the water-level I ran through punishing storms. Pure exhilaration—as I was pelted with rain, hail, then snow on the starboard side; then wind-blown/dry- cleaned double-time down along port, with sun beams suddenly bursting through the leaden sky like solid pillars; and off the stern, in the vast expanse of Cross Sound a kaleidoscopic rainbow flared mid-sky in colors Kodachrome can't capture . . . . And the summer solstice evening in the Gulf of Alaska when an endless sunset, unfurling well past midnight, painted the icy wastes of the looming 15,000 foot Mt. Fairweather fuscia and lavender and each time around the track there was added yet another staggering, luminous hue . . . . Running, late at night, through a storm of northern lights that flared in eerie splendor, iridescent blue green and red currents—electrifying both the sky and the viewer.

One morning my upper-deck run was interrupted by "The Woman With The Singing Breasts." "Are you Michael the Naturalist?" she said. "Yessss," I stammered, a bit flustered because she was very well-endowed and her breasts were chirping, peeping, singing—under her V-neck sweater! (Suddenly, I'm in a Fellini movie.)

"Oh, GOOD!" she exclaimed, reaching down into her brassiere and extracting a pearl gray bird with webbed feet. "I was up here earlier this morning doing my daily constitutional and I kept hearing a bird crying—then I found it, right over there, under the smokestack. Didn't know what to do, so I picked him up and went to the purser's desk and they said to find you."

"You did the right thing—keeping him in, uh, a warm place."

A girlish giggle. "My three husbands used to think so—they all fell asleep, right here, every night!" she said, patting her ample décolletage. "But what kind of bird is he? How did he get way out here?"

"Maybe a Storm-Petrel. He probably got blown off course and exhausted, came down to rest on what he thought was an island. If he allowed you to pick him up and allows me to do this (spread his wings out)—good, nothing broken—that means he's in shock. A wild bird, up to speed, normally wouldn't let you even near him."

"He's all done-in. *Pooooor baby!*"

We went to Meredith's cabin and made a nest of fluffy towels in her suitcase. We placed the bird inside and closed the top almost all the way; then turned up the heat in the room. "There, best thing we can do is let it have a good rest. I'll come back in a few hours, OK?"

I checked on the bird mid-afternoon and it was hunkered down, eyes-closed, sleeping away. Meredith was reading a romance novel and caring for the bird with the same protectiveness and pride she had raised four children with. We decided to let it rest and meet again just before dinner, at 6:00 p.m. It was formal night on the ship, so Meredith in a formfitting, sequined red gown and *moi* in a white dinner jacket, carried the now feisty feathered fellow back up to the jogging track. I set him down on the flat teak rail. He fluffed all his feathers in the brisk air; looked over his shoulder at us, then dropped straight down about five stories before the wind filled his wings and he zoomed straight out toward the sun. As we watched him arrow away—across the wild ocean expanse, Meredith burst into tears and I had a major lump in my throat. We hugged and I patted her shoulder: "You should feel so proud of yourself, for what you did . . . . "

"Did you see the way he *looked* at us?" Meredith smiled through her tears. "I will take that to my grave!"

Then running through the heart of RIO DE JANEIRO, striding with the 'tall and tan and lovely' girls from Ipanema, Amazonia, Paris, and St. Louis . . . hundreds of people, all dressed in white, racing the clock through the cordoned-off streets of Copacabana. Suddenly, away from the tall buildings, the night sky opened like a deep bowl, pouring down fireworks: rainbow-hued expanding plumes as I stood, at midnight, on the wide sweep of beach with two million people, reeling in Rio, the *Cidade Maravilhosa* ("marvelous city") on New Year's Eve.

To slake my thirst, I slithered through the crowds over to a beach shack and ordered a whole coconut. Like a jack-in-the-box, the reed-slim proprietor popped out the side-door and with three rapid strokes of his machete sliced topnotch openings in the football sized nut, then flicked-in a straw. I removed my shoes and while sipping the cool, sweet milk, chugged through sand, to the southern Atlantic to join in the annual homage to *Yemanja*, the Yoruba "goddess of the sea."

I passed many shrines in her honor, circular mounds or hollows in the sand, holding lit candles, offerings of flowers, food, liquor to Yemanja and other *Orixas* (African Gods) presiding atop the bowers in statutory forms. One shrine was heart-shaped, with the bottom of the heart pointed toward the sea, so that the good spirits could enter and the bad ones depart. Each shrine was as individual as its worshipper, yet the repeated elements of delicate flowers with luminous candles in such an unexpected "cathedral" raised goose-bumps on the skin.

During previous trips to Rio, it had been abundantly clear that the beach is where the *cariocas* (natives) do most of their living. They may work in the skyscrapers or apartment buildings squeezed-in amidst the mountains and rain forest, but upon the unbounded beaches is where they socialize, play *futebol*, dance, eat, court a lover, and pay homage to their gods. The beach is the great "equalizer." Whether you are a rich industrialist with a double-penthouse or one of millions living crammed together in the hillside *favelas* (ghettos)—on the sand, stripped-down without status-bearing clothes or adornments, you are as we should be: all one people. The bitter bite of poverty is softened in Rio by the blessings of nature. During a previous visit, on the beach I befriended Rico, a young boy from the "Hell Hole" favela. "The favela," he pointed, "I only sleep. Here," he smiled, arms extending like wings, "here I live!"

As I passed the many shrines I noticed more than one abandoned dog, every rib showing, approach the plates of food in the reliquaries like arrows about to pierce a target; then abruptly veer away a few feet from the circles as if encountering a visible wall.

Out in the velvet-aired, tropical night with the soft susurration of surf and such a collective calling of the spirits, New Year's Eve in Rio is like no other party in the world.

I was prepped on the way down by a flight attendant and Portuguese Speaker, Eleison Diettrich, a native carioca who left only a few years ago to explore more of the world. "Oh, what you will see tonight!" he said. "And keep this in mind— even though Brazil is the world's largest Catholic country, we have a saying that we're 90% Catholic and 100% Spiritist! The Christ statue may be on top of the mountain, but many gods are worshipped down below.

"Over the past four centuries, 15 million Africans came to Brazil, many as slaves; a far greater population than the colonial Portuguese and resident Indians, and their religions of *Umbanda* and *Candomble*—known to most outsiders as *Macumba* are very strong to this day."

At ocean's edge, cariocas were mindfully tossing flowers into the sea, mostly white lilies, gladiolus, and roses—each bouquet accompanied by wishes for the New Year. It wasn't just here at Copacabana, but all along Rio's twenty miles of beaches people were wading out into the sea; many turning around to fling the flowers like salt, for a pinch of added luck, over their shoulders. If the blossoms floated out to sea, Yemanja would grant your desires. If they were returned on the incoming tide . . . submit them again next year.

Off in the distance were hundreds of strange lights flickering on the surface of the night sea. I was puzzled as to their origin—until I came across three stooped, matronly women, filling a child-sized boat with their offerings of flowers, a bottle of champagne, a vial of perfume, a pearl necklace, a lit candle, all around a small statute of Yemanja. The friends hoisted their skirts, waded out into the foaming surf and gave their offering a resolute launch. For awhile, like life itself, it could go either way . . . . I push-*pushed* the floating shrine with my eyes— not wanting to see it returned to these lively women, their hopes dashed like the other shipwrecks at our feet. Then almost imperceptibly the boat was gone, aglow on the horizon, joining the fleet of favorability.

When I boldly asked what their wishes were for the New Year, one of the ladies gave a mathematical reply: "Wished for good twice as much and," she paused to slice her hand low through the air, "half as much the bad."

Farther down the beach, a much larger boat headed for the ocean hoisted on the shoulders of two men and guided through the crowd to water's edge by a drummer, his head half-shaved (to more easily let-in the gods). This boat, with a confident wavy white line along its hull, was overflowing with flowers and offerings; the many candles being lit right to water's edge. The bearers walked it out into the surf, and gave the bower a strong sendoff. Looking at first to be overburdened with hopes and dreams; too heavy to advance in a fickle tide, its karmic cargo must have pleased Yemanja for as soon as the barge touched water it skimmed lightly out to sea—trailing wands of foam.

As I walked along the beach, there were islands of exotic activity. In the center of one tight huddle, fronting an altar covered with both the sacred and profane: empty beer bottles and plaster Orixas, a black woman, a *mae de santos* (sainted mother) chanted wildly, extending her arm, palm-up to the sky . . . . When it was fully charged, at full quiver, she snapped her hand down toward worthy subjects—who then surged around as if struck by lightning, babbling in voices not their own.

Watching the ceremony, there was nothing evil or pagan about it. It was like going back in time when religion was in its purest and most primal form: people as humble conduits with a direct pipeline to their gods—before the ubiquitous missionaries arrived, controlling and corrupting the signal. But even though transplanted to Brazil from Africa, the Orixas proved stronger and smarter than the monotheistic Gestapos. So as to insure their survival, the African Gods went undercover, blending with the identities of the Christian Saints, themselves.

That's why, at first glance, Yemanja looks like the Blessed Virgin—but a closer look reveals a sultry, invincible mermaid surfacing from under the blue gown.

Walk on and there's a black couple, he of cloud-like white hair, she in white diaphanous gown. She's kneeling worshipfully in the sand by a loaded Orixa shrine. At one point in her prayer, he reached down and tapped her lightly on the spine. Her head snaps back and she shudders . . . her face glowing like a sunrise. The hair stood up on my head, and I had a hat on.

Further down the beach was a "psychic pen": a roped-off area full of Umbanda priestesses, middle-aged woman: their ample girths clothed in hoop skirted, taffeta dresses as they puffed on cigars, the blue smoke keeping away spirits with bad intentions. They predicted, for a small donation, the futures of a long line of mostly American and European women who eagerly stepped five, six at a time inside the circle of sand.

Soothsaying was in the very air, for outside the pen, strolling by, I overheard a white-turbaned *fashionista* explain to a friend that clearly the "dental floss" bikini was back in style; and for next year, she, herself predicted that it would give way to the slightly more conservative "hang glider."

There was no avoiding the famous *tangas*: those minuscule Brazilian bikinis that help attract millions of tourist dollars. Even on a night of spiritualism the young female cariocas wore them, softening their devastating impact by covering themselves with gauzy, see-through skirts!

When asked on the airplane why the derriere ruled supreme in Brazil, Eleison smiled. "Americans and Italians are fixated on big breasts—maybe a hunger over the loss of Mama, an infantile hang-up. Here they worship the *bunda*. It's more mysterious and complex with so many things, the luxurious lines and curves and hollows all happening at once." He then shrugged: "It's an African thing!"

Up at the top of the Copacabana beach, a large crowd gathered, magnetized by music: the famous two-by-four samba beat. A small troupe of musicians and dancers were performing—a tune-up for Carnival, only a few weeks away.

Those drums! As Alma Guillermoprieto reported in her classic book, *Samba*: "It was what one tied to the railroad tracks might hear as a train hurtles immediately overhead: a vast, rolling, marching, overpowering wave of sound set up by the *surdos de marcacao*—bass drums about two feet in diameter in charge of carrying the underlying beat. Gradually a ripple set in, laid over the basic rhythm by smaller drums. Then the *cuica*: a subversive, humorous squeak, dirty and enticing, produced by rubbing a stick inserted into the middle of a drum skin. The *cuica* is like an itch, and the only way to scratch it is to dance . . . ."

The three different root African drums transcended the ears, mere hearing—

traveling deep into the gut, the groin, and reverberating out through every bone. Even I, a 'rhythmically challenged' white man, felt a tremendous sense of well-being. The drums and flickering candles and trance-dancers and pure white lilies flung upon the sea—made you feel so free. In the thick humidity, surrounded by outrageous vegetation, juicy passion fruit, a harmonious polyglot of people—life was luxurious and porous and packing heat.

Maybe that's why guilt takes a holiday in Rio; why rigid rules experience meltdowns here. More than one vacationing male from the temperate zone has explained his aberrant, wild behaviors to himself on the plane ride home to Germany, U.S. or Japan with the saying that the early missionaries, themselves, contritely observed: "There is no sin below the Equator." Even Rio's mountains, rising out of the spuming sea, look like abundant female *bundas*—'Sugar Loaf,' indeed!

Two of the *sambistas* removed their gauzy white wraparounds with one tug. The drums quickened; their bared buttocks ("covered" in wispy 'dental floss') assumed a life of their own. Their protuberant, cantilevered hips moved as if unhinged from the rest of their body . . . . As the thick flood of drumbeats crested, a mandolin plinked-in sharply and the women stopped moving, save for their left buttocks that shuddered—then jumped and dipped, while their right cheeks remained absolutely still: a chassis with heart-stopping, independent suspension. With the return of the drums, they immersed themselves full-body-samba in the raging, tympanic rapids . . . . Then the mandolin again, and this time their only answer: right buttocks that bucked and quaked—as if the wildly plucked strings were attached directly to their flesh.

Words from a favorite author, Nikos Kazantzakis, sprang to mind: "Watching the women dancing, my temples beat like castanets!"

"This suu-*uuure* beats being all bundled up; freezing your ass off in Times Square waiting for a ball to drop!" a wide-eyed, barefooted tourist said next to me, intoxicated by both the view and another slug of *cachaca* (potent sugarcane alcohol).

"Hey Frank—new 'Best,'" his buddy announced, raising his bottle. "Instead of Iceland having the best-looking women, it's now gotta be Brazil! Those mulatto ladies are drop-dead gorgeous. Right there is the strongest argument against racism—put black and white together and whattya get? Perfect beauty!"

There is a scientific premise that "Two bodies cannot occupy the same space." Clearly, it doesn't apply in Rio when music is playing. Men and women now merged unashamedly before our eyes. However, as carnal as the couples' samba-driven motions were, their bodies, aglitter with sweat, were but open vessels that pitched forth their very souls one into the other and back again.

Samba has been said to be a derivative of *semba*, an Angolan fertility rite that involves rubbing belly buttons together. Other sambistas insist it is far more complex, emerging from the Ngangela concept of *kusamba*, meaning to move in a manner that expresses wild joy for life no matter what your earthly circumstances. Every samba, no matter how provocative, is a call to one or more Orixas. Samba also means "sacred prayer."

On New Year's Eve in Rio, it all came rapturously together: samba and *candomble*—music and religion ('religion' in its purest, root form).

Suddenly it was 5:00 a.m. The drums had ceased; the candles in the hundreds of sand shrines and in the offering boats on the horizon had burned down. With wishes and dreams securely in Yemanja's care . . . the cariocas and tourists floated like pale ghosts through the streets to their places of rest.

Later that morning to help alleviate the jet-lag, I went for a run. In the fresh blue-pearl sky an apparition appeared. "Look! Yemanja!!" said a male carioca on a rocky promontory, bowing to a cloud moving in from the sea.

We stood together, watching the goddess expand over her *Cidade Marvilhosa*, outstretched arms blessing all below. She sailed over to Corcovado Mountain, topped by the Christ the Redeemer statue and hovered nearby.

In Rio de Janeiro, there is room for both.

Amazing how far the Mind can travel, with the body set on "automatic pilot." Long distance running is such an instinctual, repetitive motion that it easily lends itself to reflection and meditations.

We continue along, meandering through low brush; the trail flowing beneath us of its own accord. Buddha said: "You cannot travel on the path before you have become the path itself." Running countless training miles on mountain trails, the knowing dance continues . . . .

Then as we enter a pocket meadow, we're startled, stopped dead-in-our-tracks by a strange apparition. I blink heavily, but to no avail. There before us, in the back-of-beyond, is a beautiful woman: a News Babe swaying towards us, microphone extended. Then we see the hulking cameraman—they must have been dropped-in by chopper. "Hi!" she chimes cheerily. "Mind if I ask a question or two?"

"Not at all," Scott says, smiling, ever-the-charmer: "As long as we can keep mov'n." (Which we do, power-walking uphill.)

"Why are you doing this?" she inquires of Scott. He's silent for a few seconds; then launches into an explanation of how too many of us settle into a comfort zone instead of pushing our limits and discovering what we are made of. Finishing a 100 miler then gives you the confidence that if you can accomplish something like this—then any other challenge that life throws in your path is a piece of cake, by comparison!

"What about you? Why do you do it?" The mike swings my way.

"To transcend the Everyday Self."

"Good! Thanks. Did you get that, Joe? Good. Thanks guys!!"

Off we run, giggling over our philosophical musings and giddy from her perfume that hits, in that setting, with twice the kick. As afternoon moves toward evening, we talk only sporadically now, gathering ourselves for the concentrated effort of staying on-pace as energy diminishes, slowly, but inevitably like sand trickling through the proverbial hourglass. And I feel the blisters building, percolating under my skin. Deep breaths . . . *shut them off with thoughts of wonder!* I smile thinking of how one of our questions has now been answered. In pre-race planning, we knew it would be near-impossible to stay together over 100 miles—for if one of us was "On" this day—the other might not be. Yet here we are, deep into the run, and we have never been more than a few yards apart, as if some sort of invisible tie connects us. And the bond is "tighter" than that—stretching into a parallel synchronicity. Silently, unannounced, all day we both reach for our water bottles and Powerbars; pause to pee; even randomly cough and fart at exactly the same time. Without speaking—we've traded-off the lead, knowing without thinking who is hitting a tired patch; who is feeling fresh. I have never felt this effortless harmony before with anyone for such an extended duration. Sure, there had been momentary flashes of E.S.P. with lovers or wife, but only for an occasional moment—not continually: all day. There had been no preliminary time with Scott to repetitiously link subconscious levels as with a spouse. I had seen my youngest brother but a few days, oddly spaced, throughout the past ten years and most of my running both in races and training was done alone, as with Scott. Now, not only are we sharing the same exact pace, but are of "One-Mind" as well! I then think of how I shouldn't really be surprised, that man is made for this: In going out beyond what we think is possible—therein lies our true destiny and fulfillment.

We come up on Mt. Wilson, better known as "the buckle buster." More than one runner, right-on pace, then falls hopelessly behind having to climb 3,000 vertical feet, 3/4 of the way into the race. Now to our weary eyes, it appears even more insurmountable, for the lofty summit is shrouded in mist: a mix of sea fog from the nearby Pacific ocean and smog from the Los Angeles basin.

Mt. Wilson reminds me that the San Gabriels are one of the youngest mountain ranges on Earth, full of abrupt climbs and descents because they haven't yet had time to get worn-down, rounded by eons of erosion and weathering. And to think that this rugged range is so close to a major metropolis. I recall that a few winters ago, a lone hiker in the San Gabriels, after becoming exhausted, hypothermic, and snow-blind—staggered down a ridge line, directly into the parking lot of a shopping mall. Crawling into a phone booth, he saved his life: dialing 911, an ambulance scooped him up moments later.

I drop my eyes from the rising incline to avoid taking-in too much at once. One of the reasons that it's easier to run 100 miles in the mountains than on a flat continuous course is that your line-of-sight (and psych-out potential) is limited to one switchback at-a-time. As the Chinese proverb states: "Life by the inch is a cinch; by the yard it's hard."

I thought of the hardest run of my life, in the Florida Everglades, where there definitely are straight lines, long endless lines in nature. I had gone into the Loxahatchee National Wildlife Refuge, 145,635 acres—the last remaining northern Glades to kayak amidst alligators for a newspaper story. The kayak was 13.5 feet in length; many of the gators hauled-out on the banks were longer. Both marvelous and terrifying to be eye-level with them as I glided by (trembling) just a few feet away! They were the exact same color as the slough-mud; and oftentimes, as large as they were, my eye didn't put all their pieces together, until they suddenly burst into action. Without exception, all of the saurian giants were non-aggresive and extremely shy. Immediately after eye contact, and oftentimes before—they exploded back into the thick green jungle, my thin-shelled boat lifting and falling over their shock-waves. While moving rigidly down the center of the waterways, gingerly dipping my paddle side-to-side, I noticed a cleared, extended area—a trail topping a built-up berm on the side of the main canal. Unfortunately, very little of the Everglades remains in a natural state. Encroaching human population and agricultural needs have sliced-and-diced the Glades into a grid of regulated levees, spillways, and swampy plots. Even though only a small remnant of the original, vast sea of grass endures, each square on the checkerboard to a lone newcomer seemed (like the resident gators) gargantuan in scale.

I returned the next day wearing running shoes instead of the kayak shell. The trail atop the canal extended as far as the eye could see. A fresh trail to an ultra runner is like *foie-de-gras* to a gourmand: it must be "eaten," each new bite/stride savored! I stretched for a few minutes in the thick, humid air; strapped on a boda-belt full of Gatorade (no pun intended); then started running past a haunted-looking stand of gray cypress trees, their many knees poking up through lime-green swamp, stumping scientists as to why roots would bend above water into the air. In places entire trees were pink with splotches of algae and I caught the red-flash of a Pileated Woodpecker as he drilled from tree to tree. Then I was out into openness like I had never experienced before. Not only was the trail extremely straight but the terrain absolutely flat on each side of the canal berm— totally displacing you. I ran mile after mile and felt like I was getting nowhere, swallowed whole by the widespread sloughs and wetlands. As if to further emphasize the flatness, clouds on the far horizons were puffed up vertically into fleecy towers. After running for an hour-and-a-half, I turned around and, even though I was heading back in the right direction, with no chance of getting lost—the anxious, overall miasmic feeling intensified, building to a panic as if, mentally, the swamp was swallowing me whole. I could see too much: too far ahead and out to the endless sides. The monotony of the topography was occasionally counter-pointed by lone Snowy Egrets, brilliant flecks of white, but as soon as they flew out of sight, the unbroken Everglades again smothered me. I felt panicked, paralyzed, as if running in place on an endless treadmill . . . . A sudden breeze whipped through the sawgrass, filling the air with an eerie, high-pitched whine. My hair stood on end and it felt like nerves were poking through my skin. I eventually made it back to the starting point feeling near-psychotic. I was shocked when my watch indicated that the return took two hours, only 30 minutes longer than the out leg. I couldn't believe it: It felt like I was running for a week straight. Einstein's theory of "Time being Relative" rang true. I felt certain that landscape affects psychology, as if the mind (at least mine) needs focal points, landmarks, switchbacks—variety to alleviate the press of distance and soothe the psyche.

(This is not to say that I dislike the Everglades. It's a place of unique beauty and I've returned many times, but I've learned to "zig-and-zag" there, instead of taking the flat immensity straight-on.)

As we stand at the base of Mt. Wilson, sizing-up the looming challenge (and not feeling my energy rising to the occasion as usual), I concede out loud: "The plaque isn't bad." (The alternative award for finishing under 30 hours, instead of the buckle for sub-24.)

"Yeah," Scott replies, drawing in a deep breath. "But for the buckle—let's die trying . . . . "

He takes the lead as we start our ascent, struggling to push through the lactic acid immediately flaming in our legs. We keep our heads down, staring only at the patch of ground directly in front of us. Breath soon, too soon, comes in gasps. To detach from the overwhelming pain coursing throughout the body, my mind creates a mantra. It's nothing I consciously try to conjure up—it's just suddenly there, delivered when needed most. On Mt. Wilson, three words arise: *Angle of Repose*—that I silently chant in a drawn-out harmony with my breathing and strides. It's both fiction and reality: one of my favorite novels by Wallace Stegner and very much an applicable geological term here for "the steepest angle that rocks can abide before they start to fall." Somehow, saying those words melds me to the mountain, supplying renewed energy to tame the pain and power on up.

Soon our flushed faces and pumping arms are bathed in mist. It pours-in from the west; swirling down along the path like ragged spirits. On the dry mountain we taste the tang of the sea. Chugging upward, one switchback at a time—we eventually pop up above the fog. High in the clear cobalt sky, we see stars brighten around us. The air is absolutely still . . . . The only sounds—our labored breathing and the amplified crunch of each footfall.

"There's the summit!" Scott says.

"This is eerie . . . . Like we're the only two people left on earth!"

"Wild isn't it! And how did we ever get way out here? What are we doing? Are we really alive or did we die somewhere along the way?!"

Our laughter hangs in the air, as we crest the summit and take the first downhill step. We then freely spend what we have just painstakingly earned—surrendering to gravity, letting it pull us along in a free-fall pace—with darkness closing fast on our heels. We take out our lightweight flashlights, only after we lose complete sight of the trail, conserving batteries for as long as possible. It is difficult to both hold a flashlight and run, for the torch-bearing hand must stay somewhat stationary to keep the light-path constant, which interferes with a dual free-swinging arm rhythm, especially required uphill—but it is the only way. (I once tried a head lamp, which projected just how much a runner's head bobs dizzily up-and-down.) There's a psychological adjustment, as well. Try as you might to fight it, at night your pace inevitably slows . . . not only from the ocular difficulty of seeing, but under the cloak of darkness, without varied visual stimulus the mind tends to turn inward, dwelling on the same inventory of miseries and woes that every runner possesses this deep into the race. During daylight, the beauty of the natural world lifts you out and away from yourself. At night, running on trails now past midnight—leaden demons come home to roost.

Our incubuses prove to be material—the flashlights, and at the worst possible time. While traversing a series of narrow ridges, with steep drop-offs to the right—my flashlight dims, flickers; then quits altogether a few steps later. *What had I been thinking—buying batteries on sale!* Then with my hand extended out to the center of Scott's back, we follow his beam—until it dies, as well! He hadn't scrimped on batteries—the bulb blew! Standing there, not able to see our hands in front of our faces let alone the narrow path beneath us . . . and knowing that one wrong step sends us plummeting out in space, we have no choice but to test a theory we both believe in: that the Mind is not confined to the brain, but primal instinct and innate knowledge permeates the body, as well; especially in time of dire physical need.

In a cold sweat, we shuffle-on—allowing our feet to have "eyes," and amazingly—they see us clear over the precipitous trail.

During the hour of intense concentration, I feel "guided" by a blind woman. As Scott and I trust our bodies to see our way clear—I feel Diane's spirit flood my being. As clear as day I see her in my mind's eye and once again heard her answer my rudimentary question: "How do you get around so well?" She said, "We see with far more than our eyes." As we jog down the dark trail, our feet proving her statement, I relax, expanding my concentration to include the life-changing conversation. I met her after giving a speech. We lingered in the hotel meeting room long after everyone had gone and the waiters collapsed every table except our's. After she was convinced I genuinely didn't care about her "handicap"; wouldn't allow it to interfere with how I saw her (admiring her all the more for overcoming what is probably *The* most difficult challenge a person can face), she invited me into her world. I peppered her with question after question, wanting to know, in detail, how she functioned without eyesight?

She explained that it was mostly mathematical: knowing exactly how many steps to her front door, the mail box, down the sidewalk to the store; pinning matching Braile numbers to clothes to color-coordinate her wardrobe. "But it's much more than that. I'll show you," she said, with a mischievous grin. "The mind learns faster with the body involved."

She placed a chair in the middle of the room and then placed a full glass of water on the forward edge of the chair. She playfully pushed me back against the far wall.

"I'll give you a 'head-start': take a good look, establish your position. O.K.— know where it is?"

"Yes," I said, repeatedly sizing-up the distance.

Diane then tied a napkin over my eyes, knotting it firmly at the back of my head. "To level the playing field," she chuckled. "Now go get the glass of water."

I stepped out quickly then slowed down, feeling almost immediately disoriented without being able to see. Concentrating . . . trying hard to sense the exact location of the chair, I then walked what I was sure was a straight-line to it, but then overshot it—so much so that I crashed into a far wall—evoking a loud giggle from Diane.

"Hey—not fair, Master!" I called. "I feel like 'Grasshoppa' on the very first day!! Where is it? Come on, just one clue."

"No clues! You must find your own way. See the chair in your mind; allow it to appear; hold it there—now move toward it . . . . "

No use—I hit everything *but* the chair. I felt like I was back playing "Pin The Tail On The Donkey"—only I was the ass. Finally, totally exasperated, I tore off the blindfold.

"You did fine for your first time."

"Yeah right. I felt totally lost after the first step."

"Spin me around," she said.

"What?"

"My turn. Spin me around. Try to throw me off."

I twirled her around and around, then led her off into a corner—a very distant and oblique line to the chair.

She calmly exhaled, gathering her bearings. One hand lifted as if of its own accord to up near her eyes, the palm flashing open, outward for just a moment. She then set off and with just a few pauses; stood before the chair and in a smooth, unbroken motion—like a bird landing, her hand swooped down, plucked up the glass filled with water and drank it down.

I applauded. She bowed, a mock curtsey, and plopped down on the chair.

"That was *incredible!*" I said. "Amazing how you-"

"Don't patronize me!" her voice flared. "I've had a lifetime to practice . . . . "

She then explained that ever since she was a little girl, she had inner visions, dreams at night that she was sleeping when a voice called to her to awaken. When she did, her eyes didn't open, but her closed hand did; and there in the center of her palm was an open eye, "all-seeing."

"I'm not Sigmund Freud or a Jungian analyst" she said, "but I know that the symbols of the dream mean that I can see, but just not with my eyes; and maybe there's an energy portal of some sort within my hands that helps guide me."

She told me how humans live largely unfullfilled lives; how little of our total potential we tap into. She spoke about Indian yogis who were so finely tuned that they could make only one half of their hand warm and could willfully flutter their hearts. There were monks in the Himalayas who wrap their naked bodies in sheets dipped in icy water and then dry them in frigid weather using only heat generated by their own bodies. And how an American cardiologist went to see them, attaching electronic measuring devices to their skin. He found that they could raise their skin temperature as much as seventeen degrees above normal in freezing conditions, even though the body would normally send blood away from the skin toward the inner, core organs to keep warm. Within five minutes, the icy sheets started to steam and in forty-five minutes were completely dry!

Diane then talked about *chi*, the Chinese concept of energy or life-force. She asked me to stand before her in a comfortable position. She then pushed me firmly on the shoulder. I lost my balance, short-stepping backward. "You're too rigid; not centered. The Chinese believe that the main energy point in the body is here," her index finger pressed against a spot a few inches below my belly button. "This is where our energy, even our mind should be gathered, concentrated like a fulcrum point. From this point meridians or pathways of energy spread throughout the body and by stimulating those paths or 'irrigating' the meridians via acupuncture or tai chi exercises you keep the energy flowing—but it all starts here." Her finger pressed again on the low spot. "Let's try something. Close your eyes and find your *chi*, establish that center point."

Like a gyroscope settling, I felt my focus spinning, then funneling down to that physical point Diane indicated; that I then pictured, holding it fast in my mind.

"Are you there?" Diane inquired.

I nodded my head.

"O.K., now open your eyes, but keep your *chi* point centered, anchored."

It was more difficult to keep centered with my eyes opened—visual distractions.

Diane then, again, pushed my shoulder, even harder than before. Instead of being knocked off balance; falling backward as before, this time my feet didn't move as I rotated at the waist; her hand sliding off my turning shoulder . . . .

"Great! Wow—you picked that up fast! Feel how balanced you are?" While we were talking, she jabbed me three times out of the blue—each time harder and each time I remained "rooted," sloughing-off her attempts to move me backward. "Is this a form of self-defense?" I asked.

"Yes. That's how I first learned it—to protect myself, but it's far more than that. It teaches you balance, ups your awareness, and even beyond that it's really the basis for everything, a way to live life. Now let's move the *chi* around. Here—try to bend my arm."

She held her right arm straight out in front of her. I grabbed her wrist but her arm was so loose, relaxed that I was confused. "Ready?" I said, expecting her to tense her muscles to fight against my strength. Instead she quietly said, "Yes, go," but kept her arm totally relaxed. I shrugged and applied force, expecting to immediately snap her arm back—but to my amazement it didn't move and then the more force I applied the looser her arm became—remaining unbendable no matter how hard I tried. "What the-?!"

"Grand Canyon . . . . " she said.

"What?"

"Water defeats rock every time! Now try again." This time she extended a rigid, tense arm. It snapped back soon after I applied force.

"What were you doing to do that—when I couldn't bend it?"

"Once you establish your *chi* spot and stay centered, you can then send that energy through your body and outward. When I had my arm extended like this (loose and relaxed), I pictured my arm as a fire hose attached to the chi point, the hydrant, and I turned it on full-blast, for you're a strong guy. But if a hose is crimped or knotted, tense or rigid it shuts down the flow of water, but if it is fully open—the force flows through. I sent the *chi* force not only through my relaxed arm but out my fingertips, through the walls, outside into the universe—as unbroken, infinite energy—all originating from here." She pressed my *chi* point again.

"Try this. Try to pick me up . . . . "

She stood before me with her arms held out to the sides. I placed my hands on her hips and expended the energy I automatically calculated it would take to lift a medium-sized woman. She didn't budge. More force . . . no liftoff. Then it was forehead veins bulging; grunt-and-groan and still she didn't move an iota.

"Now try!"

This time she flew up into the air as soon as my hands touched her hips. I jumped back, stunned.

"The first time I sent the *chi* downward into both legs as 'solid lead'; the second time upward like feathers in the wind . . . . "

As if a Doubting Thomas, I asked her to do it again, with the same results. "You mean mental imaging is stronger than physical force? Diane, this is scary! I know what I've just seen but it defies common sense. It's not supposed to be this way!!"

"Who said? Michael, there are many realities. You've just learned one way of looking at life. You know, some days I'm actually glad that I'm blind, for without my eyesight taken away I may never have discovered other levels. We have far more ability in our bodies than we realize . . . . "

The next checkpoint, at Mile 80, is aptly named "Idlehour Trail." It looks like a mash-unit, with runners reduced to gibbering wrecks, sprawled across army cots and on blankets in the smashed grass. This deep into the day, a wide-range of ailments: dehydration, diarrhea, broken blisters, blood in the urine, locked-up quads, blown-out knees—all take their toll. Strange to come across friends, who the last time we saw them looked so fresh and energized as they blew past us—now hard to believe it's the same person: lying in the dirt, many right on the trail as if they've been shot: their eyes slammed shut, moaning in misery. Just as a regular 26-mile marathoner hits "The Wall" at Mile 20, an ultra marathoner's barrier is here: Mile 80.

As I look over the carnage, I think of how at 80 miles many talented ultra runners suffer from "The Jim Howard Syndrome." Howard is an amazing distance runner: lithe but muscular, with extremely deep-set eyes, a roamin' Roman nose, and a thick mountain man beard: With a black hat on he could be a Quaker Elder and he trains with their same austere and exacting discipline. He tasted victory twice at Western States by, incredibly, running 100 miles as if it were a sprint. He put the hammer down from the start and kept it floored all day—demoralizing everyone else who even thought of making it a close race. At Mile 40, he'd have a six mile lead . . . . It's the only way he knows how to run: win or die trying. He either finishes hours ahead of the next runner or you find him 'blown-up,' lying comatose across the trail somewhere out in No Man's Land (Mile 80 on) . . . .

Ultra running strips away more than body fat. A person's approach to life, their inner psychology is laid-out bare for all to see in the way they race. Some runners, at the midway point or before, even though perfectly healthy, will suddenly DNF (Did Not Finish), snootily shrugging: "Since I'm not on pace to win, what's the sense in finishing?" Others, the back-of-the-packers, who never realistically have a remote chance at buckling are out on the trail for 30 hours or more before finishing, but 'quit' is just not in their vocabulary, as they are living embodiments of Robert Louis Stevenson's statement: "To travel hopefully is a better thing than to arrive."

Many quick-to-judge outsiders falsely label ultra runners "masochists." But unlike masochists who enjoy pain for its own sake: ultra runners have a further purpose in mind—first welcoming pain (for its arrival tells them they are on pace), then rise above it by feeding it as fuel into the running engine. The coping power of this breed of human beings is astonishing to see. They can pull a groin in the early slippery snow fields; puke repeatedly from altitude sickness atop each of the many mountain passes; trip head-over-heels over every other tree root on the downhills; suffer dehydration in the airless, heat-trapping canyons; get stung by a squadron of angry wasps; shredded with nettles; slathered in poison oak; nipped on the Nike by a rattler—heck, desperadoes could even ambush them at Chantrey Flats, whack them over the head with an oak plank and they'd be up on their moving feet moments later, not even complaining of the headache. In fact, the more horrible the obstacles, the wider their smiles! What did Hemingway say about man being destroyed but not defeated? More than anything else in life, ultra running teaches you how to carry "destruction" to ultimate victory. And how about Cowman Shirk, one of the original Western States pioneers who always runs with a skullcap holding a pair of upturned horns, and boasting a Ripley's "Believe It or Not" that at Mile 80, he always pauses for a tryst off in the woods with a curvaceous crew member, then keeps right on truck'n to the finish? "The coaches are dead-wrong," he grins convincingly, "claiming that sex takes it out of your legs! Hell—puts 'It' back in!" Then there's Tess Porter . . . . In the later stages of so many races, there she is: collapsed under a checkpoint table, limbs akimbo, her mascara the only thing still running; an earring and piece of ear torn off in the bramble long-ago; and after you move on by her, having encouraged her, yet at the same time waving a sign of the cross over her prone, barely breathing form—an hour later she's up on your shoulder, singing, cracking dirty jokes, prancing around as if she had just miraculously undergone a "total body transfusion!" *What are these people made of?!*

That's why so many runners have such great respect for Doug Latimer. In ten Western States starts (including tying with Jim Howard for a victory), he never finished out of the top ten—a new 'First' in and of itself, earning him a special gold buckle at the age of fifty. Somehow, even after tasting the addictive "thrill of victory," Latimer, no matter his position rarely DNF'ed; and considering all the variables: "The Twelve Labors of Hercules" working against you, for a decade straight, he overcame them all consistently, demonstrating a mind as strong or stronger than his incredible body. An anomaly, he thought like Aesop's patient turtle—but ran with the hare's bounding legs.

At "Idlehour," to continue on, we have to win over our minds: grapple with the psychological barrier of knowing you still have almost a full marathon to go and you're starting that distance nearly 'out on your feet.' To ease that anguish, how I wish I could now totally rejuvenate myself in some way: strap on a new pair of legs and power-on! However, overall fatigue seems a trifle compared to what we have just come through! We borrow two flashlights from aid station workers and the new, bright beams in our hands provide impetus—spike us with the type of adrenaline that only comes from having escaped disaster.

A total mind game from here on out: After running 80 mountainous miles, everyone's body is shot. Whoever can steel themselves not to give in to the exhaustion, whoever can gather or somehow produce new shreds of willpower here-and-now will finish. To brainwash myself, eradicate any energy-draining, negative vibes that total fatigue brings on—I hold in my mind how much I love running: the very act itself. I recall the technique of Psycho-Cybernetics, where it's been proven that the autonomic nervous system (Mission Control) can not differentiate between real and imagined experiences, (e.g.), before actual performances athletes picturing themselves scoring the goal, the touchdown; sinking the basket step-by-step, over and over, so that oftentimes in the actual game, they then effortlessly repeat the "grooved," familiar success. Maybe I *can* strap on fresh legs, by actually going back to the feeling of when they were new . . . to the liberation of running alone down country roads.

With my Dad retired from football, and with Uncle Dick's 14 year NFL career winding down, they invested together in a 100 acre farm, an hour's drive from our home in suburban Cleveland on the Ohio and Pennsylvania border, near Pymatuning Lake. The summer and weekend getaway provided the happiest years of our young lives. At first, the neighbors, real "salt of the earth" working farmers, were suspicious of the big-shot pro ballplayers invading their turf, but never ones to put on airs, Dad and Uncle Dick, hats in hands knocked on the neighbors' doors saying they didn't 'know squat' about farming and would you please show us how? Kermit Lewis started us out with "Tractor Driving 101" and Charles Hayes (who moved his dairy cows from far afield into the barn for twice-a-day milkings by simply uttering a warm: "Come On, Girls!") taught "Animal Husbandry."

It was both working farm and resort. We raised 60 head of Hereford beef cattle and the clover and alfalfa grasses to feed them. Dad and Uncle Dick also put in a big swimming pool and filled the barn with riding horses.

Sundays we saddled all the horses and took turns charging back and forth across the clover field, trying to keep everyone in the home-movie viewfinder. I always loved to see the four brothers, my Dad and Uncles posing up on horseback together: Ed, Dick, Gene, and Joe Mo, who, starting out speaking Polish before English, had sure ridden a long way through life. Each brother had four children (couple infants even delivered just a day or two apart . . . brothers so close, they did "everything" together).

At the farm, the entire clan gathered around the TV set every Sunday night for "Bonanza," and out in our clover field as the brothers reined away from the movie camera and galloped off, I often called-out the opening bars of the theme-song: *"Dun-Dunnah-Dun-Dunnah-Dun-Dunnah-Dun—Dunnah-Dun-DAAAAAH!"* By far, the easiest brother to match to the Bonanza boys was Uncle Dick. He looked and acted *exactly* like Hoss Cartwright, with the same oversized body and jolly-good nature.

During the farm years, Uncle Dick was playing out his 14 year NFL career with the Cleveland Browns, traded there from the New York Giants (and helped bring the Browns a world-championship in 1964). The Browns' training camp was in nearby pastoral Hiram, so during the summers he often brought some of the players over for Sunday barbecues and beer. The famous 'Gods' you watched for years score touchdowns or stop them—whose every move you imitated in your own pickup games were now sitting next to you on a picnic table, in madras shorts and V-neck T-shirts, laughing in booming baritones as they blew off steam from the pressures of a very competitive training camp, where their livelihoods were on the line. I was in awe! Nothing prepares you for seeing a pro football player in person, especially the linemen and linebackers. Their arms are as big as your legs and their legs as big around as your entire being. With necks flaring up wide alongside compact heads topped by nappy crewcuts, they exuded raw, unchecked masculinity; with a swagger in the slightest movement. Gene Hickerson, the pulling guard who led their bread-and-butter play, the sweep, looked so tough and thick that if you whacked him over the head with a two-by-four he wouldn't even blink. But . . . he'd remember, and flatten you, too, just before Jimmy Brown turned the corner and cleated you further into ground-round.

One Sunday, while taking the requisite horseback gallop across the clover, my buddy Chuck Owens took a nasty fall. Laying flat on his back with the wind-knocked out of him, he then felt the earth shake as Uncle Dick charged out from the swimming pool gate to see if he was all right. Chuck later said that, at first he wasn't sure if he was more afraid of the fall from the horse or the unknown Giant trundling his way!

The most popular villain at the time was 'Oddjob': the James Bond movie heavy. With his crewcut, bull neck and brick house body, Uncle Dick played that role, as well—in the swimming pool, coming after the kids . . . . We would throw things at him to bait him—gleefully bounce beach balls off his head and then slowly . . . Oddjob would robotically turn . . . blocking out the sun as the 6 foot, 260 pound wall of muscle moved toward you, rising in the shallows where you cowered in a corner, sending in his wake waves of water pouring out over the sides of the pool. In slow-motion, he was playing his game: rushing the passer and you were that target, the quarterback: Johnny U, as he wrapped you in a bear hug and *squeeeeeeeezed*, crushing you down into the water. Even in play Dick Modzelewski's raw, close-quarter strength was both frightening and inspiring. It was a strength developed not in a gym or steroid lab—but a genetic power germinated in the peasant fields of Poland and coal mines of western Pennsylvania. He was his father's son, maximized.

It all began with "Dzaidzi" (Polish for "Grandfather"). Joseph Modzelewski, from a farm outside Warsaw; coming to the United States at 13 years of age, was the progenitor of that physical power. In his seventh decade, with ox-yoke shoulders, a deep barrel chest, legs of knotty pine, you immediately saw where the all-American sons came from. He worked for more than 30 years in the coal mines, long before unions; when waves of immigrants were replaceable fodder—men as 'work beasts' in four foot high tunnels, with cold water drip-dripping like Chinese water-torture onto your back as you shoveled under heavy lakes. As a hungry immigrant, you may have been originally lured by the promises of 'Milk and Honey' but to actually put those goods on the table, you descended daily into Hell: America's "Heart of Darkness"— going to work in the dark of morning; coming out of the hole well into the night; with you, yourself as dark as the coal you mined, the black dust coating every crevice, lining ever wrinkle and slowly smothering frothy pink lungs. In such brutal conditions, even the protective miner's canaries flew the coop, but the many Poles, with little education, and no way out, slaved on . . . . In the prime of his life, Dzaidzi was the "stud duck." Among the other miners, he took on heroic proportions: What Paul Bunyon was to the forest; John Henry was the railroad; Big Joe was to the mines. Most men, working with a partner, shoveled ten, maybe eleven cars full of coal a day; but Dzaidzi and his partner filled eighteen, nineteen, *twenty!* cars—waging an all-out war. Dzaidzi never could find a partner to keep up with him, but no matter: By unleashing his bottomless strength and endless frustrations, he single-handedly moved subterranean mountains and in doing so, slowly widened a surface niche, a life for himself and his growing family, day by day, year after year. Out of sight, the other men slowly picked away at side veins, but Big Joe was front and center, drilling holes into stubborn bedrock, dropping in dynamite, running for cover; then returning to scoop up the broken coal, in a frenzy with a giant-sized shovel.

One day, the Mine Supervisor blocked Dzaidzi's path. "Hey Big Joe, slow down . . . . Don't kill the job."

Deep into his groove, Dzaidzi kept shoveling right up to the Super's feet. "Pleez, get oud my way!"

The Super (really miffed that he was no longer 'The Man' with Big Joe stealing his thunder), took a swing at the miner.

With both men stooped over in the low tunnel, Big Joe grabbed the Super by the throat. "CUMM ON! I PUUT YU *DUWWNNNNNN!!*"

The other miners gathered around, but the Super, gasping for breath in Big Joe's vice-like grip, backed down . . . .

The men returned to work with even more admiration for one of their own. Big Joe shoveled on—pausing momentarily to give a bull-like bellow that roared through the tunnels like a heart on fire!

Each evening, coming out of the hole, Dzaidzi was as black as the night. The only thing that showed he was a man, not a lump of coal, were the whites of his eyes and the flash of a smile. In his house, surrounded by his wife and young children he stripped to the waist at the kitchen sink for a quick washing away of coal dust, so, famished, he could dig into his first of two dinners (in a bowl big enough to feed a horse). My Dad did his back, marveling as the soapy rag dropped down into deep culverts between the raised muscle ridges erupting across his back. His coal-carved physique was legendary. Men used to stop him in the streets or local pool hall: "Hey Big Joe—take off your shirt!" Occasionally he would oblige them and strike a pose. Everyone would gasp—then rush to touch him to make sure he was real.

Decades later, with the veins of coal spent and even Big Joe's spine twisted and lungs charred he gratefully worked as the night janitor at Har-Brack High, the site of his sons first glorious successes on the gridiron, the springboard to their Big-Time. No one ever cleaned the place like he did. He mopped, then buffed the long hallways and bathrooms until everyone could see themselves reflected in the floors. He even proudly made the toilets shine. Big Joe knew no other way—always going beyond the call of duty, and full-throttle no matter what he did.

The tradition continued on our farm with the self-imposed ferocious pace of his weekday work building to a Sunday showcase crescendo. Dzaidzi was the first to rise in the summer mornings—prancing out, at first light, into his garden or the clover field—waking up by lifting the holy water of heavy dew from plants to his face and strengthening cell-by-cell in the golden light; then working straight through until dark again, but now in a world of difference—topside in fresh air and sunlight and satisfaction, for all that he did directly benefited a farm, that once, in the old country as a youth he had to flee in famished desperation—now his sons securely, bountifully owned, bringing the aging progenitor to a full and complete circle.

I followed him like a shadow, drawn to his radiating goodness and profound simplicity. We raked up profuse heaps of branches that the century old willow tree shed every day; we weeded the half-acre garden, whitewashed fences, planted flowers, cut the grass, cleaned the swimming pool, shoveled manure from the barn.

He'd always try to shoo me away, "Go—go play now!" but I would rather be with my Dzaidzi even if it meant working all day. At sundown, I even followed him into the bathroom. He was a man who after the day's labors kept himself impeccably clean and neat. Shaving, he whisked a straight razor back and forth over a long, leather strop attached to the wall—holding the bottom end of the strop in his left hand while the steel razor glided up and down the narrow hide . . . My job was to take the cup holding the soap cake, the round bar mostly shrunken down and sliding a bit inside the manly mug; add a couple drops of hot water from the faucet, then froth up the firm soap with the squat, boar-bristle brush, the handle a cool, heavy chunk of blue-veined marble. Today's high-tech, plastic disposable razors and electric shavers with enough power and gears to drive you down the street may get the job done quicker, but totally negate pleasing the senses; to say nothing of coming close to the closest shave possible. The old-fashioned way not only severed every deep whisker but quenched each sense, as well: that whisking sound of long blade on leather strop; the scent of English soap cake brushed up into lather; the sight and feel of that creamy froth infiltrating bristly beard; even the taste of said soap, looking like the irresistible foam on a cappuccino! After Dzaidzi crisply bladed the last white dollop from his upturned jaw, we then finished the ritual with him shaking out two puddles of Old Spice from a ceramic jug emblazoned with a Wind Jammer ship all sails a flyin'—into the cupped palms of my hands. Giggling, I'd then carefully, slooowly reach up . . . then suddenly go slaphappy on his face, smacking in the after shave until his cheeks glowed as red as the country sunset.

Whether shaving, painting fences or shoveling manure, Dzaidzi had a unique mannerism. He continually sang aloud, not popular songs, but emitted a pure harmonic resonance—like a hive of worker bees humming forth on each outward breath.

He possessed the hardest thing in life to find: peace of mind. His entire life was a prayer. Despite lacking a formal education and only speaking broken English, Dzaidzi made you a better person just standing next to him. He had a saintly goodness and sincerity that radiated from a heart the size of the sun. Nearly all who knew him, even if briefly, said that he was the most impressive man they had ever met.

Though deeply religious, Dzaidzi always had an eye for beauty, especially if expressed in the feminine form. His favorite summertime TV show was The Miss Universe Pageant. We all gathered around the rabbit-eared set, the scent of fresh-cut hay wafting on the evening breeze through the window screens trying to guess who would ultimately win with Dzaidzi leaning forward, elbows on knees, work-bent fingers tapping over an evening rosary, a stream of "Hail Mary's" now pouring forth in his buzzing whisper. As the pageant progressed, Dad would repeatedly try to tempt Dzaidzi away from his prayers. "Pap, what about *her*? Wow—with those legs: what do you think her chances are?!"

There would be a gradual slowdown, then finally a complete pause in Dzaidzi's litany. "No too good!" he said, returning right back to his prayers. Then when the field was narrowed to the five semifinalists and with Dzaidzi on his last bead; kissing, then pocketing his rosary, he then quietly announced his choice: "Miz Venezuela, you watch; she win. Gud-*niiiite* . . . . " he said going up the stairs to bed, a man of unwavering habits.

Two years Dzaidzi murmured "Miz Venezuela" and those two years she won. Made us wonder exactly *whom* he was praying for with that fervent rosary!

To the benefit of all the boys, we not only had daily interactions with our grandfather, but we were the growing beneficiaries of his garden-fresh vegetables (oftentimes standing out in Dzaidzi's controlled jungle with him—bare feet in warm soil; wholeheartedly chomping juicy beefsteak tomatoes right off the vine). And both grandmothers nourished us as well, with cooking "competitions":

bake-offs that you devoured for hours, then loosened your belt afterwards and rolled around out on the lawn—beyond stuffed. Babcie, the Polish grandmother, with a stocky peasant's build, not only produced two mighty all-Americans and pro football players but of her five babies, none weighed under 12 pounds. She still holds the record for biggest delivery in a hospital in western Pennsylvania. Aunt Betty Lou entered this world at 15 1/4 pounds; with the doctor having to break her little arm to free her from the birth canal!

From scratch, Babcie created a Polish cornucopia of gourmet wealth and freshness: *pierogi, gulumpki, kielbasa, kristchiki, punski, plutsky* and duck-blood soup. Then Nonnie, my Italian grandmother, would take over. Starting with nothing more than a pile of flour, water and raw eggs—a few minutes later, a blonde mane of handmade, irregularly shaped pasta noodles was draped over the wooden table. That pasta smothered in a beefsteak tomato sauce (left out overnight in the garage for the mix of herbal flavors to marry), then accompanied by 'Dago Red'—wine that Pap Pap made in the cellar of his house—why, just one taste and single sip and you were certain ya died and this was Heaven! Watching the ethnic grandparents at work was like seeing alchemists transforming basal elements into incredible, edible magic!!

Among its many pleasures, the farm also served an economic purpose, partially paying its own way, in that the beef cattle we raised were subsequently served on the menu at "Mo & Junior's," the Cleveland steak house that employed the entire Modzelewski clan (and half of East Cleveland at one time or another). I started working there at age 11, when dressed Halloween night as a bum and making the goody rounds Dad tracked me down in his car, swinging open the passenger door. "Get in—the dishwasher didn't show! One of the busiest nights of the year and as good a time as any for you to start working . . . . Come on, we're late!"

"But I can't go dressed like *this*!"

He quickly looked over my tattered costume. "Perfect—for where you'll be!"

As usual, he was right. In "The Pit" of scalding steam: emitted often from the flung-open industrial dishwasher; garbage flying off jet-sprayed dishes like errant missiles; glacial grease on the floor—'bum attire' fronted by a nonstick plastic apron clearly met the dishwasher's dress code.

As "Toots Shor's" was to New York City, "Mo & Junior's" was to Cleveland. With Dad and Uncle Dick hosting in person on weekend nights; doing the meet-and-greet at the front door, the place was packed with both professional athletes and the sports fans who loved them. Visiting teams in town to play the Cleveland Browns or Indians dropped in *en masse* for Surf-n-Turf and Brandy

Stingers the night before and after the big game.

Mo & Junior's (the second moniker being Junior Wren, a Brown's defensive back and original partner, soon bought out by Uncle Dick), was a forerunner of today's 'memory lane' sports bars, with Dad and Uncle Dick's gridiron memorabilia lining the walls of the bar. They were young when pro football was young and both grew up together. There was a newspaper headline announcing Dad as the Steeler's Number One Draft Choice; Uncle Dick's Outland Trophy as the nation's best college lineman; still photos from "The Greatest Game Ever Played" when the Johnny Unitas led-Colts finally defeated The New York Football Giants in the NFL's first sudden-death overtime, a pulse-pounding cliffhanger that convinced television to invest in a new national pastime; a bronze plaque proclaiming Uncle Dick the NFL's "Iron Man" (at one time playing in the most consecutive games); framed pictures from a famous Life Magazine spread of the 'Mud Bowl'— photos with an epic, heroic quality, one framed front-and-center in the shrine room: Dick "Little Mo" Modzelewski on his hands and knees in deep mud, head down, helmet caked, uniform number obliterated. Under the photo Dad had placed an Anonymous quotation: *"Although I may lie down and bleed awhile, I shall rise to yet fight again . . . "*

On a shelf were helmets, one from the College All-Star Game covered in soon-to-be-legendary signatures; Uncle Dick's New York Giants helmet—the cage-like face mask bent; the midnight blue plastic shell streaked with a mad rainbow of opposing colors—the colossal collisions and rhino head butts exploding through your body as you held the helmet between your hands. You followed the Mo Brothers' careers by the progression of hats; and at the very beginning of the row was head armor emitting the most powerful aura of all. It bore no famous names or big-city glamour; yet it, alone, made all that possible. It was a humble metal hard hat, fronted by a small lamp—the bulb shattered and the coal miner's cap bearing dents much deeper than those from NFL wars.

The restaurant was packed because of selling both the steak and the sizzle— the thirty tables turned over three times each on Friday and Saturday nights. Movie stars and singers stopped in. Groupies in hot pants and go-go boots packed the piano bar—catching hotel room keys from star quarterbacks and stray center fielders.

Behind swinging doors, the kitchen roared nonstop, all cuts of steaks spattering on the flaming grill five hours straight—the chaos all orchestrated by Uncle Joe, the only Modzelewski brother who didn't play football, opting instead for more direct physical contact. As a boxer, he trained in the Navy; then employing the "sweet science" all the way up the professional ranks: winning his first 12 bouts; sparring and fighting an exhibition with heavyweight champion Ezzard

Charles and was just one fight away (a loss) from meeting an up-and-coming boxer named Rocky Marciano. Uncle Joe was the head chef, and with a cauliflower ear, a roamin' nose, and a jagged scar covering a broken jaw from ear-to-ear—nobody dared mess with him. Even my Dad, who, during Saturday night prime-time, would occasionally burst through the doors like a rampaging bull, flinging menus and wondering at the top of his voice where the hell the Baltimore Colt, Big Daddy Lipscomb's special order of four steaks all rare/raw were, when "YOU DON'T HAVE TO EVEN COOK THE GODDAMNED THINGS?!"

Uncle Joe spun around from the infernally hot grill, eyes basted blood-red telling Dad to go to Hell and "GET THE FUG OUT OF MY KITCHEN!"—firing a grease-soaked rag through a crisscross of waiters—that missed Dad's new suit by an inch. Dad quickly backpedaled out of his older brother's domain before a meat cleaver came his way.

With the last of the endless orders off the grill at 10:00 p.m., Uncle Joe then unwound with his nightly ritual—a shot and a beer, keep 'em comin.' . . . He'd then call me out from The Pit and relive his boxing career, taking me through his best fights, playing himself: Joe Modzele (the full "Modzelewski" too long to fit across the back of his silk robe) and I stood-in as the assortment of pugilists he had conquered. He pulled his punches, yet taught me to box.

One night, while swinging from way back in his memory bank and/or fueled by a few too many Boilermakers under his belt, he forgot himself and tagged me full-force, bare-knuckles, with a left uppercut to the chin followed by a lightning right cross to the cheek. I woke up flat on my back—Uncle Joe hugging me back to life and slapping a cold, raw porterhouse up against my swelling face.

During the school year, I attended St. Margaret Mary Elementary, run by the Sisters of Notre Dame. The nuns, in black habits, with only their faces and hands showing, now ruled our young lives—driving into us The Baltimore Catechism. Day after day, over and over in a brainwashing manner they inquired of us: "Who Made You?" "God Made Us!" we all recited. "Why did God make you?" etc. etc. etc., back and forth; 'Q and A' straight from the blue book in a singsong, seesaw manner until it was hardwired into our soft, impressionable heads. You never questioned the questions; just roboticly uttered the rote answers, never rocking the boat or asking why? It was all about being an automaton: wearing the same white shirt and navy blue tie and having the two right legs of your desk in perfect, precise alignment with all the other desks in your row. If you dared deviate from the norm, the controlling conformity in the slightest way, you then brought down the wrath of Sister Mary Verne—who pinched your upper arm in a grip that could have torn the door off a Volvo.

All the families in the parish came to the school church for Sunday Mass. I was a substitute altar boy, stepping up when one of the regulars took sick—mostly kneeling on a purple pillow in a snow-white frock and shaking bells at appropriate times. Far more than the liturgical content, itself, I loved the overall ritual and pageantry of it all: setting out the priest's layered vestments, the spiky organ music, soaring coral chants, progressive "Stations of The Cross" aglow in stained glass, pungent incense, whispered vespers, the white wafers, ruby-red wine in a golden chalice. I nearly cried during High Mass at Christmas and Easter when Father Hofer gave it all in Latin: just the sound of that archaic language, its roots in nearly all words—shook me to the very foundation.

Saturday afternoons I went to confession, kneeling in that narrow darkened cubicle, waiting for the wooden door to slide back—the priest finished with the sinner on the other side; now turning his shadowy, all-knowing attention to me. With my penance computed; then rapidly rattled out in a church pew, I then always went the "extra mile(s)." From the Good Sisters, throughout the week, I collected prayers that had Indulgences attached to them—printed on cards with pictures of sponsoring saints, who by their previous good acts helped you ward off punishments still due for sins that had been sacramentally absolved. By reciting these prayers over and over you could, not only erase your current black marks off the slate at Heaven's Gate, but could also stockpile future good graces. I went overboard, figuring why not build a credit-line that will stave off *all* future failings? So I knelt and recited Indulgences hour upon hour, until my tongue cramped and knees turned to mush.

By its very nature, with its unavoidable minefield of sins, negative slew of "Thou Shall Nots . . . " and gallons of guilt poured over nearly every human enjoyment, Catholicism, especially to a budding teenager, seemed built on failure and constricting the human spirit from exploring the full, freshly blooming parameters of life.

However, religious brainwashing and imprisonment were counterbalanced by a father who, on my thirteenth birthday, at our suburban Cleveland home called me into his bedroom for a talk. When he asked me to shut the door I knew it was serious. "Michael, I'm going to treat you like a man until you prove me differently. It's all up to you now. I'm not going to give you a long list of rules. You're smart enough to know right from wrong, but I will take away this freedom the first time you cross me or embarrass our name in the slightest way . . . ."

I stood there blinking, amazed at what I was hearing. I felt tears sting my eyes. "Dad, I would rather *die* than disappoint you!"

"Every kid is different. I probably won't be able to say this to your brothers when they are your age, but I sense an unusual maturity in you. So I'm giving you your freedom: letting you determine your own fate."

Since it was the weekend, we then drove out to the farm. Dad was quiet; avoided eye-contact, rapping his fingers repeatedly on the big steering wheel of the big blue Pontiac. It was strange; we usually effortlessly chattered away or sang Hank Williams, Roger Miller or Johnny Cash songs, totally off-key but in close harmony together, erasing time during the hour drive. I finally broke the uncomfortable silence by asking him if I did anything wrong? He then blurted out: "You're becoming a man now. Sex . . . . Is there anything you need to know?"

I shrugged my shoulders with the feigned nonchalance of youth (while really totally ignorant of the subject).

"Well, just be careful when you're in rest rooms. Don't stay in there too long. There are men who like boys and don't let yourself be taken advantage of."

What? That's it?! What about GIRLS? But later that same day, the education continued. To stretch my legs from the car trip I went for a long run toward Pymatuming Lake, but then halfway there I detoured down a remote lane I had always wanted to explore. It really didn't seem to have a purpose—one lane, dirt and gravel and it dead-ended after about a quarter-mile. As I advanced down the narrow tunnel sided by woods, I saw plenty of tire tracks in the dirt, and then at the dead-end, found out why.

Rather than turn around at the dead-end, I stopped running. I momentarily stopped, as is my habit to this day, not because I was tired from running, but to take the full-measure of a new place. Standing still, with your heart pumping from running and all of your senses or gates swung wide-open, irrigated with oxygen from exercise, it's as if you are more attuned; can take in more, seize up the true spirit-of-place and every place has one. Here, there was something secret and forbidden exciting the air.

At the time I was midway through reading the entire series of Hardy Boys mysteries, which turned the secretive into the sinister. This deep in the woods, with so many tire tracks (why else would anyone drive down a dead-end lane?): *The perfect place to hide dead bodies!!*

Instead, I then stumbled upon dozens of "live" ones. Something foreign down in the greenery, a piece of clear flapping plastic caught my eye at the bottom of a slope in the woods. I pawed away a skimpy covering of leaves; then unrolled a large folded-over sac, and through the cloudy plastic a heavy stack of something shifted, slick and multicolored . . . . I reached down into the loam-scented sack like a pirate opening his first treasure chest, and here be Jewels:

Playboy magazines, over 20, 30 of them! Sheer excitement thunder-bolted up my spine!!

Of course I knew of their existence, what American boy didn't? Previously, I was all set to look at my very first Playboy with my neighborhood buddy, Harry Irvine, who smuggled the swollen double-Christmas issue out of his Dad's den and down into my basement. Wide-eyed with anticipation, we were just turning the cover, when my Mom's voice, like an all-seeing God, boomed out the laundry shoot: *"MICKEY—WHAT ARE YOU DOING DOWN THERE! IT'S MUCH TOO QUIET!!"* That ended that (no way to examine naked ladies with omnipresent Mom peering over your shoulder). Now finally, alone in the woods—an unadulterated peek at every boy's rite-of-passage . . . . (My brothers Scott and Bruce hid their collection in the infamous basement, in my mother's wedding dowry trunk no less, under a pile of cashmere sweaters. One day, when all-knowing Mom dropped the stack of irrefutable evidence in front of their father [who displayed his own stash openly on the coffee table at his restaurant office], Dad overruled doling out severe punishment over something so natural and instructive. However, he did promise the Mother-of-his-sons that something would be done. The next time the 'textbooks' for Female Anatomy were hauled out, my brothers discovered their Playboys gone—quietly replaced with an equal number of National Geographics. "To broaden your horizons," Dad later told them. And I have a hunch that the confiscated contraband, instead of being discarded, made its way to a certain restaurant office.)

There in the woods, away from censorship or interruptions of any kind, I leafed slowly through the treasure-trove, gazing with hammering heart and widening eyes at the spherical miracles. No male ever forgets his first look at a naked woman: It's like discovering an unknown continent that you will then spend the rest of your life blissfully exploring. I turned the pages of Playboy with a trembling hand . . . It wasn't shocking; wasn't pornographic; it didn't make me want to jump up and rape the next real female I saw; it didn't imprint impossible, airbrushed standards of perfection from which I then would judge all women by. It *did* make me want to have these same glorious feelings when I gazed at all females, real or imagined, naked or clothed—feelings of pulse-pounding awe and drop-to-a-knee thankfulness that women just existed, graced this planet with enchantment; and as a beginning connoisseur of all things beautiful discovered that day: There is nothing in this world as inspiring and beguiling as the female form, for it truly is "Living Art."

I worshipped page-by-page until dark, and then did something impulsive. From each of the Playboys, at the centerfolds I pried open the big buckle-like staples, freeing the tri-folded women. I didn't covet them all for myself; they weren't going home to be secreted away under my mattress. No, the fate of such glorious creations shouldn't be concealed or returned to smothering plastic.

I hung each of them: Miss June and July and April and November in the trees above the lane at the dead-end—poking an up-slanted twig through the tops of the glossy paper. A full moon rose above the woods making the work easier . . . . Finally, finished, I stood back to take them all in—and gasped. The two dozen pinups shimmered in the moonlight like sylvan nymphs, sylphs brought to life in the ultraviolet: all the bare skin catching and reflecting the lunar light so that the dark paper backgrounds fell away. They looked so natural, so right being there: The luxurious curves of their bodies matching the flowing contours of the trees; the stars in the sky twinkling in their eyes . . . . That day and early evening, what I saw and did down Lover's Lane, turning thirteen—plowed deep into my subconscious; later proving to be lodestars in my life, supplying the themes to live by and write about: wilderness and women; romance and adventure. (To say nothing of marrying a woman who later graced those same pages.)

As I ran back home, my feet barely skimmed the earth because for the very first time there was sacred awe and the primal power of *la femme* ashimmer in my soul.

Soon after, sex became more down-to-earth. I learned the nitty-gritty from a man of the world, a family legend who appeared out of the blue on the farm one day, like something out of Hollywood (where he actually lived and worked). When Dad was a boy growing-up in the tiny coal-mining town of West Natrona, Pennsylvania, he was already "a man among boys"—larger in size and bigger of dreams than the other neighborhood boys. He came into this world as an alpha-wolf, the leader of the pack: the one adults put their money on as "going places."

In the ethnic enclave of West Natrona, where English was definitely a second language, life offered you two choices: you either did your time, as your father or grandfather before you as a 'work-beast' in the coal mines or steel mill—or you earned a ticket out and into a better life by playing football. (Western Pennsylvania was a breeding-ground for future great pros such the Modzelewski brothers, "Iron Mike" Ditka, Joe Namath, Joe Montana and Jim Kelly.) At Har-Brack High, with Dad often out-gaining the entire offense of the opposing team, the fullback was the toast of the town, but after the Friday night games instead of going out to party, he went home; changed clothes and collected scrap metal well past midnight to sell for extra money. Wanting to be just like his father, his hero—after weeks of begging Dzaidzi to take him to work down into the coal mine, one day Dzaidzi finally lowered his protective guard. It was a 'reality-check' if there ever was one: Just one shift of backbreaking labor in the claustrophobic tunnels gave Dad the impetus to seriously sharpen his gridiron skills to get out of town, better his life, and try to further the entire family.

It wasn't all work and no play. Dad was the leader of an admiring gang of fellow ethnic boys, smaller in size and full of admiration for the town hero. A benevolent gang, their "colors" were a grateful red, white and blue; and ever-resourceful they converted an abandoned chicken-coop into their own plush clubhouse. (Girls need a "room of one's own"; boys, more tribal, want a "den of iniquity"— our basement; Dad's clubhouse.) Tommy Barto was Dad's *major domo*, his right hand man, with one of his main duties: approaching any girl that Eddie had his eye on and talking her into a date—probably where Tommy first developed his "Method-acting" skills: convincing demure, young females that "Big Mo's" intentions were on the up-and-up, so that the normally-chaperoned-at-all-times-by-their-Catholic-mother misses might slip away on the sly. Some even dared walk alone into the clubhouse: my mother being one of the early 'lambs' led into the lion's den.

While Dad went on to become an all-American and then pro football player, Tee Barto became an actor. He sent postcards a few times a year from exotic locations and we would catch fleeting glimpses of him on the silver screen (typecast as a mobster with his swarthy good looks).

At family gatherings: "Anyone hear from Tommy Barto lately?" often came up, with my Mom, Aunt Dot and Aunt Toots all giggling girlishly. The reigning female role-models at the time were Jacqueline Kennedy and Elizabeth Taylor, both in their prime, as were Mary, Dot, and Toots (her name really Bertha). They imitated Jackie K. and La-La Liz with their dark bouffant hair, tight white Capri slacks, round oversized sunglasses. Young and chic, they kept away from the dusty machinations of the farm: keeping house or sunbathing in bikinis pool-side and getting up to dance for the home movie camera to that ubiquitous Herb Alpert and the Tijuana Brass album "Whipped Cream." "Oh that Tommy! He could charm birds out of the trees!!" Mom exclaimed. "The way he always calls Dottie, 'doll,'" Aunt Toots added. "*Sooooo* dramatic . . ." Aunt Dot smiled. "He's always rehearsing. Even if he says: 'I'm going to the bathroom,' the way he draws-out each word with that perfect diction, he makes it sound like it's carved in stone for eternity!"

Talking about Tommy Barto, there was a different tone in my Mom and Aunts' voices. He infused their words with a lively lilt, a coy touch of flirtatiousness. Someday, I wanted to meet the man who made them speak that way.

One summer, when I was fifteen, at hay-bailing time, as I was wrestling the boxy alfalfa chugging up from the bailer chute; bucking the heavy monsters with knees, back, elbows into a crosshatched stack on the buckboard wagon behind me and sneezing ten times with hay fever over every pollen-laden bale— I suddenly had company. In the long, clanging racket of repetitious machinery, and my own fits of sneezing, I didn't hear his approach. Suddenly, a slender man with long, dark hair, almond eyes, and a pencil-thin Errol Flynn mustache was standing next to me on the wagon. Like a slim-hipped matador basking in the center of attention, he swiveled on the square-heel of his imported ankle boot. The bulwark hay bale charged past him through the air. At the last possible moment, his hands shot out—grabbing the parallel twine lines and in one effortless, continuous motion—he directed the heavy clover atop the swaying stack.

"No need to struggle," he said in a rich, dramatic baritone. "Let the 'mo' of the bale—the momentum work for you." He grinned and winked. My mouth fell open . . . .

He was the first man I ever saw in a pair of black jeans, silk shirt (white) and ascot (red). It was the infamous Tee Barto, a dandy in the flesh—blending into rural Ashtabula County about as well as Mae West in a Western.

"You're Tommy Barto, aren't you?"

"Last time I checked!" He extended his hand, rose up on his toes and clicked the heels of his Beetle boots. "You're Ed's oldest?"

I nodded. That afternoon as we took turns pulling (or rather, directing) hay bales; with Tommy Barto launching into a monologue, no—a soaring soliloquy that could have been entitled (like the book at the time): *Everything You Always Wanted to Know About Sex But Were Afraid to Ask*. Living in Hollywood and on movie-sets around the world provided him with subjects for his second profession: Like Sir Richard Burton, Tee Barto was a "sexual anthropologist" fascinated by how the libidinous talents of the opposite sex compared in different cultures. Rather than being a theoretician, his research was conducted hands-on and down in the trenches—all of which he shared, that hay day, with me.

For the dramatic thespian, however, words weren't enough. He needed to act-out . . . and to complete the scenes he needed to play-off of a "Leading Lady." On every hay wagon, there were a couple busted wet bales and long-handled brooms. With the wooden spines and loose, sweet clover Tommy sculpted the "highlights" of two horizontal females, one front and one back, atop the waist-level bed. Very little belief had to be suspended, so well rendered were his hay women and so convincing his method-acting. (At one point as the tractor driver, Charles, a middle-aged bachelor neighbor swung the attached bailer into a tight corner—he then had a clear sight-line back at the wagon. Right then, Tommy, with Miss Clover was demonstrating a few techniques from the Kama Sutra. Charles, so flabbergasted at what he saw, let the long rig keep turning . . . then over spun the steering wheel to get the bailer back on the hay row. The resulting whiplash toppled the full-load, Miss Clovers, Cassanova and his young apprentice onto the ground.)

After we reloaded the hay and headed for the barn (the farmer still shaking his head), Tommy announced, waving a Hamlet-like hand: "But the very best sex is when you don't have to move."

"Huh! But how?"

"Kegel muscles, boy. Find a woman who knows how to use them and marry her on the spot! There was this French girl once in Cannes . . . . "

So mesmerizing was the buckboard seminar that afternoon that despite the worse pollen and ragweed count in years I didn't sneeze once. For the first time in six summers, my sinuses were cleared/cured by dreams of distant lands and exotic ladies—hay fever replaced by fever of another sort—thanks to Tee Barto's academy-award winning performances.

I then met (as the song went): "A Real Live Girl" to practice with. At the family restaurant I quickly moved up from dishwasher to busboy. One late evening, after the last party was served, I was down in the cavernous basement laundry room bagging up all the dirty linen when I felt the presence of someone behind me. I turned around—and froze. Not just "someone," but Cindy Cooper, the hat check girl, who just turning 16, was suddenly a fully turned-out woman who swiveled heads and drew audible gasps even while standing still. Before I could utter one word, she moved right up to me, placed her mouth on mine and immediately found the right combination to unlock my pressed-together, neophyte lips (SexEd Instructor Barto didn't cover kissing, although he did call it, with typical male bravado: "Upper Persuasion for Lower Invasion!") Cindy's candied tongue then did things I never dreamed post-pubescently possible: dipping and darting; then ever so slooooow-leeee sliding and gliding her sweet soul over, under, and around mine: for my first, *wheew*, French-Kiss.

So began some serious petting sessions on Thursday nights when we both were off work and her Mom was gone (conveniently waitressing at the same restaurant). I would ride the bus down the hill and inside the apartment we would make-out, always 'listening' to "Star Trek" as we rolled around under the television on the shag carpet, never quite going all the way. (And to this day, sex and "Star Trek" are inseparably entwined, for whenever and wherever I hear the rousing opening music and that bold statement: "SPACE—THE FINAL FRONTIER!" my own, *ahem*, 'pocket rocket' readies for launch.)

Petting was permitted under my configuration of Catholicism, for rounding first, second, even reaching third base and then dangling off the bag; down the silky line toward Home were only minor, venial sins—quickly swept off the score card in weekly confession sessions—finished-off with a rapid, rote recital of a baker's-dozen "Hail Marys" and "Our Fathers" out in the chilly church pew. Swinging for the fences, "going yard": trying to jack one all the way was not permissible for that fell into the category of a grave Mortal Sin—not easily litigated away, even in a negotiable liturgy and there were far more drastic, lasting consequences outside of religion that I never wanted to face: the creation of a child when I was still 'all that' myself, and breaking the adult trust that my father had placed within my control. So, fueled by turbo teenage lust, but to the ultimate frustration of Cindy and myself: We kissed, hugged, fondled, groped, sucked, thrummed, dry-humped and deep in the throes of passion tore clumps of orange threads out of that 70's shag carpet—until a mere moment and millimeter away from 'docking,' we aborted the Mission, de-coupling; and there, right at the slippery slope of Deep Space and my curfew, I zoomed out the door at warp speed like the star ship Enterprise—thruster(s) glowing from parental gravitational pull . . . .

Sundays were showcase days at the Farm, with the entire Modzelewski clan gathering to swim, horseback ride, target shoot, play touch-football. Once I started high school and we all secured driver's licenses, I'd invite a dozen couples out for the activities. After quickly showing everyone around, I dissapeared up in the hayloft with my date to practice a few new first-to-third base moves.

Once I got my own car, I would sneak out to the farm with a girl during the week when no one was there. Every time I started to give her the tour—there would be Buck, the quarter horse or the Hereford bull, Husker Rupert the 70th with raging erections. It could be the dead of winter, with mating season long gone and nary a cow in sight but Husker's bright-red pecker would be darting in and out over his anvil-like scrotum like a flaming Chili pepper. And Buck—a gelding for crying out loud!—but no matter: out and out . . . and out some more emerged an annaconda-sized phallus. Just when it seemed it would plow a furrow in the ground; he swung it upward, thumping the full length against the bottom of his belly like banging a gong. They were incorrigible! The moment we showed ourselves: holding hands or playing kissy-face—one of the beasts would come running from some unseen pasture, brake right in front of us and unashamedly display their pyrotechnic pornographics. I swear those animals knew my intentions: that I was there on the sly; hoping to round the bases and were clearly out to ruin my chances with one swing of their mighty bats!

"Ohmygawd . . . take me home—*NOW!!*" Mary Rose, Tina or Margie exclaimed; all the color avalanching out of their faces—and my 'firm resolve' suffering serious shrinkage in the presence of such elongated male competition.

Next summer, while on a long run down to Pymatuning Lake and back, on the return I was a few miles away from the farm, when a car pulled up alongside. My brother Scott was driving (Dad letting him take the wheel on the near-deserted country roads). Dad was in the passenger seat. I slowed down, but he waved me on, "Keep going!" He then hopped out of the car, hitting the ground running; coming up alongside of me. "Go at the pace you normally would!" I did; he couldn't keep up. I was torn. *What is this? Should I run with him? Is this a test? Should I slow down? What!* I looked over my shoulder at him for a signal of some sort. Walking, he was smiling and shaking his head.

"GO, MICHAEL, GO!" he and Scott called out the open windows as they drove alongside: now I really sped-up, relieved, releasing pent-up confusion and adrenaline. I ran faster than I ever had before, with my father watching: the man I looked up to more than anyone in this world. Even though he was back in the car now he was really running with me inside, fueling my heart, my legs—faster, faster I flew. The pace car pulled into the driveway honking just ahead of me, as if I was the first to finish/win a glamorous marathon. I kicked it in, all-out up the gravel driveway, then stopped—totally spent. Dad jumped out of the car and put his arm around me. "I never knew how far or how fast you could run!"

"You were really clipping!" Scott called, with an awed look. "You blew by Dad like he was standing still!!"

Dad was looking at me in a way I had never seen before. "I didn't mean to," I mumbled, at a loss for words; wondering if I did something wrong, upset the natural order of things. But there was a warm light in his eyes and palpable pride emanating from the length of his arm slung across my back.

How does an aging father, who once made his living at the highest level of athleticism handle the emergence of three young sons "coming into their own?" He always provided us a yardstick that was also a way for him to measure himself. As we lifted weights in the basement or in the barn at the farm, he always said as he walked by, "I can lift with one arm what you guys can do with two!" He said it not as a put-down, without scorn, but as a statement of fact; and as a way to challenge us, keep us going; give us a tangible goal to shoot for: an Oedipal overthrow but in a way that would only improve us both.

As growing teenagers, whenever Scott, Bruce or I did an overhead press or clean-and-jerk lift of a new, heavy weight, we'd call Dad down to the basement—sure that *this time* we finally 'had him!' He'd come down, not as an outsider but one of us (which he really was, for he was there with us even when gone, pushing us psychologically along). He'd casually place one relaxed hand behind his back; grasp the bar with the other; stare straight ahead and up the weight would go.

We groaned loudly; and he good- naturedly chuckled, more to himself than out loud.

He set up other contests: more direct *mano y mano* exercises that he sprang on you at anytime. He stood against a wall with his legs apart; hands on his hips, elbows flared out. You stood directly in front of him, placed your hands on his elbows and pushed, trying to move his arms back to the wall. Never! He was an immovable force—even if two sons pushed—one on each arm. He would hold up his right index finger and place it inside a closed fist. Attempting to pull his hands apart was as easy as moving a slab of steel out of a tightened vise. A complete test of both strength and agility was when he placed his left foot forward, dropped into a crouch and extended his right hand. You placed your left foot up against his and took his hand. "Go!" you would say when ready. Push—pull . . . feint—until he knocked you off-balance: your anchored foot and the rest of you flying through the air!

There was Indian Wrestling—wrist-twisting after Sunday afternoon dinners, when the good china and white table cloth were removed—that never lasted more than a few seconds before he stopped toying with us and put us down, but in doing so gave us a "yardstick" of strength to measure up to. Then instead of arms, you locked legs: lying on the living room carpet flat on your backs in opposite directions, hold up your right legs; cross/lock ankles . . . *"Go!"* you'd say quickly, trying to catch him off-guard, but your leg would soon buckle under a pressing mass of downward strength.

Sometimes we'd lay for him, try to catch "Superman" after he'd been exposed to kyrptonite: late at night when he came home exhausted from an eighteen hour day at the restaurant. But he welcomed the tests, the physical interactions with his sons, his eyes lighting-up as he took us on. "Almost . . . Wow! You're getting there!!" Even though you 'lost,' you'd live on his praise for days, using it as renewed impetus to hit the weights even harder, expanding a notch: adding new platters to the bar; enlarging your arms.

Other times, we'd send-in a reinforcement. On 'Showcase Sundays' at the farm, after we were all soundly defeated (and Dad was sufficiently warmed-up), we pushed forward Uncle Gene. There were three football playing Modzelewski brothers: Ed "Big Mo," Dick "Little Mo," and the youngest, Gene "No Mo"— as in 'no more' Modzelewskis. Gene was an offensive tackle at the University of New Mexico; and the strongest of the Mo Bros. At 6'2" and 255, he was solid muscle and cat-quick. His legs, in particular, were colossal, as thick as tree trunks. When he and Dad lay on their backs and raised their legs, it was something to see: "The Clash of The Titans" as their mighty entwined limbs pummeled the floor—shaking the house at its foundations; knocking pictures off the walls;

smashing teacups; making babies cry.

Sunday guests at the farm, observing these physical rituals, tiptoed around wide-eyed, not quite knowing what to make of what they called: "The Modzelewski Olympics."

Inevitably, the days came when Bruce lifted more weight than Dad . . . Scott put him down in arm wrestling . . . and I outran him on the road. There was no gloating; no lording it over the victor who had vanquished us all the time. Instead, we felt stunned, disbelieving that we had actually accomplished what had proved impossible all of our life. Right after those sudden turning-points of surpassment, Dad immediately surrendered supremacy: wrapping us in his arms and announcing how very proud he was of us! From him we learned both how to win and more importantly how to 'lose.'

In an age of burgeoning absentee fathers how fortunate I was to have continuous physical contact with a loving father. It's been proven that when you put strange women together in a room, within fifteen minutes they will be telling each other the most intimate details of their lives. Put men together, and the first thing they'll do is play a game. So much was 'said' in our physical contests, an intimate male articulation passing back and forth through arms and legs, a pitch-and-catch from heart-to-heart.

The physical contact didn't always have a goal or a competitive pitting of one against the other. The earliest memory I have in life is flying through the air, straight up, toward the sky or within the leafy canopy of a tree. It was a real dream, created by my father. When I was very young: 2 or 3 years old, he encouraged me to stand straight-up in his massive hand. At first it was a bit frightening: "Grab my thumb and here, this finger," he'd say. "That's it, steadeeeee. Now stand up . . . ." (He was still playing pro football at the time, and his thumb had been pulled out of its socket and into a permanently bent angle by a Pittsburgh Steeler by the name of John Henry Johnson, providing a perfect handle to first, grasp; then use as a pushing-off lever to the upright position.)

Once my tiny bare feet were surfing the muscle fluctuations in his hand, he extended his arm and carried me upright before him, out the door and onto the driveway. Mom, watering the lawn, dropped the hose. "Oh, Ed! Whatever you do, DON'T DROP-" It was too late. While she was talking, Dad flung their firstborn straight up into the air. Up I went toward the blue sky and pure-white clouds . . . . Down, I fell into Dad's hands. Up, up higher into the sky, down into the Cleveland Brown fullback's massive, sure hands.

The neighbors all peered out from behind their drapes.

"At least get off the driveway! What if you drop him!? Oh, Ed, PUT HIM

DOWN!!" While continuing to launch his son, he sidestepped onto the lawn, flinging me high, higher . . . . He stopped under the big oak tree in the center of the front yard and then really snapped his back into it. I sailed up through green leaves; past big branches and a startled squirrel. The higher I flew, temporarily disappearing from Mom's sight inside the verdant canopy, the louder she screamed and the more I laughed with glee! The next time up I reached out at the apex of the ascent—plucking an acorn. As Dad then carried me past Mom, I dropped the nut into her hand. She sighed with relief and finally relaxed as "The Flying Walendas" retired for the day.

I waited nearly every afternoon at the big picture window for Dad's car to roll up the driveway after football practice. "WINGEE, DADDY, WINGEE!!" I smiled, running toward him—jumping up into his extended arms and after a hug, immediately was sent skyward again.

That earliest memory proved to be a metaphor for my entire life. Mom was always there, a loving constant but cautious presence, but it was my father who sent me flying: teaching me transcendence; that there were no limits.

The four-letter word Dad most detested his kids saying was: "can't." Obscene curse words wouldn't raise his ire as much if we cried: "I *can't* do it!"

"I DON'T EVER WANT TO HEAR THAT WORD IN THIS HOUSE!" he'd thunder. "YOU *CAN DO* ABSOLUTELY *ANYTHING* IF YOU BELIEVE YOU CAN AND WORK HARD ENOUGH!!" He said it with such resonating conviction (and with the shining example of his own life), that you had the added impetus to then conquer whatever challenge blocked your path.

One night, I awoke from sleep. A strange male voice was talking continuously downstairs. Curious, I got out of bed and crept cautiously down the stairs to see who it was. At first, I assumed it was a friend of Dad's . . . . However, in five minutes I still hadn't heard Dad respond back. To my surprise, at the bottom of the stairs it was pitch-dark and the deep voice rumbled on. Then my worries about an intruder were dispelled when I listened closer—finally placing the voice as a record on the stereo. The man was speaking about "The Power of Your Thoughts." Just then Dad's eyes made contact with mine. He snapped on the light above his easy chair; and motioned me over to sit on the couch. When I did, he snapped off the light.

"Hear better in the dark," he said.

"Who is that?" I asked.

"Earl Nightingale."

For over an hour we sat together listening. It was the first in a series of recorded motivational seminars and together we listened to them all, for seven consecutive Sunday nights, sitting united in the dark. It was as if we listened to

Nightingale's words with our entire beings—like relaxed sponges soaking up wisdom in the deep, dark depths. Afterwards, we talked about what we had just heard and how to apply it specifically to our own lives.

Afterwards, late at night, I couldn't sleep. I'd lie in bed, heart racing, alive with possibilities. Earl Nightingale had opened-up vast areas within the mind and soul. His voice, a rich basso profoundo, resonated for days, months, years inside with his inspiring lessons on how to maximize our full potential.

What a gift, how absolutely blessed I was having a father not only as hero and mentor, but my best friend. I especially looked forward to the hour drive out to the farm when it was just the two of us. Occasionally, during the winter, he would slip away from the office and I'd play hooky from school. Buried under a white blanket of snow and lambasted with frigid winds, the farm came to a standstill (Charles the neighbor feeding the cows and horses once a day in the barn). Once or twice a winter, we'd go out to shovel manure (often taking Dzaidzi with us), the barn floor rising like a solid tide under the many sheltered cows and horses. "Other men go to psychiatrists, but shoveling manure does it for me!" Dad said in a Cleveland Plain Dealer interview, now on the business page, instead of the sports.

Not bothering to restart the furnace inside the house, we quickly changed into well-worn work clothes, but not too many despite the cold, for soon our own furnaces would be roaring. Writing about the act of chopping wood, Henry David Thoreau declared with enjoyment: "I warm myself twice!" The same can be said of shoveling manure in winter—but even more so, for unlike the delayed space between chopping wood and then burning it in the stove later—both of our warmths intersected at once. Inside the barn, the heavily soiled straw, created by a herd of 4-chambered stomachs and then compacted down by the one-ton Husker Rupert and his heavy mates—released blasts of methane heat when punctured by an obtrusive pitchfork. The other, inner warmth came, simultaneously, as you broke through layer after layer of *merde* and then hoisted the heavy slabs, throwing your legs and back into it—up onto the hay wagon for dispersal out on the frozen fields. Even though we could see our breath in the barn, we were soon stripped down to T-shirts.

Dzaidzi, at 70, outworked us all. His massive, 'bread-loaf' biceps moved his pitchfork twice by the time we even stabbed together one load. I felt so proud to be working alongside my two heroes. Dad often commented how here we are: three generations of Modzelewskis, the realization of the American Dream! In those joyous moments, I thought of the Thomas Jefferson quote: "My father was a farmer so that I could be a businessman so my son could be a poet." (A distant goal to aspire to.)

Inside the "perfumed" manger; and then out in the open white fields, we three grunted and heaved; and up to our elbows in dung enjoyed the most enlightening, philosophical conversations—unfurling like lotus flowers with stems in the muck. One day, talking about youth and maturity, Dad summed it all up with a pithy parable.

"There were these two bulls," Dad said, pausing to fling another piece of ripe bovine linoleum over his shoulder, "a young bull and an old one. It was early spring. All the cows were in the back-forty and the two bulls were munchin' sweet clover side-by-side. Suddenly the young bull, hormones raging on such a fine spring day, got the 'Urge.' He quickly raised his head up out of the clover; stared keenly over at the cows and said: 'Hey Old Man, why don't we run and hump a few!' The old bull, a blue-ribbon grand champion many times over with more than a few gray hairs around his horns just kept right on chew'n. Finally, he slowly raises his massive head and looks at the youngster. 'Son, instead of running over and humping a few—why don't we *walk* over and hump 'em ALL!!'"

After the barn was cleaned and we were standing down on the original floor with arm and back muscles quivering and a deep sense of satisfaction in a job well done, we slowly shook-out fresh straw, like spun gold across the floor. Reclaiming his turf, young bull, Husker Rupert immediately deposited his opinion of our handiwork: both Nos. 1 and 2, that he probably saved-up the entire three hours we labored. Dad, Dzaidzi, and I looked at each other and groaned; then Dad, the former pro fullback, hit the flank of the bull with a forearm shiver, like he used on middle linebackers.

If we had time before the early winter darkness, we threw saddles on the shaggy-coated horses for a quick spin. Not ridden for weeks, they were ornery and wild, rearing and bucking once out of the barn. If we fell off it was usually into a soft snow drift. Once they shook out the kinks, we then lined them up to race over the full, diagonal length of a field, their anticipatory breaths stabbing out into the frigid air. The building speed cleaved a frigid wind of motion, tearing our eyes and flash-freezing exposed faces. We then whooped and hollered as Buck, Fred and Dino ran neck-neck-and-neck, fueling each other, tripling their speed back to the barn.

The next summer, a dark shadow was cast over the farm and family gatherings. Uncle Gene was drafted by both the Cleveland Browns to play professional football and the Federal government to serve in Vietnam. Despite my Dad and Uncle's best efforts to pull strings; call in favors to get their 'baby brother' an exemption Gene soon wore camouflage green instead of brown and orange. Despite being newly married; drafted by the NFL; having a metal plate in his right (rifle) arm from breaking his elbow; near-blind vision without corrective lenses; and highly allergic to nearly all green plants, at the height of the Tet Offensive, Gene was classified "1-A" and sent to Pleiku.

Uncle Gene was my connection to young adulthood. He was in college; an awesome athlete; drove a sports car; had beautiful girlfriends and played the newest, hippest rock and roll. Best of all he always played with us: lifting weights; wrestling; tossing a nurf football in the swimming pool as we took turns springing-off the diving board to snag his high, challenging throws—perfect training for this fledgling wide-receiver. "HEY MICK! COME-EER!!" he'd shout from inside his farm house bedroom. The needle on the stereo arm was biting full-blast into brand new LPs: "Johnny Rivers at the Whiskey A Go-Go" or "James Brown's Greatest Hits." The burly lineman whirled around the room on nimble feet, showing me the steps to all the new dances as he sang along, giving a bang-on impersonation of James Brown. After one side of the platter had nearly played through, soaking wet from his workout, he even had me toss a blanket (from the bed) over his shoulders just as the handlers of "the hardest working man in show business" did. Then, just like J.B.'s resurrection, Uncle Gene sprang back to life—giving the identical, wildcat-like wail as Brown launched into a funky, tight cut of "Cold Sweat."

With Gene suddenly gone, the farm was subdued, soulless. Dad told me how much Uncle Gene loved getting mail, so I decided to write him twice a week, telling him everything we were doing and how much we missed him. He wrote back just as often. I'd sprint back from the distant mailbox, unfolding the many onionskin pages, crying out the news to everyone like an old-fashioned newsboy. Deep in the back-forty woods, with my other cousins, we built a shrine-of-sorts to the exact specs of Uncle Gene's field camp: constructing twiggy lean-tos, put up a mess-tent, dug foxholes, and painted PLEIKU in red paint on a narrow plank, and nailed it to a tree. From then on, I always waited to read Uncle Gene's letters out there, the words having double the impact in similar surroundings.

One day, while riding horses, I led Dad out to the camp. He was stunned by what we did—creating externally what was always lodged deep in his mind. The encampment put him in a philosophical mood. He talked about the horrors of war and that with so many of our boys dying so far away in a fight we shouldn't even be in—a part of us should be prepared for Uncle Gene not coming home. He made it easier to understand death with nature all around: pointing out how the fallen, dead trees were feeding new sprouts, how spring always follows winter, but then he stopped midstream. Without another word said, we both slid off our horses, knelt down in the middle of the woods, in "Pleiku" and prayed for Gene's return. It was the first time I ever saw my father cry.

Uncle Gene, finally, returned home safe and sound, but 'The Times Were a Changin' not only in society but in our small world, as well. Dad and Uncle Dick sold the farm my senior year in high school. By then, the kids were growing-up. The farm was no longer the focus . . . school activities were.

Dad, Dzaidzi, and Uncles Dick, Gene, and Joe now receded into the background. A new male mentor now dominated my days and inspired my ways: Bill Gutbrod, the football coach at St. Joseph High School in Euclid, Ohio. He was right out of Central Casting: that name!; the wiry brush-cut; booming baritone; iron hard-flat-bellied-bandy-legged body—but nothing at all tinsel-town about Coach Gutbrod—he was so "Old School" that I was surprised he didn't have us playing in leather helmets. He was Ohio's version of Vince Lombardi, complete with the same techniques of making daily practice so tough and agonizing, with the full-contact "Bull In The Ring" and "Nutcracker" drills and endless wind sprints up the cliffs from nearby Lake Erie, that in comparison, the actual games were easy. Like Lombardi he was a master motivator: Coach Gutbrod's booming halftime orations, by themselves, stoked us to at least three victories a season. We won not so much with talent, but with heart; and Bill Gutbrod, after 20 seasons, knew how to reach inside the centers of young men and inspire the very best from us. When he spoke his entire body vibrated, so sold was he on striving for excellence; and turning unformed boys into shining men. Under his tutelage, I lived on a higher plane.

At all times he had the locker room (and your mind) papered with motivational reminders: "There are no shortcuts to success"; "No gain without pain"; "Fatigue makes cowards of us all." Beyond driving his players to undefeated seasons on the gridiron, Bill Gutbrod's real genius was in preparing you for life: "Character is what you do when no one is looking"; "Tell the truth and you won't have to remember what you said."—two of his all-time favorites.

Most of the teachers at St. Joes were Marianist Brothers: young to middle aged men in navy blue suits and ties, temporarily pausing or content to stop altogether just beneath the summit of Catholic Priesthood. They all had their specialties: English, Geography, Philosophy, etc. I became good friends with Brother Gerald, the Guidance Counselor, who, one day, after hours, reversed roles and poured out his problems to me. He was 34, and like most of the Brothers, a virgin—having entered the seminary as a chaste teenager. However, being "married to God," pouring his red-blooded libido into his work no longer seemed to be working. He told me that just before he entered the seminary, while walking across a park one winter day a woman in a full length mink coat stopped in front of him—flung open the coat and stood there totally naked.

Gerald was now absolutely haunted by that image, obsessed by a world he would never know.

Reading a book about Zen at the time, I copied one of the stories and slid it under his door, no comments necessary. The story went that two monks were hiking in a forest when they came across a beautiful maiden who was afraid to cross a raging stream. The older monk offered to carry her across, and she hopped up on his back, wrapping her long legs around him. The older monk with his 'burden' and the younger monk, solo, then forded the stream. Then for days, weeks, months afterwards, all the younger monk could talk about was the beautiful woman. Finally, the older monk said, "Believe me, I was not blind to her charms, but I set her down. You are still 'carrying' her . . . . "

In the '70's, many brothers and priests left the order to marry—believing that sexual libido and physical pleasure were also, undeniably, divine sacraments.

Most of my high school dates, were near-disasters, such as a double-date to the Sophomore Date-Dance with Gary Fatika, who was probably born with a beard, so manly was he in high school that he had five o'clock shadow at 9:00 a.m. and played a mean offensive tackle on our St. Joseph Vikings football team. Even though I still had yet to put razor to face, I was Fatika's teammate, going into battle lined-up alongside him as the tight end (a position of prime importance to the following tale).

As in a Greek tragedy, our power was our weakness. Sure, from an all-male student body of 2,000—22 are easily recruited to pillage and plunder on the gridiron—but tackling the complex psychological subject of young women was an entirely different matter. Shut away, with only our convoluted male selves and taught by the equally mystified Marianist Brothers, the daily halls of St. Joe's were veritable bubbling cauldrons of testosterone. Stirred by Coach Gutbrod, who even whispered in stentorian tones, we then boiled over Friday nights for football. Our only contact with the feminine gender was seeing distant flashes of plaid skirts from our nearby sister school: The Villa Angela "Angels." No wonder women were mysterious, ethereal creatures some of us dated once a week (Gary Fatika on a near-nightly basis; myself, rarely, for even though I demonstrated sure hands on the gridiron, and by the Viking legions was twice voted Class President and "Most Likely To Succeed," outside our manly encampment, around the complexity of maturing females I was somewhat flummoxed, lock-jawed and afflicted with *rigor mortis*, especially in the lower extremities when it came to dancing—what all young women live for.)

It all changed on Sophomore Date-Dance night. Fatika picked-up his date first—an absolute vision: a chiffon cloud afloat down the driveway and now perched wondrously on the front seat. A few miles later, I then opened the door for my paramour, but so flustered was I by her feminine perfection and the x-ray gaze directed at me by her parents and curious sisters that I dove-in on my side of the back seat without looking down . . . . Fatika had just pinned an immense corsage on his lady and after a five-minute kiss finally looked over his shoulder, snapping a wink—but then arched the eyebrow when he saw that my date was tapping her satin pump; looking around imploringly.

My cover was blown. I leaned forward, extracting the crushed corsage from beneath me (the rosebuds and baby's breath suffocating against the box's visquine window). Screaming inside with pain and total embarrassment—I then grasped the pearly-head of a straight pin and plucked the long, blood-red rod from my behind. Women might be from Venus, but I was from Cleveland and without a clue.

To my total surprise, Shelly wore the battered bouquet proudly the entire evening and emitted the most relaxed, down-to-earth belly laugh every time she explained what she was pinned with. Like a fairy tale in reverse, the prick of a pin, rather than putting the protagonist to sleep, helped jolt a young man to life. I boldly told-off Brother Thomas when he tried to pry this couple apart on the dance floor by admonishing: "Leave room for the Holy Spirit!"

For the first time in my life, with a woman, I felt completely comfortable in my own skin (and paisley-patterned tuxedo); and thanks to a forgiving Shelly—discovered that nearly all of my parts were in perfect working order.

Then two years later, trying to be a 'good Joe,' with Villa Angela's Senior prom the weekend following our's, I contacted the Senior Class President there and said that since most of our tablecloths weren't stained in any way, would they want to keep costs down by using ours? Chris said she would check with the Mother Superior and call me back.

She called the next day and said, "No thanks."

"What?"

Chris whispered in the phone: "I'm *soooo* embarrassed. Can you meet after school? I'll fill you in . . . . "

We shared a root beer float at a nearby diner and she told me that the nun said "Absolutely not, for white tablecloths might remind the young men of 'bed sheets!'" We both shook our heads in astonishment, agreeing that never in a million years would we have ever made *that* connection!! I then learned of the more common ban on patent leather shoes ("Boys will look up your dress by staring at the shiny toes!") and Chris then shared the nuns' instruction to departing seniors: "When you go away to college, if you have a picture of your boyfriend in your room, before you undress, make sure to turn the picture around."

My sister Nancy, a feisty free-spirit, attended Regina, yet another Catholic all-girls school in Cleveland. Sister Mary-Stifle-Your-Libido-Since-I-Must-Stifle-Mine was sending memos home about the length of Nancy's skirt. Seems the rules strictly forbade the cross-barred cloth from ever revealing a bare knee, let alone even the hint of a shameful thigh. I remember Mom the Mediator, often at her sewing table, letting out, yet again, what her daughter hoisted-up—as Nancy played a continual tug-of-war with the Body Police.

One day, when I actually entered Regina, walking unannounced down the main hall, the nuns slammed classroom doors to the left and right of me—as if Atilla the Hun was invading the priory: there to collect the maidenheads from 1,000 vestal virgins! With the girls in "lock-down," I turned and ran out—feeling totally embarrassed and ashamed to be causing such a commotion—with my only crime being that I was male (meaning to the nuns I was 'only after one thing!') when in truth, I was there for two: to drop off some papers and to give my sister a ride home.

By this time, after 12 consecutive years of being under the warped rule of the religious right, I now craved uncensored viewpoints and the liberal arts.

I accepted a football scholarship to the University of Maryland, but it turned out to be a mistake. It was the same school my father attended when he was an all-American, leading Maryland to number one in the nation, and the shoes were just too big to fill. I showed talent as a wide-receiver, but my heart just wasn't in it. Running down on a kickoff against Navy, from the outside wing position, I angled-in on the return man's blind-side—launching myself helmet-first, a technique called "spearing" that was soon banned for the following reason: my helmet hit, full-force, on the inside of the ball carrier's upraised knee and I heard the joint explode in my ear hole. As the runner lay flat on his back—his screams echoing off the roof of the stadium, I ran off the field, sick to my stomach.

In a Monday meeting, when we watched the game film, the coach kept playing the devastating hit back and forth, praising it over and over and saying that's the kind of football player he wanted at the University of Maryland. I left after my freshman year for I could no longer be that player.

I told my mother first. She seemed almost relieved. "Everyone has a calling in life. I've watched you play football and I've also watched you do something else, that makes you far more happy. When I used to look in your room when you were writing, you had a glow around you. Maybe that's what you should be doing with your life."

I then agonized over how and when to tell my father. It would be devastating news, not because he wanted his boys to follow in his footsteps, be carbon-copies of himself, but because I was giving-up a "Free Ride": an all-inclusive scholarship. And, at the time, I didn't have an alternative plan in place.

While home for the summer, dozens of times I said *Today's the day—I have to tell him today.* I'd greet Dad when he came home from work, have my speech ready to roll, but then would chicken-out at the last second. Finally, one day, when he came home beaming: with a college football magazine that forecasted his son as the starting flanker for the University of Maryland—unable to deny him any longer what I knew and he didn't; I took a deep breath and broke the news.

He collapsed into a chair. I ran through my explanation, which he accepted, but as I expected: a protective, loving father tried to make his son see all that he was giving-up; that life, itself, was not a game; it was a cruel business—and what was my plan? "I can understand you not wanting to play football, but how can you close one door without having another opened?" I had no answer. Dad was speechless and remained that way toward me for weeks.

To survive, I got a job at a grocery store warehouse, loading trucks during the graveyard shift from midnight till 8:00 a.m. At the 'lunch hour,' a few of my fellow workers, alcoholics and drug-addicts would drink or shoot-up their meal while in my car in the dark parking lot. After a month, of not having a life: working all night and sleeping all day, and suffering from the silence from the person I loved the most, reality set-it. I started to despair. Instead of being a 'Big Man on Campus,' one night, at a low point, I nearly accepted a needle loaded with smack.

Always an extremist and desperate now for a way out, I thought of becoming a priest: had talked about it once with Sister Mary Verne and she was certain I had the "Calling." I could accept the Vow of Poverty, for I was already familiar with functioning well below that line—*but*, I didn't want to be like the priests and brothers I knew who entered the seminary as virgins and were, therefore, forever obsessed with sex. Then I read in the newspaper that Billy Graham was bringing his "Crusade for Christ" to Cleveland. At the time, Graham was at the height of his powers, packing entire stadiums full of seekers and repentant sinners around the world. I often watched him speak on television and whether you agreed with his theology or not, the man was a magnetic, powerhouse force as a public speaker.

In the depths of despair, with youthful naiveté and a boldness born from blind faith, I decided that he might help and I wanted to try to talk with him personally. Reading that he was in town to meet with the mayor and other religious dignitaries, I called a friend: the minister of a Baptist church and yes, indeed, he was invited to the meeting, and yes, I could come along as his guest and he would see if he could get me a few minutes with Reverend Graham.

At a reception after the meeting, Graham was standing across the room, giving off the luminous aura of a superstar. The Baptist Minister came over, shaking his head; saying he tried but Rev. Graham's schedule was planned to the minute. For some reason, I didn't give up. I hung around and hung around until nearly the last person left and as Graham's handlers were then about to whisk him away, as a last chance, I stepped forward and called his name.

The protective phalanx paused, and then the lead handler waved them on again, but Billy Graham held up his hand, "Wait!"

A tall man, he towered above the shorter entourage. He must have seen or heard something to give him pause for he walked straight toward me; his people all looking at their watches and rolling their eyes. I told him I was Catholic and maybe wanted to be a Minister and could he please give any advice?

I've always felt that the eyes are the "windows of the soul" and very few eyes that you see emit conviction and grace. No *Elmer Gantry* here: By the look in his eyes, I could see that Billy Graham deeply believed in God and what he preached. He talked for about five minutes, telling me of bible colleges that I should write to; try to attend—lifting his hand twice to stave off the imploring handlers.

At home, I wrote to the Moody Bible Institute and while awaiting their reply, one day, the phone rang . . . . While at Maryland, when I was still (by society's high-achievement standards): "somebody," I had given the keynote speech to an Eagle Scout convention in Indianapolis, Indiana, after Richard Retterer had read a profile on me in The Fellowship of Christian Athlete's magazine and then booked me for the speech. It had gone very well: a standing ovation and the then-mayor (now US Senator) Richard Lugar presented me with the "Key To The City." Dick Retterer was now calling to see how I was doing?

I told him about the changes in my life. He offered me a job working construction, on a new Inn he was building on a lake in Indiana. Desperate, and with good memories of Indiana, I accepted.

Working outside, in the healing sunshine and wind on the shore of sparkling waters, I regain my enthusiasm for life. External energy originates not so much from food, but from inner peace and happiness, and, although we worked hard, ten hour days, I then ran five miles every evening around the lake and swam the sweat, dust and sheet-rock off my skin. Home was Retterer's small Air stream trailer on-site. Relaxed and refreshed after the day's physical exertions, we then talked for long hours into the evening over a gourmet meal he cooked-up and a bottle of vintage wine. I had never before met a man so cultured and refined. On weekends we drove to the Merchandise Mart in Chicago, where he picked-out all the antiques and fine art to furnish the Inn, giving me informal lessons in those unknown subjects.

One night, with the Inn nearly complete, he said: "Why don't you take the money you've earned this summer and go to Europe?"

I laughed, shaking my head. "You've paid me well, but not *that* well!"

"No, go on 'the cheap'—the best way, for then you won't have a comfortable buffer between you and life. Buy a Eurail Pass and stay in youth hostels and you can stretch your money; see all of Europe in a few months. My oldest daughter just did it, and it changed her life. You say you might want to be a writer. Well, over there, Europeans look at life differently. Money is not the be-all-and-end-all like it is here. The Arts are just as important. Heck, they've even named streets after writers!"

The next day, while browsing in the campus bookstore at nearby Indiana University, one title jumped out: Frommer's *Europe on Ten Dollars a Day* (still possible in the mid-70's). I bought the book and it never left my sight for the next two months.

I returned home after thanking Dick Retterer profusely (an "angel-on-earth" if there ever was one). After telling my parents of my plan to go to Europe, Dad wasn't impressed, fearing I would turn into a bum. Mom was very supportive and excited. Due to leave the next morning, feeling both scared and exhilarated, I just couldn't go . . . not without reconnecting with my father: without his approval, and it just wasn't going to happen as he said goodnight, turning in early. I tossed and turned all night; then got up early and went downstairs dejected, still undecided what to do. But there was a note from Dad on the kitchen table . . . saying how much he loved me and how proud he was of his son, and wished he had done the same thing when he was my age. I cried and cried all the way on the rapid transit to the airport, reading and rereading his letter. He ended it with a quotation from Kahlil Gibran's *The Prophet*:

> *"You may give them your love but not your thoughts,*
> *For they have their own thoughts.*
> *You may house their bodies but not their souls,*
> *For their souls dwell in the house of tomorrow,*
> *which you cannot visit, not even in your dreams.*
> *You may strive to be like them, but seek not to*
> *make them like you,*
> *For life goes not backward nor tarries with yesterday.*
> *You are the bows from which your children*
> *as living arrows are sent forth."*

On the airplane, I folded Dad's letter into my Passport, and now clear of mind—I raged to live!

In Amsterdam, my first stop, I walked along the canal district, stopping to stare at lavish window displays that the Epicurean Europeans do so well: stars of strudel; rows of dozens of different-shaped cookies; castles constructed of creamy crullers; then at the next store assorted meats hanging like organ pipes; coiled links of sausages; cheese wheel towers; and then—*Oh my! Excuse me!!* There was a nearly naked woman behind glass. Then another . . . and another . . . sitting openly, brazenly behind window after window inches away! *DU-UH*—it finally dawned on me who they were; and what "delicacies" they had for sale.

While frozen in my tracks on the sidewalk, transfixed by an absolutely gorgeous "Little Miss Muffet sitting on her tuffet"—a hand closed around my wrist and I was tugged into a doorway—face to face with a drop-dead redhead.

"Come on!" she said in English, leading me down a short hallway, into a small bedroom. As she began removing what little clothing she had on, I cried, "NO!"

"What is it?" her voice flattened.

"I . . . ah, I really don't have the money—but I'm sure you're worth it and *oh god, LOOK AT HER!* but, well, would you . . . . "

"Would I what?"

I then blurted out something that as soon as it left my mouth I wanted to catch in midair and stuff back in, for it sounded completely ridiculous. "Would—would you go out with me?"

I'm sure that the sex worker had heard many strange requests, but from the look in her eyes, without a doubt—mine was the weirdest.

At first, she looked as if she was going to burst into laughter, but then she tilted her head slowly from side-to-side while staring straight into my eyes. She must have discerned something sincere, for she finally responded with: "Maybe . . . "

Standing there, beet-red, I was shocked by her response. "REALLY?! It's-just-that-I'm-backpacking-across-Europe-and-trying-to-live-on-five-dollars-a-day-and-you're-so-beautiful-and-instead-of-not-having-a-chance-with-you-I-just-"

Stopping me from further embarrassment, she pressed a forefinger against my lips.

Back out in the doorway, she pointed down the lane to the street corner. "Meet me there at 8. And you better show-up!"

I stuck out my hand. "I'm Michael."

"Alice," she said, shaking her head as she shook my hand.

I walked and walked and walked: down the lane; over canal bridges; through downtown; all the way to the city's outskirts, not seeing a thing, burning-off adrenaline and embarassment and re-playing the scene over and over: in absolute shock at how it turned out!

I have a date with a prostitute!? I shoubldn't do it—she's a sinner! Yes, I should—imagine what she knows!!! Then all thoughts were glossed-over by the warm memory of her vibrant curves and satin skin . . . .

As I walked back to the youth hostel, the war raged on: all my years of Catholicism now clashing with unbridled curiosity. The stern visage of Sister Mary Verne appeared in my mind's eye: *"Remember one thing,"* she said, shaking her finger: *"Curiosity killed the cat!"* Then another voice, a new one, spoke from deep within: *"No it doesn't. It keeps the cat alive and purring!!"*

Inside the large communal room of the youth hostel, with backpacks and bedrolls staking-out every inch of the wooden floor; with four hours to kill, I kicked-back on my foam pad and tried to work-up a truce between the dual feelings of terror and ecstasy. Finally, what persuaded me to go ahead with it was a feeling of total anonymity: no one who knew me knew where I was or what I was doing and that was exciting—being totally disconnected from home and school—free to experiment away from "enquiring minds," and guilt-dispensing nuns, brothers and priests.(Although Coach Gutbrod's quote of "Character is what you do when no one is looking"—gave me serious pause. I cleared that hurdle by thinking: *Isn't 'Character' formed by pleasure as well as pain?*)

Once decided, I jumped up, took a long shower; put on a fresh pair of jeans and pulled from my pack a flannel shirt that had the fewest wrinkles. At 7:30 p.m., I crossed Dam Square with a pounding heart.

Amsterdam is world-famous as "Sin City," for prostitution is legal and drugs are sold openly. Even though I was in an experimental mode, drugs didn't interest me, for running teaches that the greatest high is oxygen spiked with adrenaline—and a plenitude of both were now pumping through my veins.

I kept approaching the busy corner, then crossed the street, then circled back again, calming my nerves by staying in motion. On about the fifth pass, I noticed a young woman standing there, but just when I decided it wasn't Alice—she called my name.

It was Alice's voice and when I looked closer—her eyes, but now she was a brunette and, besides shedding the red wig, also gone was the mask of make-up. She took my hand and we walked and talked and went to an X-rated, animated movie: "Fritz the Cat." Afterwards, we pub-crawled: tossing back shot after shot of *Jenever*, the national drink, a fiery gin made from juniper berries. At each stop men and women approached, hugging Alice and sitting down at our table to talk awhile. She was constantly opening her purse: buying drinks, food; handing out cash loans on the spot, no questions asked to needy friends.

Finally, well past 3:00 a.m., totally done-in—she hailed a cab. As much as I wanted to continue the evening (every time her miniskirted thigh pressed against mine in the movie theater or under a pub table, my heart palpitated and eyes crossed), but standing out there on the sidewalk with everything up in the air, I said: "Thank you, Alice, for the fantastic night. My room is just around the corner—I'll walk."

Her eyes widened with surprise and then beamed-up into mine. "Tomorrow I take the day off. We go to museums, yes?"

Yesssss! I said it right—reining-back what the alcohol pushed me to say and what she expected, so that she would know that the same goofy idiot who asked her out stone cold sober while she was "on the job" did, indeed, want to know her as a person.

We spent the entire day at the Van Gogh Museum, with Alice excitedly narrating the life and times behind each of her favorite artist's paintings. We had a wonderful dinner at a quiet restaurant. She took me back to her place and we had sex and, at times, made love in ways I never thought possible. I was nineteen years old and a virgin no longer.

We parted the next morning, both smiling—with one of us recovering something possibly forgotten and one of us with something just found.

I checked out of the hostel and walked to the train station. I stopped in the long shadow of a church, a cold chill climbing my spine . . . . I bowed my head, waiting for a lightning bolt to strike or at least the urge to rush in for confession, but neither punishment arrived, so I turned the corner—sprinting to the station feeling just born; and hopped a train to Italy.

In Rome, arriving late evening, I found the youth hostel and then went out and walked the city. I loved arriving in a new city at night, when all the grit and grime and commercial signs were softened by darkness, as if you could, initially, feel more about a place by seeing a bit less. While ambling in awe through the Forum, I tripped and fell over a chunk of marble and lay there in the grass looking up at ruined temples and arches from antiquity, spot-lit, in what was once the civic center of Roma. I climbed a hill, looking over the Coliseum, my mind filling with the rush of history and Christians being fed to the lions—but when walking down around the arena, I heard, instead, muted mewings from hundreds of abandoned cats; and from behind every dark nook, prostitutes stepped out into the light—Alice's sisters.

The next two days while touring the Vatican; staring up at the ceiling in the Sistine Chapel; descending into the catacombs; seeing omnipresent statues of saints; and walking amidst scurrying coveys of nuns and priests, I began to feel a "disconnect"—as if it was no longer the world I put my faith in. Instead of

Rome, in all its glory, dispelling any doubts I had about religion; returning an agnostic to the core of his beliefs—it was there I felt a turning point, a solid shift deep in the soul. What before I had accepted blindly, I now saw with fresh eyes. It was personified by the severe, contrasting colors of the nuns and priests' habits: black and white, saints and sinners, when instead I was seeing that life was far from being so simplistic: people and reality—all a delirious gray.

My favorite country was Spain. Spain may be in Europe, but it seems an independent continent. It has culture and refinement, but for me the soul of Spain was not found in its cities. I explored Madrid, impressed at how well-mannered a city can be. In the Prado Museum, the Goyas and El Grecos were awesome but fixed reflections. I wanted to see moving pictures—current yet ancient essences—with my own eyes.

I discovered the spirit of Spain in the wonderful people aboard a countryside train, a vision on the plain, a horse that turned into a centaur and merged with Espana itself.

On the slow train from Barcelona to Madrid, with stops in the many villages between . . . the cars packed with both short hoppers and those Spaniards going the full distance I was a novelty—an *American* sitting next to a window at the end of a row of padded seats full of natives. To communicate, we mixed pantomime and a few words of one another's language. Hands and eyes, feelings more than facts came through. After questions and answers, I couldn't decide if the people around me were related by family or village—their surnames seemed to combine both.

An older gentleman came aboard, sitting down across from me. He wore a black beret, dark suit, pencil-thin silver mustache, and kept glancing at the open book in my lap, trying to read the title.

"*Don Quixote,*" I said.

He smiled and turned his palm outward, indicating the open plains. "Where many of his adventures took place," he said in firm English.

The group was reaching down to baskets and bags under their seats for food—each person offering something to everyone else. The patriarch of the clan stood up, pulled down three large suitcases from the luggage rack, and stacked them in the middle of the aisle. The makeshift table was quickly buried under loaves of coarse bread, manchego cheese, baked quail, *churros*—Spanish fritters, and a jug of Graciano wine—a dry red.

I put out a mesh sack full of melons I had bought in Barcelona and Senor Garcia pulled out a bottle from his satchel that raised eyebrows all around. He poured Andalusian sherry. From my backpack I quickly got out my Sierra Club camping cup, catching the liquid gold—unbelievably smooth and ever so delicate.

As the train rolled along we became one big, happy family—eating, talking, drinking, singing. They saluted Dallas, New York, California—the places they knew of (via TV) in America. I raised my cup to Seville, Toledo and Torremolinos, then picked up my book—to La Mancha! For dessert, our resident gourmand, Senor Garcia, sliced the melons in half, scooped away the seeds, then took out another bottle and poured into each melon cup a dab of *Anis del Mono*—one of the finest anisettes in the world. The soft sweetness of the melon mingling with the sharp aroma of anise was ambrosia to the senses.

All the talk and musical verses died out as the Spaniards settled into their habitual afternoon siesta. The dignified Senor Garcia had his head back, snoring.

As I sipped the sherry, the train clacked past the sun-drenched plains, past yet another ancient village, past a windmill and a young woman standing barefoot in a white dress that streamed with each blast of wind stirred by the rotating vanes. She was a tawny statue; a living mirage—Don Quixote's Dulcinea.

Basking in the sun on a straw mat on the beach at Malaga, the center of the *Costa del Sol,* I dug my heels into the sand and looked at the mountains looming high above the Mediterranean Sea. Then, seeing a man on horseback trotting three other saddled horses along a dirt road, I jumped up and jogged over to the rider, who reined in his horses, removed his black, round-brim hat, and beat it free of dust against his leg.

I inquired if he rented out the horses. Yes. We arranged to meet in an hour under a big shade tree down the road. Returning to my room, I showered, put on blue jeans and a denim shirt, which chafed my sunburned skin, and I unbuttoned the shirt as I walked down the dusty road.

The *caballero* was sitting under the tree smoking a cigarette. Two horses were tethered to a low branch. He stood up, put on his hat, tightened up his bolo tie.

"My name is Paco," he said, extending his hand.

"*Me llamo es Miguel.*"

"*Habla espanol?*"

"*Un poco.*"

Paco untied the horses and handed me the reins to the roan. We mounted, rode past some large *haciendas*; and turned onto a trail that ran behind a wooden fence then dog legged up a hillside.

The roan fell into step behind the bay's whisking tail. I looked over the angular white houses—Picasso's cubism—to a shimmering turquoise sea. The horses topped the hill and trotted across a wide mesa. Ahead was a mountain that started straight up, then rolled back into the sky. The trail upward was a narrow ribbon of switch backs.

As we ascended, I loosened the reins to give the horse its head and felt his back legs swing under, hooves dig in; the push of thick muscles. Loose rocks rained down.

The mountainside continued up in a series of bluffs and mesas—a crude stairway that climbed high into the sky. A few twisted trees clung to rocky faces and withered leaves of chaparral were caked with dust. Buzzards circled.

"Stop for water up above," Paco said.

The horses charged up the bluff, catching the scent of water. When we reached level ground, Paco began to curse: a hundred yards away a band of gypsies were cavorting in a large trough of water.

"Stay close," Paco murmured. We swung in a wide arc around the group.

Fully clothed the women and children were flinging themselves into the wooden trough; their clothes were odd combinations of bright colors and the agitated water was both washing machine and bath tub. Their shrill cries ceased when they saw us. Flying out of the water, they stood statue-still, the children hiding beneath their mothers' dripping skirts. The gypsy women had thick black manes of hair and round black eyes that glowered out of thin faces.

They looked dirt-poor but their poverty wasn't the standard by which to judge them.

This was humanity pared to the essence of pride and fierce freedom. No place was home and they roamed the countryside making up their own rules as they went along. One woman suckled a baby lamb.

Once past the gypsies, Paco puffed his cheeks and then blew out the air.

"Why didn't we stop?" I asked.

"They would steal the horses and eat them right there. Polecats those women are!"

"What about the water?"

He pointed up the mountain. The horses worked hard to gain altitude and amidst their labored breathing, I heard faint bleatings. The rise topped into a flock of sheep—the woolies parted like cumulous clouds in the wind and the horses lowered their heads to navigate. The shepherd raised his staff. Paco tipped his hat.

Clear of the bleating sheep, the horses tossed heads high, snorted and pranced, reaffirming their nobility. Paco looked over his shoulder and nodded as we cantered across the wide plateau. I reined out of his dust, swinging off to the left. Seeing each other, both horses bolted—galloping flat-out—and the land suddenly dropped away; the horses sailed over an arroyo, then settled down into an easy lope up a well-worn trail.

We came to a house/cantina that served as a way station for travelers on the mountain path. A boy poked his head out from behind a burlap blind, climbed out the window, and ran to us as we dismounted and Paco handed him the reins.

"*Agua, Peppito,*" Paco said, patting the boy's head.

A heavyset woman came out of the house wiping her hands on a white apron. She and Paco spoke rapidly as she led us out to the open verandah. After disappearing into the house, she returned with a platter of fresh corn bread, a bowl of salsa and a swollen bota of wine.

Corn bread dipped in that fiery sauce and washed down with wine packed a wallop. As Paco and the woman made quiet conversation, I leaned on the wooden rail overlooking a dazzling expanse of sea and lost myself in the big sun, which hovered above a flat shadow: Africa on the horizon. Again, feeling the bota against my shoulder, I reached around and swung it up to squirt a steady stream against the back of my throat.

It was one of life's exquisite moments: high on a mountain in Spain, watching an orange sun plunge into blue sea, horses at the ready, and streaming wine—a red that measured up to the bold surroundings.

I felt a hand on my back. "We must go."

Peppito brought the horses and we swung up into the saddles as the indigo sky darkened. The horns of a new moon appeared and a cool breeze blew against our backs as the horses picked their way down the bluffs and over the mesas.

"You ride well, *amigo.*"

I told him about the horse I grew up with. He told me of how he rode before he walked, and now how many mouths he had to feed with the little money he made from renting horses.

We rode on without words. Stars glistened. The air smelled of salt and settled dust. My ears caught the muffled roar of surf as the horses swung past the glowing *haciendas* to the tree where we had started. I dismounted and put money into Paco's hand.

"Tomorrow we ride again—half price. They need to run and they need the sea on their legs," he said.

"*Que hora?*"

"Before the sun comes over the mountain."

I got up in the middle of the night, lit a candle, and stepped over cool tiles to a small desk where I picked up a pen and continued writing in my journal. A few hours later a horse whinnied so I dropped the pen and opened the window. There was Paco sitting bareback on the bay.

"*Buenas dias,*" he said, raising the reins of the roan.

I put on the denims that smelled of horse and hopped out the window. Paco handed me the reins and I swung up onto the broad back. The horses' hooves clacked over the cobblestones and the sound echoed off the rows of white plaster buildings. Cats padded out of alleys; seagulls flapped off a low roof.

As we crossed the dirt road and moved onto the beach, shafts of brilliant light fanned over the blue mountains and the sea curled in sparkling tubes that broke on the sand. I steered the stallion through the rectangles left by yesterday's sunbathers as we passed a long row of hotel towers. I looked across at Paco; it was impossible to tell where horse ended and man began.

We moved onto flat sand that the sea lapped with foaming tongues. Paco pulled back on the reins and I did the same. With robust energy abruptly contained, the horses bowed their necks, snorted, and pranced high in place. Paco flashed a smile. HEEE-AHHH! The horses bolted. My calves clutched the sides of my mount; I felt him flatten as he surged into full stride, paired hooves striking the sand. His muscles surged in waves and I rode the crests.

The horses ran neck and neck. One nosed ahead and then the other pulled even. I glanced over at Paco—his eyes were full of pride. "Let him go. Let him learn his limit."

The reins jerked through my fingers as the horse sprinted out to top speed. The horse ran and ran on the tips of his hooves. Loose sand didn't slow him—he produced more power. He ran with his nose cleaving the air, sucking that wind into himself, feeding flaming muscles. He would run until his heart burst.

"Whoa boy, slooow boy," I said with my lips in his ear, and gentle, even pressure on the bit. He slowed—rocking half-circles in the air—kicking up a shower of water. "Whoa runner . . . . " He strutted with his head up, eyes continuing down the sea-washed sand.

Pressing my right thigh against his withers, I pushed wet hair out of my eyes and slapped soaked pants in joy, jubilation. We joined Paco and walked back toward the towers as hotel beaches were filling with people.

In front of my small cottage, I slid off the roan and flipped Paco the reins. I told him to wait, and went in to bring out my own bota full of Rioja. We passed it back and forth. Never before did wine taste so good or mean so much to me. It was through the wine—squeezing the skin dry—that we finished our time together. We then wrapped hands and nodded to what we saw in the other's eyes.

The next day I was back on the train, pushing my Eurail Pass through Luxembourg, Germany, Sweden, Norway. As the trip wound down, I arrived back in Paris flush with nearly two hundred dollars. Having lived so frugally and facing the end of the trip, I felt a sudden desire to splurge, in one day, an amount equal to that which had carried me across the Continent for weeks.

After I checked into a *pension* and headed for the luxurious purge of a hot shower, I wondered, of all the temptations of Paris, where to spend my money? The mirror on the wall supplied the answer—my body was nothing but bones. I had gladly sacrificed pounds of flesh for art that had filled my spirit. Now it was time to take the aesthete in another direction.

After indulging in a hair cut and a hot lather shave, I discovered a shop with tailor-made suits on sale, where I subsequently emerged the sharp-dressed man. I donated my frayed blue jeans and flannel shirt to the nearest trash bin and took on the air of a *boulevardier*. It was early afternoon and I had a hundred dollars, which translated into francs that would serve me well.

Rounding the corner of the rue Royale, I saw Maxim's, a veritable beacon of stylish gastronomy. I hesitated, straightened my tie and walked in. I raised one finger to the tuxedoed maitre d'. He tapped his pen and looked imploringly over my shoulder before turning on his heel and leading me to a table in a far corner. A waiter materialized posthaste with the menu, which I proceeded to scrutinize as if it were a Russian novel. Curiosity piqued, I ordered the truffle sandwich and decided to accompany it with a bottle of Taittinger champagne.

I surveyed the expanse of this illustrious icon synonymous with Paris and its *belle epoque*. No expense had been spared in this solid, plush establishment, with its gold-framed mirrors and red velvet seats, accented with the finest in silver, linens, and flowers. Any minute I expected to see Gatsby stroll in with Daisy on his arm, or perhaps Piaf followed by a lively entourage. Better still, I thought I actually saw Aristotle and Jacqueline Onassis. But whoever they were . . . he smoked, she ate. And everyone else nonchalantly pretended to look away.

At surrounding table were the current reigning politicos, titled folk and of course, the ubiquitous coterie of *nouveau chic*. Bejeweled women and mustachioed men garbed in Chanel, St. Laurent, and Cardin chatted animatedly. Amidst the soft patter of worldly accents, lilting laughter and crystal glasses ringing toasts, I felt like a spy, hidden away at my table, surfacing from the underground to investigate this elegant environ: A combination of Hemingway and Le Carre.

I had to smile as I reflected that just hours before I had spent the night atop a radiator in the train station waiting room surrounded by a variety of *clochards*— a sheltered kid from suburban Ohio beginning to comprehend how far the fall to down-and-out that Orwell and so many others had evoked in their writings. I sat in my new suit in a plush chair suffering vertigo from a combination of champagne and the rapid climb to this rarefied restaurant of French gastronomic lore.

More guests stepped briskly into the dining room following the stiff-backed maitre d', heads held high, smiling—as if given a table at Maxim's was admission to some sacred sanctum.

As I savored my champagne and awaited the arrival of my truffle sandwich, I remembered the historical tidbits I had read in a Paris guide book: how tossing money around Maxim's has always been popular. For example, when the Grand Duke Serge offered a coquette named Augustine a dozen oysters, each containing a pearl worth 2000 francs; or when the American, Gordon Bennett, owner of the Paris Herald, once paid a flower girl 500 francs for a bunch of violets; and when a New Yorker named Todd flung a fistful of golden *louis* in the air, and they came down he knew not where, causing a *melee* among the *demi-mondaines*— forty years later, when workmen tore up the seats to renovate the place, they found the *louis* in nearly ever crack and cranny.

My sandwich arrived. I picked it up and took the first bite. What grabs a pig's nose from three feet under surely gives the taste buds a tingle. Bathed in a delicate red wine sauce, served on an open crisp baguette, the black truffles of Perigord were extremely tasty, with a pungent, bosky flavor.

Truffles range in size from no bigger than a peanut to splendid giants the size of an orange (although most are walnut-sized, which these had been), sliced thin enough to depart all of their savouriness.

I was reeling, deliriously pleased, ending a two-month backpacking tour of the Continent comfortably ensconced in the fabled Maxim's, quaffing the finest champagne and indulging in truffles. Though the sandwich was not very large, I consumed it as if were a five course meal, taking one small bite, then sitting back to watch and reflect firsthand a world I previously knew about only between the pages of books.

I thought about how money is a conundrum—too much of it can shield you from realities everyone should know; too little of it can do the same. I recalled a sidewalk cafe evening when a philosophical Frenchman told me: If you are down to your last two coins—spend one on bread, the other on art. One gives you the means to live, the other the reason.

I realized that those wise words perfectly described my afternoon in Maxim's—that during a few special moments in one's life, means and reason, bread and art can be one and the same.

The price of my memorable lunch was only a few francs shy of all I had. Even though the service was included in the bill, I stood up and ceremoniously placed all my money on the table—determined to leave Europe with only expansive memories. Inspired and exhilarated, I took one last survey of the room, catching the eye of an elegant Deneuve look-alike. I glided through the foyer, hands in pockets, clutching empty but expensive cloth. As I stepped out on the sidewalk, taking my first breath of a new reality, I stopped and did my best Gaelic shrug. *C'est la vie*, I thought to myself. What's money to a young writer hungry for a truffle sandwich?

What I would give right now for just a bite of that solid, succulent sandwich. The cuisine of ultra running leaves a lot to be desired. There are 8,000 taste buds on the human palate and we are only repeatedly hitting two limited areas: sweet and soft. A steady flow of glucose is required to keep the blood-sugar stable, and since nearly all your blood is busy elsewhere in the running machine, the stomach, normally an ironclad organ, but now somewhat seasick from the constant motion, just can't handle much more than baby food: body-heat-melted Power Bars, mollified Reese's peanut butter cups, mushy bananas, and GU—small pouches of pasty glucose, that you easily tear open with your teeth; then squeeze the small sacks of jazzy-flavored "Chocolate Outburst," "TriBerry," "Banana Blitz" directly into the mouth and, presto, within seconds, the supercharged GU enters the engine pipes, pulling you up out of a bonk. But you have to be careful that you don't wait too long—get overly bonked, for when the body is totally exhausted, especially at altitude, its judgment goes out of whack and, strangely, the last things it calls for are the very things it needs most to keep going: water and food. So, you have to drink and eat well before you are thirsty or hungry, for when you actually feel those two conditions, if you even recognize them through the dehabilitating fog of fatigue, it's too late: you're already dehydrated and starved, which can then trigger an ultra runner's worst fear: cramping—for a severe stomach or leg cramp deep in the woods, miles from nowhere is, for all practical purposes, *el finito*. So the trick is to keep your body both hydrated and fed around the clock, which I try to do on the hour, every hour—sucking down the sweet pap of life.

As we run on through the darkness, tanked-up once again, I tuck back into the comfort of memory.

Returning home from Europe, I enrolled in Indiana University and cleaned out my savings account—driving off in a used MGB sports car (initials really an acronym for 'Money Good Bye!' for the car, although a blast to drive, was constantly breaking down and at the most inopportune times—when I had no money). Coddling that car and protecting my rising investment, I couldn't leave it parked on the street, out in the weather (the carburetor seizing-up at the first hint of moisture), so I asked the live-in landlady of the boardinghouse I was staying if she knew of a garage for rent in the neighborhood?

She walked me out onto the porch and in a gossipy whisper said: "See that house across the street? Well, Mrs. Henley lives there or used to—no one has seen her in months. That place used to be the jewel of the university, but it's gone to seed. But there is a garage attached to the house. Try there . . . . " Mrs. O'Malley's eyes then swelled wide, "And let me know what happens!"

Curiosity piqued, on a beautiful autumn Indiana afternoon, with the trees raining leaves of crimson and gold I crossed the street and walked down the long gravel driveway through a riot of vegetation. Halfway down I needed a machete to clear a way through. Finally, stooping and at times, crawling through the overgrown greenery, I stood-up in open space and saw the house. I gasped. It was huge: a tall, ante-bellum brick mansion in a neighborhood of cookie-cutter duplexes. Standing on the front porch along rising white pillars, I turned and gazed over a half-acre lawn, or what once was a lawn, buried now under years of leaves; and around a central, bone-dry fountain were chairs and settees—total victims of unchecked vines.

I grabbed the big brass knocker on the front door, but it was rusted in place. I threw my back into it, pulled—then wrapped it down. I waited a long minute . . . no answer. I tried once more, with the same result. I shrugged and started down the steps. Then I heard the front door creak open a crack.

"Ye-ssssss?" spoke a frail female voice.

All the hair went up on the back of my neck. I suddenly felt like "Pip," for standing in the doorway was a living ghost: Mrs. Havisham—straight out of Dickens' *Great Expectations*!

After introducing myself, she invited me in. Elba Henley was 80 years old, bone-thin, wearing a sandy pageboy wig slanted off to the side and a dark nightgown stained with coffee and holed by errant cigarette ashes. Her skin was paper-white; her eyes a pale, rheumy blue.

Standing in the foyer, I asked if she had a garage I could rent and I would gladly pay her a reasonable rate?

"I have a ga-raaaggh," she said, with a King's English diction, "but I don't need your money. There is this lamp . . . . "

She shuffled forward in velvet slippers. Following her around the corner into the house proper, I was then stopped dead in my tracks. The vast living room was filled with antiques, most covered with cobwebs: English landscape and portrait paintings on mahogany wood walls; a gold brocade divan; marble tables; a crystal chandelier; Steinway baby grand piano; a Louis the IVth love seat in the bay window; and covering the central section of the wood floor was an immense oriental carpet, crisscrossed by footprints in the surface dust. Fronting a television was a modern brown recliner and all around it was a litter of empty Sara Lee coffee cake tins and glass ashtrays overflowing with dead butts.

With a bony hand, Elba Henley repeatedly yanked the chain of the floor lamp next to the recliner. "See, it just won't work!" she said. "If you can fix it you can park your little car in the ga-raaaggh."

The bulb was good (replaced from a discarded four-pack on the floor; which I tested in another lamp). "Maybe a short in the wiring . . . . Mrs. Henley—are you all alone?" I said with concern.

"I have two daughters," she pointed to pictures on a side-table, "but they're gone. And the 'Busy-Bees' used to come, but I fired them."

"'Busy-Bees'?"

"Yes, Bonnie and Barbara. They came in twice a week to cook and clean . . . .But look," she said stomping a slippered foot, "the lamp is *ruined!*"

"Why don't I take the lamp into town and see if we can get it fixed?"

At that, her eyes lit up and she smiled. "Let's go!"

"Um . . . well—ah . . . "

"I haven't gotten out much lately. Let me find my purse!"

There was no arguing with her. Clearly this was a woman used to having her way. I put the top down on the MG, held the towering lamp, sans shade, between us like a brass lance; and Elba Henley clutched her wig with both hands: *Wheeeeeeeee!* she kept shouting with glee as we rolled into town.

So began a three year "Harold and Maude" love affair.

After the first couple weeks of daily visits: cutting the grass, trimming back bushes, fixing appliances, vacuuming and dusting and getting along great, she said: "Oh Michael, why don't you just move in? Take one of the extra bedrooms upstairs and make this your home!"

I kept resisting, but the house was close to campus and I could save a great deal of money by working-off the rent . . . .

Neighborhood tongues were atwitter as one Saturday I carried all my belongings across the street. At first I slept in a Venetian gondola-framed bed in a bedroom with frocked wallpaper, but not wanting to turn into Henry James (although I'd have given anything to write like him), I then took the corner room with a conventional bed, large windows and third-floor balcony.

Since Elba had been married to prominent lawyer and Indiana University trustee, George Washington Henley, a flood of gratis front row tickets arrived in the mail for concerts, ballet, football games. With Elba on my arm, we saw Nureyev dance both "Swan Lake" and "Sleeping Beauty," and wildly cheered the Fighting Hoosiers to victory over rival Purdue with a last minute touchdown. Everywhere we went in Bloomington, the older I. U. faculty and board members waved to Elba with surprise, both over the youthful age of her escort and the fact she was still alive.

Life returned to the Henley house. The "Busy-Bees" came back: two wonderful Indiana farm ladies, who grocery shopped, cooked and cleaned (all three of us conspiring to break Elba's unhealthy addictions to sugar, caffeine and nicotine). After a leisurely morning bath, every day was a fashion show as Elba wore dresses from an international wardrobe. Evenings at home, instead of watching television, we read a book from the massive home library, taking turns reading aloud alternate chapters or we would sit side-by-side at the baby grand piano as she played music long into the night. Originally from the same Indiana town as Hoagy Carmichael, who wrote the eternally popular song, "Stardust," Elba was also a music major, playing all the standards from the early century: "How Ya Gonna Keep 'Em Down on The Farm After They Seen Paree?" "Arrivaderci Roma," "Vaya Con Dios," "Rhapsody in Blue," "The Maple Leaf Rag." The songs may have dimmed a bit in her memory, but no matter, for after decades of playing, they were all encoded in her fingers, and once she got rolling (after I hummed a few opening bars), they all flowed forth flawlessly from the ivory keys.

She encouraged me to have parties, filling the house with young students and faculty, and Elba was the life of the party: energetically spinning yarns about her worldwide travels and I.U. history; then we'd sit down at the piano and everyone would all sing-along, slaphappy together.

If outward energy comes from inner happiness, so does youth, for when Elba was playing the piano, riding in the MG or on her feet cheering at football games, I would glance over at her in amazement as years, decades seemed to fall from her face and body; and flashing forth again was the young ingenue—the same absolute "heartbreaker" on campus during the roaring '20's. (One day, in an old scrapbook I found a newspaper article saying as much and a picture of young Elba in a flapper outfit. She had those same slender, shapely legs and when happy, a flirtatious face that could still cause a young man to, in the words of Ring Lardner: "give her a look you could have poured on a waffle.")

However, with 'the child now being mother to the mom,' Elba's two middle-aged daughters: Dody in California and Natalie in Pennsylvania were getting suspicious, for during their phone calls home all Mother talked about was some 'Michael' and now he actually had moved-in! With visions of me backing up a truck to the front door and making-off with all the family heirlooms, both daughters coordinated their busy schedules and flew-in for a "Grand Inquisition."

Dody arrived first and was very standoffish, but when Natalie came in the door, we took one look at each other, and had no choice but to embrace—much to Dody's dismay. After they did a quick inventory of the house, finding everything intact, we all sat down to lunch and I was peppered with a hundred questions. What really seemed to put them at ease was seeing their Mother so happy and Elba telling them that while cleaning the roll top desk, I had found old stock certificates that she had completely forgotten about and were now quite valuable; and ten $100 bills squirreled away, which I had promptly delivered to her money manager at the bank.

That night, while studying, there was a knock at the door and Natalie came in holding two glasses of bourbon. I was in what used to be her room. It was a full-moon night and we stood out on the balcony, talking, drinking and listening to Nat King Cole and Ella Fitzgerald records. She was twice my age, but young in both whippet-thin body and facile mind, a high school English teacher in Pittsburgh and a total romantic at heart. She had been a widow for years, her physicist husband and love of her life dying suddenly, and his death devastated her to the point where she had completely shut down emotionally and sexually.

That night standing on the very balcony and with the same moon she used to dream under while attending Indiana University as I now did, she opened-up and we found ourselves kissing and embracing and she cried and cried. At four in the morning, just before tiptoeing over to the guest room she shook her head and smiled: "Strange how life works: I came here expecting to throw you out, and end up in your arms!"

Natalie became my teacher and lover (both words interchangeable). We met in New York City for Broadway plays; the museums; and evenings at the Cafe Carlyle, listening to Bobby Short sing Cole Porter: imbuing each song with verve and brio and in the process telling an entire novel in a three minute song. We flew off to Acapulco; the south of France or spent rainy weekends holed-up in the library of her Pittsburgh home, grading papers, eating pizza and making plans to visit the Oracle at Delphi—Apollo being her god and dolphins her favorite animal. I brought her my English Lit compositions and essays and she, more than anyone, taught me how to write, constantly slashing her red pencil through passive verbs in favor of the active.

With the floodgates opened, Natalie was insatiable: wanting to have sex everywhere and all the time, making up for lost years. Driven by the turbine of lust, we did it across carpets, over furniture, midair on airplanes, in elevators, down in basements, up staircases, al the while teaching me: *There! Here!! And this is why* . . . . She challenged me to see how many ways I could have her climax with my pants on: teaching me that sex to a woman, is much more than intercourse; that women have "skin hunger": erogenous zones sprinkled all over their bodies. I marveled at the power of female sexuality, far more pervasive and stronger than a man's. I read an aboriginal analogy about man always coming-up short: only having so many arrows to fire from his quiver, compared to a woman's vast, cave-like capacity.

Natalie was the first woman I ever met who employed an amazing love technique, that I became fully aware of in the writings of my favorite explorer and sexual anthropologist, Sir Richard Burton. Burton was particularly excited about Ethiopian women famous for their highly developed vaginal (kegel) muscles, whom by sitting on a man's lap could induce orgasm with sole contact of that one body part!

As great as the sex and traveling was, it was the talking that really was the most exciting. Sex can be measured in minutes, but we talked and talked for nonstop hours: having "mental orgasms" over favorite new books, movies, who was the better philosopher and man: Plato or Aristotle? Going out to dinner, the waiters often gave-up on us, for menus in hand, we just couldn't unlink our minds long enough to consider food.

I constantly thanked her and said how lucky I was to know her and all the things she was teaching me. One day she said in an entirely new tone: "Michael, every woman should be so lucky to have you in their life." That stunned me. I felt so very in over my head and quite often, intimidated by Natalie. And I knew by now that I wasn't going to be famous like my father. I wanted someday to be a successful author, but the odds were stacked against that happening. So, I concentrated on being the absolute best person I could be, even if no one ever knew my name.

As Natalie often reminded me: One of the great things about going to college is having a respite from the major responsibilities of life. For a brief time, sheltered behind ivy walls, you have the opportunity to try on new identities and dabble in courses that fill your canvas with new colors. My real goal in going to college was to take as many different courses as I could, sample all the riches of history and, in the process, try to become a complete human being. Hopefully, everything else would happen from there. The corporate world was starting to look at college graduates differently. Rather than hiring specialists who narrowly ratcheted down their viewpoint in a single field, so that all they knew was "more-and-more about less-and-less," law firms, businesses, the media were starting to hire from the Liberal Arts: wanting people who could actually see The Big Picture. Along with fulfilling requirements for an English Literature degree, like a kid in a candy shop, I relished the electives: eagerly sampling art history, anthropology, philosophy, entomology (fascinating study of what populates the world in the greatest numbers: insects) and acting.

I read far afield of my courses. I once spent four straight days in bed, away from classes, in a fevered state—devouring Henry Miller's *Tropic* novels and his

Rosy Crucifixion. Ever since Mom gave me my first library card, I'd rather read than eat. I can't agree with people who boastfully claim that they don't read. Might as well say you're content to cut yourself off from life, itself! Go into a bank and the only money you can withdraw is your own. Walk into a public library and all the riches of the world are your's for free: all the life lessons in biographies and autobios; the privilege of holding Thoreau's *Walden Pond* in your hands; the heart-soaring emotions and very pap of life packed into poetry (Whitman! Pablo Neruda!!); a novel that can rock your world (Homer's *Odyssey* does it for me). I coveted those riches like a pirate hoarding gold coins.

I took a theater class and acted in a few plays. Our student production of Paddy Chayefsky's "Noah" was so good that we toured the Midwest, putting it on at other universities. I played Japeth, Noah's youngest son. The class professor was Noah and Charles really carried the play. Seeing a glimmer of theatrical promise under my constant overacting, Charles, having totally dedicated his life to acting and teaching of the dramatic arts, worked with me on stage long past normal rehearsal hours.

We'd then go over to his place for dinner and talk far into the night about acting. He was a gifted raconteur. Charles could read the phone book and halfway through you'd be on your feet applauding. However, after downing a bottle of wine, he'd then start flirting and issuing imploring invites to stay the night.

"Charles, I'm flattered, but I have no interest. I really enjoy our friendship. I'm learning so much from you and would want nothing to-"

"If you want to be a complete actor, an artist, you should experience all of life!"

"Yes, but," I shrugged, "I'm just not attracted to men. I can appreciate male beauty but it doesn't turn me on."

"You talk about how you love women so much—well, it's all the same in the dark. And with a man, it's a lot neater—'pussy on a stick!' Come on, let's go to bed!!"

I then made an abrupt exit. The next day in class or on stage, we both acted like nothing untoward had transpired. One day, he asked if I'd like to go with him to New York City to visit one of his former students, now enrolled in Juliard and with a leading role in an off-off-Broadway play. Ever fascinated by New York, I agreed to go and why don't we stop at the family house in Cleveland on the way? Charles was brilliant and I wanted my family to meet him, but as a safeguard I made him promise that he wouldn't, well—overly reveal the side he normally kept to himself.

"Done!" he said without a moment's hesitation.

I called Mom; she was delighted we were coming. I asked if she would please cook her incredible spaghetti—but hold the wine.

When we knocked at the door, Charles extended his hand and shook Mom's: "A pleasure to meet you, Mrs. Modzelewski!"

We then walked up into the kitchen where ex-NFL football playing father and two testosterone-and-body-building teenage brothers were standing. "Dad, Scott, Bruce—I'd like you to meet Charles . . . . "

My worst nightmare then unfolded. Upturned hand on left hip, Charles slowly sashayed across the kitchen floor and stopped, dead center, in front of "Big Mo." His right hand now fluttered up into the air and eventually came down, nestling just fingertips inside Dad's massive hand.

"Sooooo nice to meet *yuuuuuuuuu!!!*"

All the blood fell out of my father and brothers' faces and their jaws hit their chests with resounding thuds. They looked totally pole-axed—as if the slightest breeze would now blow them over.

"DINNER'S READY!" Mother called, saving the day (but really only temporarily postponing my "execution.")

I'm sure there were gays living in Cleveland, Ohio in the late-1970's, but I'm also sure, other than congregating at an unmarked nightclub or two, that they kept their sexual proclivities, for the most part, undercover. The 'closet' that many eventually burst out from was waiting a few years down the road on the liberal West Coast, not the religious, ultraconservative Midwest. And I know for certain that prior to that visit, my entire family had never before met and supped with a practicing homosexual.

Well, as it turned out, Charles chose that moment: when I was most vulnerable, to pay me back for not giving in to his desires. Because he was an excellent actor, the effect was doubly dramatic, to say the least. Charles, all limp-wrists and lispy *sssssss's*, dropped very clear hints (having the effect of detonated nuclear bombs!) that we "knew" each other in the biblical sense . . . . The sham was really a shame, for my family never got a chance to know the wonderful person underneath the performance.

Rather than stay the night, as planned, we continued on to New York late that night (with no protests from my shell-shocked family). I drove on, seething in silence; speaking to Charles only when asking for minimal directions.

Jennifer was outstanding in her play; and later that night in her tiny Manhattan walk-up, knowing her former professor and assuming we were lovers, offered us her bed. Then, with Charles in the bathroom, I gave her a quick whispered synopsis on what happened. Lights out, she then slid into bed next to Charles and I took the sleeping bag on the floor. She ended a bit of pillow talk by mentioning that she was running a 10-K the next day in Central Park and asked me if I would like to join her? Charles abruptly rolled over. The next morning, off we ran . . . .

Back on campus, I stopped taking drama (so convincing was Charles' performance that for years afterwards my family assumed I was gay or certainly "bi".) I concentrated solely on writing. One day, overtaken by an idea, I sat down at the typewriter and got up five hours later with a story about my Dad's football career and how he graciously lost his job to Jim Brown. It wrote itself, because for the first time the words came not from my head, but my heart. Having the virgin confidence of a writer yet to be rejected; not knowing any better, I decided to start at the very top and send the story to "Sports Illustrated"—then promptly forgot all about it.

Weeks later, while attending an English Literature class, the Dean's secretary stopped the professor's lecture asking for me. "There's a long-distance telephone call for you," she said in the hallway, "from a Mr. Peter Carrey at Sports Illustrated!"

I was dumbfounded as I picked up the phone. "Michael, congratulations! What a wonderful piece about your Dad! It just needs a little work but we want to publish it."

I floated back into class like I was dreaming. Sure enough, a few days later the marked-up manuscript arrived; I made the corrections, and a week after that a big check came from Time-Life. As hard as it was to do, I kept the story a secret and at Christmas, rolled up the magazine and put it in Dad's stocking with the story facing out. As he read it . . . for the second time ever I saw my father cry.

Ever since we were young children, the house in suburban Ohio held western riches. Every month a new issue of "Arizona Highways" magazine arrived with glorious, hyper-real photos of things we had never before seen, let alone imagined: saguaro cactus with human-like arms rising into crimson sunsets; deserts carpeted with spring wildflowers in every hue; pure white schooner clouds floating across deep blue skies; red-rock, convoluted canyons; Navajo Indians, covered in turquoise squash blossoms, weaving 'eye-dazzler' rugs. In industrial Cleveland (at that time, before its present-day renaissance, the city was the butt of jokes with the Cuyahoga River actually catching fire from all the combustible pollution), under those gray skies and gritty winters it was impossible to believe such places actually existed: *Arizona, Colorado, 'Utall'*—just pronouncing the words transported you to other planets, worlds away from northeast Ohio. Dad eventually had all the "Arizona Highways" hard bound in leather covers and placed on the honored top row of the bookshelf.

Then a folksy young bard with an infectious laugh and huge love for all things natural and western started climbing the music charts. In the evenings, after work, Dad sat in his easy chair roaming the latest "Arizona Highways" with John Denver's celebratory odes playing on the stereo like soaring clarion calls.

At this time, Dad sold the sit-down, steak house restaurant and went into fast-food. Unlike many retired jocks who go into the restaurant business with name-only: trading on their notoriety to attract customers, then showing-up, in person, only once in a while, Dad's investment had longevity and ungrafted profitability, for he was an shrewd, hands-on businessman. He put in 18-hour days and while taking care of business today, always had his eye on tomorrow. After the restaurant first opened, he inspected the delivery of steaks and declared them top-rate. He then picked-up the phone and berated the supplier for sending over such poor meat.

"Thought you said the meat was great!?" I said.

"It is—but you let them know who they're dealing with—let 'em know right away you're on top of it, or else they'll start slipping in more and more bad cuts . . . "

One of his favorite sayings was "Timing Is Everything." Even though Mo & Junior's was doing very well, he saw that the times were 'a changin': that women were now liberated and, with careers of their own, had little time to cook at home—so the future was in fast food. He sold the thinner profit-margin steak house and started a fast food franchise chain called "The Beef Corral," specializing in roast beef sandwiches that, for awhile, throughout the northeast U.S. gave Arby's a run for their money. His Western interest was now on public display: the Beef Corral buildings wooden A-frame barns, and the workers all wore red-checked gingham shirts, bolo ties, and brown-felt cowboy hats. Replicas of old-west saloon signs covered the walls: "Don't Shoot the Piano Player!" "Best Grub West of the Mississippi" and across the bottom of "Hotel Rooms 10 Cents," in small type: "Indians sleep downstairs."

One day, at the downtown Cleveland Beef Corral, the urban cowboy had a run-in with an aforementioned hotel 'guest': Russel Means, a full-blooded Lakota Sioux, Hollywood actor and one of the founders of the militant A.I.M. (American Indian Movement) was on the warpath: in town to try to get the Cleveland Indians baseball team to abolish their mascot/symbol, Chief Wahoo—depicted, in Means and many others' opinions, not as a noble brave but a toothy-grinning, red-version of the Negro 'Step-n-fetchit.' And Means wanted the name "Indians" dropped as well. "If sports teams were named 'The New York Kikes' or 'The Denver Dagos'—you better believe there would be an uproar!" Means stated in a newspaper interview.

Taking a break from his fight with the baseball team's front office, in a surly mood, Means walked into the nearby Beef Corral for lunch. When he saw the placard demoting Indians he threw a fit: demanding in a thundering baritone that a trembling teenage cashier produce the Manager!

(This was the late-1970's well-before the advent of the P.C. [political-correctness] microscope. From today's perspective or any era, clearly, the sign should never have gone-up. But Dad was not a racist, by any means. More than half of his restaurant staffs were minorities and many in managerial positions; and his personal friends were made-up of every race and hue.)

Dad happened to be there, pitching in, slicing roast beef. When he stepped up to the counter, Means immediately got in his face: "That sign is discriminatory to my people. You have 24 hours to take it down or I'll burn this barn down!"

Dad walked over to read the fine-print on a sign he wasn't fully aware of (interior decorating of the rapidly expanding units solely the job of the architect). Asked politely, he probably would have removed the sign on the spot, but the worst way in which to try to get your way with Ed Modzelewski was to confront him in a threatening manner. (He trampled more linebackers on the gridiron after they made the mistake of verbally triggering his temper.) In response to Means' demand, Dad, anger reddening his face, responded with: "Ahh, you're overreacting! Hey—I'm Polish; I hear Polish jokes and insults all the time. But I laugh at them. Instead of having a chip on your shoulder as big as a block, why not lighten-up?"

Means jabbed a lance-like forefinger into Dad's chest and bellowed: "YOU HAVE 24 HOURS TO TAKE THAT SIGN DOWN!!!"

Upset, Dad left early for home with the sign still up. Deep in the leafy Cleveland suburb, he slowed the car, turned and ascended his driveway. As he got out and walked around the rear of his brand-new Porsche toward the house—an arrow whizzed by his nose and stuck on the lamp post. Wide-eyed with terror, Dad sprinted into the house yelling at the top of his lungs: "MARY—THE KIDS! GETTHEKIDS!! QUICK!!!" He dashed down into the basement for the shotgun.

(Unbeknownst to him, all afternoon brother Scott was in the backyard with his new bow-and-arrow set, trying repeatedly to loft one up over the garage . . . .)

When Dad finally figured out what happened, never one to ignore omens or portents—the next morning the sign came down.

That summer, my sister Nancy and I were on our way out west, as Dad's scouting party. One day he came home singing J.D.'s song, "Guess He'd Rather Be in Colorado" as he dropped an Automobile Association "Trip-Tik" on the dining room table, excitedly flipping page after page, state after state, following the highlighted route-line connecting all his dream spots: Monument Valley,

Bryce Canyon, Zion, Yellowstone National Park. Dad couldn't go himself, for he was in the complicated process of trying to close the sale of his entire fast food franchise to a corporate buyer. So he sent us as his eyes and ears. I was the writer (promising to keep a journal); Nancy the expedition photographer.

Henry David Thoreau, in his essay "Walking" described how whenever he went out for a stroll he instinctively turned in a western direction: "The future lies that way to me, and the earth seems more unexhausted and richer on that side . . . Eastward I go only by force, but westward to go free . . . . The West of which I speak is but another name for the Wild; and what I have been preparing to say is that in Wildness is the preservation of the World."

Crossing the Mississippi, driving through stagnant heat and incessant flatness, time and our mood was stretched as thin as taffy. Then like a mirage, on the horizon enormous clouds seemed to solidify until we realized the high white cumulus was snow! Seeing the Rocky Mountains for the first time, something clicked. It felt exactly like the phrase in J.D.'s "Rocky Mountain High": *"Com'n home to a place he'd never been before . . . . "* (And looking back, it was at that moment my life really began.) Bursting with excitement, we stopped atop Loveland Pass and called Dad at his downtown office and our words of shouted excitement pulled him right there, through the wires, with us up into the evergreen high country, dusted with snow and dreams.

As we moved on, it was quite a disconnect—purring around in a silver 911 Porsche, but then to save money on hotels (Dad continuing his fiscal policy of only matching the funds you first saved), we often pulled into KOA campgrounds and parked next to a picnic table, where I slept on top; Nancy protected underneath, in a 'Polish Bunk bed.' We climbed a rock mountain together in Zion; herded cattle on cutting horses at a Wyoming dude ranch; ate our first buffalo burger in Jackson Hole; got snowed on in our sleeping bags in Yellowstone—and that night almost lost my one-and-only sister in the worst possible way. Getting up in the middle of the night to pee, by habit, I lifted the seat in the 'one-holer' park latrine; then a few hours later, Nancy, unbeknownst to a snoring me, rose to also visit the outhouse and then shattered the silence with "HELLLLPPPPP!!!!" Immediately, thinking *Bear!* I ran to the source of the sound, flashlight poised as a club, but there was my sister in the deep grip of the toilet—having plunged three-quarters down into the hole, with her head just visible over her knees.

"WHO THE HELL FORGOT TO PUT THE SEAT DOWN??!!!" she shouted the eternal female lament, as I hauled her up out of the deep *doo-doo*, and turned my back as she then washed herself off with newly fallen snow.

"Some male idiot, that's for sure," I murmured, way too embarrassed to fess up, burying myself in shame deep inside the bag.

Our last stop before returning home was Aspen, Colorado. "Maybe we'll see John Denver!" we said wide eyed while singing along to his songs on the tape player, and trying out our Colorado-speak of "Wow!" and "Far Out!" as we entered the mountain hamlet. Jumping around in our seats, we excitedly pointed out the sights and bent our necks to look up the mountainsides at the quaking aspen trees, leaves like gold coins against an impossibly blue sky. I glanced over at Nancy. She never looked so beautiful, happy and radiant; and after spending nearly every moment of a month together, I would have married her, I thought, if she wasn't my sister—I felt that close to her and honored to be in her presence.

We parked the car and "NEW FAVORITE PLACE!!" we both shouted in unison, arms upraised to the encircling mountains. Starving, we followed the alluring aroma of fresh ground coffee and homemade waffles—into a cafe with framed pictures of Cleveland Browns players on the wall. Looking closely at a team photo, sure enough, there was number 36: Ed "Big Mo" Modzelewski, complete with a bristly blonde flattop that we unmercifully, eternally teased him about!

"Who owns this place?" I asked the waitress.

"Tommy O'Connell."

"Wow! The quarterback!! Could you maybe please tell him that Ed Modzelewski's kids are here?"

Tommy charged out, swooping us up in his arms and for the next three days showed us exactly why he moved to Aspen and loved it so much.

We were there just before the town went totally Hollywood and prohibitively expensive (driving young ski bums and service employees out of Aspen, down the hill to Glenwood Springs). In the late 1970's, you could see the exclusivity coming, but there was still time to actually have your own pad (instead of sharing a small studio with 4 or 5 others to keep up with the exploding rent, if you could even rent, at all). With Tommy's guidance and Dad's help we slapped down deposits to hold the last two apartments at Valley Hi. In a few months, Nancy was going to finish high school at the same time I graduated college, and with Dad about to close his deal, as well—all signs now pointed west, as we sped back to Cleveland.

After finishing high school, Nancy moved out first, and I followed a few weeks later. My apartment, across from hers wouldn't be ready for awhile, so I would crash on Nancy's couch in the interim. Having sold my car to finish school and pay rent on the empty apartment, the day after graduating from Indiana University I eagerly rode a Trailways bus out to Aspen.

Nancy picked me up late at night. She had a meal ready back at Valley Hi and there I met Robin and Ted: young guys, skiers; just passing through. I saw a totally new side to my sister that night: Nineteen years old with her own pad in Aspen; and 3,000 miles away from the restrictions of parents or nuns, she was celebrating her freedom with "wine, men and song." Way past midnight, Nancy brought out some bedding for me; and said goodnight. Before turning in, I stood there waiting for the two guys to leave. Instead, my sister put her arms around both of them, plucked-up a half-finished bottle of Wild Turkey and sashayed into her bedroom . . . .

I collapsed on the couch in shock, struggling to clamp teeth to tongue. At home in Cleveland, I had always been the protective brother, with no guy ever good enough for my sister (knowing exactly what their ultimate intentions were). But that hair-trigger reflex I now had to cut: Nancy was, clearly, on her own and being a guest in her home—I had no right to say anything or protest in any way (at least not the first night and as it turned out—ever), for Little Sis was now very much her own adult person.

That first night, in her tiny one-bedroom apartment, I kept hands over ears, but eyes wide-open thinking it all through. At sunrise, I finally made the correct mind-shift and in appreciation, sister became best friend, confidant and volunteer cook. She included me in her burgeoning social circle around Aspen and introduced me to the other Valley Hi residents, as well.

None of us had any money, so we "pooled" the little we did have. Nancy's apartment was the communal gathering place, with a party almost every night. Lynyrd Skynyrd played nonstop on the stereo, with "Free Bird" the anthem of the day. One of our friends was Aspen's garbage collector, nicknamed, what else?: "Trash." The rich people living up in the million dollar mansions on Red Mountain, once they tired of something or if it broke, rather than bother having it repaired, simply tossed it away. Thanks to Trash's generosity and ability to fix anything, our poorly furnished apartments were soon filled with state-of-the-art stereos, chipped china, and Nancy and the other girls had designer jeans in their closets. Nancy got a job at Carl's Pharmacy behind the soda fountain; Sandy was a nurse at the clinic; Jodi, a bank teller. Weekends, we all banded together for outdoor concerts, mountain hikes, nude sun bathing along the Roaring Fork, sing-alongs around campfires—living on J.D.'s "Poems, Prayers and Promises."

To survive, I washed dishes, shoveled snow, made beds—those dead-end jobs only fueling my desperation to somehow get a job as a writer. I kept applying at the "Aspen Times" newspaper but so did about 500 other journalism graduates across the U.S. who wanted to live and write in Paradise.

Many of the local homeowners in Aspen left town for the winter, getting rich by renting out their houses for the ski season, while they traveled the world. Meeting a girl in the grocery store, she invited me out to one such house where her family was having a party. The house was a few miles west of town and unseen from the road, built into a hillside. I parked next to a "landmark" car and boot-skied down the slope.

I spent more time that evening getting to know the absentee owner than I did the girl. Once inside, you felt you were "outside," but with all the comforts of home: Large glass windows looked out across a sloping valley, down to the Roaring Fork River and across a wide expanse, studded with elk, to the Rocky Mountains; great books and music LPs filled shelves; the bathroom was wallpapered with maps of the solar system; a large studio in the rear of the house was crammed with film making equipment and finished nature films "in the can(s)."

"Oh, here you are!" Melissa said.

"Who owns this place?"

"Bob Lewis. He's a wonderful man! A friend of the family. He does so many interesting things. You know those nature film strips we saw in school? He made all those. He invented the 'Braille Trail'—where blind people can appreciate nature by following a rope through the woods with knots at signs in Braille that tell them to reach up and touch a pine cone or a bird's nest or smell a certain herb. And here—look at this . . . . "

We walked over to a studio wall covered in blueprints. At first glance you thought them to be designs for either a spaceship or something subterranean. They turned out to be both.

"Bob started The Wildwood School here in Aspen—it's incredible, revolutionary really. Made of ferro-cement, it's built totally into the hillside and the only way in is for the kids to slide down a rabbit hatch on the roof, here—like *Alice In Wonderland*! Once inside there are all these learning nooks and no formal teaching going on. Under the guidance of teachers, the kids learn as they play. Bob's really a genius. To teach them History, he has 'His-Story' and 'Her-Story': actors that dress up and suddenly visit one day, bringing the local history alive. A mountain man in full buckskins, traipsed through looking for beaver; and the most popular was a Ute Indian lady who lived in a teepee on the land. Here, the kids can see all the wildlife in the pond by simply walking up to this wall of glass. John Denver's son, Zack, goes to Wildwood . . . . I've been there at the end of the day and the kids all cry cause they don't want to get on the bus. They don't want to go home! How many schools can say *that*?"

I had to meet this man, and asked Melissa when he would return and could I please have his phone number?

I called about a month later and he invited me out for lunch: delicious, macrobiotic vegetables and miso soup and a jug of wine that we enjoyed while sitting cross-legged on the rug in the afternoon sunshine, looking out over the snow-covered valley. I left two hours later totally drunk and with a dream job: writing the scripts for Bob's nature films.

To keep in shape I decided to run to work: a 5 mile jaunt out along the main highway. The road followed the curves of the Roaring Fork River. One morning, on a rock poking above the rushing water, a chunky slate-gray bird with a brownish head started doing deep knee bends, abruptly lifting its body up and down, up and down over spindly legs—then plunging directly down into the stream. I stopped dead in my tracks, not quite believing my eyes.

About a half-minute later, the bird exploded up out of the water farther downstream, winged strongly back to the rock, and once it touched down on top, opened its beak and out poured a melodic, celebratory song: *bzeeet . . . zeeeeeet zeeeeeeeeeetttt!!!* It's vibrancy and mastery of two different elements was stunning!

I burst into the studio, babbling excitedly about the bird. Bob looked up from editing film; reached above him and handed me a finished film: "The Water Ouzel."

"Aren't they incredible! The Water Ouzel was John Muir's favorite bird and I think you saw why today. It's a land bird that spends a lot of time underwater, flying down through the current to walk on the bottom of rivers to feed on flatworms and snails and small fish. When we were researching the film, we came across stories of the Ouzel nesting on ledges behind waterfalls. They enter their homes by flying right through the falls—the water curtain protecting them and their young from predators!"

We worked side-by-side in the studio and the biologist brought all of nature to life with his films and stories. Like most creative people, he was a mass of contradictions; a harmony of opposites. He grew up in Los Angeles, went to Hollywood High, but felt most at home living where there were few people and not much tinsel or glamour. During World War II, he first came to Aspen with the Army's 10th Mountain Division, training/skiing on the slopes long before the commercial ski runs went in. So taken by the beauty of the place, he vowed to return after the war—and did, buying for cheap his spot in Paradise and other parcels of land—now worth megabucks. But money didn't matter to Bob Lewis: Animals, the Environment, Education and a choice part of Humanity did.

One day, I asked, "Bob, of all the animals that you've studied—what's your favorite?"

A wide smile split his face. "One would be the bull elk! When they rut in the fall, it is something to see—and hear! The real 'Call of The Wild' is the bugle of a bull elk. Once you hear it, you never forget it. For about a month up in the high country, the bulls are totally taken over by fighting and fucking—might say they are 'Male' in its most flagrant form. Filled with lust, their necks swell; the hair bristles up on their ruffs; they slobber and urinate and stomp the earth and all the woods reeks of their musk. They fight to gather their harems of cows and bugle to advertise their presence to other bulls." He cupped his hand around his mouth and tilted his head back: *"EEEEEEEeeeeee UUUUUPPPPPPP!!"*

After running out to the house for the first time, I asked Bob if I could take a quick shower before getting down to work?

He led me into the master bedroom where there was a waterbed on a raised platform and a large wooden tub recessed into a nook. The narrow wall fronting the tub was made up of rocks, with a series of split-bamboo pipes exposed among the stonework, an intricate indoor waterfall to fill the tub.

"Does it work?" I asked

"It never fails!" Bob said, his eyes gleaming.

I had never before met a middle-aged man with so many girlfriends. Every man I knew over 40 (and in nearly all cases, married) seemed sadly resigned to the fact that they would never again know the wide range of feminine joys they had once experienced in their youth. They reminded me of placid, plodding workhorses given over to the harness of monogamy. Reined-in; domesticated—something essential in them had gone slack. But even with silver hair, Bob still had a dashing air about him: a joyous spring in his step, salubrious timbre in his voice: the youngest and most energetic of 50-year olds, with the source of his energy, both personal and creative, very abundant.

There was nothing sad or deceitful about Bob's passion for women. He wasn't a smarmy player or sex-addicted "collector." He simply knew what he wanted and was honest with his paramours from the start, explaining: nothing personal, but he was not the marrying kind, valuing his independence and celebrating women in all their varied glory too much to ever settle down with one. Like the bull elk, he had a harem and because of being true to his nature, his up-front honesty and communication skills—none of the females protested. Quite the contrary, I was amazed at how all of his lovers, whether past or present, also remained his good friends. There was no double- standard: If a lover moved on . . . married or had a new boyfriend, both she and he were most welcome at the house. And there wasn't the slightest locking-of-horns with the new younger "bull"—rather a warm hug and hearty congratulations!

Bob Lewis was the first man I met that loved nature and women with an inseparable passion and was courageous enough to follow the laws of nature rather than the artificial, guilt-ridden constricts of man. One day he said to me: "Deep down, we're all animals—we just dress it up a little. And the biggest reason for so much unhappiness is the difference between the way nature works and the way man thinks." Even for his "nooners" there was nothing hushed or rushed. I'd be working in the back studio and the phone would ring: a female friend of Bob's calling from the Denver airport, there on business and a long delay between homebound planes; should she take the shuttle over to Aspen on the chance that she could come out?

While she was en route, Bob whipped-up a quick picnic and after falling into one another's arms at the door, in deep conversation they headed down to the meadow by the Roaring Fork. Awhile later, even though the river was living up to its loquacious name, the air was ruptured now and again by high-pitched, rapturous female cries. They returned an hour or so later wrapped-up together in a blanket, sunburned, the stressed city woman with a glorious grin and wildflowers crushed in her hair . . . and Bob prancing around up on his toes.

When Natalie, my "Mrs. Robinson" from college came out to Aspen for a visit, I took her out to Bob's for dinner. She was totally charmed by his stories, films, music, house, home cooked meal—his blend of the wild and urbane. The same age, they had a lot in common. That midsummer night, through the bacchanal filter of wine, I saw Bob as a human satyr, with his upturned eyebrows, pointed chin, broad shoulders and effortless powers of seduction. After the third bottle of wine, with Nat and Bob making oogle-eyes, I whispered in Nat's ear that I was going home. She didn't protest. After I cleaned-up the kitchen, while walking up the steps to the car, I heard the bamboo waterfall *splish-splashing* into the Japanese tub . . . .

The next morning, running out to Bob's to work, his car entered a curve just as I did. Natalie, in the passenger seat, smiled brightly as she waved; and Bob, dropped his left arm straight down out the open window; out of Natalie's sight-line. Just as they passed by, his wrist flicked upward; and he touched thumb and forefinger in a circle: saying it all.

Bob taught me to ski—in one day. "I'm not going to give you a lot of talk to tie-up your mind," the educator said. "You're a natural athlete. I'll give you pictures instead; and just follow my moves down the mountain." I did and he was right: Watching his "silent movies," undistracted, my body mimicked the actions and only at the bottom of the runs did we talk, fine-tuning, mainly, the stem christie turns.

Far more than downhill (lift tickets exorbitantly expensive), I enjoyed cross-country skiing, a continuous workout and free-of-charge. A favorite day was spent kick-and-gliding all the way out to Maroon Bells, the awesome mountain peaks looming high above an alpine lake. On a sunny day, with the sky that deep cobalt blue only seen in Colorado, I'd call George, a Bavarian and former Winter Olympian at Mountain Haus, a purist who sold me on wood skis (with bamboo poles). He said that plastic skis with the built-in cross-grips on the bottoms: too artificial. Skiing on wood, kept you closer to nature, for you had to wax them to match snow conditions; different color waxes to grip different types of snow.

"George!" I'd inquire, still learning: "What color wax today?"

"Green, Michael, *Green*!"

I'd wax up; singing as gleefully as the Water Ouzel; pack a lunch; fill a bota of wine and then work over the creamy snow through air like cut-glass—eighteen miles out to the Belles and back. I'd top off the day with a hot, juicy hamburger at Little Annie's; then under the cloak of darkness a front desk buddy would slip me in the back gate of a fancy hotel for a hot Jacuzzi soak. It was "Livin' Large" on little money!

One Saturday night, subzero, with the air scented with pinon pine smoke from condo fireplaces and serious skiers now turned fun-seekers, slip-sliding uncontrollably all over Aspen's icy streets, I went into a throbbing Disco—stumbling onto something that became my routine all winter. The place was packed, wall-to-wall with people from all over the world. Once inside the door, I then had to retreat . . . step back out onto the street, to allow the voluminous "cloud-people" to pass: a silver-haired, full-length-sheepskin-coated man with his padded arms around two stunning, fur-clad women, one black; one white (*their* skins). A bit wobbly even before they hit the ice, the man, probably/ normally the CEO of a Fortune 500 company, leaned back and matter-of-factly said to me, in a Texas drawl: "Son, if you can't find someone to lay in there, then Howdy Doodie ain't wood!"

While I was lifting my jaw off my chest, Cher and Greg Almon slithered by, holding hands; with Diana Ross gliding in, inches away, a few minutes later.

Instead of feeling encouraged, suddenly I was discouraged. What could I possibly offer—an impoverished scribe competing with deep-pocketed captains of industry and famous stars of the Hollywood screen? Finally, driven more by curiosity than confidence—I pushed my way into the packed Paragon (originally a bordello that serviced silver miners now updated to a strobe-lit Disco but with the original, restored ambiance of ruby-red velvet couches, frocked wallpaper, long mahogany bar), and eagerly ordered a Coors (at the time impossible to get east of the Continental Divide and even though hard to believe by today's far more sophisticated beer-tasting palates, *THE* reason many came to Colorado!) While standing near the packed dance floor, sipping the "Colorado Cool-Aid,"

I eventually made eye-contact with a pretty young miss also on the perimeter and because of the off-the-chart decibel throb of the music and a couple hundred exclamatory fun seekers—we drew closer to communicate: shouting intimately into one another's ears. Women came to Aspen in droves (the main hooks being J. D.'s musical P.R. again and whispered tales back home of lusty adventures from their girlfriends/predecessors of 'knocking boots' with a real cowboy or at least the ski instructor—proof again that no better advertising than word of mouth).

Their usual stay was a week, Saturday to Saturday. After dancing and conversing with four different ladies that first night, I found out that they all bought the same expensive "Learn-to-Ski" package. With their lips pressed against my ear and sweet perfume wafting up into my head (thank goodness for noise!), they shouted how nervous they were about their first lesson tomorrow morning and how much it cost to stay here and having to hire a ski instructor on top of it!

"WELL, THERE ARE ALTERNATIVES . . . . " I shouted to Sally, a knockout legal secretary from Chicago.

"WHAT DO YOU MEAN?"

"WELL, I'LL TEACH YOU TO SKI FOR FREE." *Hey! Yes, maybe I did have something to offer, after all!*

"WOW, REALLY? BUT I MUST GIVE YOU *SOME*-THING . . . . "

(After choking on my beer): "JUST COVER MY LIFT-TICKET? AND YOU KNOW—INSTEAD OF SPENDING ALL THAT MONEY FOR A HOTEL ROOM AT THE HEIGHT OF SEASON, WHY NOT STAY AT MY PLACE? WE CAN SKI RIGHT OUT THE DOOR TO THE CHAIR LIFT; BE THE FIRST ONES UP INTO THAT FRESH, VIRGIN POWDER!!"

Their eyes swelled . . . then their brows crossed.

"OF COURSE: YOU SLEEP IN MY BED; I'LL TAKE THE COUCH."

Oh, it was glorious: skiing all day, every day and with a different woman each week. (When I informed Bob Lewis of my miraculous social life, with his blessing he granted his employee "flextime"—but [with his satyr-like eyebrows arching with interest] only "If you ask if they have a girlfriend!") Many were from the Midwest, their first vacation away from home, fresh-faced and innocent (but with my sister Nancy's same pent-up-Catholic-nun-induced-repression simmering just beneath the surface; and ever-so-ready to erupt with wild abandon). A few were older and married but temporarily sans husband; and therefore, wide-eyed over the change of scenery. Although attired in designer outfits, and top of the line Head skis, rather than ski, many were there solely for the '*apri*.' (The telltale sign of the poseurs was their fresh-tread: bottom ridges of ski boots not worn-down in the slightest way.) One 'widow' was a bona fide countess from an Eastern Bloc country who did ski—like an absolute angel. It was heaven just *schussing* in long, crossing parabolas together over the silken snow, starting the process of seduction with widening smiles on our way down.

It was the tail-end of the era of Free Love and the counterculture revolution was running on a second-wind. As remote as Aspen was, it was "in the loop"; on the direct consciousness-raising pipeline to cutting-edge California. Timothy Leary and the-less-drug-more-eastern-religion Ram Dass were the popular gurus. Werner Earhard's "EST" seminars had huge attendances in Aspen. Transcendental meditators were filling entire mountain meadows. *Jonathan Livingston Seagull* was flying high . . . . Whether it was the ubiquitous 'poem' "Deserata": about you do your thing, I'll do mine and if we meet in the middle—fine! or Crosby, Stills, Nash, and Young declaring that "If You Can't Be With The One You Love, Then Love The One You're With!"—the message from all the varied 'Far Out' messengers was simply the same: "Follow Your Bliss!" I was—getting paid to write and skiing for free with females eagerly seeking adventure!!

Saturday morning, after cooking my breakfast specialty of Eggs Benedict always served to Mademoiselle, gratefully in bed, I took Karen, Stacey, Judy or Countess Irina to the airport. A final kiss; then at home: a nap, shower and the Alpine Gigolo was shamelessly on his way back to the Paragon to offer his services all over again. (I can hear the hissing from feminists—but it went much deeper than mere sexual gratification. It was a glorious time for a young man to learn a few things about women, inner intricacies that men rarely have the time or opportunity to experience. I was blessed. As one incredible, forty-something lady said, with four days/nights left: "Most men know how to tune-up a car, but don't know the first thing about turning-on a woman. Wanna learn?" The lessons didn't end in bed. I learned, again, that "Foreplay is what you do all day.")

When spring arrived, with the slopes and my sheets mostly barren, I returned to running. I didn't miss a beat, for the skiing, especially cross-country used many of the same muscles and certainly kept you aerobically fit. During the summer, with Ajax Mountain looming over the town like an emerald green giant, every Saturday morning I attempted to run up the fire trail that ascended the peak in steep switch backs. Struggling, each week I tried to tangibly gauge my fitness level by pushing higher, farther up the mountain. Usually alone on the upper reaches, one morning a young man came charging by like a locomotive—whooshing air in vast measures. He passed me as if I was standing still. I saw legs like I had never seen before on a human being: horses, yes—humans no. His thighs and calves were all separate, striated muscle flexing and counter-flexing without the slightest covering of fat, fed by thick veins—open pipes delivering immense amounts of oxygen, and between the large feeder veins were hundreds of smaller capillaries spread like filigrees of lace across the smooth surface muscles. Then I saw the pack—pulling on his shoulders, bowing his back severely on the steep slope. No small day pack, this was a serious alpinist's deep rucksack, filled with a lot of equipment. Just then a cloud slammed into the mountain, erasing the ascending colossus.

He reappeared on the way down. Even though I had turned around, demoralized, near the spot where he blew by me, on the descent he quickly caught me again, even though he had gone all the way up to the summit. This time, I was determined to stay with him on the descent. As I moved up on his shoulder, I expected him to surge, compete *mano y mano*—but instead, he slowed a bit and grinned: "It's a great day to die!" He exhaled forcefully, then laughed. As we swooped down the switch backs, Aspen opened-up before us and we enjoyed the eagle-eye view across the Shangri-La valley, familiar landmarks: nightclubs, ski shops, hotels flaring through the crystal air and enlarging with each stride down. We stopped when the ground was finally level. "Fritz," he said, extending his hand. I introduced myself and he invited me to breakfast.

We sat at an outdoor cafe near the base of the mountain. After we ordered half the menu, Fritz went to the men's room. I couldn't resist. I grabbed the top of his parked backpack and lifted. It didn't budge. I slid my chair closer and heaved upward with both arms. It had to weigh fifty, sixty pounds. I peeked inside—the pack was chock-full of rocks! Fritz reappeared, smiling.

He was a world-class mountain climber. A German native, by the age of seventeen, Fritz Stammberger had climbed every major mountain in Europe. A few years later, he had bagged nine peaks in North Africa, the Middle East, Tibet. He climbed alone. And unlike the majority of mountaineers, he climbed without supplementary oxygen above 20,000 feet, the death zone.

"Why alone?" I asked. "Isn't that a death-wish, not having a partner to bail you out when in trouble?"

"Other climbers just hold me back," he said, matter-of-factly. "Being alone in the mountains, for me, is like going to church for others—it cleanses my soul."

As we ate and talked we were constantly interrupted by a procession of beautiful women: "Hiiiiii Faa-ri-iiiiiiiiiiiitz!" they said, their bodacious curves extending into their words; and hale-and-hearty young men patted him respectfully on the back as they walked by. He was one of the 'gods' of Aspen. The gonzo-journalist Hunter Thompson ruled the night, holding court in the bar at The Hotel Jerome; Spider Sabbitch, the Olympic skier (and soon to be victim of Claudia Longet's gun and tabloid trial) owned the ski slopes; and Fritz Stammberger, famous for his bold solo ascents was the mountain climber supreme. The town was full of outdoor wannabees: many Hollywood actors and moguls who played in Aspen on long weekends and holidays, and *nuevo-riche* Texans who parked the biggest Learjets at the airport (size always mattering to Texans) to throw their cowboy hats and buckles around town. (Inside a western-wear boutique, owing its sudden success to role-model John Denver's 'uniform' of yoked and pearl button western shirts, and insulated vests, a Dallas man walked in wearing a weathered white Stetson, perfect sweat-stain on the outer hat band. When the store owner asked if he was a working rancher—pointing to his hat, the honest Texan took it off and chuckled at the stain: "Oh *that* . . . That's Bernaise sauce!")

Fritz was for real. He lived in Aspen year-round. He owned a printing business and was active in many community affairs and benefits. However, he wasn't totally immune to glamour, recently marrying Janice Pennington, hostess of "The Price Is Right" TV show.

As we finished breakfast, I asked about his closest call in the mountains? He described a hair-raising tale about surviving an avalanche in the Himalayas when he and two other climbers, in their sleeping bags, were suddenly buried under chunks of ice, rocks and suffocating powder. He clawed his way out and then saved the others. "You have to be careful you're not digging your own grave, digging down. The only way to tell which way is 'Up' under all that fallen mountain is to spit and watch which way it falls . . . . "

"See you on Ajax some Saturday!" he said, abruptly jumping up and nearly crushing my hand in a farewell shake. He was busy preparing for his next expedition, a big peak in Pakistan.

I walked away with a hop in my step—totally energized and inspired. I wanted to be as fit as Fritz, in peak condition, and shine with *élan vital*. I wanted to climb high mountains in foreign countries and then be able to tell stories of real adventure and risk while sitting totally relaxed over breakfast in the sunshine. And maybe, like Fritz—someday earn the respect and admiration from both women and men.

Back at my apartment, along the Roaring Fork River on the back deck I laid-in a cache of round river rocks; and each Saturday ran with an increasing stack in my pack. Up in the thin air of Ajax, carrying the heavy ballast, I felt my lungs expand; legs harden.

I looked for Fritz on the mountain trails but never saw him again. Neither did his friends or wife. He disappeared. Other climbers from Aspen, including my landlord from the Valley Hi apartments, searched for him, scouring the mountain in Pakistan, but to no avail. Janice Pennington didn't give up; she just knew he was alive. Her search lasted nearly twenty years, including frustrating, labrynthic dealings with high-level government officials from the U.S., Pakistan, Soviet Union. Even "The King," her friend, Elvis Presley tried to get information from his sources in Washington. This was during the era when CIA agents had doubled as mountain climbers (one expedition of CIA alpinists were caught installing nuclear blast monitoring devices directed at China). Finally, Janice discovered for a fact that, totally unbeknownst to her, Fritz was recruited by the CIA in 1974. He collected information in Afghanistan and Pakistan; he was involved with the U.S.-funded Afghanistan rebels in the war against the Soviet Union. And he *was* alive, dying in the early 80's inside Afghanistan. (Their love story and the essence of a complex man is recounted in Janice Pennington's courageous, best-selling book, *Husband, Lover, Spy*.)

As much as I loved the mountains, after a year in Aspen I began feeling landlocked and restless. Out on the western horizon, the Pacific Ocean was calling. I felt this Shangri-La to be a false one: many residents by living the 'Strenuous Life' in all that snow and sunshine had the bodies of teenagers, but many succumbed to acting just as immature in the eternal Aspen playground. I needed seasoning. I needed to grow-up, especially if I wanted to mature as a writer.

For three months, I lived on peanut butter and top raimen, so as to save enough 'bread' to make my move. Then to stretch my cache of cash even farther, I planned on hitchhiking west and camping out along the way.

How great it felt to walk into one of the mountaineering shops on a Saturday morning and, for the first time, finally have enough money to outfit my dreams—purchase a top-of-the-line, internal frame pack; a warm yet lightweight sleeping bag; Redwing hiking boots (the color of an Irish Setter); six oleaginous pairs of rag wool socks; tiny camping stove (that roared like a fighter jet); lightweight aluminum cooking pots, fitted one into the other as shrinking concentric circles; a soft-sided canteen that kept cool your water; shiny pouches of freeze-dried astronaut food; a Swiss Army knife with twenty folded-in implements enabling you to both butcher a side of beef and sew on a button. "Do you want it all in a large bag?" the clerk asked.

"No, all inside the pack, please—except for the boots."

I gleefully threw-off my old, heavy four-pound clunkers and slipped into the light, butter soft Redwings that smelled as good as they looked. I stepped into the harness of the new pack with the clerk showing me how to customize the crosshatch of padded straps and pressure tabs to evenly balance and tote your entire world. Walking out of Mountain Haus, as the door shut behind me—Aspen no longer had a hold.

It was time to move on, for the open road was calling and everywhere ahead was unknown country.

Since so much of life is "mirroring": we attract what we first project, I decided to put my best self forward while standing thumb-out on the side of the road. So many hitchhikers I had seen looked like greasy 'road-kill': laying back against their pack, digit up defiantly. A high-speed driver only has a split-second to decide if they're going to feel safe with you in their car, so I always tried to be freshly shaven; wear clean jeans, a textured sweater, topped off with a black mountain man hat (flat-brim rather than the pretentious curved wings of a cowboy hat). I kept a fresh found feather (red-tailed hawk at first; white seagull plume later) perched up in the brim band. And like the English landscape painter John Constable, who always worked a daub of red into all his canvases, I tied a short crimson scarf around my neck, knotted to the side.

The first ride out was a good one, a long-hauler all the way to the Utah border with a man, half white and half Sioux Indian. It was clear from Mile One which side of Jesse dominated. We talked for hours about the struggles of the First Nation. He told me a parable that has stayed with me ever since. "There was a Chief sitting on the porch of a western B.I.A. (Bureau of Indian Affairs) outpost, staring off at the horizon. The Agent came out and sat behind the Indian in a rocking chair, eating his lunch. The Chief's nose began to twitch; he reached-up, pinched closed one nostril and blew a stream of snot out of the other . . . that hit the dusty ground and rolled up, covering itself. The B.I.A Agent made a big deal of it: 'GAWD! HOW'S A MAN SUPPOSED TO EAT HIS LUNCH!! THAT'S THE REASON RIGHT THERE WHY YOU SAVAGES WILL NEVER EVER BETTER YOURSELVES!!!' The Agent then leaned over and made a big show of fluffing out a white cloth handkerchief and honking long and hard into it. After the Agent then carefully folded up the lace-trimmed hanky and slid it back into his pocket, for the first time, never taking his eyes from the horizon, the Indian spoke: 'You white people save everything, don't you?'"

Out past Grand Junction, Jesse apologized for leaving me in the middle of nowhere, but after talking with him I was actually looking forward to slowing down and meeting the land.

There was no better feeling than standing there all alone in that high desert in the late afternoon. After Jesse's car disappeared down a dirt road, silence reestablished itself—unbroken across the vast void. I had read somewhere that when you hold a seashell to your ear, you're not hearing the roar of the sea, but your own bloodstream echoing back to you from the tiny enclosure. Well, this "enclosure" was colossal, the sky arcing above like an endless blue bowl and the scrub land running flat to far horizons, but I could hear a roaring in my ears and it was so still that I heard my muscles slide one over the other, when I moved.

The slanting sun cast long shadows. I was thrilled: Everything was ahead of me and I knew I could do this! Reality was pared down to basics. I had everything I needed on my back and I felt as free as the hawk that floated overhead. Walking, I spouted Walt Whitman: "Afoot and light hearted/I take to the open road!"

A few cars passed, leaving contrails of rushing speed in that slowed-down, solid silence; none stopped, but it didn't matter. The world was now my home. *Be nice to keep moving on, but hey—I just might pitch my sleeping bag behind that bush right over there . . . .* A big semi-truck, an eighteen wheeler blew by—then stopped with a series of downshifting, rattling groans and an air-brake hissy fit a quarter mile down the road. I sprinted in the new Redwing boots; the internal frame pack flexing perfectly with each twist of my back and ground-eating stride. The passenger door popped open. Never having been in a long haul truck before, I did a slow, clumsy climb up toward the high cab.

"HURRYUP! FORE I CHANGE MY MIND!!"

I finally wormed in across the seat.

"Where ya headin' kid?"

"West."

"Totally aginst insurance rules, pickin' up hitchers, but hey—what are rules for, 'cept to be broken! Fuck 'em all but six; and save those for pallbearers!!"

The trucker then double-pumped a massive clutch and muscled a gear shift like a bent barbell through a dozen changes. With the truck back up to speed, the roar from the engine was tremendous and so were the vibrations.

Occasionally, conversation erupted in brief bursts. Seeing pictures of kids and a smiling woman taped directly onto an open spot of the dashboard, I shouted: "YOUR FAMILY?"

"YEP. MY 'REASONS FOR LIVIN'!"

"THAT'S GREAT."

Then further down the road, a half hour later: "YOU HITCHED?"

"NO, NOT YET."

"'LIVE FREE OR DIE!'" punctuated by *"AAAAARRRR-UUUUUUU"*—a lone wolf howl.

I settled back in the spacious, bucking seat and enjoyed the view—incredibly high above the road. A few miles later, roaring over a hill, there was a metallic flash in the distance, the sun glancing off a car half-hidden in the brush.

"DUCK DOWN!"

I laid out across the seat, as we rolled past a Highway Patrol car.

The trucker grabbed up a CB mike, clicked a few knobs on the dash unit, then proceeded to chatter away to his unseen brethren in a rapid-fire warning code. The only word I made out was the driver's identifying handle: "Preparation H."

At sunset, the trucker pushed in a cassette tape and Waylon Jennings sang of a good hearted woman in love with a good timin' man . . . .

Across the desert of southern Utah, we rolled the windows down and cool air carried the sharp, pungent scent of sage throughout the cab. Owls fluttered like giant moths across the windshield.

Then off in the distance there was a strange luminous glow, that looked out of place in all the empty darkness. As we moved closer, the brightness intensified.

"WHAT'S THAT?" I inquired.

"LAS VEGAS. BETTER KNOWN AS 'LOST WAGES'!"

A few hours later, the light bent, then wrapped around us as we pulled into a Truck Stop, crawling into a corral of giant rigs, most unoccupied but with their engines still running.

We climbed down and walked stiffly toward a big building. The trucker stuck out a massive hand: "Clarence." I gave him my moniker—smiling at how there was no need for proper introductions until the end of the journey.

Inside a restaurant, a line of truckers were waiting impatiently to be seated. A waitress with a boxy figure and a 'take no guff' attitude approached. "AHH, HOLD YORE HORSES!" she said in a gravely voice. "YOU TRUCKERS ARE ALL ALIKE—NUTHIN' BUT A BELLYFULL OF COFFEE AND A HARD ON!!"

"HEY, FLO! POUR ME SOME AND I'LL POUR IT TO *YOU*!!" Clarence called, hitching up his low-slung drawers. (Like most truckers, he was no-butt and all-belly.)

She guffawed and seated us. "Dinner time," Clarence said, sliding into the booth with a painful wince. I looked up at a clock on the wall: 2:10 a.m. I looked around the mess hall filled with mostly silent loners tucking into huge platters of food. With many of the men in leather vests, Tony Lama boots and weathered faces they looked like the last of the cowboys riding through the West at all hours, herding the goods into Dodge.

After dinner, Clarence snatched the bill in a meaty fist; and handed me a peppermint toothpick at the counter. Working the slaw out of our teeth, we went into a general store attached to the restaurant. He bought a big bottle of No Doze and a Hustler magazine. We went out to the truck and I pulled my pack down from the cab. "Good luck, kid. As my pappy used to say: 'Keep your horse in the barn—but if it breaks down the door: keep it in a tight saddle!'" At that, he mounted his steed; roared off the wide tarmac, 'ballin the jack'—away into the night.

I shouldered my pack with that excited tingle of anticipation and strolled into Las Vegas.

At that time, Vegas had yet to even think about converting to its present-day reconfiguration of "Disneyland," and men with no necks, hoarse voices and out-of-place bulges under slick coats ruled the roost. You didn't take the kids, for the main attraction was its dangerous edge and total anonymity. You came to Vegas to take a break from your normal, responsible self; do things that were totally out of character and illegal back home. It was Sin City and Sinatra still packed 'em in at The Sands.

I walked the neon Strip in hiking boots and backpack in the middle of the night, shaking my head in disbelief. Having come in on a slow approach across the desert instead of dropping out of the sky, I just couldn't believe that all these colossal buildings, garish signs, masses of night crawling humanity were actually *here*. 'Circus Maximus,' indeed!

Displaying enough firepower to turn night into day, I felt totally disoriented as I ducked in and out of the big casinos, the 'muscle' at the doors telling me to "lose da pack." With my body-clock crapping out, I didn't bother arguing or stepping all the way in. (Although I did hear a lounge singer do an utterly lifeless rendition of "Send In The Clowns." Sinatra should have had him retired on the spot for brutalizing that poetic song.) It was August and infernally hot. I checked into a cheap motel out on the edge of the desert (just behind the Strip) and then bolted out of the room: a hot-box smelling of stale beer and vomit. I spent what was left of the night reclining on a swimming pool air mattress. I dozed on and off: Every time I rolled over, I took a plunge into the cool pool, which felt great.

A couple hours after sunrise, I checked out, and took up one of the incessant billboard offers of a 99 cent casino breakfast. After downing a couple rubbery eggs and battery acid coffee, I decided I had enough of Las Vegas and would move on. Out on the strip, in the roaring heat, I came up on a woman in a full length sheepskin coat walking a thick-coated Siberian Husky dog. "Hello," I said, tipping my black mountain man hat and petting the panting dog, who looked up alertly: one eye sky blue; the other hazel brown.

"Oh, hi there!" the woman said, looking relieved seeing one of her ilk amidst the sea of stretch pants and polyester leisure suits.

"Where ya headin'?" I inquired.

"Out of town!"

"Me too."

"Oh yeah? Where?"

"West—California. Hitch hiking . . . . "

"That's where I'm going—to Barstow, but by train."

"Oh, didn't know there was rail service."

She guffawed. "There isn't! Hopping the next freight train out of here."

"Hey, want a cup of coffee? Let's talk about it."

She tied up "Taku" in the shade in front of a small diner and we went in. 'There's a million stories in the Naked City', and Mary's was a doozy. She was from Alaska, married a pipeline worker; lived the high life on the good money: big, handmade cabin off in the bush, winter vacations in Hawaii, Thailand, the Mexican Rivieria. Life in both the slow and fast lanes and a vague description of a contraband "Import/Export" business that suddenly went bust with her husband's arrest and seizure of all their property. She escaped in the nick of time, but with no money and a couple addictions to shake, cold-turkey, in the process. In Canada she took up with another man who soon began beating her, so on the run again.

"What's in Barstow?" I asked.

"Nuthin' much. Maybe someone who owes me money."

One part of me wanted no part of Mary's business, but I had always been fascinated by Alaska and thought of maybe hitchhiking all the way up there. My curiosity about The Great Land and a protective, chivalrous side toward the misplaced woman won out. I threw-in with her travel plans.

We bought some sandwiches and filled our water jugs in the rest rooms on the way out. We then left the strip, walking out to the rail yard. I followed Mary and Taku into a patch of tall weeds, where we crouched down. "Yes, this is the one we want," she said looking at the long line of train cars. "Union Pacific will take us to California—leaves in an hour or so."

"Are you sure?"

"Yep, rode it out of here this spring. Now let's pick out the one we want. Need a boxcar with an open door . . . . "

We crept through the weeds for about 100 yards, then Mary pointed and stopped. "There, that one! Now we watch for 'bulls'—railroad dudes on the lookout for 'bos.' You don't wanna be in their clutches!"

"You mean this is illegal?"

"They say so. I guess their insurance for freight trains don't cover no riders."

"Why don't we wait until dark when they won't see us as well?"

"Because the train leaves *now*." She looked at me as if I was a moron.

We waited five minutes, looking and listening—then made a quick beeline to the car. Mary lifted Taku up in a practiced move; then we hoisted ourselves in. We placed our things in a dark corner of the empty boxcar. "*Shhh*, no talking," Mary said. "Now we have to watch that they don't close that door on us. If they do, we die in here."

The tall metal door was half-open. I never once took unblinking eyes from that opening and keened my ears for the first crunch of footsteps. Mary was more relaxed, fiddling with her small pack and glancing over at Taku, an infallible "early warning system."

Time was suspended as we held our breath . . . . Then the train suddenly lurched forward; and we rolled out of Vegas on steel wheels and a rush of adrenaline.

We sat down cross-legged on the grubby floor, shared an apple and settled in for a long haul. The repetitious *clickety-clack*, *clickety-clack* rhythm and sideways sway felt as comforting as a cradle as we moved west out into the Mojave desert.

I asked Mary how many trains she had ridden? "Too many to count," she said. "And yes, I did get nabbed by a bull once. Gave him a blow job on the spot and he let me go. In fact," she grinned, "after that he helped me find the best car! . . . Now doncha be gettin' any ideas," she said as a stern afterthought.

I had never before met a woman like this. She had lived in so many worlds and social stratas, high and low, and each of the eras of her life took turns revealing themselves in a facial expression or her different manners of speaking. Occasionally and clearly you could see underneath the road dust, heartbreaking defeats, chemical addictions to a woman who once had total happiness.

For the first time, Mary removed her sheepskin coat. I was shocked. Even though I knew the coat was thick, she seemed to fill it out solidly as well—but now she was bone-thin underneath. She looked like a "Troll" doll and I saw that hair was an overall 'buffer,' her padding against the cold-cruel world, along with the sheepskin and Taku's shaggy pelt. On the interior walls of the long coat were sewn-in pockets and thick elastic bands holding a bowie knife, a can of mace, a pistol, a box of bullets, pill vials, a sac of trail mix, a can of dog food, a copy of "Glamour" magazine . . . . A little bit of everywhere she'd been: disparate elements that coalesced into all she needed to exist.

As the day wore on, I thought we were going to die in that boxcar. The sun was directly overhead and through a cloudless sky it beat down unmercifully on the hardpan Mojave. Intense heat radiated from the metal walls around us, and out the open door the far horizon swam in torrid waves. The desert floor was cracked and peeling in irregular, upturned scabs and as we went further in, there was mile after mile of blanched, sodium-crusted beds. I removed my T-shirt, sprinkled it with water and wrapped it around my head, Beduoin-style; Mary stripped down to just her panties. The dog was panting a mile-a-minute.

Taku was named after an Alaskan glacier and I was afraid he would melt just as fast. Mary sliced off the top of the plastic jug and placed the gallon of water in front of him. We shared my canteen. I had a small thermometer: a zipper-pull attached to my jacket. I pulled it up from the bottom of my pack: it had topped-out at 110 degrees.

We stood in puddles of our own sweat. Looking out the open doorway pained the eyes, a white heat searing everything. As thirsty as I was, I then lost the impulse to drink, slumping over in a corner, burning my back on the hot metal wall but not even caring. With Mary and me down—Taku took over, padding back and forth between both of us, licking our faces or shoving his dry, cracked nose under our trembling hands.

When I awoke from a sleep I didn't remember falling into, I was actually surprised to still be in the boxcar, still alive. Taku was lapping more water. I watched Mary's bare chest—yes, still rising and falling. I half-grinned now sure I was alive, having taken a second to admire the beauty of her breasts. I walked over to her, lifted her head and she hungrily chugged the last of the water from the canteen. The tide was turning—the light out in the desert had softened; and inside the boxcar the air was nearly breathable again.

A few hours later, as the air cooled dramatically toward evening; and with Mary still asleep behind me, I sat on the open edge of the rail car, pulled out a White Owl cigar from a tube that I'd been saving for a special occasion. Taku came over and laid down, releasing a deep-seated sigh as he rested his head on my thigh. I thought how I could love Mary and Taku with ease. *That's all they need—constant love and all the crustiness and road scabs and fear will fall away and they'll smile and their dry hearts would fill again* . . . . I started crying over all the pain from the lack of love in this world.

When I looked up, outward again at the heat-seared hills on the horizon— they had been transformed. The setting sun was turning them deep purple, magenta, bright ochre. They glowed with divine fire. I woke Mary up to come see! The air so cool that we put our coats on. Sitting there, watching the colors, swinging our legs in the open air and passing the cigar back-and-forth, I knew Mary and Taku would be all right and that those gleaming hills, *Nature* was the lover that called the most and I ached to embrace and learn all I could about her mysterious ways.

As I puffed the last of the cigar and watched the shifting hues, I thought of how this ride through the Mojave totally changed my mind about the desert: Before I thought it was an empty void, but now I knew it to be a place full of answers.

Reaching Barstow, California I wished Mary and Taku well, bolted the rail yard and stuck out my thumb alongside I-15. A couple short hops west, and then off in the distance—a tangled freeway cloverleaf, a concrete knot meaning a big city—L.A.! was near. As I daydreamed off in the distance, a Lincoln Continental crunched to a stop in front of me—the passenger window powering down. *Wow—that was easy! Didn't even lift a thumb!!* I leaned-in to check out the driver, then did a double-take. Behind the wheel was Jesus Christ: the identical long hair, angelic face, wispy beard, white toga and sandals. In a relaxed baritone he asked where I was going?

"L.A.," I said, wondering if I should genuflect.

He flashed an ultra-brite smile.

In shock, I tossed my pack in the back, and then just as my butt hit the black leather seat, the George Harrison song "My Sweet Lord" (no kidding!) started up on the radio. *My God—what is happening here?!* With a sandaled foot, Jesus pressed the accelerator and the big Lincoln floated out into the traffic flow. Then a few miles down the highway, 'God' blew his cover, flipping open an ashtray on the center console; pulling out a joint and firing it up. After a deep toke—he held it out. I passed. Clearly, I needed all my wits about me.

Now emboldened, I asked: "What gives? You're a dead-ringer for Jesus Christ, but driving a Lincoln Continental and smoking a dube?"

He put his head back and gave a hearty laugh, now looking exactly like the 'E-Z Man' on the front of the rolling papers. "I'm heading to Laguna Beach for the annual Sawdust Festival. Every year they re-create a painting with actors— 'Living Art.' This year it's 'The Last Supper.' Hey man, afterwards me and the Apostles are going out—to hunt down some pussy, wanna come?"

I declined, but what a way to enter L.A., ("The City of Angels") for the very first time—with none other than 'J. C.' in the driver's seat!

For my next ride, having finally run out of west, my thumb now swiveled north. I couldn't wait to see the ocean, but held back—wanting it to be away from any "divine disillusions" or the eye-watering smog of the L.A. Basin. My hitchhiking karma must have really been working that day but with a twist, for the next ride was, again, totally surreal. Gazing across the eight lanes of freeway I watched a Porsche Carrera swerve from the fast lane to my feet in about four seconds. A black tinted window slid down, revealing a female fantasy in a short dress! I got in, clutching my bulky pack in my lap, totally blocking my view out the window and pressing my head left, but who cared with such feminine pulchritude pulsating inches away. We roared up into a canyon and entered a hacienda-style house.

"Make yourself at home; got to make a few phone calls. There's beer and food in the fridge," Toni said, flinging down her sunglasses.

"Thanks for being so nice! Is everyone in California this way?"

"Well, we do have our motives . . . . Why don't you whip us up some lunch from whatever's in the fridge?"

At first, I grabbed a beer and wandered around. On all the walls were photos of absolutely gorgeous women and a repetitious, black-haired swarthy man who looked vaguely familiar. Then it hit me: *That's Bob Guccione and those—those*, I gulped, *are Penthouse "Pets!" Oh my God, Toni is . . . .*

I then busied myself constructing sandwiches and a salad; then walked over to stare closer at the women in the pictures: At least six feet tall, with overt, flawless curves; clad in leather miniskirts and see-through halter tops—they carved and quivered the air, even from a flat wall.

Looking at the "Pets" up close, every muscle in my body went hard except one: my heart . . . drooping down like a gob of honey onto my shoes.

Playboy advertises their models as "the girls next door." No matter what street you live on, you will never see a Penthouse "Pet" washing her car or ringing your doorbell. They take 'Fantasy' to new heights. With bodies right out of Boris Vallejo, they are castle-in- the-clouds sorceresses whose purpose is to harden earthly swords. And no future soccer moms these: With the wardrobes and whiplash grins of a dominatrix, the only balls they'll be kicking are your's.

When Toni returned from her calls, we sat down to lunch. My hands were trembling so much that the plates shook when I placed them on the table. Toni asked if I was O.K.? I asked if she was a Penthouse Pet? She laughed and laughed. "Michael, I'm totally flattered, but I work in another department: I'm the west coast editor."

We then talked about books and writing. "Michael, if you want to be a writer, I'll give you some advice: Live a life without limits and read your ass off. Young people don't read anymore. 'In the beginning was the Word.' Words are sacred. It all starts there: 'If it ain't on the page, it ain't on the stage!'"

Toni asked what it was like to hitchhike? I told her about my ride with "Jesus." She laughed. "That is *so* L.A.! 'The Land of Illusion.'"

I asked what it was like to work for Penthouse? She said that in many ways it was like any other job. "Don't get me wrong. The pay is great and there are a lot of perks, but in a lot of ways it's not real."

"What do you mean?"

She looked over at the pictures on the wall. "Well, 'Tamara Irons' is often 'Karen Kowalski' from Normal, Illinois . . . . People re-invent themselves out here. And if you live the illusion long enough you wake up one day and it's become real. The challenge is not to lose touch with who you really are, deep down, in the process, for that's all we ever really have."

"You mean like Jay Gatsby?"

"Very good! Let's go . . . . I have to run some errands."

As we swerved down the hill, I shook my head. *Only in L.A. can your fortunes turn this fast!* After making a few stops, the wind carried a salty tang and we followed it a few blocks to the Pacific Ocean: The first time I saw the ocean as an adult; and from the trim seat of the Porsche, alongside a beautiful woman—the heaving aquamarine expanse looked as fresh and unlimited as my dreams. A rage to live crested up inside of me in rhythm with those wild waves and I knew I wanted to be a writer, even if I didn't yet have the slightest idea what to write about.

Then Toni dropped me alongside I-5. A nice kiss and "Michael, you will be a writer someday—I can just tell. But don't let the world knock away your sweetness and fresh vision . . . . "

The Porsche sped off. I stood there, reshouldering my backpack. Nearly dark, it all seemed a dream, a movie—which quickly came to an end. A cop scolded me for hitching on the freeway and drove me off the highway. "Catch you out there again, pal, and you're in the 'steel motel!'" I then thumbed for three hours, yards away from an on-ramp, with no luck. Finally, near midnight, a car pulled over.

Just like you should never go grocery shopping when you're hungry, when hitchhiking you should never immediately jump into a car no matter how long it's been between rides. So far, I avoided trouble because I always trusted my gut—previously turning down two drivers because something about them just didn't seem "right". . . . Peering into this car, I started to back away, but glancing around at nowhere to sleep but under a ratty freeway trestle—that sight overrode my caution and I hopped in.

An hour later, speeding up I-5, I had a hidden hand on the door handle, pondering how many bones I'd break hitting the concrete at 80 m.p.h.? Two men and a girl—one guy driving, the girl up front; the other guy next to me. They looked like 'Bonnie & Clyde' and 'Sonny Corleone.' 'Clyde' cracked open a bottle of Jack Daniels; 'Bonnie' fired-up a spliff that would have choked a Rastafarian; and 'Sonny' whipped out a loaded gun and waved it in front of my nose. *This is it. I'm done! They'll take my money and that's all she wrote* . . . . I pretended to take sips of the Jack and tokes of dope when it was passed around; and that seemed to ease the hopped-up storm a bit. Then unaccustomed to a slack of tension in their lives they began confessing some of their past transgressions, trying to elicit a harsh, judgemental opinion; give them a reason to do me in—but my response was always the same: a supportive, yet unexcited: "Cool."

Then, suddenly, out of nowhere: sirens and flashing lights directly behind us—triggering ear-piercing shrieks and a burst of babbling inside the car. Windows went down; the open booze and packets of grass and white powder went out. 'Sonny Corleon' whipped the gun behind his back and forehead veins snaked as he frantically tried to stuff the gun down the seat crack.

Once we came to a stop, four cops—guns drawn, lights in our faces ordered us out and muscled us up against the car for spread-eagled searches. "Sir, what is this about?" I said, shaking in my boots. Just then, 'Clyde' spoke-up: "That guy had nuthin' to do with it. He's just some hitchhiker we picked-up." One of the cops asked for my wallet and went over to his car radio.

I was astounded that 'Clyde' did that, when he could have done just the opposite: pinned whatever the entire rap was all on me. When the cop returned he said, "You're free to go; cuff the other three and let's take 'em in."

While standing there, trembling and totally incredulous, a female officer came over and said: "You're very lucky. That's a stolen car you were riding in. And all three are ex-cons. Hitchhiking is extremely dangerous, especially along this stretch. Come on, I'll give you a ride into the nearest town . . . . "

I holed-up in a motel near Lost Hills, California rethinking my travel plans.

Winston Churchill once stated that "Nothing in life is so exhilarating as to be shot at without result." I hadn't been shot at, but just being a squeeze away— now, instead of triggering fear and depression, filled me with happiness, brio, a boundless *joie de vivre!*

As I awoke to a new morning, everything looked fresh and newly minted— even the stained carpet in my room and the dead flies on a sticky strip hanging in the corner. I lay there in a lumpy bed, belly laughing: Didn't know where I was or where I was going—hell, couldn't even remember my name; and that total disconnect felt absolutely marvelous!!

In the dead silence of the room, I heard my breathing . . . and started from there. I moved slow and deliberate . . . out the room, onto the highway—savoring each step, each breath, the pure gift of simply being alive.

After the 3-cons and stolen car incident, I decided to change my M.O.: Get off this long-haul, desperado I-5 by cutting over to the coast and once there, near the comforting ocean I'd hitch not alongside the road but from the parking lots of rest stops and restaurants—chat a bit with people out of their cars before jumping in.

I crossed the deserted road, stood under the Route 46 West sign and prepared for a long day. *Not a lot of traffic passing through Lost Hills . . . .* Just then, a battered pickup swung around the corner and stopped. The front seat was filled with three smiling adult Mexicans.

I dipped into my high school Spanish. *"Hola, amigos!"*

"Hola!

"La Mar? (The Sea?) I said, making a rolling motion with my hand.

They chattered rapid-fire among themselves. *"El Paso del Robles?"*

I whipped out my map. "Close enough! *Si, muchas gracias!!"*

The driver got out from behind the wheel, shook my hand and escorted me to the back of the truck bed. It was loaded with lettuce crates and kids. I hopped in and away we rolled under a robin-egg blue California sky.

I passed out candies to the kids and played Patty Cake with them. The cab window slid open and spicy burritos were passed back. Freddy Fender had the number one song in the land and "Before The Next Teardrop Falls" played repeatedly on the tape deck. They proudly all sang along with Fender's heartfelt vibrato and I chimed in after a couple silent passes to refresh my *Espanol*.

At Paso Robles, I hopped out and took a precious ten dollar bill (money running low) and handed it to Juan, with profuse thanks. He shook his head and pushed the money away. When he went off to the rest room I gave it to his wife, instead. I high-fived each of the kids; then walked away, choked up inside over the goodness of the common man.

I caught a quick hopper ride over to San Simeon, then a long hauler all the way up glorious Highway 1 to Los Gatos, just south of San Francisco. I spent a day with Natalie and her new husband; then they took me into San Francisco.

They prepped me about all the sights to see as we drove in. "Where would you like for us to drop you?" Natalie asked.

"Anywhere in North Beach!"

I had a pilgrimage to make and the 'Cathedral' was open long into the night. "Oh, Michael—*do* be careful!" Natalie said as we hugged good bye. "What are your plans? Where will you stay tonight? You can't just walk away into the night . . . . "

I did, after hugging and kissing and thanking her. I was eager to again lose the controls, simply live in the world—out on the wing of serendipity. I hiked uphill to City Lights bookstore, the temple for all travelers of the heart and spirit, and eternal home of the 'Beats.' Owner and poet-laureate of San Francisco, Lawrence Ferlinghetti had reprinted in affordable paperback all the works of Kerouac, Ginsberg, Burroughs, Corso, Rexroth and Snyder—heroes all, and to walk through their old neighborhood; then step into City Lights and hold their works in my hands—I was the richest impoverished rucksack wanderer on earth!

Benet's *Reader's Encyclopedia* defines the beat movement as "A group of American writers and artists who found a voice during the 1950's and proved to be culturally influential during the turbulent 1960's. Although they never had a stated manifesto or program, the beats' creative efforts and lifestyles bespoke a vehement rejection of middle-class life and values. With a few exceptions, they were not considered respectable by the literary or social establishment until the 1970's. Then the ideas they championed—pacifism; reverence for nature at the expense of sophisticated technological pursuits; and stress on enhancing one's consciousness, whatever the methods employed—became ideas much of the nation championed as well. They came to be venerably regarded as descendants of American Transcendentalism, Thoreauvian in their distrust of the machine and Whitmanesque in their faith in America and the individual."

A coda to adhere to!

I wanted to buy every book in the store, but finally settled on a fresh copy of Kerouac's *On The Road*, as pages of my previous copy had to be sacrificed for toilet paper when I was surrounded by a patch of poison oak at an urgent off-road pit-stop. It was sacrilegious and I was depressed all day afterwards, but now with a new copy in hand I looked up at a poster-sized head-shot of Kerouac on the wall. I swear I heard his forgiving laughter! I stayed inside City Lights half the night reading; sprung for one more book: Ginsburg's epic poem, "Howl"—then walked down Broadway to the former beat-haunt, Vesuvio's cafe, and sat outside sipping and reading.

At Vesuvio's, I met two sisters: residents of San Francisco and spent the weekend with them, but that's a whole 'nuther book! I left Deborah and Donna, sad to end everything we did, but happy to move on across the Golden Gate bridge. At the last minute, I decided to savor the fabled crossing. At night, I scrambled up into the Presidio Army base, with a high and wild view of the full length of the Golden Gate connecting San Francisco with the Marin headlands and Sausalito and everything North. I sat there on the edge of the aerie-like cliff for hours, just thinking about life and the wonderment of it all—the bridge strung like a bright harp between now and tomorrow.

I bounded across the Golden Gate; turned down a gay guy in a Jaguar coming out of a bar in Sausalito; caught a ride with a man who asked me if "I knew Jesus Christ?" "Yep, drove into L.A. with him!" deflecting his conversion efforts on Highway 101 up to Ukiah. Then the land expanded and the forests returned tenfold. Just across the Oregon border, in Grant's Pass, I met another hitchhiker with my same plan of hanging out by roadside cafes, trying to hook safe passage.

Gary looked just like Bob Dylan and he'd been on the road for years and had it down to a science: one change of clothes, a thin blanket, a towel, and toothbrush (handle cutoff) that he carried under his arm in a folded brown paper bag. Suddenly, my pack felt as big as a house. Even though two take up more room than one, we hitched together and flowed from ride to ride in an unbroken rhythm up through "Cascadia"—the Pacific Northwest, where every day it rained a fine mist and we drank in the land. We camped one night under a big Doug Fir we found up a logging road to shelter us from the weather. Gary filled a hat full of morel mushrooms as we walked in and we cooked 'em up over a smoky fire; then picked sweet salmon berries off a bush, hand-to-mouth, for dessert.

Gary was from a wealthy family on Long Island, New York but had been caught with a lid of grass as a senior in high school. His Dad, a prestigious lawyer, kept him out of jail, but then imprisoned him far worse, physically and mentally, at home. So, Gary, with near-genius-level I.Q. and a scholarship to Yale, hit the road instead and had been living free for three years. We told our life stories late into the night and then fell asleep on beds of deep moss to a great horned owl's lullaby hoots overhead.

Most drivers pick up a hitchhiker because they are bored: want to move their trip along with new conversation. Tired of telling our own lives over and over, I told Gary's and he was me—which gets you thinking: hearing your life through another voice. In Yakima, Washington Gary actually called his Dad for the first time in years from a pay phone and hung up with happy tears.

We parted ways in Canada . . . . I went on to live for nearly two years on a wilderness island in British Columbia (recounted in my first book, *Inside Passage: Living With Killer Whales, Bald Eagles, and Kwakiutl Indians*).

After leaving the island and settling in the San Francisco Bay Area, I dug-in, nailing my butt to a chair day after day, trying to make it as a writer. I could only endure the frustrating, resultant rejection slips if I still had adventure as an "antidote." I started running because it was cheap and mood-lifting and showed me that I could bear the restraining harness of civilization and work if, on the near horizon, I had a marathon to look forward to or a mountain to climb.

On the weekends, I became a wandering "run-bum" with 'Have Marathon/ Will Travel' my motto. Articles in "Runner's World" magazine advised that you should do only 1-2 marathons a year, so depleting was the toll on the body. But I was running at least a marathon a month, and often two, on back-to-back weekends. Where else but California could you run The Big Sur Marathon—striding along the closed-off Highway 1 on the edges of cliffs above heaving ocean and soaring hawks; then seven days later drive up into Humbolt County and do The Avenue of The Giants: running under redwoods: the world's tallest trees, with the lofty architecture and amber light—pure cathedral.

Then after running out of all the big organized marathons, in nearly all the open lands and parks of northern California, Dave Horning of Tri-Sports loosely organized long-distance races, with the trails barely marked: a ragtag lot of 30-50 runners starting early on a Saturday morn, clutching a blurry mimeographed map and if you didn't get lost your first time in yet another preserve or wild sanctuary—there was a keg of beer and a yet another T-shirt awaiting you at the Finish.

Then I started going out of state—over to Colorado for the Pike's Peak Marathon: sunny and hot at the start but a foot of snow atop the mountain and soul-shaking, quaking aspen forests in-between.

Family and friends were somewhat critical and often psychoanalytical: Why all this running? What is it you running away from? Why devote all that time to something that doesn't make you money? True, on the surface running didn't make sense, but it did directly affect my ability to make cents. The main reason I ran was because it helped me write. The satisfaction of finishing a marathon swept away the rejection and self-doubt that piled-up on my writing desk all week. The more I ran, the deeper I was able to progress resolutely with my work. It was like the ink in my pen and the blood in my veins were one-and-the-same; and running supplied an elevated flow . . . .

While living in the Napa Valley, there were miles and miles to run off-road, through the glorious vineyards, shoe-slicing through carpets of mustard plants during the post-harvest winter slumber; and then in late-spring, with the weeds roughly tilled into the soil for nitrogen, I toughened ankles over the irregular surface and broken clods of dirt. By summer, with the grapes fully set and the vineyards all groomed like country clubs, I ran over soil as soft as sifted cake flour (kept loose to aerate the vines). I'd then go into the vineyards for speed-work: bound all-out down a quarter-mile long row, then jog easy up the next; sprint again, recover. On hot days, never took water—just reached out and plucked a few grapes . . . dropping them one-by-one onto my tongue and pressing the orbs slowly up against the roof of my mouth—gasping over the explosions of warm, liquid sweetness! I was a run-bum, totally drunk on life.

During the sprints, I'd flush jack rabbits lying in under the leafy vines. They'd explode out full-throttle, helter-skelter, and I'd surge and dodge to keep up with them down the rows: like Rocky Balboa chasing the chicken across the yard. Just before harvest, in early September, Indian Summer would unfurl across northern California with a big heat wave. The grapes would suddenly swell with juice, and the vineyardists feeling the pressure, rushed to get their 'money in the tank' before mildewing rains, sugar-lowering cool weather, or the storms of starlings came.

One day, deep in an Inglenook vineyard bursting with fruit, the sky overhead darkened and then it rained—birds. Hundreds of starlings poured down onto the vines gobbling grapes and cackling with loud joy. They were an identical motley crew, dark and greasy; giving off a free-for-all gang mentality. The rootless hooligans didn't stay in one place long. Obeying a cryptic command, they all lifted-off together—the vast flock twisting and turning with one mind through the sky . . . then in the distance, plunging down again to suck-up more sweetness.

The vineyardists viewed the starlings as plagues of locusts. They tried everything to drive them away: statues of great horned owls on vineyard row posts; tall, humanoid scarecrows placed mid-vineyard; loud recordings of shotguns banging-off nonstop or ear-piercing heavy metal music. One vineyard alliance even hired a falconer on horseback to try to put the starlings on the run, but the plan backfired: seeing the falcon, terrified, the flocks all dropped to the ground, taking cover in the leafy grapevines.

Long-distance running down country lanes and remote corners often led to surprising sights. To keep from getting stale while exercising, personal trainers suggest "Muscle Confusion": varying your routine to spark continual growth. Always on the lookout for new terrain, I ran down Stanley Lane in the Carneros region: a dogleg mile through a tunnel of eucalyptus trees (planted originally as windbreaks along edges of fields after *The Grapes of Wrath* era when all the topsoil was blown off Oklahoma). A summer afternoon, I came up on a UPS truck parked off to the side in the shady depths of the lane. At first, I thought it might be abandoned way out here but then approaching from the rear, I saw another car parked in front . . . The back door of the truck was fully open and there was the driver, brown pants down around his ankles, delivering *his* package to a bent-over housewife. I held my breath and went by on tiptoes, so as not to interrupt their tryst down "lover's lane."

After harvest, with the vines all in tatters from being shaken by mechanical harvesters or migrant workers, there were still some grapes remaining, small clusters that had been overlooked. With most of the leaves gone from the vines, the remaining grapes now stood out in full magenta. Miles into one of the vast Mondavi vineyards, I swung down the very last row, rising across a hillside. In all that space and solitude suddenly someone stepped out in front of me—grape knife bared. It was a middle-aged woman with wild black hair shot full of silver; wearing brightly colored, mismatched clothes. Turned out she was a Rumanian gypsy, who was picking the second set of grapes for her homemade wine and plucking the largest leaves to bake around rice and lamb. She was as startled to see me as I, her—but after talking awhile we parted friends and compatriots, both of us working the outer fringes.

One day, Dad now living in Sedona, Arizona, sent a newspaper clipping about a woman who had just run across the Grand Canyon, from rim to rim.

The accompanying photo showed her just emerging from what the Hopi Indians called the "Womb of The Earth." I wrote to Kay Alderton, asking how she did it and a wonderful friendship began.

Inspired by the intensive care unit nurse and bold adventurer, six months later, in the first flush of daybreak I was in a small plane, lifting-off from the south rim of the Grand Canyon. Running out of runway, the Cessna temporarily dipped into the gorge, then regained altitude to reach the north rim, 1,000 feet higher and eighteen miles distant. During the short hop, I pressed my nose against the window in absolute awe of the spectral beauty below. I could see the trails I would be running on all day: the North Kaibab down; and Bright Angel back up to the south rim, where my family waited. The trails were thin zigzags down amidst the bases of bulwark buttes, jagged ramparts, towering turrets, and sacred temples—the wind-riven rock glowing vermilion in the first rays of sun.

Touching down on the 8,200 foot high north rim, I walked away from the plane through a ponderosa pine forest and found the trail head. The south rim was a faint blue curve in the distance. I peered down; it was all straight down—a vertical mile to the river and with the hairs all raised on my arms and legs, I took the first step in . . . .

Every moment of the next four hours was a spiritual experience, physically expressed. With each stride down; I felt myself dissolve into the immensity and monumental silence—my legs falling away, torso lightened—leaving only my heart thudding through thin air. I raced the light of day that slid in an even illuminating line down the broad rock walls or abruptly bolted like lightning into narrow cul-de-sacs—lit only a few minutes each day. I paused in one rock chamber just as it was struck: the dark, vault-like air suddenly aglow with molten light. I shuddered, for it was like showering in a golden radiance.

I ran on, lost to myself. Time expanded into new dimensions, measured in millenniums, not hours. The deeper you plunged, the further back in time you traveled. Here was the complete geological record of the earth: the strata in the lofty walls displaying every known class of rock, from every era. Totally transparent, I felt spirits in the wind, pulses in the rocks, stars in the dust. I ran alongside a creek, then pivoted abruptly at a switch back as the rushing water flumed out into space, raining down to the Colorado River below. I ran to its roar and danced down there amidst bluish outcrops of ancient shale.

Down was a controlled fall, but up—another matter. Flayed by the afternoon sun on the exposed Bright Angel trail, my skin felt cut away and my tongue turned into a flame. I was consumed by steepness that never seemed to stop. Finally, coming up out of the Canyon, my body came back to me. Taking *flat!*

steps, I flung my arms around my family and then opened both hands, releasing two egg-shaped, black rocks—possibly 2 billion years old, from the Inner Gorge. Before leaving, I spent a few moments alone on the canyon rim, savouring the journey through the folded layers of time. With fingertips—I flung tears out into the void . . . overwhelmed by how deep the feeling of being alive can really be.

I called Kay from the first pay phone, babbling excitedly about the crossing. Our conversation had everything to do with the poet Franz Wefel's saying: "For those who believe, no explanation is necessary. For those who do not believe, no explanation is possible."

A few months later, Kay invited me to climb Mt. Shasta with her and a group from Arizona. Halfway up, on a steep snow slope as she was pulling away from us, leading the charge: "DAMMIT, MOM—SLOW DOWN!" 25 year old Allan called.

"What?" I said, huffing and puffing alongside of him. "Kay is your *Mother*?!"

"Yeah, and I've never been able to catch her yet!"

Kay mounted an expedition to Mt. Orizaba in Mexico, at 18, 855 feet, the third highest mountain in North America. After resting in a high hut to get acclimatized to the altitude, we roped together in two groups of three, and set out for the summit in the middle of the night when the snow was firmest. Many a lazy or lackadaisical climber has slept in and with the sun's rays softening a skimpy snow bridge over a crevasse—cracked through the deceptive cover, plunging to his or her death inside a vast, icy casket half-a-mile deep.

We set-out at 4:00 a.m. in the frigid darkness. In the tiny beam of your head lamp you couldn't see the climber in front of you—only the rope connecting you snaking forward across the snow as if with a life of its own. Kay's group was climbing about a hundred yards ahead of us; she was in the third position with Greg and Frank ahead of her. You put your very best climber in the third position and I soon learned why.

In the coral-pink twilight, we could now spot the lead group ascending a steep, 50 degree slope high above us. Kay's colossal energy had already driven them on ahead by 400 yards. They were small specks in a vast white amphitheater. Just when Peter, Marilyn, and I paused to take a blow and look up to check their progress: we took-in something the eyes saw, but our brains refused to accept as really happening . . . . Frank, the lead climber in Kay's group fell—zipping down the icy slope in a nylon shell jacket. He committed a climber's cardinal sin by not yelling as he came off the mountain . . . . Greg, next in line, about twenty yards of rope behind Frank, had his head down and didn't see Frank go by. Frank is only about 140 pounds but his acceleration was enough to rip the 210 pound Greg off his feet and send both plummeting downward. Still, in total shock, sliding helter-skelter, neither man uttered a sound . . . . Kay, giving full concentration to the icy patch in front of her, saw a blur out of the corner of her eye. Without looking up to see what it was (then too late), she immediately did an ice-ax arrest (driving the sharp tip of your ice ax down into the mountain with your prone body weight, just behind the rope). Thank god, the ax 'took' and Kay's 130 pounds were anchor enough, for a split-second later: the rope stretched taut—and Frank and Greg, turned upside down—came to a halt.

Even though it all took place in the blink of an eye, somehow, as we watched it seemed to unfold in slow-motion. If Kay hadn't acted without thinking, exactly when she did she would have been peeled-off th mountain, as well . . . and with the three of them speeding down the slope there was no way we had time to get over into their distant path to try to stop them. We would have had to watch them slide by us and free-fall thousands of feet off the glacier lip to their certain death: a sight no one should ever have to live with. (A month later, two climbers slipped in the very same area and plunged to their deaths.)

We power-climbed up to them. They were back on their feet; Kay shrugging off all the gratitude and praise with a simple, matter-of fact statement: "Next time you guys—please yell!"

I was the rookie climber of the group, having only done the Mt. Shasta "walk up" before this. As we continued up the steep icy slope, I began to sweat in the cold air. *If Frank and Greg can fall—where does that leave me?* It then got worse, with the slope steepening even more and the surface all hard blue ice. No matter how hard I kicked, of all the crampon points covering my boots—only one of the very front fangs went in . . . . Each time I pushed up, I stared down—wide-eyed at that one small point of steel, incredulous that it would hold my body weight plus heavy pack. I started to lose it, all my muscles going rigid with tension; panic climbing my spine. And being roped together, after what I had just seen, was an added burden: the link now more a curse than a blessing, for if I fell . . . a bad chance I would take Marilyn and Peter with me.

Just as my mind was bottoming-out, I heard a strange buzzing sound. Suffering from tunnel-vision, I stole a glance out to the side and, incredibly, there was a bumble bee, a black and yellow aeronaut meandering up over the slope . . . . Seeing that plump, vibrant bit of life on the frozen mountain—broke the ice within. There wasn't a flower within 18,000 feet, but that didn't seem to concern the bee. Its steady, hum-like buzz unknotted my clenched nerves. I relaxed and moved on . . . following the bee in the updraft that carried it here.

We all made the summit without further mishap. And every time I see a bumble bee, I murmur a silent word of thanks.

A few months later, Kay organized an Orizaba reunion climb on the highest of the Kachina Peaks, above Flagstaff, Arizona. It was a playful day, with much teasing from Kay toward Frank and Greg. Noticing that I didn't join in on the merriment, I confessed my fears I had after the fall on Orizaba. We then reenacted the near-disaster but on a much lesser snow slope, with Kay showing me exactly how to do the lifesaving ice-ax arrest. We then tried it "live." With Frank and Greg sailing past, I plunged into the slope with the ax held firmly under my chest. I drove it home with the rope looped around it, but then could barely hold the falling weight of the two men. From that point on, I marveled even more at Kay. Forewarned, my ax went up to the hilt in pre-chosen soft snow; hers without time to choose; and only the tip penetrating blue ice. I weighed at least 50 pounds more than her yet she stopped the guys traveling much faster on a steeper, slicker slope and in real time, "crunch time": with lives on the line.

Atop Humphreys Peak, the views were dazzling. Air loses 1/30th of its density with each 900 feet of altitude gained. At 12,643 feet we looked through air not just humidity free, but it had lost nearly half of its weight in oxygen and carbon dioxide. We could see into the Grand Canyon and the Painted Desert's multihues flared-up through the transparent air. It was clear why the Hopis believe that their Kachina gods resided up here, in an elevated environment, yet very close to home.

Kay Alderton was a great mentor, spending every spare moment on a new adventure. Whatever we did together in Arizona, afterwards, we usually stopped at Dad and Joanne's house in Sedona on the way back to the Phoenix airport or Kay's home in that burgeoning burg. At Dad's big house, in the shadow of Grayback Mountain, we burst in, babbling about the latest climb; hit the Jacuzzi; chowed down on Joanne's killer spaghetti; sipped great wine—and the next morning Dad led us on a hike through Western movie scenery (Sedona second only to Monument Valley as a celluloid backdrop) to explore Indian ruins set in high caves within that extraordinary pumpkin-colored rock.

Much has been written about Sedona being a mystical, new age power-place: "The only place with 1,500 channels and no TV stations," so says Jorgen Korsholm, director of a group of psychics and healers. The Red Planet Diner serves "mothership margaritas" and Earth Wisdom Tours takes you out to supposed vortexes and medicine wheels made of stones arranged in circles. Dad and Joanne, residents long before Sedona became a trendy spiritual Mecca, kept an open mind and if there was anything happening on a mystical level the avid hikers felt it might be due to all the pulsing quartz: the rock shot full of "electricity."

During one visit, while running the steep hill up to the Sedona airport topping a flat mesa, I detoured out to a vortex: a rising column of rock looking out over a vast tree-studded valley. It was a gray, leaden day and my mood matched the weather. My first book had just been rejected for the 17th time, currently by HarperCollins. Standing at the very peak of the vortex, I closed my eyes and prayed that the book finally find its way into the light. I opened my eyes to a staggering sight—a 'god beam' shot down from a parted cloud and hit a medicine wheel on a lower cliff—dead center. The sky-laser intensified for a moment, glowing with white light; then was snuffed by the closing clouds as quickly as it had appeared.

Then a day later, at home, on my answering machine this message: "Michael, this is Dan Bial, HarperCollins. After your book was rejected a few months ago, just for the hell of it I resubmitted it again. That never works and I can't even explain why I did it, but congratulations: You are now a published author! I still can't quite believe it—the other editors that were previously most against it, now sang its praises! I've been in publishing twenty years and have never seen anything like it!!"

Another call came that also played a big part in changing my life. Seeing a picture of a runner, in a local Napa Valley newspaper emerging out of the Grand Canyon wearing only shorts and running shoes, a sculptor called, asking if I might be interested in modeling for his life drawing class. "It's without clothes but you will be 'anonymous'—we're not looking at you, personally, just the lines and shadows you present," Joseph Query said.

With the start of class weeks away, I agreed to do it, not really thinking about all the details (or lack thereof). Finally, the night before, reality set-in: I couldn't sleep and broke out in a cold sweat at the thought of being totally naked in front of a group of strangers with all eyes upon you. Morning finally arrived and I was about to call Joe and tell him I was sick (which I was), but then just couldn't bring myself to cancel on him with such short notice.

On the drive over to the restored barn where the class was held I agonized: *What if I get a hard on? What if I can't hold a pose? Oh my gawd— buck naked in front of strangers!!! No way—what was I thinking! Must have been out of my mind to agree to this . . . .*

What delivered me to the door was my faith in Joe. In the intervening weeks I had visited his studio in Sonoma. There was a sculpting class in session, the final session of finishing a standing male nude (the model no longer present). As the dozen students set to work finishing the details on their statues, Joe announced. "They are all good, but fixed, static. Now work from imagination— abstract the figure; totally reshape it. Be bold!"

Thrown off course, the students walked slowly around their work—looking for a way in; the catalyst to begin anew. At the very point of finishing, they were hesitant to mar their creations, and asked the teacher to show them what he meant. Without hesitation, Joe snatched the damp cloth off an abandoned, half-finished sculpture, grabbed up a wooden knife and quickly slashed and stippled the clay, then dropped the tool to bend the wire armature with both hands, not pausing to step back, think, analyze—but surrendered to a force that seemed to grasp the positions in the sculptor first, then sent the energy rippling through him into the clay.

There was total silence, stillness beyond him in the room. Creative Power, a palpable presence was flowing beyond Ego, in its purest form. Under Joe's hands, from the depths of his being, the male nude was merely a point of departure—transforming now into a winging bird, a musical note, then a blossoming flower.

After the class, a woman came in to have her portrait done. Rather than a long, drawn-out, traditional affair requiring many sittings: it was finished in twenty minutes. Again, restless with realism, Query drew a spiritual interpretation. His portraits were done in pastel chalks on brown paper and eyes glued to the subject, he felt the colors' vibrations with a moving hand and then would suddenly snatch-up a vibe that matched the one he saw emanating from the subject in front of him. I could hear him drawing as I walked around the large studio—chalks rapping the paper, often snapping to pieces as he worked powerfully from within. The result was an intense upward showering of colors above her recognizable head that swirled with energy. He then spoke aloud: interpreted the meaning of each color to the woman and how the vibration levels applied to her life.

After the woman left, Joe looked tired. "I feel as if my head opens-up like a fan during the creation—then closes down afterwards and then I'm back to being plain old Joe again."

"Hardly," I said sweeping my arm around at his finished work: an eagle in brindled marble about to spring into flight; a snow-white, squat marbled penguin; a bronze Pan playing his flute, with fingertips and one cloven hoof uplifted; exquisite facial drawings of St. Francis in a range of moods.

As his day's work was done, we sat down together with a glass of wine to talk. As a young boy, while his friends dreamed of growing up to be soldiers and firemen, Joseph wanted to be a Trappist monk—like Thomas Merton, and wrote to an Arctic monastery. They turned him down, but he soon found spiritual expression as an artist—studying at The Boston Museum School of Fine Arts under the renown sculptor, George Demitrios. Joe then went on a two year scholarship to Italy—Pietrasanta, Tuscany as an apprentice to the Italian marble carvers—extracting his stone from the very same quarry that Michelangelo favored.

Although in his 50's, his education had never stopped. He constantly immersed himself in the great works of literature and mythology. His teacher was Gil Bailie, the scholar/poet who directed the influential study-group, TEMENOS. Joe's readings often sparked his drawings. He pulled out a large folio and showed me a haunting "Veiled Beatrice" who emerged from Dante, and a series of startling portraits of a modern-day Job. Along with his readings, Joe's dreams and meditations directed his art, which was clearly his spiritual biography.

It was an autumn afternoon, with slanting sunlight. The big sliding door to the studio was open. Joe's face was in shadow but his eyes caught and held the golden light with that intense gaze of artists and visionaries, possessors of the "Holy Madness": what Kazantzakis called the creative spirit.

We talked about animals and then as he spoke of his admiration for St. Francis—a sparrow flew into the room and perched on a beam above Joe's head. His eyes turned upward and he smiled. I clicked the 'snapshot' in my mind's eye: the portrait of the artist as Joseph Query; the rare reflection of a man who knows his own soul.

Inspired and emboldened by the visit to Joe's studio, I showed up at The White Barn in St. Helena, undressed and stepped naked up onto a small stage in front of 20 students. The music helped: Mahler, Bartok, Sibelius, Debussy, Schubert. I lost myself in the symphonic vibrations, let them play through me and *"There!"* Joe would say; I would hold that pose and charcoal sticks then glided over paper. Disappearing deep inside the process, two hours passed like a few minutes.

During a break midway through, at first, I immediately dashed over to my clothes and redressed even for ten minutes but by the third week; the sixth session, I was so relaxed that at break, I didn't even bother covering up. Sipping a cup of tea, I walked around looking at the easels. Joe was right: It's not about 'You' and everything to do with impersonal lines and angles, shadows and light.

Only once did I get self-conscious, but it was in an instructive double-perspective manner. At break, I was standing down on the floor talking to two women who were still seated on low chairs behind their easels—my penis at their eye level and just a few inches away. I thought of how normal it felt to be there naked in that context, but to a stranger suddenly walking in with the usual hang-ups and guilt-trips—it would appear totally different. Emerson advised us to "Be a good animal"—for a reason. The Transcendentalist knew that we are so far removed from the Age of Innocence, dominated by our overly analytical minds and artificial morality that we've lost the pure instinct that carries animals, in many ways, far beyond where we now go.

The Jesuit priest and philosopher, Teilhard de Chardin wrote: "The Animal knows, of course—but it doesn't know that it knows." Is it our self-awareness: our *knowing* that we know that therein lies the disconnect from playful naiveté to self-entrapment in snares of a thousand rules and constricts, either laid-out in the open or camouflaged (by religious conditioning) in human consciousness? We need to return unafraid to the untrammeled Garden and let the wizened beast romp free!

While on magazine assignments in Europe, in hotel rooms I'd often flick on the television—shocked to see how freely and naturally the naked human form was displayed in shows and commercials. Early on, while Eurailing across Europe, I checked into a youth hostel in Stockholm, Sweden in dire need of a shower. After signing-in, I asked the clerk where the shower was? "Down the hall; first door on your left . . . . "

Eagerly pushing the door open, I then closed it just as fast: seeing three naked women soaping-up in a large shower stall.

I strode back to the front desk. "Um, where's the Men's shower?"

"Hey man, you're not in Kansas anymore!!"

Instead of bounding back down the hall to join "The Three Graces"—as any healthy red-blooded male would do, proclaiming *This is mah luckee day!* instead, I dragged my feet and a soul burdened by Catholic conditioning: all that guilt over seeing a naked woman (in triplicate, no less!!!) before marriage was a sin; three nude women alather—downright dirty. Then reminding myself that the whole purpose of this trip was to try to break the chains of my past, I stripped (with my back to the women); took a deep breath—and slithered in past all that nubile flesh to the open shower head on the back wall.

Pinching a sliver of soap off the tray, I then held onto it for all I was worth, actually afraid if I dropped it I would have to see more *(my gawd how the brainwashing of the Good Sisters lingered!)* But then after surveying through a soapy, squinting eye—the luxurious, flowing contours around me . . . I finally relaxed and rather than being cast into Hell, it felt more like glimpses of Heaven.

Why in America is it all backwards? Turn on the television or go to a movie and every five minutes someone is being blown away in slow, glorified motion— but show a bare breast and *that's* obscene?! Most Americans came from Europe, so why the prevalent, present-day Puritanism? Why do we prefer to watch death over life? And then wonder why our desensitized children are killing one other at school? The Center for Media Education estimates that a child sees 8,000 simulated murders by the time he or she completes elementary school. To me the nude female form is the ultimate in design, "Living Art"; something totally sacred (and proof there is a 'God,' for no human artist could create such awe-inspiring lines)—but instead of watching a couple make love, we're more comfortable seeing "Jason" or another horrid psycho snuff people in the very act (or doing it ourselves with a 'Joystick' in hand). It's sad—ism and it's insane.

We enter and depart this world naked; and the human body is setup for blissful pleasure during the time between those two portals—yet how often we deny and denigrate the very bodies we wear. Why? Are we so lacking in self-worth or crammed-full of religious guilt that we are too embarrassed to accept and freely exercise the sacred gift?

As the adult film actress Nina Hartley said in an interview: "The penis is multipurpose: procreation, recreation, pleasure, elimination, but the clitoris is completely there. It has only one purpose. Pleasure. Do you believe in a god that makes mistakes?"

Mark Twain: "Nature knows no indecencies; man invents them."

Posing for the Life Drawing class loosened me up off the stage, as well as on. I felt freer, more in tune with nature, more in my body and less entangled in a worrisome mind. I regretted that we humans are cursed with wearing clothes. I would much rather go through life wearing the permanent hide of an animal, say the sleek (always fashionable) black pelt of a panther! (And Joe felt much the same, wearing on the drafty winter mornings in the barn a beautiful long sweater made from the fleecy hair of his dog: a Norwegian elkhound that a weaver spun from the daily brush-hairs Joe had saved.)

With great abandon I now romped through the class, so much so that Joe was shouting *"There!"* with just about every pose that came through. Occasionally, he would hurl himself on stage and draw directly on the model with a blue magic marker. "Look at the way this line continuously spirals *here!* and over *there!!* The body is as vast as the Universe, with the very same patterns and characteristics." Joe would then momentarily snap out of his consuming passion, recap the pen and murmur an apology for marking me up, but I smiled, waving it off; wearing the blue strokes like badges of honor.

After the last class, Joe said that he wanted me to meet friends of his, both writers.

We drove over to the Sonoma Valley and I met Rebecca and Fred Latimer. At first, we talked shop while sipping tea. They had lived for years in Turkey and they then told stories; showed pictures of the historic architecture and natural beauty from "the crossroads of civilization."

As we were leaving, Rebecca opened the closet door to get our jackets, and there taped to the inside of the door was a course map of The Western States

100 Mile Endurance Run. At the time, Western States was chosen by "Outside" magazine as the toughest endurance event in the world (superseding the grueling Ironman Triathlon in Hawaii, because instead of switching off from swimming to biking to running, Western States was all one repetitious motion and with the cumulative uphills and downs, was equivalent in effort to climbing Mt. Everest in one day). There on the foyer table were family pictures with a red-haired runner in many of them.

"That's Doug," Rebecca said.

"*The* Doug Latimer?" I said, excitedly explaining how he was a legend among marathon runners, either winning or always finishing in the top ten of Western States!

Rebecca chuckled. "He's just 'Doug' to us, but he is some runner!" As Rebecca and Fred showed me other family pictures, Fred said that their son John was Doug's crew chief, and Doug's daughter Allison helped as well, as did Rebecca and Fred. From their exited tones it was clear that Western States was a family affair and the high point of their year. Fred had just turned 80 and was laid low from various ailments, but come race day he always rallied—trotting energetically through the woods in support of his son like a proud papa wolf.

I met Doug a week later at his parents house and was most impressed. If there ever was an ultimate long-distance runner's physique, Doug had it: six feet tall, 150 pounds, with legs up to his shoulders and whipcord strong. He wore glasses, had red hair and freckles and resembled a slender Robert Redford. I grilled him for about two hours all about Western States; he asked about my marathons.

He called a few days later and asked if I might want to pace him at this year's Western States—run with him for the last 30 miles?

"Really? It would be an absolute honor—count me in!"

The night before the race, with Doug and his crew holed-up in a mountain chalet-style hotel in Squaw Valley, we held a final strategy session in Doug's room. He had spread charts; altitude profiles; an exact time line; a list of other elite runners' strengths and weaknesses out across the bed, which we stood around. With the efficiency and planning of a military strategist, Doug took us through his plan: including the exact times he should be arriving at each checkpoint; what supplies he needed at each; the precise positions we should be in to shave off a few steps and the energy-draining stress of trying to find us. From previous years he knew exactly what rock or tree we should be parked by, with coolers, fresh socks and shoes at the ready. "And Michael, be ready to pace at Mile 70. I should be O.K. until then."

Clearly the man was driven As the meeting broke up and we were walking to our rooms, as if reading my mind, his mother whispered to me, "You should drive with him. He won't stop until he picks off—passes all the cars in front of him!"

The next day went by like a blur— if running 100 miles can possibly proceed that way, but it did with Doug Latimer one of the front runners, racing all the way. Previous to Mile 70 where I would start running with Doug (each entrant allowed a pacer for the last 40 miles), I pitched in with mixing batches of Exceed (electrolyte replacement drink); made sandwiches; toted lawn chairs. Sometimes we got to the deep forest checkpoints only minutes ahead of Doug's arrival. The man was a machine and each successive hour into the race my admiration for him increased by leaps and bounds.

Then in the late afternoon, I put on fresh running shoes, stripped down to a singlet and shorts and joined Doug, who hardly paused now at the checkpoints. He had said in last night's strategy session that the race really began with 30 miles left, with the majority of the mountains and steep canyons behind you.

As we ran off together, I marveled at how fast he was moving. He was covered in a sheen of sweat, dried mud-splashes halfway up his long legs, blood trickling down from a small gash on his shin. As we moved on through the remains of the day, Doug was a power plant pumping out molten energy. He emitted a red-orange glow, like a blacksmith holding steel to the fire. I kept him drinking, and continually pushing the pace he didn't even stop to pee—stutter-stepping, dragging a leg while hosing down the trail!

Voices carried through the still forest and at the first sound up ahead, Doug would increase his speed and we would surge by another runner and pacer: Doug patting Rae Clark, a good friend and world-record holding endurance runner on the back and Clark, in turn, cheered Latimer on. Then with just a few miles to go, there were voices behind us and then a runner visible in his flashlight beam: Richard Spady, from Montana closing fast. Doug, who just a moment before was vomiting on the side of the trail from a sour stomach, now with Spady in sight sprinted as if he was just starting, uttering, "That Spady—he's tougher than wang leather!" He then had me turn and run backwards every five minutes, giving him a progress report on Spady.

We hit the streets of Auburn in the clear and as we entered the Auburn high school stadium, there was one final lap around the track to the finish. Latimer's name was boomed over the loudspeaker, bringing loud applause. I stopped running; stepped-off the track and cut across the infield. It was Doug's day. Unlike most runners hoping to buckle, rather than desperately depending on a pacer to help get him to the finish, Latimer was a self-propelled force-of-nature. I knew I was along far more for companionship than dire need. John,

Rebecca, Fred, Allison—all of Doug's family crew hugged me with great thanks; then we all gave Doug a conquering hero's welcome! Finishing fifth overall, it had been another great year; great race.

Instead of relishing his success (or even acting the least bit exhausted!) after a quick shower at the nearby hotel, Doug Latimer showed what he is truly made of—returning to the Auburn Stadium and standing at the finish line to cheer on runners for hours longer. Whether they were friends or strangers, it didn't matter, for Doug and they were linked by the shared experience, irregardless of their ranking. As we joined him, welcoming in the back-of-the-packers, brother John turned to me and said, "So, you're going to run, yourself, next year aren't you?"

"I . . . ah—well, it was incredible out there! That country is so wild!!"

"I saw it in your eyes when you guys came up from the river. You're hooked! You have that wide-eyed, hypnotic look."

"Michael, you can do it," Doug added. "Let's train together next year; I'll show you how . . . . "

There's a saying that an ultra runner can best train if he is divorced and unemployed. I was both, but Latimer was neither. A former vice-president and editor at Harper & Row in New York (the classic *Seven Arrows* by native American medicine man Hymothius Storm, one of his projects), Doug was now the publisher of "Women's Sports & Fitness" magazine, putting in 18 hour days; traveling incessantly across the country. He was also a husband and father with two young daughters. During the week he stole time to run on his lunch-hour; and by Saturday morning when he picked me up, he went up into the mountains exhausted, carrying the frazzled aura of office stress, so much so that he often asked me to drive while he passed-out for a few hours across the back seat.

Doug's winning training method was to start getting serious about 10 weekends before Western States: then running every step of the toughest sections of the course, itself. His theory was that by training at high altitude, even for a day or two, you triggered the build-up of additional oxygen-carrying, red blood cells and you definitely felt that incremental increase each week, for returning to sea level your local neighborhood runs were then done with ease—PR (personal records) set on most. Torture tests: each run up in the high thin air, but we built-up to it: taking it somewhat easy the first few weekends.

Up near Hodgson's cabin (an actual abandoned cabin) we took a detour, Doug smiling as he led me off the trail, to a small stream cutting through a sylvan meadow. He pointed down into a clear pool. Rainbow trout flickered back and forth.

"Someday when I stop running, I want to backpack up here. Just live off fish and sleep under the stars."

Some weekends we ran our route in reverse, to take on more uphills. One time we pushed all the way out to the top of Emigrant Pass, and from 8,900 feet looked down over deep canyons; steep mountains; forest veldts—our starting point lost in the distance, the trail itself, erased by immensity. We stood like castaways on the high peak, voicing disbelief that we actually *ran*—moved ourselves over those mountains. I concluded our awed comments with *"Wagh!"*— (an old mountain man superlative expressing surprise or wonderment: half word and half buffalo bleat it spoke volumes!) We then felt that familiar, addictive surge of adrenaline lifting through our fatigue as we started back over a trail that showed itself only one turn at a time.

After running 30-40 thigh-churning, lung-burning mountain miles, on the drive home, famished, we'd whip into a tiny Sierra cafe above the American River, wade in amidst rafting parties up from Sacramento, their dirigible-like, rubber galleons anchored outside on long trailers. We'd tear into juicy buffalo burgers and mounds of French-fries and thick milkshakes. Fat is the steady fuel that an ultra runner burns hour upon hour and fat, salt, grease—all the things normally bad for you are what the body craves most right after an all-day, high-altitude run. So great were the caloric outputs during our bouts with the mountains that nothing was safe afterward: all foods, dead or alive, were fair game for miles around! The sateen-thighed college coed rafters, picking with restraint at salads shook their heads and fingers at us. Doug and I smiled back with full churning mouths; then we'd slaughter yet another buff and platter of fries; topping it off with huge slabs of wild berry pie—and were still down 4 pounds on our scales at home.

For our first training run, we went into the high country early that year, too early as it turned out. On the cusp of May with winter still hanging-on, we started out in sunshine clad in shorts and thin long sleeves, but then soon were moving through a snowstorm, joyfully following cougar tracks, suddenly visible, dusted by snow; splayed wide and fresh before us. In hoping to catch a glimpse of the cat, we ran with "blinders" on, oblivious to the worsening weather. Fifteen miles out we were soaked to the skin from the blizzard, and thoroughly chilled. We then turned around; struggling to stay ahead of hypothermia. Cold to the core, we constantly monitored each other's numbness, strange pains, uncontrollable teeth chattering; then total lockjaw as we kept moving, our only salvation: to keep moving through the frigid, white forest back to the car. I never thought I would ever be so happy to see a car—that we dove into as if it was home-sweet-home. Driving down out of the mountains, we then blasted the heater for two hours straight before we completely thawed-out.

A few years later, a cougar killed a runner on the Western States course between Rucky Chucky and Highway 49. Barbara Schoener, 40, a mother of two, was attacked from behind while was running alone. The petite woman was thrown down a slope, where she fought back, but eventually succumbed to the cougar's second attack. Just one month before, Barbara had completed her first ultra, The Cool Canyon Crawl, over the very same section of trail. To have her die in the same wilderness that enlivened so many of us, was just too difficult a dichotomy to accept.

I recalled, while living in a cabin in the Mayacamus ("howl of the mountain lion") Mountains above the Napa Valley, one night, I broke a sound sleep, sitting straight up, instantly awake in bed, the guard hairs on the back of my neck extended and vibrating like wires . . . . I then learned why. A sound shattered the night like no other I had ever heard. It was a train rumbling, a woman shrieking, a baby bawling, birds softly chirping—all rolled into one. After the caterwauling—dead-silence, then a similar but shorter response from higher up the mountain. Back-and-forth, the immanences called. When I looked out the bedroom corner window, in the moonlight a long tawny tail passed by the cabin. The tail, alone, was six feet long and flicked side-to-side with a wild, irrefutable life-force.

I tried to accept Barbara Schoener's death by justifying that since we all have to die, what's the worst way to go: slowly rotting away with terminal cancer one organ or limb at a time or seized by a cougar in mid-stride? I thought of the Native Americans and Japanese samurai, when in life-threatening situations, "froze the moment" by looking around at the sparkling sunshine, leaves dancing in the breeze, white clouds billowing overhead and declared it: "A Good Day to Die!" Death was the last thing Barbara Schoener desired while running the trail, with so much to live for; so much life ahead of her, but at least the ultra runner was taken out on the trail, a place she loved—as shocking as it may be.

This was extremely rare. No cougar-related death had been reported in California for the last 80 years. A study by Paul Beier of the University of California-Berkeley documented 53 mountain lion attacks on people in North America, 11 of them fatal, over a 100-year span. That's far less than the annual total of people killed by lightning strikes or rattlesnake bites.

Cougar attacks on wildlife are far from rare. According to the Department of Fish and Game there are more than 5,000 adult mountain lions in California and each kills and eats approximately one deer a week, equaling 250,000 deer a year or a quarter of the estimated one million deer in the state

A Canadian woodsman once told me that cougars attack from behind and above, biting through their prey's spinal cord and raking a razor-sharp thumb/

"kill-claw" through the jugular vein. From our perspective it seems cowardly to attack someone from behind, but from the cougar's point of view that's the area where it least endangers itself—away from the victim's own retaliatory teeth, arms, claws. Recently in India, remote villagers under fatal assault from man-eating tigers fought back; not with guns or poison—but with papier-mâché. When wandering out into the forests to gather fire wood or fish along the banks of the river, they wore facial masks on the backs of their heads, unnerving the man-eaters. And this is a predator not easily fooled. Professional hunters called in previously to kill man-eating tigers wrote that the great cat's hearing is so acute that before beginning the hunt, they would trim their nose hairs, lest they give themselves away with fife-like breathing.

In the Americas, the cat of many names: cougar, mountain lion, panther, painter, catamount, puma ranges all the way from Canada to Chile. At the very tip of South America, in Chilean Patagonia, while hosting an episode of Outdoor Life TV's "EarthWise," I learned that there the puma's presence remains pronounced, as well. At the turn of the century most of Chile's southernmost Region XII, "The Region of Last Hope" (last land before Cape Horn) was covered by immense sheep ranches. Each ranch employed one or two *leoneros*—whose job it was to track and kill marauding cats, especially destructive in the spring when the mother puma, instead of taking one sheep to abate her hunger, slaughtered an entire flock while demonstrating to her cubs how to hunt. In 1980 the killing of pumas in Chile was prohibited by law, although occasionally ranchers still retaliate for lost sheep. However, inside Torres del Paine National Park, a magnificent 935 square miles of towering granite horns; tidewater glaciers; undulating steppes; and deep blue lakes, the puma population was strong. Its main prey: the wild guanaco, a camilid relative to the llama free-ranged over the park's steppes and mountainsides. Even though guanacos are big of eye and long of eyelash, no Bambis these. The adults stand 5 feet tall and weigh 250 pounds. They were fond of chest-ramming, neck-wrestling, suddenly dropping down into steppe potholes for dust and dung baths, and communicated with weird humming and stacctato-like neighing sounds, including a bizarre, unimitatable mating noise called "orgling." No matter the activity, the herds never totally surrendered to their fun-and-games. With the tightly wound energy of animals accustomed to being preyed-upon, they continuously swung their large ears like radar-beacons and while grazing paused, mid-chew, to probe the air with elevated noses.

Wildlife ecologist William L. Franklin and his Iowa University research team began studying guanaco behavior in Torres Del Paine in 1976. After 9 years, Franklin and his team expanded their study to include the chief predator:

the Patagonian puma, the southernmost of 27 subspecies of cougars and one of the largest. At a remote cabin deep in the park we filmed an interview with Mike Banks, a young man holding down the research-fort alone. Just like a stripped-down sourdough's cabin in Alaska, the space was small; the views out the window immense. Creature comforts were gladly exchanged for close encounters with exotic wildlife. Guanaco family portraits papered the walls. Towering condor feathers dwarfed a jar. The host served a lunch of homemade bread as fluffy and sweet as cake.

After we ate, Mike placed a puma skull on the table. He swiveled the jaws open and closed. Four canine teeth as long as daggers pierced the air. "There are 13-18 pumas in the park. The adults weigh about 150 pounds and can move in bursts of 40 mph when charging guanacos." He then showed us a guanaco skull—or what was left of it. "Of 1,000 guanaco skulls we've studied, 1/3 had puncture wounds from pumas, so this is a very active predator in the park."

Many of the Iowa University field-researchers go years following the guanaco herds without seeing a puma. Mike Banks is the embodiment of "beginner's luck." His very first day out with the guanacos he spotted what, at first, he thought to be a kitten. Then when his eyes adjusted to the immense landscape, the puma that he had walked by now fully "materialized" out of the scrub. He looked directly into its inquisitive amber eyes and was hooked.

Now he didn't have to go far to find them. As we were leaving I noticed a battered metal bowl in the meadow alongside the cabin. It was horribly bent and twisted. "What on earth did *that*?" I asked.

"Puma," Mike replied, kicking the twisted metal with his shoe. "I set out grapes for the fox to eat, but a puma came by that night—not only ate the grapes but totally destroyed the bowl. They have amazing power in their jaws!"

TV shoots seem predestined to either succeed or fail, soar or plunge. Either nothing goes right from the onset and only worsens from there or everything falls into place as effortlessly as checking off a Wish-List or the daily shot-sheet. The talents and chemistry of the crew have much to do with how things proceed. On the Patagonia shoot, we had a very balanced mix. There was Rob, the young director, an edgy, high-strung New Yorker with his butt on the line: this being his big chance, very first show. He was constantly saying over and over, rapid-fire to the videographer: "Enrique, didja get the shot?! Did you get it, *didja*?!?!" Enrique, from Caracas, Venezuela and with the same swarthy good looks, cocksure confidence and deep, stentorian voice as fellow countryman Fernando Llamas, straightened up from the camera booming forth the same riposte: "ARE YU KIDDING ME! *UN—BAH—LEEEEEFV-ABULL!!*" Then there was Ron, the sound man: very quiet, steady and an equipment expert who kept combing, with a wire brush, his long microphones covered in dog-hair covers that muzzled the incessant, howling winds. It was really Enrique who was the heart of our team. He backed up his boasts, for when we watched the dailies in the hotel room late each night—his footage *was* unbelievable! Unlike many cameramen who work only set hours and never go the extra mile—Enrique shot around the clock and didn't hesitate to sprint all-out, uphill or have us grab his legs while he leaned out an open window of the careening van with a camera that he mortgaged his house for—for nature and film-making wasn't a job: it was his life's passion . . . along with the "fairer sex." An extreme extrovert and absolutely fearless, he would approach women in airports, hotel lobbies, hiking trails, churches and temples; and within five minutes have their phone numbers and a date—along with a coy wave and blown kiss as he sauntered away!! Our guide from The Explora Lodge, the most remote hotel in the world, was Giovanna Ranieri, a devastatingly beautiful half-Chilean and half-Italian woman. Clearly, Enrique was smitten but she was well-practised in fending-off the advances of Latin-lovers. Whenever she was around, which was quite often, Enrique would none-too-subtly air his intentions by singing the Spanish song: "*Cuando, Cuando?*" ("*Tell me when will you be mine/ Tell me Cuando, Cuando . . . Cuando???*") We then all picked up the infectious melody and were soon suporting Enrique's cause by coming-in on the chorus: "*Cuuuuuuan— do?*" Giovanna just rolled her almond eyes . . . . Finally, unable to bear her refusals any longer, the fourth morning with a long day ahead of us, Enrique playfully said to her in the van, "Gio, if you don't fall in love with me today, then—" he paused to cast down his gaze: "Then all the film I shoot will be underexposed . . . ." At last, she smiled!

On a tight schedule, the next three days we drove, hiked and rode horseback all throughout the vast park; the filming continuing to be (as if Enrique bent it to his will): *UN—BAH—LEEEEEFV-ABULL!!* The glaciers calved colossal icebergs; not one but dozens of Andean condors, the largest raptors in the world with ten-foot wingspans were perfectly back lit and spiraling in the thermals like feathered 747s; a young, fledgling eagle played "tag": continuously dive-bombing and extending its legs at the last second to slap at the ears of a galloping guanaco; *El Viento*, 100 mile-an-hour winds tore wraithlike spirits off a thunderous back-country waterfall; a fiery sunrise torched the soaring granite horns crimson, giving credence to the region's original name: "Tierra del Fuego."

As we bombed over the park's dirt roads, intermittently we saw Mike sitting like Buddha amidst a guanaco herd. Once we stopped for an hour, hoping to film a puma, but the biologist soon waved us on, shaking his head at our 'checklist' impatience.

The last morning, as we were packing up the endless camera equipment in front of the lodge, Mike's battered pickup truck came speeding over the dirt road, screeching to a halt in front of us. He stuck his head out of the window wide-eyed and grinning ear-to-ear: "You guys missed it! This morning—the closest ever! I was just walking toward a guanaco herd, when *wham*, a puma charged right by me—actually slammed into my leg as it went after a guanaco! It was stalking behind, using me like a tree!!!"

Still resonating with that rare, wild event, Mike explained that he didn't feel in danger, being exposed to stalking pumas on the vast Patagonian plains; that maybe in an Edenistic environment with plenty of prey around and nature's balance unbroken, the great cats viewed man as just another "tree." It made me wonder that if in the very few remote places where wild animals haven't been exposed to man's bad side: shot at or had their wide-ranging habitat stifled by a cancerous human growth—then maybe wild animals are not 'wild' at all. After a hungry Patagonian puma bounced off Mike Banks, I could no longer scorn the entire species, for the cougar that killed Barbara Schoener was a different animal in an entirely different place.

On weekends when Latimer had family obligations, I drove up alone to join a group run along the most challenging section of the Western States trail. Pulling into the tiny mountain hamlet of Forest Hill or the Michigan Bluff checkpoint, by 9:00 a.m. Saturday morning there were a dozen runners stretching, filling water bottles with strange-colored concoctions or night owls with bloodshot eyes stiffly extricating themselves from vans or campers that they had slept in. Talk would be about muscle groups; electrolytes; vitamin supplements. Ultra runners understand the body the way a mechanic knows a high-performance engine. Amazing how "in-tune" you get when you are testing the physical limits on a daily basis. You actually hear your body speak out: requesting specific satiation for its deep-seated needs.

I often thought that a sociologist or psychologist could do an interesting study on the subculture of ultra runners. In the era of instant-gratification and big-payoff, why would this small (but growing) group give so much time and effort, subsume their entire lives to repeatedly run races that rarely made the papers and rewarded them with nothing more than the effort, itself?

Reinhold Messner, the premier alpinist of the 20th Century explains: "How many of us suffer in one form or another from the fact that our energies and skills are not being properly utilized? More than ¾ of all people in the Industrial West, say the statisticians. I don't know. I only know that under-realisation of the bodily and emotional resources promotes a cancer of the soul, an unlived life. There are many ways one can safeguard oneself against this: Climbing Big

Walls, for example, is one . . . . "

Or running ultra marathons.

Many ultra runners are responsible professionals: dentists, doctors, nurses, lawyers, engineers, policemen, publishers, computer programmers, but, in spirit they are all mavericks, misfits—only able to step into the harness of the 9-5 workaday world because on weekends and vacations they range free, far into the mountains under their own power. Most feel they were born a couple centuries too late; really belonged with Lewis & Clark's "Corps of Discovery," the first party to explore wild America or should have been Pony Express riders (some of these enduros would probably feel sorry for the horses and run the mail just as fast on their own backs)! Favorite books discussed out on the trails were Louis L'Amour westerns (my brother, Scott, took the nickname "Hondo" after the L'Amour hero); Vardis Fisher's *Mountain Man* was spoken of with awe, as was the related film, "Jeremiah Johnson"; *The Way of The Peaceful Warrior* by Dan Millman was read, reread and passed around until copies crumbled. Preferred music was U2's heroic album, "Joshua Tree," and before training runs Bob Seger and his Silver Bullet Band boomed out of car stereos and portable boom-boxes with the powerful anthems of "Against The Wind" and "Like a Rock" supplying soulful inspiration and running impetus.

There was great sympathy for the Donner party as we ran over some of the very passes they had expired on. Modern-day mountain men and women, we were training on the very same trails and trade routes that Indians tribes originally traveled; through much the same wild country—with the entire Western States trail stretching from the Sierra Mountains east to the prairies. Later came the gold prospectors whose encampments, such as "Rucky Chucky" and "Last Chance" are the same checkpoints used today along the route of The Western States Ultra Marathon.

Training in protected wilderness and park lands, how marvelous to be able to run across land that is unfenced, uninterrupted—wild rather than enfeebled. I'd fall in with a group and out we'd go in the early morning, chattering away as we pushed through the steep canyons—stopping midday in a pocket meadow where a friend had driven-in ahead with food and drink. On the way back we'd hydrate at a natural spring burbling out of a rock wall: ice-cold from snow runoff and tasting of granite, pine needles and lightning. As I sucked the sweet elixir and splashed it against my sun-burnt face and fatigued legs, I thought *This is the "Yardstick"—how I want to always live my life: with water tasting like a great reward!* Sometimes I added tears of joy to that mountain stream, feeling so happy and overwhelmed by nature.

Those late-spring mountain runs, with your actual race comfortably anchored months away on the distant horizon—guarding against over-training you went a good distance, 'fur piece,' but at a leisurely pace: catching up on winter, flatland marathon and 50-miler results; discussing the merits of a new miracle drink, energy bar, the latest bota-belt or trail running shoes. Those early season runs were times to shake down your gear and buildup your stamina slow and sure.

Then six weeks out from a 100 miler, I'd really push it: running two 40 milers in the high country back-to-back, Saturday and Sunday. Saturday night I stayed in nearby Grass Valley with the artist Tim Bowles, whom I called "Mother Nature's Son."

For centuries, great paintings have stimulated and inspired mankind and long ago, from the cave walls on, the artist was revered as a magician who shaped reality in a sacred and magical manner. Tim is such an artist for his wildlife paintings approach the supernatural.

I met him at a small showing of his works in the Napa Valley and was staggered. Here was a shaman: a chrome-domed, red wooly-bearded hippie trembling in the public shower of compliments. I said nothing to him—instead holding out my arms and hugging him.

A few days later, I visited his tiny cabin at the edge of his father's property in the foothills of the Sierras. In selecting works for the show, his entire *ouevre* was exposed inside the cabin. It was like entering a pocket Eden, with the Animal Kingdom alive on the walls. Using watercolors, he created paintings that look as tight and precise as oils. In "Mountain Goat" the beast's wind-blown fur took your breath away. "The only way you could paint that fur; know that yellow-white and texture is if you are a goat, *yourself!*" I said in amazement. His "Red-Tailed Hawk," wings unfurled, showed the exact red and russet color combinations and the texture of its feathers brushed softly upon your eyes. "Snowy Owl" was depicted in mid-flight: a Lord of the Arctic peering down with a predatory gaze that made you thankful you weren't a lemming!

"The first thing I paint is the eye," Bowles explained. To see the entire painting I have to start with the bird's eye. Then it's as if I'm taken over; disappear in the process. I don't create the bird—it comes through on its own."

I picked up "Herd of Fur Seals," a small drawing of eighty-six seals. He spent more than *six hundred hours* forming the lifelike herd, dot by dot with an .06 rapidiograph pen. At a recent show, after Richard Sloan, a best-selling wildlife artist, picked up the drawing and studied it closely, he said to Bowles, "It's beautiful, but you're crazy!"

Bowles always knew he wanted to be an artist. "In grade school I took the desk by the window with north light so I could draw birds in my notebooks. At home, I started looking through a set of encyclopedias and got no further than 'B'—discovering birds. They were illustrated by Arthur Singer and I mimicked his style. I spent all my free time up in the trees watching birds." As an adult Bowles took a job driving a forklift, but would get up at 3:00 a.m. to draw for five hours before going to work. He quit his job after a year, and hiked all the way from California to Colorado and like John Muir, spent six months wandering in the mountains.

"I had no money or food and came close to dying," Tim recalled, "but I found my purpose."

Bowles came down from the mountains, from his Vision Quest knowing his purpose: to devote his life to painting, to show others the power and magic of animals; the beauty of the earth. He painted twelve hours a day, giving birth to a tremendous outpouring of animal scenes and landscapes. In 1974, he sold his first painting, of a peregrine falcon. The appearance of the peregrine in his art signaled an important change in his life.

Hiking on Mt. St. Helena in the Napa Valley on a spring morning, Bowles spotted a male peregrine falcon. For the next four hours, he watched through a spotting scope as the bird soared and plummeted past the female on the nest, repeating the sequence again and again. It was the courtship flight of the, then, 12th know pair of nesting pure peregrine falcons in California.

The next day, the U.S. Fish & Wildlife Service drove Bowles back up the mountain with his steamer trunk full of supplies. He set up a primitive camp, moving his blind closer and closer, until by the tenth day he was able to observe all the falcons rarely seen movements. Through the lengthening days, Bowles kept his eyes fixed to the scope and recorded everything he saw. Over the next three springs, watching the same pair, he recorded more than three thousand hours of observations, some of the falcon activities seen for the first time. The experience transformed him. At the top of the mountain, in the heat and the silence, Bowles lived out beyond himself—inside the falcons. He came to understand every nuance of their movements, could predict what they would do, and felt their thundering flights as if they were his own. "It was the best time of my life," he said. "I woke up every morning knowing I was going to learn more about the falcons. That time was the pinnacle for me—I've never felt closer to nature."

The emotional experience of living with the peregrines was captured in Bowles painting, "Grandfather," a tribute to the North American Indian combining totemic elements with the symbol of infinity: an elongated figure eight, the pattern the artist discovered in which the falcons fly.

"Someday I'll have a studio up in the Yukon with animals all around and no one will be able to find me unless they're good trackers. I want the work to be famous and myself to be unknown. The paintings are spiritual—putting my name on them is the hardest part."

Occasionally, Tim tore himself away from painting to sell prints at weekend art shows, but money meant little to him. For the honor of being in his company, I'd arrive with sacks of groceries, bottles of wine, secondhand running shoes. His eyes crossed from ten hours at his easel, and bone-tired from my long run in the Sierras, but both of us effusive of spirit—we'd cook up some grub, down a jug of vino and talk deep into the night. His single-minded intensity about birds and art changed my life. He showed that finding your passion in this life is all that really matters—everything else grows out of that. Tim Bowles is a living embodiment of what the naturalist John Burroughs wrote: "If you want to see birds, you must first have birds in your heart."

After an exceptionally hot and strenuous run I pulled into Tim's place one afternoon, downing a gallon of water and wanting more—through the pores. I lingered long in the shower . . . .

"Michael, come here—QUICK!" Tim called from outside.

I hurried out of the bathroom, wrapping a towel around my waist. Unbeknownst to me, Bowles had just filled a dozen bird feeders along the back wall and roof of his cabin, as he did every day, precisely at 6:00 p.m. Exiting the bathroom, I heard a loud hum. *A power line down?* Then behind the building, I stepped out amidst a feeding frenzy, into the direct line of fire. I stopped, swept into a dream: A hundred hummingbirds were zooming in for dinner, filling the air with blurs of ruby red; swabs of iridescent blue and scintillating green. They alighted on the yellow towel around my waist, buzzed my ears and lifted my hair. It was beyond beautiful. I felt like an Aztec priest—with only an artist/shaman like Bowles capable of orchestrating such a gift.

After the hummers gorged, moving on as quickly as they appeared, Tim gandy-danced in front of me. "Wow, man! What a painting *that* will make!!"

Totally recharged and inspired, I'd leave Tim's cabin early the next morning to hook up with another group of ultra runners training incessantly in the spring and early summer along the Western States trail. In between visits, just knowing he was up there, painting in 'Bird Land' was comforting—as if he steadied the world in its wayward wobble: Bowles, at his easel balancing environmental destruction, like cloistered monks shut away on mountain tops cleansing sins.

Driving up to Michigan Bluff in the fresh mountain morning, knowing I was going to run all day and make new friends along the way was exhilarating! I joyfully crooned sad Hank Williams songs at the top-of-my-voice while swerving around hairpin turns on tread-bare tires. In my early-thirties I was still broke; owned nothing of value, but on mornings like this felt like I possessed all the riches of the world.

One Sunday I fell in with a group that was mostly women. Asking if you could join them, they looked you over head-to-toe, as if you were naked (which you nearly were) to see if you were a real runner or a "hanky-panky" man . . . . One lady stepped forward extending her hand, "Hi, I'm Tess. Sure, come on—if you can keep up!"

Tess Porter exemplified the term "free-spirit." She was a nurse, a high burnout profession, so she could find work just about anywhere. She migrated around the country in a truck with a camper shell or took short-term leases on apartments, with her permanent base a teepee hidden in the wilds of Vancouver Island, Canada. In her late-thirties, she dated a string of 'boy-toys' long before Madonna even invented the term.

No matter how tired I was, for the last half-mile I always tried to kick it in—not to race or beat anyone, but to establish the habit of always finishing up strong. At the end of the hot, arduous 20 mile canyon run our entire group was slagged. As was my custom, with the end in sight, I started to sprint. As I swung out wide and away from everyone to signal that this was a solitary challenge, I felt another runner zoom up on my shoulder. In a split-second an old competitive and chauvinistic remnant that I thought was long-gone, reared its ugly head: *Can't let a girl beat me!* Tess Porter surged ahead. I tapped the last fumes in my tank and regained the lead. Then she put the hammer down and won going away . . . .

One of the many benefits of the coed runs was learning about women from a very different perspective. Starting with segregated gym classes in elementary school, rarely do men get to share athletic endeavors with women. Sure, we workout side-by-side at health clubs, but rarely really 'bust-a-continuous-gut' together. One of the biggest surprises was that out on the mountain trails, as strange as it may sound, I learned that exercise is more likely to get a woman aroused than a romantic dinner. Approach these same females in normal everyday circumstances; even wine-and-dine them and you're either turned down flat or the 'knocking of boots' postponed until she "gets to know you better." However, after running just a few hours together out on the trails, many of the ultra ladies were darn-near rapacious. It was physical accomplishment as aphrodisiac; their own feel-good endorphins helping to spark erotic flames.

I thought of the old vapid expression: "Women don't perspire, they glow"— when females were put-off by normal body functions in that neurotic Victorian era of willingly wearing wasp-waist corsets and swooning to their beds for days with the "vapors." None of that from these liberated, kick-ass gals. Their very perspiration, pouring sweat was what made them glow and glisten. One of the most erotic, breathtaking images I've ever seen was right after a tough training run: watching a single bead of sweat travel so slooowly . . . down over Julie's sculpted, nut-brown thigh . . . *"Wagh!"*—like a melting pearl. Sportswriter Heywood Bruin wrote: "Sweat is the cologne of accomplishment." The 'perfume,' as well!

During those training runs, I saw female sexuality in its most raw and potent forms. I saw that far more erotic than a woman spreading her legs in some gyno-porn magazine, those same legs, carrying her vast distances, opened a deeper floodgate of sexuality. At the end of the day, turned inside-out from the colossal effort, these women's very spirits soared out through their pores. Back at Forest Hill, as we pulled coolers out of our cars to get at food and drink, I saw women as if for the very first time: Awash in sweat; hair all matted; tattooed high-and-low with trail mud; bleeding at the knee from a downhill fall—their smiles and crystal-clear eyes flashed around like klieg lights on opening night.

This was Woman at her most primal and powerful, and the effect was devastating. In the presence of men, their concern was moving over mountains, not with the petty frivolity of *"Ooooh, look at my hair!"* or *"My make-up is suuuch a mess!!"* (And gone were the prevalent body image problems plaguing nearly the entire female gender: *"My thighs are so fat!"* *"If I could just lose these last ten pounds!!"* or the serious, widespread devastation of bulimia and anorexia.) No, these were women with bodies honed by exercise not extreme denial. After a mountain run these sleek gals ate, guilt-free, with the lusty gusto of linebackers and since food was "their friend"—never put on a pound. Without the artificial masquerade, for the first time, I saw females unbound and fully juiced. No damsels in distress or coyly playing by *The Rules* to trap Mr. Right, rather these were women being true to themselves: unafraid to be real and as strong or stronger than men, and sacrificing none of their femininity in the process— actually increasing it by having the courage to display it at its most unadorned, molten core. Like splendid animals, totally unconscious of their beauty, the force and purity of their *élan vital* took my breath away.

Many a date on Friday evenings, I'd been previously blessed to see feminine perfection walk down the stairs and into my car, but some of the most alluring women I've ever dated have been out on the trails—clad not in DKNY, Manolo Blanik and "Obsession," but in blood, sweat and pine needles. And running together accelerates the courtship process. No need for a guy to wait 3-4 dates for his 'trial-period' to end. Running together on the trails: your proving-ground has just been compressed, your true nature revealed to a potential paramour over 30 miles by what you say; or when you are both totally fatigued, by the inner mettle you reveal. At the end of the day, many a male ultra runner has galloped off into the sunset, hand-in-hand with a lady he met just a few hours earlier—but with the women usually doing the initial bidding, (e.g.), Tess Porter, right after kicking my booty, made it clear that she wouldn't mind seeing it "in action" again, later that night!

Running has to be the most erotic of sports. You're wearing very little clothing, muscles are contracting; breath rising and falling; the skin flush with blood. Look at marathoners' faces as they finish and it's a fine-line between distinguishing agony from ecstasy. A photographer friend took finish-line photos of marathoners' faces. As I looked at the close-up prints, revealing no traces of their actual origin, I saw visages not in pain, but totally orgasmic: head-back, skin aglow, teeth-bared through rapturous grins—the 26 mile finishers looking to be at the very peak of orgasm, what the French call "the little death." The only change the photographer made was to show the faces horizontally instead of vertically. She submitted the runners' portraits in a photo-contest and won first-prize for the "Eroticism" category!

In training for an ultra marathon it's not the number of miles you compile per week, but the quality of those miles, and 'quality' means hills. After the long training runs up in the Sierras on the weekends, midweek I'd drive an hour or so around the Bay Area to ascend the gentler slopes of Mt. Diablo, Mt. Tamalpais or Mt. St. Helena in the Napa Valley, working up above the vineyards when at harvest, the "Crush," you'd get inebriated just breathing the air; chugging past the site of Robert Louis Stevenson's cabin (where he researched *The Silverado Squatters*) up to the summit where Tim Bowles' peregrine falcons nested and occasionally jetted overhead.

Or the phone would ring and it would be one of my absolute heroes, Galen Rowell, calling from Yosemite: "Michael, let's run Half Dome!"

"What? When!"

"In a few hours—first light. Leave now; flash your lights twice when you pull into the campground; we'll go at dawn!"

It was a five hour drive but I gladly hopped to it—would have run all that way on foot to be with Galen Rowell. Growing up in Berkeley, California, with a city youth spent as a hot-rodder and hooligan; and cutting his hands on every rock face in Yosemite every spare day or weekend, he eventually sold an auto repair business, giving himself one year to try to turn a private hobby into a public profession: succeed as a photojournalist. He beat his self-imposed deadline with months to spare, completing his first major magazine assignment: a cover story for National Geographic on rock climbing in Yosemite.

The early '60's was the "classical era" of climbing in Yosemite. Many impoverished rock bums that Galen pioneered first ascents with turned out to be the founders of very successful companies: Yvon Chouinard of Patagonia; Doug Tompkins of The North Face and Esprit; Leo Lebon of Mountain Travel—all first formulating their "business plans" on the challenging Big Walls of Yosemite. Galen grew with them—filling their catalogs with jaw-dropping landscape photos; field-testing equipment; and leading adventure travelers on expeditions around the world.

He's participated in more than 1,000 climbs, including many first ascents and has made over 100 journeys to the mountains and wild places of Nepal, India, China, Tibet, Africa, Canada, New Zealand and Patagonia. When Robert Redford was looking for a guide for a month-long trek in the Himalayas, he chose Galen Rowell.

His photographs have appeared in numerous national magazines and he's shown in all the major photography and art galleries around the world. He is the author of a dozen text-photo books, including my two favorites, *Mountain Light* in which he gives away all the secrets behind each dazzling shot and *In The Throne Room of The Mountain Gods*. (Is there a better title for a book?!)

In person, with the compact build of an astronaut, Galen Rowell exudes *purpose*. He's a photographer with inexhaustible energy and enthusiasm, for he has answered his calling: showing that the ultimate life is when the life and art are one.

In what seemed only minutes after I crawled into a sleeping bag in my Honda Hatchback, I heard a door slam, and there was Galen strapping a camera into his chest pack. I rolled out of the rack already dressed in running clothes. As we stretched in Yosemite's icy air, my pulse quickened. Even though Galen was a decade older, I had to be in peak condition and even then I was hard-pressed to keep up with one of the world's top high altitude climbers.

As we moved up through the trees . . . the light increasing like an organ note, we caught up on our lives. Galen was a bit battered having just survived a wild and woolly float trip down the Bio Bio River in Chile. The outfitter had been shaky from the start and, sure enough, the flimsy raft flipped in the fierce rapids. Barbara, Galen's gorgeous wife, had all her top teeth knocked out against a rock; Galen, unconscious, spun away down river and would have drowned if an Indian who happened to be where no one went—pulled him up onto land! Then, somehow, Barbara drinking her own blood, flew them out in her small plane that they had flown-in all the way down from the U.S. That was just last week . . . . The week before that they were in Antarctica photographing penguins, or the North Pole aboard a Soviet nuclear icebreaker . . . . The Rowells cover more ground in a year than most of us in ten lifetimes.

Our talk was cut by intermittent thunder, then a constant roaring rip-rap that turned into Vernal Falls. We slip-slid across a wet wooden bridge and just a few yards below, the boiling cataract plunged over a granite lip—free-falling hundreds of feet through high air . . . the roar drowning our words. We then ran through rainbows—flaring and arcing in the rising mists like fireworks. Galen's camera clicked with every step. That pocket plateau was nature's perfection: the sun on tall trees, tarting the air with warm pine resin; white clouds caught in the tree tops like cotton candy; the surging waterfall releasing a storm of ions that inflated the spirit with cool wafts of well being. The place was the very apex of life. It was like the entrance to Asgard, the home of the gods in Norse mythology, reached by crossing a bridge of rainbows. We emerged from the roaring, chromatic mists soaked, slaphappy; feeling born again.

We then hit the toughest section totally refreshed, sailing up steep pitches, pushing off giant tree roots, pirouetting atop pointed rocks—digging in, pushing on up and then we were exposed, out in space, skirting a waist-high cable rising up the flank of granite. We ran on unaided—hands flailing forward; and thighs afire.

Suddenly, no more 'up': Atop Half-Dome, hearts hammering, we stopped and looked around at what Edward Abbey called: "The place where a man should count himself lucky to make one pilgrimage in a lifetime. A holy place." Below were the awesome granite massifs of El Capitan, Cathedral Rock, Three Brothers, Royal Arches, Clouds Rest. In shining air, rock was rising; water falling in sheer verticality. *"Wagh!" "Wagh!!"*

We then swooped down, down, down the trails like two spiraling hawks . . . . Reaching the valley floor, we sliced out across the day in progress—jumping from a bridge into the icy Merced River. Galen then combed his hair and went off to a park meeting. I drove home singing.

I first met Galen at one of his photo seminars—along with twenty other students in a 4-wheel drive caravan back behind Bishop, California, on the Sierra Nevada's eastern slope, following Galen Rowell through a maze of dirt roads—stopping abruptly to photograph a herd of high cirrus clouds, snap portraits of Indian petroglyphs and climb through a massive boulder field for overview vistas.

A gusting wind stirred the sharp scent of sage as we rumbled in separate clouds of dust following our leader, whom by unanimous consent we nicknamed Galen *Romell*—"The Desert Fox."

Galen is known for his portraits of mountains, high-altitude snow and ice, but we were about to add an opposite element. From the southern horizon, smoke billowed across the sky, a purple, then orange mass veiling the snowy Sierra.

Galen didn't stop until we were in the midst of the fire. It was late afternoon but dark as night, as a legion of photographers fanned out across the road, burning film as fast as the fire. Galen was running, looking for *the* shot as he put a Nikon F3 on a battered tripod near a barbed-wire fence, attached a zoom lens and shot away. "Fill the frame!" he shouted to nearby students on the verge of asking questions.

It resembled a war zone, with trees bursting into fiery corpses, acrid smoke and adrenaline filling the air. Feeling the heat, some of the students forgot about taking pictures, worrying "What's next? What's the plan?"

With a gleam in his eyes Galen turned to the class and asked, "Should we go through?" He answered his own question with a smile, and the class dashed pell-mell back to their vehicles. My then-wife, Ronna Nelson and I jumped into our jeep with Ronna insisting that we turn around and break the security of the group to photograph a fresh inferno farther down the road.

By the time she quickly shot a few frames, the caravan was gone. We sped back into the black smoke, passing a fire truck, screeching to a halt at a stop sign. *Did they turn right or left?* We went right . . . and it turned all wrong as the wind shifted the fire, burning the oxygen out of the air moments before flames roared over the jeep . . . .

My red-haired, Aries wife, immersed in her astrological element, never lost her cool—slamming the stick into reverse and flooring the accelerator. We zoomed back to life, again reaching the stop sign; clinging to it now like island castaways.

Then ahead on the roadway, like mirages, we saw a crowd of men in yellow slickers. A bit shaken, Ronna and I had switched seats. I drove over to them. Ronna rolled down the window and asked, "Could you please tell us how to go to town?"

They all looked at each other and smiled. "Get out of that jeep and I'll show you how to 'go to town!'" one man said, making an obscene gesture with the pole of his shovel.

"GET AWAY FROM THOSE MEN!" a fireman said, running to us; waving a pistol. "They're convicts—convicted felons—and they haven't seen a woman in years."

Fire to the right, aroused convicts to the left—so we stayed in the middle, Ronna pushing fear away by continuously pressing the shutter on her Nikon.

"Your best bet is to follow our fire truck. We're going on through," said the warden. "Bishop is only two miles away. Stay right on our bumper."

We made the end run, following our interference. Clear of the fire, we drove north on Highway 395, then followed a road up into the Sierras to the parking lot of the Rock Creek Winter Lodge where the photography seminar started. The rest of the group was there waiting.

Dazed and shaken, we walked away from the jeep, wearing the smell of charred sagebrush amidst snow banks and frigid, alpine air. Surrounded by the group, we groped for words to describe all we had seen.

"Did you get the shots?" Galen inquired.

Ronna and I put our arms around each other, nodded and smiled—having received our "baptism under fire"—knowing full well the fear and addiction of being front-line photographers.

You can always tell a fledgling photographer, for upon seeing a great picture they'll immediately ask: "What kind of camera do you use?" Galen always had a string of the latest Nikons around his neck, oftentimes systems that were months away from being in the stores: Nikon Inc. field-testing cutting-edge equipment with Rowell, who in just one short hegira into the nearby Sierras would take new gear the full range of 'Fire and Ice'—but a Galen Rowell photograph isn't about cameras. It's about eyes and insight. The man has those Pablo Picasso eyes: that same wide-angle and open aperture gaze that takes in and transforms the world. And like Picasso, his art originates deeper: from what's behind those orbs. Rowell's best images are created because he first pre-visualizes them and then projects them onto film, into reality. He sees a masterpiece in his mind's eye (focused by thousands of climbs and campsites; scientific and philosophical readings), and then shows up ahead of time waiting—to click the shutter, to match 'inner light' with outer luminosity and an earthbound subject.

It's in the filaments behind his eyes and in the fibers of his legs. Where another shooter is too out of shape to hike a few yards uphill from the car, Galen is sprinting all-out across a Tibetan plateau to get ahead of a flaring rainbow he knows full-well will soon strike the Potala Palace . . . .

Going back in time, to "new legs" and through the strata of building-up those legs to this point worked! Miles had rolled by while I was lost in thought. My legs are as sore as ever, but we have progressed well beyond the barrier, the "Wall" of 80 miles. A reporter asked me just before the start of Angeles Crest: "How long have you been training for this?" "All my life," I answered without hesitation. And I now run *with* all that life—for a 100 mile ultra marathon taps into every formative fiber of mind, body and soul. The total *gestalt* of a person's life is grist for this grinding mill.

For most of the race I'm able to dwell in the moment, revel in the basic hypnotic rhythm of breath and heartbeat. But now, near exhaustion, more often I set my legs on automatic-pilot and depart the present, seeking the comfort and distraction of the past. Like having your life flash in front of your eyes when threatened with death, "dying" slowly now produces the same effect, only the speed of the filmstrips slow down in the overworked projector.

This deep into the race I now feel relief. One of my biggest worries coming in was if my blood: the engine "oil" would holdup under the stress, for my oxygen-delivery system had once been severly damaged—nearly all of my red blood cells destroyed. As we run on into the darkness, I return to Africa:

That splendid safari with the famed English guide, Robert Carr-Hartley, when Ronna and I brought over a group of Americans and we enjoyed the game parks of Kenya for three weeks, seeing wildlife up close and in great numbers. The only disappointment was that we didn't get to view the wildebeest migration in the Serengeti. There had been so much rain that year that the wildebeest stayed south with plenty of grass to eat. So much rain, standing water, puddles in all the camps . . . mosquitos everywhere. At the end of the safari we put everyone on the plane for home but Ronna and I stayed an additional day with appointments to interview leading African environmentalists who lived in Nairobi. That morning I awoke with a splitting headache and a feeling of overall malaise. The house doctor at the Norfolk Hotel in downtown Nairobi was puzzled by the symptoms. He thought it was the flu, but then sent us downtown for a blood test, saying that when he received the results he would come to our room. I told Ronna to go ahead and photograph the environmentalists—the interviews I could do later over the phone. She left reluctantly, sensing trouble.

I then tried to catch up in my journal, but couldn't concentrate. My mind was overpowered by intense, physical pain. I was on fire. I stripped off my clothes and lay down on the bed. Sweat rose out of every pore, pooled together, then fell off my body like rain. The sheets were soon soaked. Then when the fever broke, there were chills so severe that I shook the bed.

Then and there I knew I had malaria—nature's torture wrack. I had taken the daily preventative medicine but to no avail. There was a super-strain of mosquito immune to chloroquine. In a fit of black humor, I laughed: To be out in the African bush surrounded by large carnivores and man-eaters, only to be done in by a minuscule mosquito!

The fevers were absolutely frightening, but I tried to "go with the flow," welcoming the fever and sweat, knowing that runners, body builders and other habitual exercisers are sick far less than sedentary couch potatoes, due to creating a daily fever—one of the main benefits of working-out. When your body temperature is elevated and you sweat, you're burning away germs and illnesses, incinerating them in the furnace before they can set in and take hold. The old wives saying of "Feed a fever; starve a cold" is wise, for when sick, fever is the body's way of fighting-back when under attack, the front line of defense; main weapon for upping the ante against viral invaders. I knew it was malaria and knew it was serious by the rampaging fevers. I had to be under serious assault to have the furnace blasting so high. Progressively, the body turned the heat up a few degrees with each new attack by the malarial parasites imploding my blood cells. My fevered skin turned ice-cold towels lukewarm within seconds. My eyeballs felt like fried egg whites. I was sweating so profusely that the entire *mattress* was soon soaked . . . I wouldn't have been surprised to see flames burst from my fingertips. It was a very fine-line between fighting the micro-invaders and being totally consumed in the process.

The only saving grace in surviving the pain were the Fever Dreams. At the extreme peaks of the infernos, there then was a short respite, a plateau to cling to before sliding down into the pit of icy hills. For a few moments I was lodged on the paradisial plateaus, where 'inside' the agony I felt ecstatically happy. I saw the world as if never before: When I opened my eyes right after the fevers— it was as if everything in the hotel room, even though stationary, was in motion, vibrating at a molecular level that somehow I was able to witness. My eyes were able to see both normally and as if through a microscope and shift back and forth between the two perspectives. The dresser directly across from me was no longer solid wood—it was composed of particles, vibrating slowly. The very walls were now oscillating; and as they vibrated I saw loose openings in amidst the plaster. The glass mirror atop the dresser was whirling faster, in tighter patterns: like sand in a windstorm. I could restore the objects to solidity by simply wishing them so; then I would see everything as we normally accept it as being. It was like a veil had been removed (burned away?) and I was granted some sort of extrasensory perception. Near-death, I was provided a glimpse into what life was really made of. No external drugs were involved (they came later and when they did the fever dreams ceased, the burned-away clarity snuffed by narcotics to combat the malaria). I sensed that this new reality-pathway was paved with endorphins. The same natural brain chemicals that create the "runner's high" and have been proven to be 12x stronger than opium were now all enlisted, full strength in the fight against the ferocious fevers. It was probably why I was so attracted to ultra running, which gave me a daily dip into the endorphin stream. I now sensed that the life-or-death, elevated powers of these natural, internal drugs had something to do with it—"hinges" that flung open doors of perception.

I had long been a student of human potential, sensing that we are here for far more than the reality we've settled for. One of the cornerstones I tried to build my life on was the premise of the psychologist William James that we lead lives inferior to ourselves; only living a small part of the colossal life we are given.

Albert Einstein said that we only use a tiny part of our brain's immense capacity. What about a woman you read about every once in awhile, backing her car down the driveway, unfortunately, god forbid, pinning her unseen child beneath a wheel? The woman rushes out, small, petite; grabs the back bumper and lifts a 2-ton vehicle off her child, saving its life . . . . What of the doctor I read about in the newspaper: while playing tennis at a country club, heard the horrid sound of a head-on car crash on the outside road? He leaped a fence in one motion to come to the aid of traffic accident victims. After he was sure they were alive and in the competent hands of the ambulance paramedics, he turned to go back into the club—but the fence he just cleared was eight feet tall and 'slick-brick': without the slightest handhold . . . . What of the yogis of India who have performed miracles on the level of Jesus? In the 19th Century, Sadhu Hiradas was buried alive underground, sealed in a stone chest. When the guarded chest was opened six weeks later and the great yogi was examined by French and English doctors, he was declared dead. At that moment, Sadhu Hiradas blinked his eyes and came back to life.

Don't we all possess the powers to truly be Supermen and Superwomen? If so, why keep them only in reserve—why not exercise those powers on a daily basis?

We're meant for more! had long been my mantra while struggling to make money, pay bills, work jobs I disliked to buy time to write, commute two hours a day, etc., etc. Yet refusing to die under the daily pile of slag-and-dross, deep within glowed one bright mote: *More!*—never losing it's heat under the burned-out detritus of life. A high school teacher always admonished us with that common cliché: "The worst sin in the world is to have talents and not use them!" Words become clichés because they usually hold a grain of timeless truth. Don't we all have talents asleep within that we don't use? I don't mean specific talents to make a living, but the talents that make living worthwhile: the miraculous powers that make us divinely human, encoded into the very fabric of our beings— the real reasons why we are here.

What about the woodsman I knew in Canada who healed himself of cancer using only the powers of his mind; and was flown occasionally to Vancouver General Hospital to hypnotize patients in open-heart surgery who were allergic to anesthetic? One morning, at breakfast in his wilderness cabin, when I asked if he would show me how he healed himself; and how he guided patients through such a traumatic operation, at the very center of their beings without numbing drugs, Will Malloff led me in a state of light hypnosis (really my own letting go into self-relaxation). He then said he was placing a hot butter knife atop my bare arm. As soon as the metal touched flesh, he immediately snapped his fingers ending the trance and said to grab the knife. It was stone-cold and had been all the while—but there on my forearm was a perfectly formed burn-blister: The Power of Suggestion . . . The Power of the Human Mind. Is it any wonder where cancer comes from? It's all within us to decide: how high or low we want to go.

The man healed himself and others of cancer by burning the tumors away with mental laser energy (documented, in Will's case, by the head of Vancouver General Hospital who watched his chest tumor shrinking in size on the chest scanner). I learned from Will that the key is mental focus. Remember eating Crackerjack as a kid? Remember the toys hidden within (almost as good as the peanuts!)? My favorite was the small magnifying glass. I used to take it out into the backyard on sunny autumn afternoons to try to burn through leaves. I was successful only when I got the magnifier tilted at the exact, precise angle where it focused the sunlight into a concentrated beam—then, and only then, did that sweet smoke curl up from a tiny hole in the crisp leaf. Will said the 'sunlight' is comparable to our inner energy and the 'magnifying glass' is our mind.

How immune we are to the miracles that compose our own beings! If all the blood vessels in a single person were stretched end-to-end they would encircle the world . . . . In a single human cell there are 100,000 coded messages known as Genes. If the directions contained in all these genes were written down they would fill 10,000 volumes of the Encyclopedia Brittanica . . . . The most powerful super computer someday may be a container of human DNA, for just one pound of DNA molecules has more capacity than all the memory in all the computers ever made.

Why do we ignore the Miracle of Self—why search outside of ourselves: for the more powerful computer, the "Ecstasy" drug, when all of that and so much more is already hardwired within, where "The Kingdom of God is within you" (Luke 17:21). Where "Jesus saith, Ye ask who are those that draw us to the kingdom, if the kingdom is in Heaven? . . . The fowls of the air, and all the beasts that are under the earth or upon the earth, and the fishes of the sea, these are they which draw you, and the kingdom of Heaven is within you." (The Oxyrhynchus Papyri, Part IV, No. 654)

In the grip of a horrid disease, with death an increasing possibility—instead of pressing to renew my religion, an "insurance policy" I had long ago let lapse— I questioned Catholicism even more. The fevers burned everything down to clarity. The message of Jesus Christ was a simple one and one that I deeply believe in. It's man that has since corrupted Christianity by interjecting his own self-serving ego, greed, exclusivity—many Popes included. When I visited the Vatican I was appalled. If Jesus walked into the museums today, he might throw out all the gold carriages, gilded icons, all the plundered spoils from far-off Crusades and fling-out a few of their 'owners,' as well—toss them like the money changers from the temple; melt down all those showy riches and feed the poor.

And what of the lost years of Jesus, the young man who wandered through India, Nepal, Ladakh and Tibet (the biblical account that possibly was deleted by papal authority)? Why conceal his most formative years? (In the New Testament, Jesus is age 12 in the temple and then *zoom*—he's suddenly 30 at the River Jordan?) Was it among the eastern holy men, the yogis and sages that for 17 years Jesus perfected his Humanity by learning from other men how to exercise a common Divinity: learning to perform miracles? As Elizabeth Clare Prophet wrote in *The Lost Years of Jesus*: "And if we read between the lines and consider his extraordinary acts—most certainly not denying but fulfilling the laws of material and spiritual physics—it is also quite clear that he sought and attained adeptship over the elements and elemental forces as well as control of the heartbeat and body functions. And that he mastered the arts of biolocation and alchemy—observable later in his sudden appearances and disappearances, in his transmutation of ordinary water into the finest wine, and in his conversion of lukewarm 'omni directional' souls into one-pointed fiery devotees.

"All this he did and more, not as a god but in fulfillment of a known path of self-mastery, a natural soul-evolution unto the unleashing of the imprisoned splendor within . . . . "

Did what Jesus often do, in the most advanced manner, a God-given birthright open unto us all? Again, why the disbelief and fear of the treasure trove within? Why buy into worshipping something outside of ourselves: 'up in Heaven,' with all that space in-between corrupted by controlling ideologies based on exclusivity and hypocrisy—when the powers, the answers exist purely within us all, children of the same, indivisible, cosmic Over-Soul?

God is much too vast and unified a force to be conviently 'shrunk-to-fit' within so many splintered "We are the Chosen One(s)" religions—like sports fanatics each shaking an exaggerated, contentious foam-finger: "We're Number One!" All religions should be abolished if mankind is to have a chance at attaining worldwide peace, for religion, at it's very heart, is racism 'undercover': based on exclusivity and division. The two motivations that have killed more human beings throughout history are tribalism and religion, which political leaders then blend together and whip-up into the emotional froth of nationalism. "Holy War" is an oxymoron if there ever was one, yet most wars, from the Christian Crusades (sanctioned by the Pope) onward are conducted 'In The Name of God.'

Just as the astronauts first photos from space of "Earth Rising" showed there to be not a trace of arbitrary borders or dividing lines carving up the Earth into sovereign nations—there should also be no demarcations upon the spiritual terrain of the Earth's inhabitants.

Each and every human being is made of light, flaming directly from the divine fire. Why then is already having everything within—not enough? Why get entangled in the artificial constricts of religion—when every moment is a miracle; each breath a prayer?

As the Pueblo Indian potter, Popovi Da wrote: "To the white man, religion is a method, a system which he can employ . . . when necessary. But to us there is no word in our language for an isolated dogma: all we can say is that we have a way of life, and that this is life itself. If we fill our minds with pure materialism and accept a convenient religion, then the backbone of our way of life, of our perception of beauty, will be broken and we will disappear as unseen winds, gone . . . . "

And if a man or woman dared exercise that life outside organized religion: attempted to tap into his or her vast potential alone or with other kindred spirits, unshackled by sanctioned controls, the church denounced it as "the work of the devil"or witches to be burned at the stake or a nation of wild savages to be exterminated, or failing that—converted. Spiritual is to religion as freedom is to jail.

At the peak of yet another fever, I flung up my hand before my eyes. The outline of the fingers and hand were still there, but now I looked in on the very dance of life, a human hand shot-full of particles of light, *yes, go ahead; call them 'god-beams' for that's what you and everyone are made of!*—far whiter and brighter with energy than the inanimate objects around me. I thought of Walt Whitman's line: "I sing the body electric!" I felt so gloriously alive, and so directly connected to a spiritual Source that all I had done in my life and accepted as 'true' or 'real' was mere infancy compared to what I now knew to be possible! And those feelings probably saved my life, for I just *had* to survive, stick around to explore these new dimensions opening now before me. I then felt the strongest urge to get up and make a true "leap of faith": place my hand into the wall—suddenly knowing with absolute certainty that if I could only zap-up my overall vibration to be faster than the wall's atomic motion, I could pass right through!

Then, a knock on the door. The hotel physician, Dr. Shah, from India, stepped into the room wide-eyed and talking rapid-fire. "You have malaria and it is the worst kind—cerebral. It doesn't stay in your liver but goes after your brain. It's called 'kill or cure.' You have a 50-50 chance of living or dying. It's now a race against time."

He took my temperature: 103 degrees. Then a shot of Fansidar. "This will lower the temperature and buy you some time. When is your flight Home?"

"In a few hours."

"Good. You belong in a hospital right now, but I must tell you, the hospital here in Nairobi is not like those in America. It is somewhat primitive and I cannot guarantee you that every needle will be sterilized. AIDS is epidemic here now. With malaria you have a 50-50 chance. With AIDS—none. You are very fit and strong. Get on the flight and if you don't make it all the way home, you'll at least reach London where there's a very fine hospital."

Ronna returned from the photo shoots to find her worst fears confirmed. Dr. Shah gave her instructions on how to keep her husband alive: ice-cold towels during the fevers, blankets during the chills and water, water all the while to keep the patient hydrated. He then added: "The airline won't let you out of Africa if they know you have malaria. It's not contagious—but they don't want a death on their hands. Be careful."

The malaria parasite is a wicked creature. It attacks, withdraws, then attacks again. In a lull between battles, we left for the airport.

It was a 10-hour flight from Nairobi to London, 18 hours total to San Francisco. Our plan was to check my condition in London, then decide whether I could make it all the way home. We were optimistic until we boarded the plane. The flight was delayed. After an hour it was determined to be engine trouble. "A part is being flown up from Johannesburg," the pilot finally announced. We sat on the runway for a total of three hours; then the flight was canceled. We were bused back into Nairobi and put up at a hotel. We would be called when the plane was ready. In this race against time, at the 'Start,' I was already falling way behind.

A few hours later we were back at the airport to try again. There was one small hitch. I couldn't sit up. Under the siege once again from the malaria parasites, I felt as though all the destroyed red cells had turned my blood to sludge; the only way to get oxygen to my brain was to be horizontal. Sitting up straight I could feel my brain begin to suffocate. I had no choice but to surrender my pride—stretch out down on the cold, filthy floor, watching a wide array of sandals, shoes, and military boots step by my head as I struggled to keep my brain breathing.

Ronna reported that the flight was only half-full, so I could get three seats to stretch out across—if I could get past the customs officials. From my prone, pale and sweat-soaked appearance, clearly there was something wrong with me. On the spot, Ronna hatched a plan. I'd fake an ankle injury with my wife explaining that the severe strain was why I looked so pained—but then in my delirium I kept forgetting which ankle it was, alternately limping on both. As she talked fast, I slowly hobbled by them . . . then collapsed across three seats, steeling myself for the long flight—that then grew longer. This flight was inexplicably delayed an hour and a half, and the air-conditioning was not operating. In the stifling hot cabin, another wave of fever hit. And then something I have never seen before or since: The interior of the British Airways 747 was sprayed to kill all bugs trying to immigrate to England. *If only they knew what was incubating in row 24!* I thought as a man with a spray can walked by. Fever-maddened and recalling Kafka's "Metamorphosis," I upgraded the insect, picturing myself turning into a giant mosquito that terrorized the plane.

Finally we took off. Ronna kept me in both cold towels and warm blankets. About halfway into the flight, wracked horrendously by pain, I knew I was in trouble. In the semi-darkness, I reached out and grabbed the pant leg of a male flight attendant as he walked down the aisle.

"I have malaria. Do you know if there's a doctor aboard?"

"No, there isn't. I just checked the passenger list for someone else. But there is a flight attendant who used to be a nurse—I'll go get her."

After taking my temperature, she gave me a big horse pill that she guaranteed would lower the raging red line. When the stewardess returned, she pulled the thermometer out of my mouth and held it up to the light. Her eyes widened. She shook it and looked again.

"I can't believe it. The temp is even higher—105!" She stepped back for a moment, glanced at Ronna, then knelt down next to me. In a clipped English accent she whispered: "There are five hours until we land in London. You're going to have to fight for your life. I don't want to scare you but no one can help you now . . . Fight it. It will get very bad, but fight it. I'll check on you often. I'm going to tell the pilot to radio ahead to Heathrow."

Crying, Ronna held my hand. I squeezed back, wincing from yet another attack. Again fever raged as the parasites ravaged my bloodstream. The veins at my temples were distended like mangled wires. The back of my neck felt pole-axed. Then—chills so severe the tremors curled my feet and actually chipped my teeth.

To save my life, I reached for images . . . trying to visualize some sort of shield against the pain. I recalled an old invasion movie and made it my own. My brain was the castle and I had to keep the door closed to the invading army—but I was outnumbered and the barbarians were now slamming against my firm resolve with a battering ram. I felt the parasites right there against my brain and knew for certain that if the door opened a crack, I'd be finished.

In the darkening cabin and with the unchanging hum of the jet engines, time seemed suspended: 5 hours an eternity to endure.

I floated in and out of consciousness, and at 35,000 feet I had 'visitors.' Gerhard Kiesel, an adventurer who died trying to set a sailing speed record from California to Hawaii, a close friend who had 30,000 miles of blue water sailing under his belt was suddenly there. I saw him in my mind's eye: a vision who inspected my 'castle door' nodding his head. Then my father was next to me. I heard his living voice loud and clear in my ear: "Michael, you have the strength to make it. Take my strength too." I did—attaining confidence and peace.

I was jolted awake by the landing gear hitting terra firma. I opened my eyes to see Ronna.

"I'm alive . . . right?"

"Yes!" she said, laughing and crying at the same time. "But now we have to rush to the hospital."

Flashing lights in the night—speeding past stately palaces, hotels, rows of Victorian houses on rain-soaked streets . . . up a flight of stairs, taking one-at-a-time forever, then collapsing into a bed, surrounded on all sides by expert care. I let go, giving myself completely over to The Hospital For Tropical Diseases.

Malaria-carrying mosquitoes have killed more humans than all the wars combined. As many as 2.7 million people die annually, worldwide, from malaria, with children and the elderly especially vulnerable. One child dies of malaria every 12 seconds in undeveloped countries. Prior to the 17th Century, malaria ran rampant in the fever-ridden cities of Europe, claiming many lives each year. Alexander the Great died of it. The collapse of the Greek and Roman empires is partly attributed to it. Yet despite Hippocrates familiarity with malaria in the 5th Century B.C., for much of the modern era the cause of the disease was a mystery. The Italians in the 18th Century referred to the cause as *mal aria*, bad air. The African explorer Richard Burton thought it had something to do with sleeping in the moonlight. It wasn't until 1897 that an English doctor discovered that malaria was caused by mosquitoes. A cure had long proceeded the cause. In 1663, a Jesuit priest in the pharmaceutical forest of Amazonia learned from the Indians that an extract from the bark of the cinchona tree defeated fever. The Jesuit shipped quinine to England in time to save the life of Charles III, but not Oliver Cromwell, who did not trust the medicine of the Catholics.

Around the clock, this traveler (and former altar boy) swallowed mega-doses of quinine as if it were Holy Communion.

I was lucky, very lucky. I landed at the best place in the world to treat malaria. The Hospital for Tropical Diseases has been in service for more than a century, acquiring its expertise when mad dogs and Englishmen stayed out too long in the tropical sun, struggling to expand the British empire. If they didn't altogether expire in "The White Man's Graveyard," as Africa was then called, many pith-helmeted colonialists recovered in these same hallowed halls.

Located in a Gothic brick building on St. Pancras Way, the hospital has wooden floors, slightly slanted; old, ironclad radiators rumbling and hissing heat; window glass rippled from the long march of time. Not one beep or byte from computerized hardware . . . instead, a plenitude of TLC from a most knowledgeable staff.

It is also a teaching hospital. The morning of the second day, with the tree bark extract having delivered me from death's door, but with my temperature still sky-high and spleen fully swollen and protruding outward like a football, my physician stopped by and in his best bedside manner, asked if I would "mind terribly if a few of my students pop in for a visit tomorrow to examine your spleen? They only get to see such a thing in textbooks."

"Sure, Doc, what do I have to do?"

"Nothing. Just be yourself. A spleen like yours just doesn't come along very often," he said, delivering a sound two-fingered thump as if testing a melon for ripeness.

The next morning I awoke to find my spleen—an organ I had previously never given one single thought to—now the subject of a lengthy discourse by the good doctor to a group of med students all gathered around the bed, fresh-faced in white frocks. Amid the medical jargon, the gist of the message was that the spleen, along with the liver, are the body's two main filters, straining out harmful substances from the bloodstream. From it's swollen, ovoid shape, it was clear that my spleen was clogged—by a multitude of ravaged red blood cells.

The students then formed a single file line and under the doctor's (and my own) watchful gaze, they each stepped up and with both hands, studiously followed the spleen's protuberant shape. (The female students: all leggy blondes with the famed peaches-and-cream English complexions, seized me up downright proper. They giggled and I blushed, as the organ's location extended a bit "south-of-the-border.") And after they left, from the cumulative effect of such lovely lasses laying-on-of-healing-hands, there was a delayed, but undeniable reaction from another neighboring organ. I now knew I was going to live; make a full recovery. 'Here, here—may there always be an England!'

The next afternoon, I got out of bed for the first time. I stood up slowly, then shuffled to the bathroom feeble and spent. I felt battle-weary, robbed of a vital essence. I cringed under the spray of the shower; shaved with a trembling hand; struggled into a clean robe and tottered down the hallway to the communal dining room, where I sat at a long table running the length of the room.

The hospital was a regular United Nations, with seven different nationalities seated for supper, speaking in varied languages about equally diverse afflictions. I sat across from two young, rugby-player-big Englishmen, their faces wrapped in bandages—muscular mummies.

"Hey mate, what you got?"

"Malaria—cerebral," I said, tapping my head.

"Oohh, the bad one!"

"What brings you here?"

"Sand fleas. Can you bloody believe it? We were in Panama on a reptile collecting expedition for museums, when along a riverbank this cloud of fleas drops down, biting us. Thought nuthin' of it. Then a couple of weeks later we started scratchin' our faces off. Turns out the fleas lay their eggs in your blood when they bite, then later the larva hatch and want out . . . . "

"Skin is thinnest around the eyes," the other man said, pulling a bandage back to reveal an exposed white facial bone.

"Cheeky bastards!" the other said, both 'mummies' erupting in muffled laughter at the pun.

I looked down at the spaghetti and pushed it away. The next morning I told the doctor about dining with the "Sand Flea Boys." He nodded his head saying, "If you're from North America or the temperate zone, you basically live in quarantine. In comparison, the tropics harbor some monstrous diseases and with no built-up resistance, you're constantly under attack from one or the other. Our case files are full of horror stories. This hospital has seen it all—and then some."

The around-the-clock doses of quinine steadily chipped away at my high temperature, but they did so with a strange side-effect, an eerie repercussion. My ears buzzed constantly. More than an intermittent ringing, it was as if all the dying mosquito parasites themselves were chorusing en masse in my ears. As my temperature dropped, the quinine doses were decreased and my hearing cleared.

I was then shocked to her my own voice. It was garbled, sloppy, out of control. The words all had chipped edges or were slurred in their entirety. When Ronna arrived later that afternoon, I asked if I had sounded like this all along?

"Yes," she said, looking crestfallen. "The doctor told me, but said he didn't want to worry you. The malaria did get into your brain, to the part that affects speech." She burst into tears.

I lay there stunned. Words formed perfectly in my brain but then fell apart on my tongue.

"Ish id puhmahnant?"

She cried more, then shook her head. "The doctor doesn't know. He said everyone is affected differently. He said that part of your brain was suffocated from lack of oxygen during the last attacks—probably on the plane here to London."

We held hands and cried together, but then I refused to get discouraged. "I con beet dis ting!" I said, sounding like a punch-drunk fighter. To cheer Ronna up, make her laugh, I recited a line (now genuinely equipped so to do) from one of our favorite movies, "On The Waterfront": *"Ah cudda ben a contendah!"* I mumbled, swinging a feeble left jab through the air.

The next day, during lunch, I had one of the wonderful nurses, on her library card, check out "The Collected Works of William Shakespeare" and for hours each day I struggled to wrap my tongue around those marvelous sonnets and soliloquies. But no matter how hard I tried, how long I read, my speech remained slurred. The doctor suggested I see a speech therapist when I got home—that I might need to learn how to speak all over again. "But consider yourself fortunate. You're alive. You got here in the nick of time. If you had arrived an hour later—well, you might have been totally impaired—or dead."

A week after entering the hospital I was released. Ronna and I rode in the roomy back seat of a London cab to the airport. I was 22 pounds lighter and very, very weak.

At home in California, Ronna fielded all the phone calls, covering up my impairment—saying I was OK, resting. I was panic-stricken. Words were literally my life—written mostly, but I also earned a good part of my income lecturing across the country, and how was I going to pitch intelligent story ideas to magazine editors when I sounded like Joe Palooka?

To feel useful, I helped Ronna with the housework and moved two large houseplants outside for watering. But afterward I collapsed on the bed, exhausted. Now I cried. Before the malaria, I was an Iron Man: running marathons and lifting tons of weights daily in the gym. Now I couldn't even tote two houseplants 20 feet.

At that time, this mostly vegetarian suddenly developed an insatiable craving for meat, and the redder the better. I was astounded. What previously was repulsive was now all I wanted to eat—but not just any carcass of cow. I had to have prime filet mignons—not cooked but merely warmed-up for twenty seconds on each side. The beef had to be sitting in a pool of blood and grease or it wasn't appetizing. After devouring the raw meat, I then lifted the plate, tilted it, and gulped down the blood. As sick as it sounds, I somehow sensed it was making me healthy.

This went on for a week. I looked forward to the raw repasts and drinking blood with all the relish of Count Dracula.

At night, I began having childhood regression dreams of putting together Tinker Toys, excitedly inserting spindles into the wheel knobs—which proved to be my subconscious mirroring what was actually taking place in my brain.

One morning I awoke speaking clearly. The words were full formed!

I then saw a doctor who set me straight, both about the vampiristic tendencies and the Tinker Toy dreams. "Right now, in your bone marrow, your body is working overtime to rebuild all the red blood cells the malaria destroyed. And the ingredients to make red blood cells are iron, salt, B vitamins, certain fats—all found in your raw filet mignons. I saw a lot of malaria cases as a medic in Vietnam. Did they drill a hole in your head?"

"What?!"

"Frequently with *Plasmodium falciparum*—to counteract the swelling of the brain—a hole is drilled into the cranium to relieve the pressure."

"How I wish!" I then told him the case history, the entire story.

"You're very fortunate. Cerebral malaria is a real killer. It can suffocate the brain in short order, setting up massive strokes. The way I see it, you survived because you were in great shape physically from marathon running, and that also prepared you psychologically—being used to carrying pain through time, as you do in a marathon. So many people die because when those waves of intense pain hit, they panic; their pulse spikes and that opens the floodgates to the brain. As far as your ability to speak coming back—the brain is actually able to figure out what's wrong and then among all the unused neurons—reroute circuitry to reconnect that ability. Your 'Tinker Toy' dream reflects that . . . . Your brain may have lost a battle but it ultimately won the war."

Then, as suddenly as the vampirish craving started, it vanished. I went back to mostly vegetarian fare, and watering the plants was a piece of cake. With new red blood cells being manufactured every day, my strength began to build. I no longer needed to sleep after the slightest exertion. I began eyeing my running shoes . . . .

The first run was pitiful. I could barely finish a mile at a snail's pace. Breath came in gasps; leg muscles cramped from lack of oxygen. But I stayed with it— each day pushing further and faster against my limitations. Out on the trails I soon felt progress like a palpable companion. I marveled at the human body and its recuperative powers. Exercise and stress it on a regular basis and the body only gets stronger. Do the same to a machine and it weakens and breaks down.

We continue downhill into a steep ravine, the switch backs glazed-over with damp, slick leaves that tug sharply at the groin as your foot slips in the darkness behind the flashlight's beam. Then we get the *yips*—two coyotes off in the night, talking in edgy laments.

"Hear that?" I say.

"Wow!" Scott slows. "Awesome!"

We pause, listening. A duet of short, plaintive wails—then they are gone.

American Indian names for coyote translate as "song dog." I had heard wolves howl in British Columbia and Minnesota; and with their rolling range of intertwined ululations they composed the entire woodwind section of nature's orchestra, but the coyote now is the piercing flugel horn, cutting through the woods, the short, high-end notes bypassing the ears and quickening the heart directly. The masters of adaptability: where all the larger predators have been killed off; the land enfeebled, the coyote has filled in, sparking the wilds where they flame no more. The clever "Trickster"of Indian lore, Coyote will have the last laugh: endure long after we're gone—but not until he picks off the last poodle in Beverly Hills. (I had read of one trotting down Sunset Boulevard in broad daylight with a 90210 "FiFi" in its jaws.)

Near the bottom of the ravine, alongside a creek the trail dissolves out into a vast hodgepodge of giant boulders. Feeling bonked, bottomed-out, we stop running—staggering around amidst the chaotic rocks: an outward display of inner thoughts.

"We're ten minutes behind the buckle," Scott says slowly, staring at his watch. "Feel terrible."

"I'm wasted, woozy. Where the hell's the trail?"

"The plaque's not bad," Scott murmurs.

"Yeah, could live with that," I agree, wanting to get out from under this constant, draining burden—the tyranny of time.

Then we both look at each other. *"NAHHH!!"*

Scott hands me two pills. "Vivarin. Maybe clear our heads; pull us out of this."

"Where the *hell* is the trail?!"

We continue staggering aimlessly amidst the boulders in search of Onward; the caffeine having no effect, for it finds no scraps of energy left to assemble, let alone amplify. We then hear voices—our legs immediately turning like tuning-forks, homing-in on the inherent comforts of human sound.

"A checkpoint?" I wonder aloud. "Down *here*?"

We come upon a large tent pitched on the only patch of clear ground within the jumbled boulder field. The ranks have thinned: Only three runners are inside, munching cookies, cursing, considering dropping-out, but really playing Mind-Games: trying to psych each other out, gain one last leg-up in the standings, for the final push to the Finish Line. Inside the tent, under a Coleman lantern's roaring glow, I catch Scott's eye. He reads my thoughts and nods: *Big Dogs! We're doing better than we think!!* That realization boosts us enough to resist caving-in—sitting down in two empty and ever-so-inviting chairs. Magnified by the fatigue of being in constant motion for over 20 hours, a simple aluminum lawn-chair is suddenly now one of man's greatest inventions and temptations. But still, we resist, knowing full-well we'd lose precious time, surrendering too long to seductive comfort.

We palm bananas, murmur our thanks to the solo checkpoint volunteer, then slip away . . . . From outside the tent, we see three shadows straighten-up out of their chairs.

"Eight miles," Scott whispers. "And twelve minutes off buckle pace. Let's get it!"

Again, climbing . . . glancing back from atop a steep switch back to see a trio of flashlight beams swinging resolutely through the darkness behind us. We all feel a palpable connection. Physical exhaustion unites our minds. Even though more than a hundred yards separates us, we are inside each other's heads. It's a tradeoff: They renew our energy by closing behind us; we supply them the easier fuel to chase.

As we move out of the ravine, I think of how something is missing. Unlike the other two 100 milers, tonight I haven't hallucinated. At Western States, each time beyond Mile 80, I experienced things, sensed things that weren't there or were they? Before, intermittently along the trail; mentally wandering in "No Man's Land," I felt raccoons and fluffy rabbits—their soft fur rubbing so real, so soothing against my aching ankles. When I looked down—only things touching my skin were mud-caked socks. Then the second year, further-in, deep in a canyon full of trees, tall timber, with a night breeze blowing through the dense forest, I heard the trees singing—eerie, awesome susurrations as they communicated one-to-the-other with all the dazzling, aggregate tonality of a Bach harpsichord concerto.

As we run on, I think of how ultra marathon running places you in the shamanic trance. The Shamans or "Seers" of aboriginal tribes were the bridges between the natural and supernatural worlds. They would first endure similar conditions: exhaustion, dehydration, fasting, and then in a wide-open, vulnerable state were transported over by the deep, continual rhythm of a drum and irregular shakes of a rattle. I place my palm over my heart and feel the same throbbing beat, punctuated by the 'rattle' of a few pebbled aspirins in the tin square inside my botabelt . . . .

And while midway into my first Trance (Western States I), pumped with endorphins, every hair flaring out on my skin—I felt flayed, as if my skin was all gone and I was exposed to everything. I totally surrendered—letting myself free fall down into a canyon, my wheeling legs barely staying under me as I sang out joyously with that year's mantra, a Sioux Indian chant: *"Hanta Yo! Clear The Way/In a Sacred Manner I Come/The Earth Is Mine!"* A moment later, I entered a tight turn—with no time to react, for a rattlesnake, forearm-thick, with an immense triangular head was stretched halfway out across the trail. I tried to freeze my leading stride in midair, but my foot was already descending . . . . When I struck the ground—miraculously the snake didn't do the same to me! Like a bolt of lightning in reverse—in a split-second it had flashed back, out of the way, allowing the sudden intruder to pass unharmed. I was on the rattlesnake so fast that it didn't even have time to rattle (an unmistakable, hair-raising warning ultra runners hear often on long training runs). When my foot did touch the ground, I then triple-jumped about twenty yards down the trail; then came to a dead-stop—my legs trembling; chest heaving as my adrenaline-drenched heart continued somersaulting. Then that instinctive "fight or flee" response quickly evaporated—and I shocked myself by walking *back* up the trail! After having not seen the fluffy raccoons and bunnies, this time I wanted verification, which totally overrode any cautionary reflexes; and there was something more . . . . I calmly walked up the trail and sure enough— there was the enormous snake coiled off to the side of the trail, right in the bend of the switch back. We made eye-contact and it's red, forked-tongue flicked upward as if to pierce your heart. For the first time in my life, the actual sight of a serpent didn't send a cold shiver up my once-Catholic spine. Rather, I felt strangely emboldened: somehow certain that I could pick up the snake and it wouldn't strike, as if for this one moment we were totally entwined. Then remembering I was in a race—I bowed to the snake and sped on.

I thought of how after the run when I asked a Native American friend, John Swift Turtle about it, he smiled and said: "It heard your prayer; your mantra from the Sioux. And it didn't strike, for two reasons: it knew you had hold of the Power and you were totally vulnerable at the same time . . . . "

We come out of the ravine, running level now. I now know why this time I haven't hallucinated or danced with the serpent. For the last 50 miles, constant pain from the blisters engaged nearly all of my endorphins, keeping me firmly rooted in reality. Each step now is agony, especially over uneven ground, which it all is. The slightest twig or pebble hits my inflamed feet like a blowtorch. Compartmentalizing, boxing-off the pain, as I had done mile-after-mile, is no longer working. Fatigue has finally lowered all of my defenses. Instead of free-flow running, it's now a forced march. I am reduced to clenching my teeth and shuffling along.

"Six more clicks," Scott says over his shoulder. "Easy training run at home!"

But coaxing more effort from our battered beings makes six miles seem like sixty, especially having to regain 12 minutes (an extra mile in effort) to finish under 24 hours. So close; yet so far, and extreme fatigue is magnifying everything. As if looking through a telescope from the opposite end, distance feels distorted, distended. I'm groggy, feeling external parts of myself shutdown to send what little energy is left to the legs, the running factory. Ultra running reveals what is true and deepest within a person. Struggling on levels rarely reached in daily life, a man's veneer is gone. Everything extraneous is whittled away, melted down until only the core of who you really are remains. The core-self that, for the most part, is buried; that we deceive and deny with the consumer-fed comforts we accept as Life—is now laid bare in the primal woods. Here you are: either strung-out, quivering protoplasm refusing to go on and cursing you for placing it in such madness or now you find your finest self—solid gold with the slag all chipped away.

I'm a mixture of each. Floundering, searching through my worn-down, dimming brain for fuel to go on—minutes later, all I can recall is an unwelcomed quote from Vince Lombardi: "The body can stand most anything; it's the Mind you have to convince."

What we are running-on, I don't know. We are reduced to perpetual motion machines, uncoiling now the same motion we had built-up all day. I feel my brain shutdown, go into a "Screen saver" mode, but without the flowing, rhythmic pictures: one Flying Toaster emerges; then quickly sputters-out. To keep the runners on course through the night, the day before, race organizers had attached glow-sticks to low tree branches every few hundred yards. It is eerie chemical light, smears of yellow-green abob in the night breezes. That light; its flashing motion clears my head; then prickles my skin as I thought of Sabrina and Famke.

While living in Kensington, a small hamlet in the Berkeley, California hills, up above the University, I did many training runs in one of my favorite places: Tilden Park, a 50 mile network of wooded vales and mountain-ridge trails that offer incredible vistas of the San Francisco Bay Area. I loved to run up into the gold-colored hills on late-summer afternoons, with fog pouring-in from the ocean, filling the canyons with foamed cream; casting you adrift on high skylines—a red spire of the Golden Gate Bridge poking up through the white blanket in the distance. In that chilled air, redolent with the tart fragrance of eucalyptus oil, you could run fueled, mile after mile to your heart's content.

One such late-afternoon, nearing the end of a fourteen mile out-and-back run, I was swooping downhill elevated with endorphins and loving life. Sometimes while running alone, to release my high-spirits I sang out loud, launching the lyrics on outward breaths; my legs falling in step with the songs, striding along on music of my own making that helped defeat time and dissolve long-distances. That day I was belting-out Crosby, Stills & Nash's "Diamond Girl" when suddenly I had accompaniment—a sound like a shaken tambourine backing my hoarse vocals. I stopped dead-in-my-tracks . . . nothing. But so sure I had heard something, I started singing again—but now the words fell flat, for

I felt totally self-conscious—as if sensing the presence of another person. But no one, no response, so I stopped singing—shrugged—and then just as I pushed-off running again the sound returned like the tintinnabulation of crystal bells. Then it grew more precise: turning/tuning into female laughter! I didn't hear it with my ears, but directly in my Mind. I swung around and but there was no one there—until I turned my head to the side . . . (While star-gazing one night with an astronomer I couldn't see a distant nebula until he told me to turn my head slowly to the side: something to the effect about the eye's arrangement of rods and cones, that sometimes things come into focus if we view them from the side, instead of staring at them straight on.)

This was one of those times. There in the air (please bear with me) was a woman with dark hair, and olive 'skin' that was really vibrating light. *What the —an Angel?* But there were no feathery wings or corporal body, rather she was pure electromagnetism. Then for a split-second, she intensified, deepened into pure gold with dazzling emerald eyes that emananted the deepest wisdom and love. It was the most beautiful thing I had ever seen in my life, *If I'm really seeing this!?* It was as if I was seeing in a totally new way: not just with my eyes, but as if an aperature had suddenly opened so wide as to encompass my entire being. Then I heard the tinkling laughter again, like tiny crystal bells that seemed to emanate from all the atoms in the air as if they were being shaken, chimed together . . . and then she was gone.

What?! I vigorously rubbed my eyes. *Am I going Nuts????* I cautiously walked back up the trail to where she had been, looking from all angles; turning my head this way and that—nothing there, *nothing, no one—THAAAANK GOODNESS!* Then standing just below where I thought she had been, my eyes were drawn down. The grass looked different. Well into a drought-cycle, the California hills were as dry as straw, but where she had been, the grass underneath appeared somehow vitalized, bearing a light-green sheen! My right arm then lifted, as if of its own accord, extending straight up—then immediately, as if plugged into a light socket, all the hairs on my arm stiffened like wires and a surge of goose bumps prickled my flesh from the back of my hand all the way down to my shoulder.

I wish I had had a stopwatch, for I must have sprinted the final mile back to the car in world-record time!

Back inside my small one-bedroom apartment, I burst into tears, feeling totally overwhelmed with awe over what I had seen and, at the same time wondering if I had lost my mind? I felt bone-tired, and without even showering or removing my muddy running shoes and socks, I stretched out across the bed and fell immediately into a deep sleep. I awoke three hours later, feeling strange, as if everything was totally different, even though it was the same: same books on the shelves; same clock ticking by the bed; same loud hum from the refrigerator, but with the "Vision" still flaring on the screen behind my eyes, I knew that everything was indeed, different: as if a door or portal had just been flung open; a new life about to begin.

I was surprised that I had no desire for the habitual urge to make strong coffee, to jolt my consciousness into the "wake up!" mode after a nap so as to get to work. I felt strangely exalted, fully juiced, as if all my cells were singing—my body thrilled. Trying to carry on as normal, I stepped over to my desk and pulled out a blank piece of paper and pen. Sometimes to get started with my writing, as a warm-up, I begin scribbling the first thing that comes into my mind . . . letting a stream-of-consciousness flow forth; not editing, censoring or even caring if it makes any sense. Sometimes what emerges from this uninhibited, freeform exercise is the spark of a good story. Occasionally, it is total "automatic writing," with the words pouring forth, finished, in final-draft—seeming to come *through*; not from me, in what Borges called "A guided dream."

This was one of those times—and beyond. As soon as my pen touched paper, the nib released words, as if they were stored-up, waiting: "*I've been with you a long time. What you saw and heard is my Happiness for you, for what is ahead. You will find your Way and many Truths soon from Women and the Earth. You are ready now and deserving. Keep your Heart open to what will transpire. It is time for the Changes. Fear not what you will experience, for many Worlds are above this plane—but not detached from it.*"

The pen fell from my hand. The words went blurry from an upwelling of tears in my eyes. I felt electrified. All the hairs on my arm were upright; my hand was trembling. When I looked at the paper again, I slowly read and reread the passage trying to absorb the meaning; and noticed that even though the words came from my hand, they looked strange, foreign: not my usual handwriting. I sat there struggling to come to terms with it all. I felt lost, as if reality had completely shifted and there was no familiar ground to stand on. Then rereading the message yet again, I relaxed. I began thinking that, in spite of what had happened I never once felt any fear. The Vision and the automatic writing somehow felt perfectly natural—and that normalcy astounded me more than anything! I closed my eyes and saw her again: those magnificent colors oscillating, wavelike and with such splendor and glory!

I had seen ghosts before and there was no comparison. While on magazine assignments in Jackson, Mississippi and Stratford-on-Avon, England, late at night I awoke to witness vaporous visages in the room. The southern ghost, a gentle, inquisitive, somewhat protective soul was the ante-bellum mansion's original occupant who lived a long life; then died in the house (mother's often-seen, lingering presence verified by her son, the present owner, the next morning over breakfast); and in the 350 year-old Shakespeare Hotel, nestled in the charming hamlet of the Bard's birthplace, with all the rooms named after characters from his plays, a younger ghost, again feminine in gender, stood bedside peering aggressively down. Seems a girl had committed suicide there at age 15 over unrequited love for a man. "Oh, you saw her?" the innkeeper said, arching an eyebrow. "I should have known, for she only goes into a room if the guest is a man . . . . " In both cases the ghosts appeared gray, saddened, sodden, bogged-down in the nether world between life and death—whereas the Vision was alive to the Nth Degree, the very apex of scintillating life-force even while having to slow (as I later learned) that glorious *élan vital* to a crawl to be visible in our plane of existence.

In *Great Ideas: A Lexicon of Western Thought* by Mortimer J. Adler, in his opening essay, "Angel," I read: " . . . Their existence is necessary to fill out the hierarchy of natures. They are links in what has come to be called 'the great chain of being.'

"Angels are also said to go from one place to another without traversing the intervening space and without the lapse of time. Considering their immateriality, such action is less remarkable for angels to perform than is the action of electrons, which, according to modern quantum mechanics, jump from outer to inner orbits of the atom without taking time or passing through inter orbital space."

I turned to *The Divine Comedy* and sure enough, speaking of Angels, Beatrice tells Dante: "The Primal Light that irradiates them all is received by them in as many ways as are the splendors to which it joins itself. Wherefore, since the affection follows upon the act of conceiving, the sweetness of love glows variously in them."

Permeating each passing day were wonderful thoughts about "Sabrina" (what I named the Vision, for she had an exotic quality to say the least!) and I read and reread her cryptic message daily. I told no one of what had happened. I wanted to understand it more; wrap my mind completely around it before daring to talk about it with anyone. At the time most of the phrases seemed as easy to decipher as Abstract Expressionism: *"It is time for the Changes . . . . Many Worlds are above this plane—but not detached from it . . . .* HUH?! But what puzzled me most was the line: *"You will find your Way and many Truths soon from Women . . . . "* At the time, I had an on-and-off relationship with a woman that had been increasingly "off" and there was no one else potentially on the near horizon and certainly not in plural.

Six months after Sabrina appeared, "Cosmopolitan" magazine made me a

'Bachelor-of-The-Month' and I received 5,000 letters from women all over the world!

Please, dear reader, laugh—for that's exactly what I did when the phone rang one morning at 7:00 a.m.

"Yahhhh . . . . " I suspired, having pub-crawled with friends into the wee hours the night before.

"This is Lisa Simmons—Cosmopolitan Magazine, and we want you to be our next 'Bachelor-of-the-Month'!"

"*Ha!* Who is this—really?"

"Here's my number in Manhattan . . . . Call back if you don't believe."

I did; she answered and I said: "Lisa, I'm totally flattered, but you've got the wrong guy. I've seen the Bachelor feature and it's always some rich Texan, a stock broker or oil baron with a boot-up on the bumper of his Ferrari Testarossa. I'm an impoverished freelance writer with a beater car!"

"Money isn't everything. In fact, we're placing bets here, Michael, that you're going to break the record for the most mail, because what you do is so adventurous and romantic! *That* has great appeal to women."

"Please give me an hour and I'll call you back."

"O.K.—but quickly: we're going to press very soon."

I called my publicist at HarperCollins. My first book, *Inside Passage: Living With Killer Whales, Bald Eagles, and Kwakiutl Indians* was just out. I explained to Janet, Cosmo's offer and said I was hesitant: "I want to be taken seriously as an author, especially with my first book." Janet laughed with delight. "Michael, not to worry! See if they will mention the title of the book. Cosmo is the number one selling women's magazine on college campuses and nearly around the world. Women purchase about 90% of all books. We couldn't *buy* this kind of publicity! Besides, it could be your next book. Freud asked: 'What do women really want?' Take notes, sweetheart—you just might find out!"

After talking with Janet, I did what I always do when I have to clear my head or make an important decision: I went for a run—a fast three-miler down and back up the hill. During the moving meditation, Sabrina re-flared in my mind and I heard her words clearly: *You will find your Way and many truths soon from Women . . .*

Back home, I picked up the phone and told Lisa I would do it and apologized for my hesitancy.

"No, I'm glad you thought it over. Michael, you have no idea how much mail you are going to get. And you better get an unlisted phone number and a P.O. box, for your life is about to change—big-time!"

Her last words were an understatement, to say the least.

So began a journey more enlightening, intense and terrifying than any I had embarked on before. I soon learned that being surrounded by killer whales, wolves and grizzly bears was tame—compared to entering the dating jungle.

When the November Cosmo hit the stands, a blizzard of letters began. I had never before seen so much purple and pink ink, revealing photos and padded mailers holding bras and racy panties or gifts of silk boxer shorts! Even the stationary was enticing: lacy paper that was sealed with a kiss (the red lipstick impressions providing very personal postmarks). Many of the missives were scented—so much so that one day after picking-up the latest avalanche of letters that spilled onto the floor of a copy center from the rented postal box, I re-poured them into the car to run other errands for an hour. It was a warm day and I returned to an odiferous outpouring: "Poison" mixing with "White Shoulders;" "Obsession" clashing with "My Sin."

The Cosmo girls' mothers must have been avid readers of romance novels, for many of their daughters were named *Mandy, Chantal, Desiree* . . . . I learned U.S. geography all over again reading letters from Indian Orchard, Maine; Truth or Consequences, NM; Bountiful, Utah. Then airmail envelopes started arriving from the Cayman Islands, South Africa, Tahiti, Germany, Japan, Mongolia, Poland, England, the Philippines.

It was "Every Man's Fantasy" that, finally, I loosened-up and embraced.

Then, like an architect's blueprint, Sabrina's cryptic message unfolded 'true'—line by line.

One day, I opened an envelope and there was something very different: the head of an eagle, in profile, its bold eye staring up at me, a beautiful rendering on the front of a card. The handwritten message inside started off with the usual: "Dear Michael, I saw you in Cosmo; and I've never done anything like this before . . . " but then abruptly changed: "When I looked at your picture I saw an eagle superimposed over you with its wings unfurled."

The eagle was my Totem Animal. How could this woman know that?

Curiosity piqued, I picked up the phone. After talking just a few minutes, we clicked. She was as compelling and mystical as the card. She was going to be in the Bay Area in a few days and would I like to get together?

"And Michael, when we first meet—I don't want to talk for about ten minutes. I just want to look into your eyes; then we'll go from there."

As strange as the request seemed, I found myself agreeing to it immediately.

It was a winter evening when I drove over to Tiburon, a small island on the north side of San Francisco Bay, covered with exclusive homes facing The City and a stone's throw from the Golden Gate Bridge. I parked on the street across from the house. As I walked up a rising driveway, my eyes went to the sky. It was a cold clear night, and the stars were a million deep. Out of the upper corner of my right eye I detected rapid movement. I turned my head and followed a shooting star—that "introduced" me to Famke Logan.

Exactly where the streak of light ended, there was a woman standing in an open doorway. At first, I only saw her in silhouette, but it was a telling first impression—as if seeing a person's very essence, isolated, before all the details were filled-in. She appeared lit from within, with brilliant white light flaring from her tall, striking figure—as if her physical form was a veil concealing greater realities.

"Famke?"

Now in solid form, she placed the tip of her forefinger on my lips. With her other hand she led me inside the house, to a small couch in the foyer. With her face only inches away, sure enough—high-beam blue eyes locked onto mine. We sat in silence and I felt all the rooms and closets of my soul opened and inspected, from attic to basement. Occasionally an eyebrow rose, but her grin soon fanned into a smile and then, finally, she broke into a laugh like a burbling mountain brook.

She cooked dinner and we talked as if we were old friends. We had the house to ourselves—her uncle and aunt out for the evening. We talked of Native Americans, Druids, animal intelligence, Scandinavia, Norse mythology, pine-needle tea. Although having made a very lucrative living as a Ford Agency model, jet-setting to shoots all over the world, for the past few years Famke had rejected things material and superficial for a quest deep into spiritual realms. She glowed with happiness and purpose; and even though I had known her for just a few hours—she was one of the most impressive people I had ever met.

The following night she came over to Berkeley to have dinner with family. While they went on to a movie she called and asked if she could come up to see me? When she entered my small studio, it was as if she filled the entire space, her presence was so enormous. "Michael, I can't stay long, but last night I noticed something. You have a blocked Chakra—at your Heart. I can help you clear it, if you want."

"Chakra?"

"The Hindus believe that there are seven energy centers in the body that parallel the spine. 'Chakra' means 'vibrating wheel' or 'circle.' Picture lotus flowers—either opened or closed and this one," she pointed, "has definitely slammed shut! Maybe self-defense?"

"O.K.! What do I do?"

That giggle, again like a lilting brook. "You're still a little boy—so trusting and willing. You just leap into life heart-first, don't you!"

"'High risk, high yield.'"

"I love that about you! But you've been bruised and battered a bit. O.K.—standup."

She stood directly across from me, nearly my same height. "Unbutton your shirt." Her right index finger then extended straight-out and traveled in upward sweeps repeatedly over my torso. Her finger never made contact with my skin. I watched it closely for I couldn't believe the effect. All the while, her fingertip stayed an inch off my chest, but it left a trail of heat, a fire that penetrated deep inside. Then just over my heart, at the center of my chest, her finger paused to swirl in tight spirals as if untying a knot . . . . Then all of a sudden I felt molten energy blaze up through my throat and shoot out the top of my head!

"There! That should do it!! Gotta run—bye!"

She was out the door before I could speak—a gleaming smile hovering in the air like the Cheshire Cat's.

Three nights later, Famke was inside my studio again. She worked for a major airline and had unlimited free-travel. Airplanes were her "magic carpets," flinging her from coast-to-coast, with an Air Porter van then delivering her right to my door!

We ate a casual dinner that night, sitting cross-legged on the living room carpet, with pasta salad and ice water before us. Sitting directly across from one another, at first, we hardly spoke, for our eyes kept locking-up. We had entire conversations without speaking; the discourses ending in giddy laughter. I felt completely inebriated, sky-high, without having a drop of alcohol to drink.

Then, while looking down, picking at her salad, she said slowly, cautiously: "Michael, do you believe in extraterrestrials?"

I set down my knife and fork. "I've never seen one, but . . . . "

"What?"

I felt an upwelling of conviction rise from my heart into my throat. I then spoke rapidly and with great force. "If a Spaceship landed *right now* in the backyard, I'd take off all my clothes and walk totally naked up the gangplank into the ship absolutely *beaming LOVE!* They could do with me what they want, I wouldn't care, but through every cell I would just keep beaming-out *LOVE!!*"

My statement seemed to hang in the air, resonating for a few moments; then Famke's eyes widened and she gasped: "THEY'RE HERE!!"

Just as I was about to say, "What?!" there was a sound in the room. It was a tone, a beautiful, pure, ringing tone. I had lived in that apartment for years, and knew every single squeak, creak, refrigerator shift, but this sound was totally foreign and contrary to human hearing that automatically pinpoints the location of a sound (*that's* the gurgling of the hot-water heater in the closet; the refrigerator's ice-maker, *there*, kitchen; car horn, *outside*, etc.) Even though hearing it clearly, I was unable to place the sound—it was all-pervasive, somehow coming from everywhere at once, as if defying limitation. The ethereal tone ended and then after a few moments of silence another began, identical to the one before, but slightly louder in volume and now transcending the ears. I heard it with my body, all throughout my being. It was dazzling, golden, molten with feeling. Then it ended and another: a third tone totally filled the room—and us. It was beyond beauty, music, the singing of the Sirens . . . . It was like experiencing the very Source of Love.

Even though Famke was sitting directly across from me during the 2-3 minutes? of the Tones, I had lost track of her: totally taken over with listening, she went out of focus. Now our eyes met again and simultaneously we said: "WOW!!"

"Did you-"

"Of course!" she said.

"What was-"

Famke's smile was dazzling. "Oh, Michael! They heard what you said—the unconditional offering from your Heart. And they responded!!"

My hands went up to my temples. I felt lightheaded. I had never suffered a headache in my life, but suddenly there was a noticeable change, something different—not pain, but more a change of pressure, pushing against my temples from the inside-out (a feeling I was to experience often in the coming weeks).

"'They'—'Them?'" I asked. "Right before the Tones, you said 'They're here!' Who are '*They*' and how did you know that?"

Famke lowered her eyes. She shifted around on the floor, ruminating. "Michael, maybe I should leave right now, slip out of your life before you get involved." She stood up, crossing her arms, looking away.

"No, stay!" I said, leaping-up to embrace her. That physical contact was shocking, so magnetic and electric that we immediately started making love, and all the while I felt a sense of recognition—that her body, even though that of a stranger was somehow very familiar to me. She felt the same, as if in our deepest places, we were reuniting.

Afterwards, on the bed, we then fell together into a deep sleep. I then had a "dream." I was sitting alone in some sort of hospital waiting-room, staring at a double door ahead. There was brilliant white light pouring out the top and bottom; and I sensed Famke was behind that door. I started feeling anxious, wondering if she was all right. I then saw that I really wasn't alone. There were other "beings" there with me. They were shadowy, short, gray in color; with huge, upturned, glassine eyes. Without speaking, telepathically, they told me she was fine. Just then I heard a loud, penetrating scream!

Now awake; with my eyes open I saw Famke run from the bed to the bathroom holding the back of her head.

"Are you all right?" I said, jumping up and striding over to the closed door. "WHAT HAPPENED?!" She finally came out with a look of apprehension mixed with awe on her face. She turned around and with both hands parted her thick, flaxen blond hair, shaking the ponytails. "Michael, tell me what you see!"

There on her central scalp were small drops of blood coming from one or two tiny puncture holes. "What the? . . . Oh my, looks like a bite of some sort. What! Maybe a spider—I'll look in the bed."

She stopped me with a hand on my shoulder. "Michael," she paused to take-in a deep breath, "It wasn't a spider. I . . . I've been . . . . "

"WHAT?"

"Probed," she mumbled.

"*Probed*?!"

After handing me a Band-Aid to place across the tiny punctures, she took my hand and we returned to bed. It was 2:45 a.m. and years before the "X-Files" TV show; prevalent abduction stories; the reopening of the Roswell Case; ubiquitous alien faces and inflatable wide-eyed and pointy-headed figurines turned into the new 'kewpie dolls.' We talked nonstop for the next five hours.

"It all started when I was a little girl. For a time, I disappeared. My mother was frantic: called the police; the whole town was searching for me. Then I remember walking home, in the door with no memory of what happened or where I had been—with a bit of blood on the back of my head. And it's continued all my life. And not just limited to me. When we lived out in the country, was when they were most active, coming into the house very often. My daughters saw them; so did my mother. One night we stood at the window and watched the disc, a spaceship hovering for a long time directly over the pond. Another time, I had a dinner party and friends drove out. One guy had an old car, and the radio never worked from the day he bought it. He locked the doors before he came in. Well, hours later, we all saw the UFO whirling around the property, and at the same time his car horn was beeping, the lights flashing off and on and the radio blasting at full volume!

"No matter where I've lived or traveled they continued to be there. And as I've matured, the probing has intensified and became more intimate."

"Didn't you ever want it to stop? Tell them to go to hell!"

"No. It was never like that. A trust developed. An awe in being able to be with them; and seeing how the experiences were changing my life—making me a better person, far more spiritual and, in the process, developing and accelerating the powers that we all have within.

"One day, a very ordinary day, I went over to the window and looked out. There was a beautiful blue sky, white clouds, green grass and cows grazing. Then right in the center of it all . . . it's hard to explain in words, it was as if a curtain had been parted down the middle—there was a huge flame shooting up through 'normal reality'—like a flaming oil well, but much more glorious! As if it was within, a part of reality all the while, somehow feeding or creating what's real and at that moment I was getting a glimpse of the Source of it all. I thought I was seeing things. I looked away; rubbed my eyes, and looked again. It was gone."

"What did you mean when you said the probing became more 'intimate'? I don't understand."

"I'm missing a vertebrae in my back, my body temperature runs lower than 98.6 and I'm always lactating, even though it's been years since my last child. I went in for tests. The doctors checked me over head to toe, inside-out, backwards and forwards and were shocked. They had no explanation. They said I showed many of the signs of being pregnant, but there was no visible fetus.

"Michael, I know you were there tonight in real-time, in your 'dream' of being outside the operating room just as I was being probed. That they didn't switch you off—included you in the experience is amazing! I think they've interacted with you before."

"No, this is all totally new. Believe me!"

"My sense is that it happened when you were younger, and that's why now you're not freaking out. I'll bet that deep in your subconscious, if you went under hypnosis, they would be there!"

"But why? Why is this happening?"

She sighed. "For years I asked that question of them. Then, one time after being abducted I was in a big nursery—there were babies everywhere. And 'They' were there alongside me, holding my hands. I asked them: 'Whose babies are these?' 'They're all yours,' they replied."

She began crying. "Michael, this isn't easy. There's so much that defies common sense, that I don't understand that it's enough to drive you crazy. But, deep down, I sense it's all for the Highest Good. I think they are very concerned for the future of our planet, being able to see what our future is. It's related to how rapidly we are destroying the environment, devastating nature like a cancerous blight across the land. Maybe they are preserving some sort of human gene pool, like a zoo holding the last few Snow Leopards so that someday they can be replenished from that stock. I just know that the way to save our world is let them in. They want to help us . . . . And I'm not the only one. There are women and men across the world having similar experiences. I also think that maybe they need us, in some way, to help themselves, too: That, in their own evolution, they chose the high-tech road and in doing so, they lost some of their vitality."

"You mean the 'Spock Syndrome'—like in Star Trek, when Spock scoffs at human emotions?"

"In a way—yes. Michael, think about it. We have bodies, genitals, secretions—we're a juicy lot. But corporal flesh is a very slow vibration. Maybe in their evolution they turned from that, from intimacy requiring physical contact, and now somewhat regret it, need us to help balance, revitalize their own existence. The babies that I saw in the nursery were hybrids, a combination of us and them. Who knows—maybe a new race to 're-seed' our planet or another world."

"Do you know where they're from?" I asked.

"My sense is from the Pleiades star cluster. Earth and our entire solar system orbits the central sun of the Pleiades, Alcyone. Our sun is the 8th star of the Pleiades. As the farthest removed of the Pleiadian cluster, we are now just coming into a Spiritual Awakening. And for the next few years we'll be entering a photon band with extremely high frequencies that will cause accelerated growth and weird time warps—we're all going to see our precise sense of time get stretched far beyond what we're used to. There will be a single hour that will seem a week long and entire weeks that speed by in an hour; and many cataclysmic natural disasters all over the planet, intensifying more and more each year.

"What's very important to keep in mind is what Einstein discovered—that 'Time' really doesn't exist. You don't see bears running around wearing watches! Time is just something man invented because he compartmentalizes and thinks in a straight line. There really is no such thing as 'Time'—it's elastic, elliptical. We're living in a universe where there are parallel worlds happening simultaneously, not in a linear fashion. And 'They' can move back and forth between these parallel dimensions by changing the speed of their vibrations."

"So, the Tones earlier tonight were their way of responding—with vibrations?"

"Yes! Precisely! Michael, the real reason why they manifested themselves tonight was your statement of unconditional love that you said with such conviction! Didn't you feel much more from the Tones than words could ever say?"

"Yes—it was the most amazing thing I've ever felt. It went way beyond words—from a much higher plane—like Plato saying that music is the highest form of the communicative arts; Schopenhauer and Nietzsche believing music was the voice of the Cosmos, itself. But then to have that dream; and you being 'probed'—Famke, it's just all too— "

"Maybe I should leave," she said abruptly, sitting up and turning away; her thick hair closing around her face like a curtain. "As much as I don't want to, but I will if this is overwhelming or frightening you in any way."

My entire being was spinning and I remained silent for a long minute. Then I got up and walked into the living room, sitting alone on the couch. I wanted to be absolutely sure that my response to her would be true to myself . . . . After a few minutes, I returned to the bedroom: "No—it's not frightening. And that's the strangest damn thing! As 'out there' as it all is, I don't feel the slightest bit of fear. It doesn't feel evil—dark or destructive in any way. If it did, I would want no part of it—and, yes, I would want you to leave. It's like a door has been flung open to a Universe I never even knew existed and now I want to walk through that door. I want to know *more!* "

Famke gave a long sigh and hugged me tight.

I started laughing.

"What?" she said, pulling back.

"I was just thinking how we met. It's too weird—a magazine: 'Cosmo' bringing us together! I mean what are the odds of that!?"

"It makes perfect sense," she said through a sloe-eyed grin. "Add an 'S'."

"To what?"

"The magazine, dummy!"

"*Cosmos,* " I mumbled, a step closer to being a true-believer.

We slept for just a couple hours and woke-up feeling totally energized. Starving, we threw on clothes and bolted down the hill to a small cafe in downtown Kensington, a favorite of Bay Area "foodies" for its scrumptious Sunday brunch. As usual, the place was packed. We lucked-out, getting a table by the window. While ordering, my eyes kept returning to Famke. The adjectives "luminous" and "radiant" were pale shadings of what she looked like. Her white-blond hair streamed with light; her blue eyes were sparkling clear and beaming. She looked like Perfection—just born.

After ordering, again, we couldn't eat—this time interrupted by the other diners. Incredibly, people were getting up from their tables and walking directly over to us. Total strangers, they just naturally started chatting away, their full attemtion on Famke. It wasn't "in passing" (after eating; going out the door and we were there on the way.) All the visits were deliberate and strangely ecstatic; and after a few minutes, people then returned to their tables and carried on with their meals. After the third group of visitors, I sensed there was more going on here than what met the eye: The real reason they were coming over was not for the conversation, but to subconsciously bask in Famke's presence. The woman was so luminous that everyone was drawn to the light.

After we left, finally finishing a meal, ever the skeptic journalist, I asked: "Are you sure you haven't lived out here? Those people acted like they knew you—were old friends!"

She smiled. "Never lived in California, at least not in this lifetime . . . . " Famke then broke into the trilling giggle. "That sounds *soo* 'Shirley McLaine'!"

One of the reasons Famke had come west was to see if she could relocate. Later that afternoon, she had a job interview with her airline to try to transfer to San Francisco. In the meantime, she wanted to get some cash from an ATM machine. We drove down the hill into Berkeley, proper, and with some time to fill, toured the University of California, famed during the 1960's as a catalyst for political protest and a hotbed for Flower Power, nurturing, in the climate of "Make Love, Not War," "Question Authority," "Tune-in, Turn-on, Dropout" a full-bloom Hippie Movement. Those times are still somewhat alive on Telegraph Avenue, the main artery leading to the campus and famed Sproul Hall, where upon its steps, via rebellious speeches, America's consciousness was changed forever. On Telegraph, amidst the now-trendy Gap and preppy Brooks Brothers— you can still buy tie-died T-shirts; Jimi, Janis, and Jerry Garcia black-light posters, and head-shops are redolent with smoking bongs and patchouli oil.

We parked alongside Peoples' Park and took a short cut: zigzagging down back streets until we reached a money machine on Telegraph. Famke slid her card in and started pressing numbers—but when her fingertips touched the keypad the machine abruptly went dead: the screen blinked blank, the keypad frozen. She stepped back, giving a nonchalant shrug. From the look in her eyes, I saw that this wasn't an uncommon occurrence. I insisted that she take my cash. We turned to walk back down Telegraph Avenue. It was slow-going, for street-people, the downtrodden slumped over on tattered sleeping bags and pieces of cardboard, were now abruptly jumping to their feet and directly approaching. One by one, they smiled, overtly bowing before her! Famke giggled, and hugged them all.

Further down the street, she tugged me into a bookstore; then asked the clerk for the New Age section. "Ah-ha!" she said, plucking a book from the shelf. She hid it behind her back. "Michael, in your Dream—was *this* what you saw?"

She then held-out the front cover of the book. There was a portrait of one of 'Them'—the very creature(s) I saw in the dream: the identical ovoid head; gray skin; oversized glassine, up-slanted eyes. Immediately, the pressure returned to my temples; the same lightheadedness as before. She paid for the book: *Communion* by Whitley Strieber (which I had never seen before), then tucked it in under my arm as we walked out. I didn't need to speak. She could tell from my reaction that it was exactly what I saw.

Walking back to the car, she said, "Michael, this isn't your first time—I see it in your eyes. You were all 'lit-up' when I first met you! You've had these experiences before."

"No . . . not this type, at least I don't think so—but . . . . "

"But *what*? Don't hold back—please tell me."

I took a deep breath and, for the first time, told another person about Sabrina. Famke stopped walking. When I finished, she wiped tears from her eyes. *"I knew, I knew. . . . "* she said, as if thinking out loud. "That is so *Wonderful!* Michael—you've been blessed. There are many hierarchies or levels of ethereal beings. You saw what the Hindus call a *deva*—"shining one." They are a lower order of angels that handle the more elemental nature spirits and protect us as well. And when you talked about seeing her, at first, unclearly that's because you were breaking-in your 'etheric eyes.' Everyone has them—they're like concave disks around the eyeball. They are what gives our eyes their vitality; their life and shine, and occasionally they operate independently enabling you to see what you did. Children see instinctually with their etheric eyes—before they 'know better.' "

We walked a few steps, then I stopped. "Famke, are you . . . some sort of-"

She laughed, reading my mind. "God, no! I'm very, very—all *too* human! It's just that right after I'm probed, as if to take good care of me they leave me 'over-amped!'"

I dropped her off at the BART (Bay Area Rapid Transit) station. I wished her luck in the interview. She gave me a quick kiss and said: "Call you before I leave!" After she was gone, driving toward the exit I suddenly swerved into a parking space, turned off the motor and just sat there, stunned, for over an hour overwhelmed by the day's events.

I finally went home and caved-in, taking a long nap. I awoke to the phone ringing hours later. "Michael!" I could 'hear' Famke smiling, "you won't believe what happened. I was late for the interview. I'm on the train and we're zipping along when we suddenly stop, dead on the tracks; and there's a red light blinking in the wall panel right above me. An engineer finally makes his way back to where the light is, saying, 'That's funny—never seen this before!' He tinkers around; the light goes off and then we're moving again.

"Famke, what's going on?"

"I'm not sure—it's never been like this! But the interview went real well. They may offer me the position out here. I have to run, my flight leaves in five minutes. I'll call you tomorrow!!"

Late that night, the phone rang. Not expecting it to be her so soon, I didn't awaken; let the answering machine pick it up: "Michael, I know it's late and you're probably sleeping, but just have to tell you something. After I arrived at the airport, I went down into the crew lounge to pull up my schedule on the computer and the moment I touched the keys, *wham*—the computers died—all of them! It's happened before—everything electronic I touch goes down. Oh well . . . . Michael, I keep thinking about the Tones. They were absolutely incredible! The first time ever for that—and to hear them together! Oh my— what else lies ahead for us?!"

During her next visit, with just a short time before we parted again, we made love in the bedroom. It was intense and rapturous, as always. However, this time, as we fell back on the bed, just as our heads hit the pillows, the ceiling 'changed.' . . . What had been for years an ordinary, drab, stucco ceiling, 10 feet high, was now covered with electric blue lights: like Van Gogh's spiraling whorls in his painting "Starry, Starry Night"—but animated, sped-up, in rapid motion, a collective pulsating dance! After getting over the initial shock, I sensed that somehow the lights were conscious entities of some sort—stripped-down to pure electric matter; charged waves of being. There were no identifiable features: head, eyes, bodies, wings . . . . It was like seeing the very sparks of life, itself; dare I say souls? or living essences of some sort, that normally, I sensed existed on another, elevated plane than us, but now for some reason, chose to make themselves visible in our realm. There were so many, coming full force in continuous, shimmering waves so as to keep the ceiling completely covered as they swept over us. Again, there was no fear, horror or anything the slightest bit upsetting. Just looking at them: their beautiful, swirling motions; their electric-blue hues created pure bliss—a feeling a hundred times more rapturous than making love, and yet I sensed that *that*: physical love had everything to do with *this*: somehow, it was the trigger or catalyst for what I was seeing. After a minute or so, I tore my eyes away, quickly swiveling my head on the pillow. Famke was gazing upward, transfixed, with the blue whorls reflected on her face and dancing in her eyes like entire worlds!

Without looking away, her hand found mine under the covers. Just as we squeezed our palms together, they were gone. The ceiling was suddenly white and roughened again. We both turned to each other and burst into tears, holding each other tight.

Attempts at analysis came later during long-distance calls. "Michael, of all these experiences I've had my whole life long, I've never shared what I've shared with you, and especially a man, in such a short time. All I know for sure is that you and I—we vibrate at the very same, exact pitch; like two tuning-forks struck together and what we can do uniting our energy—well, absolutely anything seems possible now!!"

While traversing an exposed ridge, a cool wind puffs intermittently. It perks me up, as if delivering animated energy. I open my mouth, sipping the wind and run with my arms held out; palms of my hands turning like dishes in the direction of the wafting vigor. Even wind now seems much more than wind—filled with spirit, and caressive as a lover as its *élan vital* coruscates through my body, energizing each atom. I think of how the Native Americans, living so closely attuned to the earth—the wildness we are running through for just 24 hours, they lived *in* all their lives—and how it made them realize that everything is imbued with spirit, no matter how "lifeless" it appears to the obdurate white man. Moving across the high ridge I feel certain that even Wind, Rocks and Clouds have pulses if you live close enough and surrender freely to them.

I now know that running and the paranormal experiences are directly connected. I may still have had them if I was a non-runner, but long-distance running, since I was 12, has opened me up: it is expansive, carrying the body, mind and spirit past measurable boundaries and self-imposed limits, creating a portal into all possibilities. As physical limits are transcended, I'm convinced that the limits we put around consciousness and reality are elastic, as well. I'm now certain that the only limits we have are the limits we believe. And when we run we are *more* of ourselves, the good parts, and chemically, the near-daily release of endorphins stream like sparkling tributaries into our life-force, increasing the channel—making us much more receptive and attuned to the Universe. Swift Turtle had once told me that "Where your ultra marathons take place, the First Nation ran before you, the originators of the trails—for trade and communication with other tribes. Most of all, Native Americans ran through such places for the spiritual exercise, creating a living cord between the earth and the sky."

Nights after the appearance of the "Blue Whorls," as they now are named, inside my apartment, alone in bed, I crossed my hands behind my head and stared upward at the ceiling. The Blue Whorls never returned, but they didn't have to. Tears poured readily from my eyes—a continuous upwelling from my heart because for the first time in my life I now felt connected directly, daily to the very Source of Life, itself. It transcended religion to a much purer, higher state (where man "in the name of God" didn't meddle and "admission" to Heaven was open to all): A Unified Field of pure Spirituality, rather than contentious-holier-than-thou-religous-factions. Some nights, before sleeping, I felt awash with a molten, unconditional Love Energy inside me and flooding outward into the room. A man who, not long ago, was very cautious about expressing his emotions, now found himself crying all the time. Weeping with tears of joy in bed, I raised my right arm straight up into the darkness of the night; opened my hand and extended my fingers . . . . God now squeezed back.

My picture of God was changing. I no longer saw him as the bearded patriarch on Michelangelo's Sistine Ceiling. Now God transcended the outward form of the body to the higher state of our inner composition of light and energy. God Knows All and Sees All, because He/She is *in* all, infusing everything with consciousness. In *The Book of the Twenty-Four Philosophers* (a 12th Century Latin hermetic text), I read: "God is an intelligible sphere whose center is everywhere and circumference nowhere." God is Light; God is Love and when we are emanating the feeling of unconditional Love, our overall vibration elevates and the Light within us glows brightest. It has everything to do with Love. Love is the bridge that connects us to the Divine.

In a state of extended excitement, for weeks, I slept only a few hours a night. My mind was racing. Books were piling up bedside like the Leaning Tower of Pisa. Twice in succession I read Paramahasa Yoganda's *Autobiography of a Yogi*, radiant with guidance, peak performances and miracles. My soul ate its way through the works of a clairvoyant with so many answers, Rudolph Steiner: "The more human love there is on earth the more food there is for the gods in heaven; the less love the more the gods go hungry."

I began to have a reoccurring dream that was both terrifying and rapturous. It had that totally real, 3-D, in living color quality. I'm running up a mountain in Alaska: it's summer, the sun is warm; the trail a soft pine-needle trampoline. Suddenly, out of the blue, I'm attacked by a gigantic grizzly bear. A blur of fur; a bellowing growl loud enough to freeze your heart, and he is on me. After the initial jolt of hellacious fear, realizing that I'm in the grasp of the bear; his long claws slashing, fangs snapping—then, instead of striking back or trying to escape, I find the bear's eyes mere inches away in the center of a massive head and lock onto them with mine. I emanate nothing but Love, beaming an unbroken bridge of love and understanding into his raging eyes. Then immediately everything changes: the bruin's violent fury vanishes and we begin dancing playfully in each other's relaxed arms!

Upon awakening from the dream, I have total recall and each time it happens I am astounded anew! Brown bears can be ten feet tall and weigh nearly a ton, yet I, a puny human, can totally replace rage and violence with the power of Love.

I didn't know what the dream meant, but I sensed somehow that it was linked, an amplification of the other transformative experiences at the time. I had long been a 'student' of Carl Jung, reading many of his works, being an instant believer in his dream-analysis: interpreting our nocturnal movies not literally, but as symbols surfacing from our subconscious like signposts. I came to see the Bear as a "Big Test," the last obstacle to see how I would react when I didn't have time to intellectualize or analyze: in the face of death what would I call upon, instantaneously, from the instinctual level? I sensed that the Bear also symbolized Liberation, immediately following my lead: returning the love; setting me free in the moving hug. What lingered the longest each time from the dream, was that miraculous turning-point when Attack turned into a wild forest Polka!! This more than anything disarmed these new paranormal experiences, showing me there was no danger whatsoever, but an unbounded joy that now infused my days, putting a bounce in each step and a feeling that I had even swapped tickers with the bear—that my heart was now too big for my chest! I was bursting with life, bounding through the days; leaving honey in every footprint!!

As a carry-over from the dream, without conscious thought (as Jung said: "Proceed from the Dream outward")—I then began love-beaming all the other 'Bears' in my life, effortlessly ending opposition and ongoing arguments with business associates and family members by simply keeping Heart-Energy alive-and-glowing.

Then two other women appeared in my life—"satellites" to Planet Famke. One night the phone rang. A hesitant female voice on the other end: "Is this . . . Michael?"

"Yes . . . . " I knew it wasn't a Cosmo Girl, for my number was unlisted.

"Who are you?" she blurted.

"What? Who are *you*?!"

Silence. "This is the weirdest thing. I came home the other night and there's this message on my machine from a male voice to call 'Michael' and then your number. The caller didn't identify himself—no one I knew and he had the weirdest fucking voice!"

"How so?"

"As if he was from another planet—very etherial, and too damn calm for anyone I know!"

"You're not a 'Cosmopolitan' magazine reader?"

"No, why? I already *know* how to have orgasms! But why do you ask?"

When I told her, she burst into lascivious laughter. "Honey, I don't need to call a man. They are lined-up out the theater!"

"Theater? Are you an actress?"

"In a way . . . . A ballerina for a major dance company and just about to retire."

So began a long-distance phone friendship with Solange. We talked, totally open and brutally honest, for 2-3 hours a call. She was fascinated with the Cosmo dates and wanted to hear every detail. I was enchanted with 'The Life of a Ballerina' and she filled me in. Struggling with withdrawal from center stage, and instead of having roses tossed at her feet, Solange just had all of her toes purposely broken and reset, just so she could walk normally after a dozen years of being "on pointe." She was in reminiscent moods, flinging back the curtain on a fantasy figure: how in ballet female masochism is often taken to the furthest extremes, with nearly all the dancers in a vicious cycle of dieting, taking diuretics, laxatives and thyroid pills to stoke their metabolism; the prevalence of anorexia and bulimia. "The goal is to be a 'Stick-Bitch'—that's what we call ourselves. Some of us even eat Kleenex to blot out any traces of hunger . . . . But you go through it gladly for the few moments on stage, when it all comes together: the music, you, the audience all entwined—that flings your soul right out of your body! There's nothing else on earth that can touch it."

Deep into the experiences with Famke, one night I asked Solange if she believed in extraterrestrials? She went silent for a few seconds; then said: "Yes, very much so." As I then described what Famke had experienced; Solange repeatedly cut me off, completing the very sentences exactly as they happened. Finally, we couldn't go on, for she burst into tears and deep sobs . . . . I felt helpless, once again in over my head and feeling absolutely awed.

I asked if she would like to talk with Famke directly? "Oh, yes, please!"

A few nights later, Solange called to thank me for saving her life.

"What? I didn't do any- *Ahhhhh*—you talked to Famke! How did it go?"

Her voice was different, softened, the hard-edge completely gone. "Michael, now I know why I called you. It must have been an Angel or some sort of spirit that left your name and phone number on my answering machine, for, through you, I found a sister! As weird as it sounds, we have both been leading the same parallel lives with this other Reality. I can't tell you how wonderful it is to know I'm not alone and more than anything, after talking with Famke, for the first time in a long while I know for certain I'm not insane! I've spend a small fortune on psychiatrists over the years, describing the abductions and they all told me I was certifiably crazy. I even agreed to be medicated for a time. But now, after talking with her . . . . " I could barely hear her over the loud music: Tchaikovsky, booming in the background.

"Solange, I can't HEAR YOU! WHY ARE YOU BREATHING SO HARD?
"*YES!*"

"ARE YOU HAVING . . . sex?"

It was the last time I talked with Solange and her final reply left a lingering image . . . She was running down the long hallway in her home, in a nightgown, carrying a portable phone as, again and again, she arced above the hardwood, "*YES!*" "*YES!!*" "*YES!!!*"—repeatedly reaching performance height for a *gran jette . . .*

Some days I was exhausted—*I can't take any more!* It was all good. It was all wonderful, but, oftentimes, it just was all too much. I felt like I was drowning in the riches of women. I had always made it a habit, as common curtesy, to answer every piece of mail I received. But now I was falling hopelessly behind. So many letters to answer, and 50 more in the mail every day, and dashing off on dates, and late or not even started on my magazine assignments—falling way behind in all the other areas of my life, including money; then "AlaskaMen" magazine called: "Saw you in Cosmo; how would you like to be our next centerfold story; we'll plug your book and you'll get another couple thousand letters—you poor thing!" Pablo Picasso said something to the effect that a man should have as many women as he can keep happy. In my case, it was none.

To try to gain some perspective, to clear my head, I hit the road for a week, taking only water and fruit. I needed to fast: get away from the rich overload and distill down to a vital essence. I filled the trunk with climbing equipment and clothes for all weather; placed a road atlas on the passenger seat and two of my Top Ten favorite books on the dash: Jack Kerouac's *Dharma Bums* and *On The Loose* by the Russel brothers, Terry and Renny. Both books about deep yearning for adventure and direct experience with nature. I preferred Kerouac's *Dharma Bums* over the more popular *On The Road*, for *Dharma* relies less on the artificial: drugs and cars and more on the natural highs of being a "Rucksack Wanderer." So often had I turned to *On The Loose* for it's life-guiding wisdom that the binding had split and the pages were all out of order, but didn't matter with this masterpiece. You could dip in anywhere and the Russel brothers' assemblage of color photos from their wild wanderings, amplified by matching quotes from great thinkers and their own journals was a book to steer your life by.

I spent the first night and day in Yosemite, and drove away charged and pumped by the thundering waterfalls and soaring granite. Then a descent down past Tuolumne Meadows to the Mono Basin, once the site of an inland sea. I spent a day at Mono Lake, the oldest continuously existing body of water in North America. Even if you aren't aware of its history, you know something strange is going on, seeing hundreds of California seagulls nesting on the lake's north shore, hundreds of miles away from present-day ocean. I hiked slowly among the lake's *tufa* towers, eerie calcified rock formations, exposed since 1940 when Los Angeles began diverting Mono's inflow streams, shrinking the lake drastically and threatening the state's gull population by killing, through increased salinization, its main food source: brine shrimp.

I headed south on the magnificent Highway 395, gaining a new perspective on the Sierras by traveling along their eastern slopes, rising abruptly from the Great Basin like a snowcapped wall. Reaching the town of Bishop, I turned east up into the White Mountains, stopping when the road ran out at 11,000 feet. I hiked across a barren lunar landscape looking for the oldest living things on earth: bristlecone pines. At first, I thought I was too late; that the 5,000 year-old trees were all dead. I came upon a grove of straggly, amorphous shapes: the golden wood cracked into deep lines and knotted fossilized muscle—with branches flung up to the cobalt blue sky like anguished arms. At first glance you would declare these ancient arboreals long-gone, but look closer and you see a vitality more astonishing than a lush, towering redwood. In a windy, freezing cold and bone-dry environment, with few nutrients in the scant soil, bristlecone pines survived five entire millenniums by each tree sacrificing much of itself in order that one or two limbs might live. Out of a hunched-over old hobgoblin there was one single branch sparkling with green needles and small brown cones! This was life at its most tenacious and I drove away pondering the life lessons: Whatever lives in the richest, easiest soil usually expires early (clogged arteries), but have the proving ground be high-altitude and hard pan, and out of extreme difficulty, tested sap rises, proving the fiercer the challenge, oftentimes, the longer the life.

I continued south on Highway 395, marveling at the richness and variety throughout California. I then drove all throughout Death Valley, parking anywhere in that empty immensity at night and simply rolled my sleeping bag out on a salt flat and closed my eyes. At Badwater, I stood in the lowest spot on earth—282 feet below sea level, gazing up into the distance at the highest point in the continental U.S., Mt. Whitney at 14,494 feet. I then drove west and in the Sierra foothills, spent a carefree day bouldering on the varied shaped bulwarks in the Alabama Hills as a tune-up for an ascent of Whitney.

Coming down through the healing balm of alpine air with a bounce in my step and feling sky-high, having summited Mt. Whitney, I was not quite ready to go home. Back on Highway 395, I turned east down a dirt road and drove toward white clouds low on the horizon that turned out to be sand dunes, the Eureka Dunes, some rising as high as 700 feet! As if in a daze, I walked away from the car, leaving the door open, and stepped up onto the sand, pure white and flowing in female contours to the distant Panamint Mountains.

I looked closer and saw traces of life—nature's hieroglyphics on the smooth flanks of sand: tiny bug tracks, every jot-and-tittle perfectly preserved, and then a bold swaying 'S' of a snake that had traveled through, hours before, in the cool morning. Clomping on, I was started by a solitary plant, a vibrant lime-green stalk amidst that clean white contrast, growing in a thrifty hollow that collects just enough moisture for life to survive. I gazed upward at artful "pour patterns" along the dune ridges where wind and gravity had avalanched dagger-like tongues that overlapped the sand and were baked into place by a fiery sun.

Totally alone and in such a sensual environment, I wanted to absorb more: take it all in through my skin. Still transfixed, without hesitation or thought, I stepped out of my shoes and all of my clothes and walked deeper into the dunes.

Feeling totally unbound, I began running, chugging to the top of the highest dune, "music" issuing from each step as the loose sand squeaked and piped underfoot like organ notes. Then atop the high ridge, like a gleeful child, I dropped down and rolled sideways, all-out, along the white curve, coming to rest at the base of the dune, half-buried. I lay there, covering myself with loose sand, until my body was erased completely.

I closed my eyes, giving myself over to the warm weight of the sand, heavy as water; feeling the sweet surrender of living death. The hot sun pressing on my head like a stone disc and the roar of desert silence—all that mattered.

Then a stirring . . . my penis—hardening down inside the warm enclosure. I laughed, watching a new 'dune snake' shift its way up through the sand! In a state of total tumescence, I laid my head back on a soft pillow; scooped up a handful of sand and watched the tiny grains stream through my open fingers. *These are our cells! And this*, I paused to look around at the flowing dunes, lavender mountains, azure sky, *This is our Body, our very Being!!*

I stood up, breaking through the pure white earth and walked. I walked covered head to toes in sand, the fine silica a second skin. I walked, wearing the history of the earth: sea shell bits, rounded mountains, ground-down dinosaur bones, the basal makings of computer chips . . . . I walked not knowing or caring where my clothes were—feeling overwhelmed, with two vertical rivulets—mud gullies flowing under my eyes . . . .

I got into the car and drove north through the desert still naked and scoured clean by the sand, by the sweet caress of open land. In Bishop, I stopped in front of a convenience store for water and very reluctantly—put on clothes.

Back home, I felt like a new man.

Because of a lot of national and local media attention, the San Francisco chapter of The March of Dimes called, asking if I would join their "Bid for Bachelors" auction, in which the Bay Area's "most eligible males" were auctioned off (with donated date packages) to raise money for the very worthwhile charity. I readily agreed to participate, catching a second-wind after the desert hegira and getting caught-up on work. With the auction date fast approaching and being the 'Cosmo Guy,' I felt I had to come up with a bit more than the usual evening of limousine ride to dinner at a fancy restaurant. As a travel writer, I pulled a few strings and landed a 4 day; 3 nights stay in Cabo San Lucas, at a new beach hotel; round-trip flights included.

While renting the tuxedo, it hit me that I was going to have to actually walk down a long (endless!) runway in the heart of The City, at the swanky St. Francis Drake Hotel in front of 500+ strange, sizing-you-up females. And no matter being fancily dressed or how many layers of cloth-armor: before deciding to fork-over money for you, their gazes would be piercing! (Believe it or not, this scribe is extremely shy. The naked moments in my life had originally been conducted in private or as anonymous posings for art. And I could easily and most happily spend all my allotted hours, sealed-off in a small garret writing away. But there's life to be lived and people to be learned from, so I've trained myself to be outgoing—because, deep down, I am shy—like the outverted concept that "courage is a form of fear turned-around.") Then to fling away the last vestiges of shyness (and help publicize the geographic location of my offered date), I decided to top-off the conservative black tux, with an enormous ten-gallon, cherry-red satin, rhinestoned, trimmed-in-gold-braid, three foot circumference Mexican sombrero. ("Where's 'Dawn?'" another customer said in the costume store as I was trying to get the right tilt to the mobcap in front of a mirror. "Who?" I said. She smiled: "You look just like Tony Orlando!")

"Knock three times on the ceiling if you want me . . . . " then became my nervous mantra chanted over-and-over the night of the Auction. I had to stand backstage nearly all night, in last place. A total basket-case, I watched each of my eligible amigos part that stage curtain with trembling hand when called to face the music (a song that they had pre-chosen to best represent their personality or date-package), and then they undertook the endless march straight down the center of liquored-up women, wolf-whistling and waving their credit cards if they saw something they liked, as your name and vital-statistics were announced over top the music. It was a total role-reversal and the women relished it, playing it up for all it (and we) were worth.

Finally, with no more bachelors lined-up ahead, and feeling like a buck private facing his moment-of-truth—about to parachute into the field-of-fire, I tugged open the curtain (very wide to clear the sombrero) and jumped. The music helped: Joe Cocker's lusty rendition of "You Can Leave Your Hat On." The song and sombrero broke the tension and as I strode boldly down the runway I was awash in a wave of laughter. (The second greatest physical pleasure for me is coaxing merriment from *la femme*. Hearing a woman laugh carries the same exciting undertones of what she might sound like when "going to the gods" as D.H. Lawrence termed orgasm. I first noticed the similarity from two young Finnish masseuses staffing the spa at the Explora lodge in Patagonia, when each time they merely giggled, sounded absolutely 'divine!')

The bidding climbed; and then a few shoppers actually asked for a closer inspection of the goods. (I blushed as *rojo* as the sombrero as I stepped down from the stage to stand before them—my ass pinched good-naturedly along the way!) Then the bidding narrowed: back and forth, higher and higher between a black-clad young vixen and a middle-aged woman (and one of the organizers of the event). Back up on the runway, blinded by klieg lights, it was difficult to track further specifics . . . . However, I kept seeing, very clearly, a pair of enormous pale blue eyes jump from across the room, disembodied, as if without a face. *Wow—those Eyes!!*

The bidding was over. The Mexican package was purchased by Karen, who had a deeper purse or more persistent interest than the younger lady. After thanking Karen, chatting for a while and then exchanging phone numbers, I staggered off to the bar, in desperate need of a vodka martini, feeling both shaken *and* stirred! When I looked up after that first, much-needed gulp, there before me were those eyes, even more striking now set in an olive-skin face, accentuated by jet-black hair in a chic, asymmetrical cut.

"Sonia Sierra," she said, extending her hand. "You did a wonderful thing! I would have bid but I'm already going to Cabo."

"Are you Mexican? Spanish?"

"Nicaraguan," she said, properly rolling all the vowels. "I really must go, but here, call me sometime?"

Another exchange of numbers and the beginning of a wonderful relationship. Sonia was a Forecast Analyst at an international corporation based in San Francisco, along with being, as her mother before her, a *Curandera*: a psychic, a healer, a fount of arcane knowledge, a Woman of The Spirit. For our first date, I went over to her apartment. She cooked an incredible gourmet-Italian meal, with three different wines perfectly accenting each course. She was extremely well read; had traveled the world and our conversation roamed in all directions. While conversing, I was totally captivated by her eyes—the palest blue; and so translucent that they seemed to gather light from the air and beam it directly into your soul. Eyes that followed you around the room without moving. Eyes that are open even when closed. Then after desert of homemade tiramisu, Sonia asked if I wanted her to read my Cards?

We sat side-by-side at the end of the table. She brought out a silk sac and there before us was the first deck of Tarot I had ever seen. The rectangular, oversized cards looked and felt (Sonia had me cut the deck, "your vibrations will guide them") magical. The colorful figures and symbols were things I had never seen before. Vices, virtues and elemental forces from ancient times now came alive under Sonia's gaze. A bit skeptical, at first, as she spread the cards out on the table what then won me over was the overall environment: this wasn't "Madam Zora" with the hokey soothsayer sign in a weedy front yard; crystal ball and tacky flocked drapes inside. No, the Madam here was as hip and altruistic as they come.

The reading was lengthy and never literal—Sonia viewed the card as it came off the deck as merely a springboard—her eyelids fluttering like wings of hummingbirds as she launched into specific details of my life (most now proven to be true). The one card that kept appearing over and over was the Hierophant. "Michael, this is really you; your role in life," she said tapping the cowled man. "You are the Hierophant: a man who has insights into the female; the bridge between the two genders and energies, acting as the balance of them both."

We often canceled conventional dates of dinner-and-a-movie, caught-up in the excitement of simply sitting side-by-side for hours on the couch, looking through her library of metaphysical books. I learned how Tarot influenced modern psychiatry; and another art book displayed dazzling *Apsaras*, heavenly female bodies, seductresses in stone, exquisitely carved in the sides of temples at Angkor Wat. Called both 'Celestial Cancan Dancers' and the highest expression of femininity ever conceived by the human mind, they waited in heaven for dead heroes to reward them for their good lives on earth with supernatural sexual pleasure!

"Now *that's* Heaven!" I said.

Sonia smiled and nodded. She believed that sexuality was extremely important in spiritual practice, but that Puritanism in America had stunted this radiant growth and physical liberation was key to attaining total fulfillment.

"Here," Sonia said one day, handing over an autobiography. "Your 'alter eagle' is Aleister Crowley. He was a mountain climber, a writer, a Magus. A man of both action and passionate words!"

In time, after getting to know Sonia, trusting her, I told her all about Famke; and told Famke all about Sonia. Both wanted to meet the other immediately; and neither flung-up the usual proprietary: "Are you *Sleeping* with *HER!?*" They had evolved way past all that . . . and seeing them together, hugging for the first time was a dazzling sight—total opposites: Famke, the blonde Nordic Valkyre and Sonia, the dark Latino. Oh my, I felt like genuflecting—in the presence of totally opposite, yet divine fems (and after experiencing the 'Three Tones' and 'Blue Whorls' with Famke, I now came to view *all* women as Goddesses)!!

At that moment, Famke and Sonia both opened their arms and invited me in. Famke then moved us over to a mirror. Near the same height, we all leaned-in: Three faces, completely different, but the windows or lamps to the soul were identically lit: with high-beam blue eyes. We all laughed, seeing the linkup. I thought of the lines from Richard Bach's *Illusions*: "The bond that links your true family is not one of blood, but respect and joy in each other's life. Rarely do the members of one family grow up under the same roof."

I usually saw Sonia on weekends. One Saturday, we toured the hidden soul of San Francisco, visiting "Botanica and Religious" stores, sprinkled like holy water in back streets and alleys. They were *apothacarias* selling incantations, spells, potions, lotions and magical herbs. Shelves were crammed full of statues of strange saints; exotic Macumba gods and goddesses; papier-mâché human skeletons and leering *diablos* from Mexico's "Day of The Dead" celebration. The artist Frieda Kahlo was making a resurgence and reproductions of her paintings hung on the walls in unbroken rows like her linked eyebrows. Isabel Allende's masterpiece, *The House of The Spirits* was just published, with copies everywhere. While Sonia chattered in rapid-fire Spanish with a shop owner, I dipped into the book. "Hey, Sonia! Listen—here you are!" I read aloud: "'Clara lived in a Universe of her own invention, protected from life's inclement weather, where the prosaic truth of material objects mingled with the tumultuous reality of dreams and the laws of physics and logic did not always apply . . . .'"

We never stayed in a store longer than a few minutes, before leaving for the next. Sonia was in search of "Damiana," a potent herb purported to be an aphrodisiac, but as we discovered there was none to be had in San Francisco—so she'd just have to go to its source, Mexico—where it grew in the wild.

Sonia really had previously scheduled a vacation in Cabo San Lucas at the same time as my "Bid for Bachelors" auctioned date, and had booked long ago at the same new hotel.

"Sonia, as much as I love being with you, I'm going all-out to make sure Karen has a great time."

"Michael, that goes without saying. But—hey, let's just let the cards fall where they may . . . ."

"Cards? Falling!" You know something I don't?" I said through a squinted eye.

She grinned. "The script has already been written; let's just play our parts!"

I then met with Karen to become further acquainted and talk about our long weekend together in Cabo. Our banter was loose and easy, but the "three nights" part of the package hung over our heads like a lead balloon.

I took a stab at it. "Uh, Karen, I just want you to know that, well, I don't want you to think . . . . Ummmmmmmm we-have-two-separate-rooms."

"Thank you. I *was* wondering . . . . And, Michael . . . . "

"Yes?"

"Serendipity."

"How so?"

"Let's just 'play the moment.' " Her coy smile floated up, expanding lightly through where the heavy-pressure had just been.

I nodded and gulped, praying that "playing the moment" didn't intersect with "playing our parts."

After landing in Cabo, (Sonia two rows back on the same, one-flight-a-day plane) and checking in at the hotel, Karen and I changed into swim suits and wandered out to the pool. After excusing herself to go to the ladies room, on the way back, of the two dozen people randomly scattered pool side, whom does Karen strike-up a conversation with? *Sonia*—sunbathing solo by the deep end! As women so often and so effortlessly do, they immediately bonded; became buds, then Sonia got up and they both walked over. Sonia didn't let on that she knew me at all as Karen introduced us; and totally at Karen's invitation (feeling sorry that "the poor dear is here all alone"), Sonia then joined us each day for either lunch, dinner or shopping. (And, unplanned, our three rooms turned out to be on the same floor, with Sonia directly across from us!)

I learned invaluable lessons about the war-between-the-sexes from the battled- seasoned, 5-time married Karen, who was not in good shape, as, just a short time before, a firestorm in the Oakland Hills tragically took her house, all of her possessions; and nearly her life. She escaped with just seconds to spare. "Michael, you have no idea how much I need this . . . just to relax and forget." Yet, despite her losses, she still showed an undaunted spirit and marvelous appetite for life: a female Zorba whom after tossing back four fishbowl-sized margaritas in a beach-shack bar, announced to the entire resort in a throaty roar: "I BOUGHT THIS MAN FOR TWO GRAND!!" (Normally, I would have slid and hid under the table, crumpled with embarrassment but instead, I comfortably and wholeheartedly laughed along over the sheer surreality of it with the crowd— who sent over four more celebratory fishbowls.)

A young adult in San Francisco during the late 1960's, Karen summed-up the era of free love: "I could have any man in the bars I wanted—once they saw me tie a cherry stem in a knot with the tip of my tongue!" She then applied her talent for figures to California politics, being the finance chairwoman for many a campaign. "I should write my life story about all the rich-and-famous men I've known, both 'biblically' and professionally. I know—I'll send a letter out: 'It'll cost you $100,000 to be in the book or $200,000 *not* to be!!"

We went whale watching, with the tropical early evening air like crushed-velvet and a setting sun and a full moon sharing the sky. We went step'n out to the nightclub, "Cabo Wabo" where absentee owner, Sammy Hagar of Van Halen dropped in to play. We rowed a boat out past broken, towering cliffs to Playa del Amour and walked barefoot on the beach where two seas meet, holding hands and Karen completely letting go, crying for the first time over her severe losses, her tears falling into the surf swirling over our feet. As sad as she was; and as helpless as I always felt in the presence of a woman's tears, I was glad I could simply be there for her.

Karen's one "non-negotiable" was to go deep sea fishing. As we headed out through a newborn morning to where the Pacific Ocean flowed into the fish-rich Sea of Cortez, I was first up to fish, but we then went all day without a single bite. It didn't matter, for suntanned and wind-swept in the salt air, Karen had reached a turning point. She was smiling and laughing and telling raunchy jokes that would have made a crow blush (and had the crusty captain repeatedly shaking his head). Then, turning for home we were startled to see, a hundred yards away, a long bill suddenly burst above the surface like King Author's sword! The first mate quickly re-baited the line with a fresh ballyhoo from the live box and flung it overboard. *Pow!* In a matter of seconds, the captain is yelling: "FISH ON!" and the mate struggling to hand over the throbbing pole that flung him all around the deck.

For the next two hours, while fighting a Hemingwayesque 400 pound blue marlin off Land's End, strapped into the big barber chair with Karen tossing buckets of cool water over me, I thought of how I was in over my head. *What had become of my simple, near-monastic writerly life?* In the lulls between the fish's monstrous runs, I thought of how even my mother had baited me.

One night, at home, answering the phone I heard the most sultry, provocative voice imaginable: "Hiii Mi-kal, this is Maaan-dee—from Phoenix. I saw you in Cosmo and just had to call. Ohhh . . . you are such a-"

I tuned-out the words to listen closer to the voice, itself. At the risk of forever ruining my chances with Mandy, I said: "MOM—is that *YOU?*"

A pause, then a shrill giggle.

"MOM—STOP IT! YOU CAN'T TALK LIKE THAT. IT'S—IT'S ILLEGAL!!"

"Son, everyone I know has seen you in the magazine and they tell me how sexy you are—but in a good down-to-earth, wholesome way. I know it will help your career. What great exposure—being on the same page with Robin Williams, Lisa Hartman and We Three."

"It's U2, Mom. They're a rock band."

"Oh, they all sound the same. But, son, I do hope with all this attention—you are being 'careful'?"

"Yes, Mother, very careful . . . . "

Then brother Scott called, very impressed with the latest findings in his coat pockets. His agent, to make sure he was a sharp-dressed man on modeling and acting castings, bought Scott an exquisite Giorgio Armani jacket that he shared with me, since we both wear a 40-regular. The Armani not only fit, but brought out the best in both of us. It was the ultimate "weapon" in the war-between-the-sexes. No way could you walk out the door wearing that jacket and not feel on top of your game. It was as if thousands of years of Roman creativity and Etruscan expression had distilled itself up though time, into the mind of Armani and out the nimble fingers of his tailors. The unstructured jacket was sculpture in cloth. The color was that debatable navy blue that is black, no blue, that kept a woman guessing. When one of us had a hot date that required reaching deep into the wardrobe to make a lasting impression, we'd call the brother who currently had the coat, and Armani FedEx'ed from Arizona to California, or vice versa, would save the day (or night). And we tracked one another's progress within the coat, itself. We purposely left Big Event ticket stubs from concerts, ballet, the opera; rose petals, champagne corks, match book covers from clubs de riguere—all went into the pocket archives. In less than a year, due mainly to the accelerated Cosmo dates, the Armani jacket had acquired a romantic history all its own.

"Scott," I'd call, "I need The Jacket."

"Who is she?"

"Laetitia Lavaggi. Going all-out. Taking her to Italian opera, "La Traviata"—orchestra seats, then pasta dinner at midnight."

"You got it, bro. It'll be on your doorstep tomorrow by ten. Full Report?"

"Yep—top pocket. Could be that kind of evening!"

With the latest buildup of date detritus, Scott called and I filled him in on some of the latest trysts and asked his advice about doing "AlaskaMen." Then no more than an hour later the phone rang again.

"Michael, it's Mother."

"Hi, Mom."

"*What* did I raise? First, the Bachelor-of-The-Month—now a centerfold in 'AlaskaMen!'"

"Mom, the staple in my naval goes through ski clothes—there's no bare skin!"

"Your brothers and sister are all married and have children and you, you're the oldest and you've become a wild man. What did I raise? What happened to that little Catholic boy who wanted to be a priest?"

"Well, he discovered that the 'Gates of Heaven' are here on earth!"

"Oh, son—I'll pray for your soul . . . . "

The marlin made another run, peeling line off the reel until it smoked; then came up . . . and up—out of the water, tail-dancing and shaking its leviathan-like head. The line stretched taut; then went totally slack as the hook whizzed past my ear (relieved, since we were going to release him, anyway).

With confusion about my love life at its very height, hell—I asked for a Larger Size! The final night turned into a Noel Coward play, a roundelay of too much imbibing of alcohol and tiptoeing back-and-forth across the hotel hallway. The next morning we flew home to San Francisco . . . Karen feeling totally rejuvenated; ready to rebuild her life . . . *moi* with marlin-cramped forearms and a splitting headache . . . Sonia cradling a bottle of Damiana—finding it not in the care of a high-desert, Castenada-like don Juan, but in plain sight at the very last minute in the tiny Cabo airport gift shop! (Back in San Francisco, we ceremoniously tried a nip; the stuff worked—Nature's Viagra!)

Unlike the many people who appear-then-vanish during our lifetimes, Sonia has remained a constant friend and trusted spiritual adviser. She's a force of nature and *La Curandera* of the highest degree.

As we run on into the night, besides employing memory to help breakup the pressing labor, in the flashlight beam I begin kicking a rounded stone, imitating the Tarahumara Indians. Living in Chihuahua, Mexico, about 300 miles from El Paso, Texas, their home is the Copper Canyon: actually deeper, steeper and more rugged than the Grand Canyon. Centuries ago they took refuge there in remote caves from the Spanish looking for forced labor for the mines. In a near-vertical world, traversed by vertiginous trails, it's actually safer to travel on foot, rather than endanger horses or mules. They call themselves *Raramuri* or "foot runners" in their Uto-Azetecan language. In the old days they would hunt deer by running after it for days . . . until the prey finally dropped from exhaustion. Their main sport is *rarajipari*, kicking a wooden ball for 200 miles or more in continuous days-long races.

Every few yards—as I kick the round stone ahead again, I now understand why the Tarahumara did this while running: It takes the mind off the immense task at hand, diverting it with incremental play.

Two Tarahumara men represented Mexico in a regular marathon (26 miles) at the Olympic Games in Amsterdam. But no one told them when the race ended. They crossed the finish line and kept running until they were stopped. The men were incredulous that the marathon was over. "Too short!" "Too short!" they said. An American agent recently entered Tarahumaras in 100 mile trail ultra marathons in the US—a distance more to their liking. Not only have the Tarahumaras been winning, but they've shattered records, especially in the Leadville (Colorado) 100 miler, "The Race Across The Sky," where the *lowest* parts of the course are at 10,000 feet.

With everyone else wearing the latest state-of-the-art Nike Air-Max or Reebok Pump $100 running shoes and drinking high-tech electrolyte concoctions, the Tarahumaras race in 'barely-there' huarache sandals and take an occasional nibble of a native corn-gruel. Watching a Tarahumara run is like seeing the Earth, itself, sprout up two spindly-strong legs and a smooth heart of clay, thudding only a few times a minute . . . and a smile like an unbroken sunbeam all the while, all the way.

I spent long hours at a new bookstore down the hill: "Gaia" (named after James Lovelock's theory that the Earth, itself, is a conscious, self-regulating entity). I had always been a voracious reader, but now my appetite was way out of control. I was spending far more money on books each week than groceries. It wasn't random reading. Books now fell into my hands like lodestars, blazing with answers.

I couldn't wait to take Famke into Gaia (both seemingly one-and-the-same). Immediately, upon entering the store, she twirled around, her burbling-brook laugh flooding the place as she took-in all the wisdom-of-the-ages titles; shamanic drums and rattles on the walls, sage and incense bundles, meditation music, tarot decks, Nordic rune stones, African Goddess/fertility dolls. She was clearly on home-turf. Pressed for time, as we always were, she danced down an aisle and plucked-up a book. "Michael, *this* has a lot to do with the Blue Whorls!" I immediately ran it over to a cashier: *Kundalini: The Arousal of The Inner Energy* by Ajit Mookerjee.

Answers were immediately forthcoming: " . . . Liberation while living is considered in Indian life to be the highest experience—a fusion of the individual with the universal. The individual manifestation is like a spark of the cosmos, as the human organism, the microcosm, parallels everything in the macrocosm. The complete drama of the universe is repeated here, in this very body. The whole body with its biological and psychological processes becomes an instrument through which the cosmic power reveals itself. According to tantric principles, all that exists in the universe must also exist in the individual body. If we can analyze one human being, we shall be able to analyze the entire universe, because it is believed that all is built on the same plane. The purpose is to search for the whole truth within, so that one may realize one's inner self, unfolding the basic reality of the universe.

" . . . The Sanskrit word *kundalini* means 'coiled-up.' The coiled kundalini is the female energy existing in latent form, not only in every human being but in every atom of the universe. It may frequently happen that an individual's kundalini energy lies dormant throughout his or her entire lifetime and he or she is unaware of its existence. The object of the tantric practice of kundalini yoga is to awaken this cosmic energy and cause it to unite with *Siva*, the Pure Consciousness pervading the whole universe.

" . . . A dynamization, transformation and sublimation of the physical, mental, and spiritual state is only possible with the arousal of the Kundalini Sakti and her reorientation from downward to upward movement as she rises to unite with Siva, resulting in the flooding of the whole being with indescribable bliss. The aspirant raises himself from the grosser elements to the subtlet, and realizes, in a transcendent experience, his union with Siva-Sakti, to become a 'cosmic man.'

" . . . Through the ages, the sex act has been generally associated with procreation or gross physical satisfaction. Tantrikas, however, realized the immense potentiality of sex energy, and, through tantraasanas, transformed the energy of sex and freed it to a plane of cosmic awareness. Sex is seen as divine in itself, and a source of vital energy capable of acting with tremendous force on the physiopsychic state which in turn reacts on the higher cosmic plane.

" . . . The manifested Kundalini becomes Kula, an all-transcending light of consciousness . . . . "

As I discovered in further readings, knowledge of Kundalini transcends cultures and centuries. From D.H. Lawrence, in his poem "Terra Incognita": "There are vast realms of consciousness still undreamed of, vast ranges of experience, like the humming of unseen harps, we know nothing of, within us . . . ."

From Stephen and Robin Larsen, in *A Fire In The Mind: The Life of Joseph Campbell*: "The person in whom the Kundalini has arisen may have strange experiences of lights and colors, visions and emotions which seem to be out of control."

From Michael Murphy, in *The Future of The Body: Explorations Into The Further Evolution of Human Nature*: "Many people say that during deep moments of love new energies or entities materialize in the space around them."

From Alex Jones, in *Seven Mansions of Color*: "In ordinary humans . . . chakras or wheels of light . . . spin just enough to bring in the required energy for living. In spiritual masters [*Famke*] of all religions, however, these same chakras are swirling balls of light like luminous suns . . . . "

From Rudolf Steiner: "Every substance on earth is condensed light. Inasmuch as man is a material being, his substance is woven out of light, condensed light."

From Albert Einstein: "E=MC2: Energy is equivalent to mass multiplied by the square or velocity of light—or simplified: All matter is merely condensed energy."

From John Milton in "Areopagitica": "The light which we have gained was given us, not to be ever starting on, but by it to discover onward things more remote than our knowledge."

From Ibn al-'Arabi the Murcian (Greatest Master of the Sufi): "Angels are the powers hidden in the faculties and organs of man."

From Buddha: "Make of yourself a light . . . . "

I now began to look at halos in a new light. My minor in college was Art History and after graduating I lugged around in various moves, and continued amassing, lavish art books: portable museums. (Could there be a better way to spend an evening than listening to Vivaldi's "Four Seasons" while reverently turning the pages/paintings of Fra Angelico or Piero Della Francesca?) Halos began catching my eye. In Renaissance paintings what distinguished Jesus and other saints were the auras of light around their heads. Before, I never thought halos were real, merely symbolic coronas showing enlightened souls. Having been raised a Catholic, I thought that these mysterious auroras were divinely ordained, not humanly attained but now I wondered if halo bearers aren't human beings who through meditation, prayer and/or sex (with the proper partner: divine worship of the highest degree!)—uncoiled their own kundalini that shot up through the chakras, to bloom above the head like a luminous crown?! I now felt convinced that halos aren't just for saints, but that everyone has one, if we just learn how to turn the Light(s) on. And in reaction to the rare souls who do, the muddled masses, so quick to believe in a god but never in themselves—put these souls up on pedestals as plaster statues, when the 'gods' are merely being perfectly human: lit to peak illumination!

Nothing now seemed too fantastic. I read like a detective following clues to the greatest mystery of all: Life, itself.

I discovered profound wisdom about the Dream Bear, that I continued to dance with in James Redfield's *The Tenth Insight*: " . . . Animals reflect our own level of consciousness and expectation. If our level of vibration is low, the animals will merely be there with us, performing their ecological functions. When a skeptical biologist reduces animal behavior to mindless instinct, he sees the restriction that he himself has put upon the animal. But as our vibration shifts, the actions of the animals that come to us become even more synchronostic, mysterious, and instructional."

I was in a perfect place: a reader's paradise. Berkeley is chock-a-block with bookstores; and not just to service the students at the University of California, but to supply the second largest book-buying public (after New York City) in the U.S. There, in the era of monopolizing chain stores—independent, idiosyncratic book shops still thrived. (For where more indie thinkers than 'Bezerkly?'") One day, deep in the secondhand stacks at Moe's Books, a veritable Temple of the printed word, I picked up a tome that totally blew me away! The title is what first caught my eye: *Occult Chemistry* (first published in 1895, with subsequent reprints). I sat there, astounded, for the entire day reading how two theosophists, Charles Leadbeater and Annie Besant, through psychic ability, described and diagrammed the subatomic composition of all the chemical elements, down to the level of quarks and beyond (years before these very elements were scientifically 'discovered' and then *Occult Chemistry* fully validated by particle physicists)! Leadbeater and Besant had developed, within themselves, a yogic power called *siddhi* enabling them to attune their vision to subatomic levels!! (The Theosophical Society, founded in New York City in 1875 by mystic Helena Blavatsky, was devoted to "the study and elucidation of occultism, to vindicate the preeminent importance of Eastern religions, and to explore the hidden mysteries of nature and the powers hidden inside the physical human.")

It's time that all these powers are recognized and respected and taught in schools, alongside reading, writing and arithmetic. What could be more important than maximizing full human potential and thus provide a Quantum Leap, so needed to advance our consciousness and heal an endangered planet! What required a billion-dollar supercollider to penetrate the mysteries of the atom, nearly a century before, two human beings did with no cost (other than traveling to India to learn the *siddhi* techniques). We're so quick to place our faith in machines, depend on hardware outside of ourselves when we 'ware' the answers "softly," within.

Then, in further readings of Leadbeater and other *siddhi* masters like Blavatsky, Paracelsus, and Rudolph Steiner, they all stated, unequivocally, that the elements, from hydrogen on up, are aided, nurtured, transformed by nature spirits—actual conscious entities acting as the matrix for the growth of plants, flowers, trees, the richness of soil!!

This I struggled long-and-hard with . . . . That these credible clairvoyants, proven subatomic seers, also saw (via direct personal experiences) that fairies, sylphs, undines, and gnomes, "the little people" of the Third Kingdom *did* exist; and not as Tolkien fiction but real fact—*that* I had extreme difficulty and reluctance wrapping my mind around. The fey world of fairies is real?! The portly, apple-cheeked gnome figurines on lawns and gardens were far more than ceramic?!! *Hey, keep an open mind,* I then kept telling myself: *Did you not see Sabrina and meet Famke and experience the Blue Whorls, when just a year ago you wouldn't have believed any of it in the slightest way?* One of my favorite novels is Thea Alexander's *2150 A.D.* As Rama, one of the main characters states: "The measure of a mind's evolution is its acceptance of the unacceptable."

The more I read, the more things became clear.

In a New York Times article entitled "Casting an Eye on Sights Unseen," George Johnson wrote: "Gazing at the edge of a rainbow, one can almost feel the presence of another color just beyond violet, a hue that can't quite be seen because human eyes were not made to register the light waves called ultraviolet.

"And beyond violet and ultraviolet are the higher frequency "colors"—X-rays and gamma rays—all vibrating too fast for the eye to catch.

"Traveling down the spectrum in the other direction, the eye quickly bumps against another barrier. Where red leaves off is an ineffable redder red, called infrared, slow invisible undulations that can be felt against the skin as heat. And beyond that are even lower unseeable frequencies called radio waves.

"The brain paints its pictures with a paltry palette. We are surrounded by a world we cannot see . . . . We'll always be a few levels removed from a reality we ultimately can only imagine, trapped inside our bodies looking out."

Is this the Territory where Angels, Fairies, Gnomes reside (not cutesy Hollywood versions, but awesome spiritual power-plants)? Vibrating faster or slower than the human eye can track? Doing their work on parallel planes, undisturbed by man, but occasionally experienced by us when they enter our limited realms of perception or we occasionally breakthrough—climb the "Kundalini Ladder" to visit theirs?

No matter what I was reading now, relevant passages leaped forth. In *Gone Whaling* by Douglas Hand: "There is a contemporary American philosopher, David Lewis, who is an exponent of possible worlds. He believes that what makes this world an actual one is simply that it is the world we are in. In his view, there are many other worlds with other people in them, which are actual for those people. Lewis's position is known as 'modial realism.' I felt as if I had just seen an example of it. There, in front of me, ants were crawling through the brown grass and over my feet, although I couldn't even feel them, not the slightest trickle. The ants were in their own world. They had their own rhythm of life, as did the hawk, the crows, the orcas. We were all in the same place, but for each one of us that place was different."

Then, like never really noticing a word until you lookup its definition, then with your awareness turned-up you start seeing it everywhere—an entirely new color entered my life, as if to drive home a point. It started while fishing for salmon one day, out past San Francisco Bay. Having subsistence-fished while living along the British Columbia coast, I knew the quest for salmon to be both art and science, but Joe, the first mate, was a downright physicist of the piscator! When I asked why all the trolling lures were such a bright, garish color, he smiled: "Chartreuse catches fish!"

"Why""

"Good question. Hmm . . . . Let's see—O.K., let's try it this way: The visible electromagnetic spectrum shows up as colors. Still with me?

"Yep."

"O.K. The light spectrum runs from violet through shades of blue, green, yellow, orange to deep Red. Fish see underwater pretty much like we do above. So the most effective color, most easily seen is going to be what falls in the exact middle of the visible spectrum, between green and yellow, and that's chartreuse. Doesn't matter if it's cloudy, sunny, if you're running deep or through soupy seas—chartreuse," he paused to dangle a lure, "catches fish!"

Then the next day, I drove by a fire station that I passed a hundred times before. The big main truck was jutting halfway out the garage. What color? Chartreuse. I turned abruptly into the drive and rolled down the window. "What happened to *red* fire engines? When I was a kid they were always red!"

A fireman, polishing the side of the truck, nodded and said: "Asked the same question myself when I started working here. Chartreuse is the most visible color. Falls right in the middle of the spectrum . . . . "

I focus on the next glow-sticks in the trees, marking our route. What color would they be to catch the attention of bleary-eyed, brain-dead runners on their last legs? As the lights streak in the breeze, again: CHARTREUSE.

Man doesn't fool around with fishing lures, fire engines and ultra running glow-sticks. With livelihoods and lives on the line, they aren't painted just any random color. So, instead of mere words; theories on paper, there was gaudy proof that the human eye doesn't see all things equally; there are gradients to our sight and many things that don't even show up on the eye chart at all. Artists, the color and perception wizards of the visible world, know and show this. As Paul Klee told us: "What is visible is only a sample of what is real."

"Superman" was my favorite comic book as a kid. Of all his powers (*Faster than a speeding bullet! More powerful than a locomotive!! Able to leap tall buildings in a single bound!!!*) it was his X-ray vision I was most fascinated with: being able, at will, to see through the surface of things. I've yet to outgrow Superman, for as incredible as his powers are, the longer I live the more I sense that they are based on truths latent within us all: the woman, backing the car down the driveway, runs over her child, picks up the two-ton car to save her flesh-and-blood; the doctor who leaps over the tall wall in a single bound to save car crash victims; 'X-ray/*siddhi* vision' psychics who see atomic particles and nature spirits;

yogis and other enlightened souls who fly out the window (without a cape!) and zoom around the world on the wings of astral-projection.

Why should we outgrow the influence and belief in the benevolent Superhero?

German philosopher, Friedrich Nietzsche didn't. He was the first, in 1883, to coin the word Superman, *Ubermensch*, describing the individual whose creative powers broke the chains of human limitations. Elvis didn't. The role-model who took him to the top was "Captain Marvel": The King wore the same wing-collared jumpsuits and capes on-stage (give-or-take a few rhinestones) and incorporated Marvel's very same thunderbolts in his mission-statement logo of "T.C.B." (Takin' Care a-Bizness). Jane Goodall didn't. When interviewing her for a national magazine, and not really getting anywhere, I threw caution to the winds blurting-out: "Jane, when I was a teenager you were the first pinup on my bedroom wall; not Farah Fawcett with the cascading curls and chicklet teeth, but, YOU, Jane!" The zoo officials standing around us nearly fainted. But I finally had her full attention. She stopped walking; tilted her head to one side and fired me a look that she likely gave in the jungle to a threatening baboon. My brain then kicked into overdrive, trying to fill-in my audacity. "As a kid I used to go to Saturday matinees: Tarzan double-features and walking out of the theater afterwards I thought Tarzan was Tarzan; Boy was Boy; Cheetah—certainly Cheetah, but I could never buy Maureen O'Sullivan as Jane: she always looked like the Hollywood actress that she was, fresh from 'Makeup.' Then one day I opened an issue of National Geographic and, finally, there *was* Jane—Tarzan's Jane! (The famous Hugo van Lawick photo of the gorgeous and gamine Ms. Goodall with a chimpanzee peeking under her blouse, not sexually, but for the bananas she used to carry there to help accelerate the acceptance process.)

She smiled. Taking a blind-stab I had totally lucked-out. Jane Goodall then told me that as a little girl in England her Mum read her to sleep at night with Edgar Rice Burroughs' Tarzan books. Someday she dreamed of being Tarzan's Jane . . . The interview was smooth sailing after that.

The NFL football player, Andre Risson's hero is "Spiderman"—the elusive receiver striking Spidey's sticky pose on the base of the goal post after his many touchdown snags. David Bowie sings: "*We could be Heroes!*" And many are. The most prevalent super hero today is "Wonder Woman." I see her everywhere: American females putting forth miraculous energy while juggling a full-time job, raising children, and being a loving, supportive wife. Third-World women are the strongest super-heroines of all: carrying firewood and other burdens twice their body weight on their backs; making something out of nothing for their children, often with no support from a slacker husband snoring away under a shade tree.

And there are animals, certainly heroic in my eyes, who actually use X-ray vision in real life. Whales and dolphins see with sound. While studying killer whales off the coast of British Columbia and swimming with dolphins in the Florida Keys, I realized that there is another intelligence on this planet that equals or is, quite possibly, superior to our own.

In controlled studies with captive cetaceans, blindfolded, solely with their sonar (streams of sound sent into the water through their lower jawbones, bouncing off an object and the echoes returning to their brains as "sound pictures"), they were able to distinguish between submerged plates of copper and aluminum: infinitesimal differences in thickness. There is now something magical going on off the coasts of Florida and the Bahamas: "Dolphin Therapy." Wild dolphins, of their own volition, with no manipulation by man are free-swimming with people. The human beings they are often most attracted to are the physically or mentally challenged or pregnant women. How and why? With their sonar they can full-body-scan themselves and us, and what Plato called "the creature with the perpetual smile" seems to enjoy putting that same 'wrinkle' across our faces! And it goes much deeper. A boy with an inoperable brain tumor, who had totally shut down, closed up in his darkened bedroom, silently rocking back and forth—as a last resort, his parents brought him to Florida. He reluctantly entered the water. For a few days a dolphin "adopted" him and brought him back to life, so much so that the boy was speaking, smiling, laughing, alive again. In another case, in connecting with a mentally challenged girl—not having an itinerary (yet someone knowing) the last day when the girl was about to leave, the dolphin gave his pal a parting gift—diving down to the bottom of the sea and bringing up an emerald strand of seaweed, that he lay across the girl's open palm.

After lecturing on a cruise ship about Dolphin Therapy, a woman came up to me crying, with her teenage son. "Micah is autistic. He didn't speak—until we took him to Hawaii where people swim with wild dolphins. One dolphin singled Micah out and worked with him, and Micah came out of that water, talking excitedly! We are so fortunate to have him in our life," she said, putting her arm around her beaming son, "for we learn something new from him every day!"

After researching and meeting Dolphin Therapy 'patients,' I'm convinced that dolphins help to heal humans by lovingly revving up our vibration levels; set our chakra wheels spinning on higher frequencies, a form of "psychic-surgery." Bottlenose dolphins have bodies that weigh up to 600 pounds; humpback whales, 40 tons, but despite such massive size they are totally buoyant in saltwater: if you swam up to one, with one finger you could move that tonnage around. Afloat, it's as if the cetaceans have shed their solid bodies and are free to then to vibrate on the astral plane. We are weighted down and ravaged by gravity, what Jacques Cousteau called the true "Original Sin": when our progenitors, first forms left the water for land—unlike the whales and dolphins (who evolving from terrestrial creatures), ultimately opted for water over land. Do they know something that we've yet to even ponder, let alone discover?

Whales and dolphins have been on this planet for ten million years; man approximately one million, and the jury is still out whether we'll last much longer, for the byproducts of our life, all the toxic pollution is devastating the environment. People say: "Ah, but we're so much *smarter, more evolved* than the whales and dolphins because we build buildings, have culture, create art." But in the long run, are we smarter? Could it be we are measuring intelligence from a narrow, egocentric perspective? Could it be that the cetaceans have no art— because they do all things beautifully? That it's built directly into their life: That they sing when they speak; dance when they swim; paint when they breach on moonless nights with phosphorescent plankton in the water? And most importantly, they've never broken their umbilical cord to the Environment, to Mother Earth. In search of an advanced "extraterrestrial intelligence," we might do well to look no further than our own oceans.

Just three centuries ago, man believed that the Earth was the center of the Universe. Then after an Italian named Galileo looked through one of the first telescopes, he insisted that the Earth and Man were *not* central to the Universe— that we revolved around the Sun. For this landmark discovery, instead of being made a hero, Galileo was denounced by the Catholic Church as a heretic and imprisoned.

That egocentric attitude, to this day, continues to influence the way we think; the way we treat nature and the animals—as 'lower' life-forms, subservient to man. How arrogant of us to think that we are better than any other species we share this planet with.

As we're entering a new Millennium, if we change our thinking: throw off the narrow constricts of ego, and the paralyzing controls of religion and science we will see animals for what they really are—and it will be an Age of Enlightenment and Amazement.

The dominant, rational Scientific viewpoint should now expand to include the Intuitive and Spiritual if this planet is to survive. Science doesn't have all the answers. Scientists always believed that whales live in the wild 50-60 years. But since 1981, Eskimo whalers have found harpoon heads made of stone or ivory embedded in the blubber of arctic bowhead whales they subsistence hunted.

Recognizing that these harpoon points were from a much earlier time in the Eskimos' culture, scientists ran an aging technique by testing amino acid levels in the eye nucleus of the bowheads. Four whales were found to be more than 100 years old; one at 180 years. And how much longer would the whales have lived if they hadn't offered themselves up to the hunters up at that point-in-time?

Another new dimension came into view one day in a very ordinary way. (Where most 'secrets' reside. As Sherlock Holmes advised Watson, when looking for clues: "The best place to hide something is in plain sight.") I was sitting in a small plane on an airport runway for the third and final flight of the day, on my way to give a speech out in rural Texas. From a window seat just behind the left propeller, I looked up from a book, casually watching as the four black blades of the prop began to turn; then spun into a blur as the plane zoomed down the runway. Once airborne and leveled-off, up to speed, it suddenly hit me that what Famke and others had been explaining (about the extraterrestrials and astral entities being invisible, "off the screen" of our eyesight, by moving at a faster vibration or speed), I was now seeing demonstrated before me.

As the four individual propeller blades spun at top-speed for half-an-hour they became invisible. I could see right through them. They were there-but-not-there. The blades were certainly propelling a multi-ton aircraft across the sky, but right through where the blades were actually whirling I saw blue sky, clouds, distant green fields uninterrupted, all of a piece. When we landed, with the propeller slowing its spin as we taxied down the runway, the black blades reappeared. When we came to a complete stop, there they were again—four solid entities. Yet, up in the sky, their whirling speed had cloaked them with invisibility.

Later that night, after the speech, in my hotel room I read from the poet Richard Purdy Wilbur's "Love Calls Us to the Things of This World": *"Outside the open window/ The air is all awash with angels."* It was no longer a flight of fancy. I now was convinced that the air could be awash with angels/astral beings, for possibly with their own 'cellular propellers,' they are vibrating faster than our limited eyes can see.

As I was interacting with Famke and Sonia and devouring metaphysical texts, I noticed that the hardest box to burst out from was opening the Mind to the 'strange' and 'foreign' here on earth. Imprisoned by the limited self, we cling to the familiar and are threatened by the alien (the crux of racism). We look only for what reinforces our own attitudes and beliefs and shun what challenges them, when, instead, we should be purposely seeking-out and embracing the different, the opposite to become complete beings. In this stage of accelerated growth, I now wanted to smash open that locked-box, discard the limiting ego and let all the world in, no matter how different or threatening it might appear at first glance.

In my reading, I now turned most often to the cultures of India, China, Japan, the Jewish Kaballah—at first, because it made mathematical sense. Anglo-America is roughly 200 years old, still in a pioneer period compared to cultures that extend back for thousands of years. It simply stands to reason that those cultures may have had enough time to transcend materialism; delve deeply into the human consciousness and surface with sagacious discoveries. Sure, at first, the strange new vocabulary of *chakras, kundalini, apsaras, golem, dybbuks* takes some getting used to, but I soon began to see that no matter how far-afield, we're all really on the same page. Jung called it "Collective Unconscious," Emerson "The Oversoul" . . . that each human soul is a sparkling cell of the same cosmic body. In India, you greet a stranger with the word, *"Nomaste"* : "I bow to the Divine Universe within you."

We, Americans, are so isolated in our thinking; wrapped-up in we're-number-one-nationalism that, of all the countries on earth, our students score worst in Geography—unable to even locate the unavoidable Pacific Ocean on the map; and the Way of the Tao, the path to spiritual fulfillment has been superseded by the Dow-Jones Industrials. The height of one's stock market investments, rather than the depths of one's holdings within are the measure of success. The one American that I kept reading and rereading was Henry David Thoreau, he of soul-*universalis*. So many of Thoreau's statements continue to ring, centuries later, with clarion truth: "In wildness is the preservation of the world." "Let your life be a friction against the machine." "Beware of any enterprise that requires new clothes." And then I met one of Thoreau's modern-day male progeny, (with the 'mother' being of Pagan descent)!

Famke called and asked if she could come out for the Spring Solstice and could I find a spot to have a small outdoor celebration and she'd like to bring a friend? "I want you to meet him. He's a Witch."

"A *what?!*"

"A *Wicca*. You'll see!"

For the next week, my imagination ran wild. *A male witch! Isn't he called a 'warlock?' What?! Does he wear a cone hat and eat toad-soup? And fly around on a broom! No, probably since he's a man, bigger, it'll be a tree trunk . . . . And what will the neighbors think?*

In the meantime, I pondered a place for the solstice celebration. While scanning a map, looking over the many splendid choices that northern California offers, it didn't take long before my fingertip tapped The Pt. Reyes National

Seashore: 79,000 square acres of preserved coast lands, bays, and estuaries only a 30 minute drive north of San Francisco, but worlds away. High, forested ridges plunge down to surf-pounding ocean. Red-tailed hawks patrol the fog-washed skies; gray whales migrate under the lighthouse on a promontory jut; the largest pinnipeds in the world: elephant seals with two-foot long inflatable noses and harem bulls weighing 5,000 pounds with pink callused chest-shields haul out on the beaches at Chimney Rock; a herd of five hundred Tule Elk, a native California species, graze amidst wildflower-splashed meadows; Great White Sharks ride wide-body tides into Tomales Bay. Pt. Reyes was named by Spanish explorer, Sebastian Vizcaino, who first sighted the headlands on The Feast of Three Kings (*Reyes*), January 6, 1603. Many subsequent ships were wrecked on the alluring shoals, for the peninsula's outcroppings are often erased by "thicke mists and stynkinge fogges" as Sir Francis Drake complained when he visited the area during his circumnavigation of the world in June 1579.

After doing weekday business in San Francisco I often returned home over the Golden Gate Bridge, dipping briefly into Pt. Reyes—parking out at Limantour Beach with a hot latte, a hand and soul warmer from a bakery in the gateway town of Pt. Reyes Station. Mark Twain once wrote: "The coldest winter I ever spent was a summer in San Francisco!" The fog is the Bay Area's natural air-conditioning. I'd burrow my bare feet down in warm sand; sip coffee, while being chilled to the bone by thick billows of fog, with the horn at the lighthouse emitting a plaintive groan to offshore mariners. Fog is produced from a clash of contrasts: the water temperature along the coast is lower than the ocean farther west, and when the warm moist air moves east over the cool coast the "thicke mists" are born. After just 15 minutes of standing out on the edge of incubation, I then jumped back into the car feeling totally renewed, mentally washed clean.

At Pt. Reyes, along with baptisms in the fog, I had galloped horses in the surf; kayaked the lagoons; hiked and ran many of the 140 miles of trails throughout the preserve and always came away happy and high.

Two of my favorite people in the whole world lived atop it all: Nory and Jacquetta Nisbet. She is Scottish and a direct descendant from the poet, Robert Burns; he, formerly the British personification of a stiff upper lip and life: an upbringing in a lordly manor (Harperley Hall, complete with servants) and English boarding school with all its inherent horrors, and a fighter pilot with the Royal Air Force flying Thunderbolts over Germany during W.W.II. Now in their 60's, they lived high atop the Inverness Ridge in a pine-wood aerie on a forested acre, complete with separate studios. Jacquetta was a weaver, her studio dominated by a large upright loom that looked like it could also play Bach harpsichord music—by itself. The high walls were covered with skeins of yarn in elongated coils, dazzling Navajo blankets, backstrap-woven Peruvian belts and purses, and Jacquetta's latest creations: soft sculptures of lizards crawling the walls—inspired by the residents of the Keet Seel ruin in Arizona. It was one of the few times Jacquetta had gone three-dimensional and expanded her earth-tone palette to include metallic threads of turquoise, gold, and amethyst. I was drawn to the lizards, eyeballing them up-close, convinced they were breathing and swore I saw a forked pink tongue dart forth! A reminder quote on the wall, described the weaver to a 'T': "Form is shaped by the spirit that inhabits it."

To balance long stationary stints at the loom, Jacquetta volunteered at the Morgan Horse Ranch down the hill in Pt. Reyes, a working ranch for the horses used by the National Park Service rangers for back country patrols. Morgans, the first American breed of horse are thick of neck, deep of chest, with the sweetest of dispositions. Jacquetta's favorite was "Kitten," a mare that she exercised for hours (swelling J's spirit) over the mountain and seaside trails.

Nory, a graphic artist and the former editor of the magazine "California Living" for the combined Sunday San Francisco Chronicle and Examiner newspaper, released the first stories of the blossoming of the Hippie Culture in Haight Ashbury in the early 60's and gave many writers a start, such as Frank Herbert of the *Dune* tomes. Now 'retired,' he designed books, catalogs, credit cards, gardens, and wrote magazine and newspaper columns on gardening, his true passion. The man not only had a green thumb but fingers and toes, as well! His own garden was something to rival the magical Findhorn, with beans climbing to the clouds, zucchini as large as elephant trunks, and he was always pressing upon you surplus bags of exotic surprises like purple potatoes from Peru. No drapes on the large, sky-filled windows and the house was exquisitely perfumed by outdoor heather and lavender bowers high and low; and 'outside' was brought inside by such cuttings afloat, center-table, in a thrown pottery bowl.

No matter where I was in the world, I would fly in to spend New Year's Eve and day with Nory and Jacquetta. The last night of the year we would stay up well past midnight, sipping wine, and as we lounged back on large throw-pillows woven by Jacquetta into multicolored clouds—we'd float away in deep conversation. Our words became birds and the hours flew by in the excitement of melding Minds. The next morning, in celebration of how we originally met (at the finish line party of The Dipsea, the second oldest foot race in America behind the Boston Marathon, that goes from Mill Valley to the sea), I would jump up from my bench bed, put on my running shoes and slip out the door, flowing down, down the ridges to the cold, crashing ocean. I'd fling a beach stone out into the sea with all my yearly resolutions pressed into it; then climb arduous miles back up the mountains to their pine-aerie, where Nory was pouring the fresh-squeezed and Jacquetta already had two hours in on the loom.

From their U. K. beginnings, they had both come so far, not only to coastal California, but immeasurably within. I had never before met a couple (especially in the showy "Golden State") that measured success by the unseen: how much you possessed within. There was no lavish furniture or impressive knickknacks in their house. Everything was built-in—so people stood out. Nory and Jacquetta had worked on themselves, did "hard labor" for years; after trying various disciplines became serious Hindus, studying for long stretches under a Swami whose last name ended in "*ananda*" meaning bliss. And it all showed. Unobstructed, their souls glittered up in their eyes. Although nearly septuagenarians, there was not a wrinkle on their faces, and their short, compact bodies were as firm as stone. They greeted each day with meditation and yoga; then Jacquetta set the tone(s) for the day by playing a flute to call the Koi (colorful Japanese carp) to feeding time in the small deck pond. Nory looked like and emanated the wisdom of Yoda, the "Star Wars" sage (George Lucas' Skywalker Ranch just a few miles away).

Then they would contrast their soul-searching-Hindu-seriousness, with a bawdy side, howling over a lusty joke that would make a crow blush. "And you know, Michael, how you love women so," Nory would grin, "well there actually is an order of Buddhist monks that believe you can attain *nirvana* solely through orgasm!" "Now that order," I responded, "I'd shave my head for!" Despite all their talents and accomplishments both were totally self-deprecating and Nory, especially, had a whimsical honesty that took your mind to places it had never gone before, much less imagined. Living in Marin County, California ("Land of Hot Tubs and Peacock Feathers!" one national TV special entitled the place), Nory and Jacquetta had good-naturedly gone along with all the new fads. During the era of "body work," Nory, suffering from a bad back, decided to get Rolfed— a series of fascia realignments administered by a very capable, trained therapist. After the fourth session, with millenniums of memories stored in muscle, now released under the rolfer's spade-like hands, Nory had gone deep, way back— regressing into a primal beast. "Starving, on the way home, I pulled into a bakery. Right after the session I started feeling very strange—like my extremities were changing . . . I began losing track of myself while driving. I was convinced that I was sitting on a long tail, my forehead elongating, and I had to keep looking at my fingers, for they suddenly felt like raspy claws on the wheel. Inside the bakery, I'm eyeing a fresh cinnamon roll, and out of the blue, standing in line, I suddenly made an abrupt stabbing motion with my head, convinced I could spear that roll with my 'beak'—I was so certain I could reach it; then flap large leathery wings, flying out of the place! It lasted about 16 hours, and even though the mirror showed plain old Nory, I knew exactly what it felt like to be a pterodactyl!!"

A dinner party at N & J's was a mixed salad of people you couldn't find unless you picked through the entire world, but the dazzling melange was just an impromptu throw-together of local "ridge people": Neighbors from across the road, he a computer engineer and building their house with hand-tools on weekends, she getting her Ph.D. in Philosophy, her treatise: "The Appearance of The *Doppleganger* During Paranormal Experiences and Extreme Sports"; A couple of cutthroat lawyers, criminal and corporate, who melted into baby talk about their herd of woolly llamas; Gay lovers, Steve with an antique business and John, a Pt. Reyes park ranger (his sexuality kept way undercover); A Hollywood Film Director, a progenitor of the "teen-scream" genre; An Indian shaman who lived in a teepee on an ocean bluff in nearby Bolinas (where the residents are so private that they continuously tore the town's highway sign down) and who was helping Nory replace widespread invasions of foreign, parasitic plants with original natives throughout The Pt. Reyes Seashore; A sexual therapist working with Nory on his elocution to help his big audition as Host for a new TV series on Gardening: (She was advising him "to breathe through his groin"); and Sandy Kaufax's ex-jet-set-wife now studying Peruvian weaving with Jacquetta. The conversations were so stimulating and fulfilling that oftentimes I forgot to eat.

I stumbled across an underlying reason why people live so intensely near Pt. Reyes, one day, while running through Bear Valley. I strode along the Earthquake Trail and at one spot, stopped to straddle the San Andreas fault, standing simultaneously on two separate tectonic plates. Pt. Reyes is literally a 'land apart.' With the San Andreas fault active for the past 30 million years, the peninsula has moved about 280 miles up from the south. The rocks and soil originated in southern and central California; and sliding northward at 2" per year, if the plates hold their present course, Pt. Reyes will eventually collide with Alaska. Standing astride that cleft separating the peninsula from the mainland of California, I could see why residents here had an island mentality and knowing full-well that the lightning-shaped fissure could flash outward at any time—lived as if there were no tomorrow. The complexity of the residents was reflected at "Five Brooks," an area named for a wild pattern of streams. As the result of the spastic San Andreas fault, two parallel currents, only a few yards apart, flow in totally opposite directions! If "Anatomy is Destiny" might local geography manifest our moods?

Most impressive about Nory and Jacquetta was their dedication to their arts. No poseurs or hot-tub talkers, these. There was time to play and mostly time to work. When Jacquetta was preparing for a show, I wouldn't see them for a month. Then at a toney Bay Area art gallery, opening night, with many of the patrons overly-patronizing—we'd be off in a corner getting irrevently smashed together. On the wall, Jacquetta's "Artist Statement" said everything that needed saying about her work (and their combined commitment to attaining higher consciousness): "The path of the Native American weaver is as complex, varied, beautiful and arduous as the routes of the many migrations from the Arctic Circle to Cape Horn. It is simultaneously idealistic and practical, and expresses the integrated nature of Native American cultures of both hemispheres where religion, art, and daily life are all of one cloth—inseparable. Over the last four millennia it has evolved the most sophisticated and elegant weave structures imaginable, particularly in Peru.

"For 35 years I have studied, analyzed, and deeply admired the work of these master weavers, and sought to learn from their attitudes, and skills—to go beyond the narrow concept of time, and to work in the spirit of the oneness of all life."

Jacquetta, being a Master Weaver, was often invited to give workshops all across the country (even by the Navajos, themselves, who wanted her to re-teach a few forgotten techniques). As much as she loved Nory, she also enjoyed driving away on her own, camping solo deep in the Canyon lands and staying with Navajo friends in their simple hogans throughout the Southwest, the very soul of America. You could always tell when Jacquetta had just returned from such a trip, for the white schooner clouds, lavender buttes, pinon pine smoke worked their way into the warp and woof of a new work on her loom or additional bold dragons flamed-up her studio walls.

With Jacquetta about to embark upon one of her peregrinations, she would call, asking if I'd come up for the weekend to keep Nory company? At first, we would do "manly chores" that Nory had saved-up, like bucking wind-toppled trees into firewood; digging out a new septic tank; widening the dirt road to their house, joking all the while how we should be in loincloths and face-paint and passing a 'talking stick' as, just then, "Wild Man," male-bonding weekends in the woods were all the rage. The catalyst for such celebrations was the poet Robert Bly. In his great book *Iron John*, he hit a nerve, writing how many men, in response to the feminist movement had overreacted: became oversensitive, soft, and confused as to their true identities and needed to get back to their roots, bang the drum, stir the ancient fires of male brio and vitality. Men had lost touch with their wildness and maleness, mainly due to the Industrial Revolution severing the close bonds with their fathers, now working away in offices when, for generations, fathers and sons toiled side-by-side together out in Arcadia: the fields, the woods, a farm; and that in these shared moments out in nature, it was from his father or another male mentor that a boy learned to be a man; not so much from the individual acts of work, but in the process itself, an overall osmosis like a shared pheromone in the air.

As Bly wrote in *Iron John*: "The ancient societies believed that a boy becomes a man only through ritual and effort—only through the 'active intervention of the older men.'

"It's becoming clear to us that manhood doesn't happen by itself; it doesn't happen just because we eat Wheaties. The active intervention of the older men means that older men welcome the younger man into the ancient, mythologized, instinctive male world.

" . . . During the sixties some young men drew strength from women who in turn had received some of their strength from the woman's movement. One could say that many young men in the sixties tried to accept initiation from women. But only men can initiate men, as only women can initiate women. Woman can change the embryo to a boy, but only men can change the boy to a man. Initiators say that boys need a second birth, this time a birth from men."

I was so fortunate to have many "Iron Johns," a succession of diverse male mentors who shaped my life profoundly: My father and grandfather on our summer farm; Coach Gutbrod on the gridiron; Richard Retterer who paid me double the going rate to work construction with him in Indiana, as long as I spent the money to go to Europe via backpack and Eurail Pass; Bob Lewis, who taught me environmental ethics in Aspen and the inseparable relationship of loving nature and women; Will Malloff who turned a cheechako into a sourdough on a wilderness island in the Inside Passage of British Columbia; Galen Rowell who revealed his Yosemite soul; and now Nory Nisbet, the "Lord of Inverness Ridge."

As much as I adore women, during those weekends with Nory it felt wonderful, so restorative to take a complete reprieve from the delicate truffles of *yin*, to root and wallow whole-hog in a sloppy trough of *yang*! Besides grunting and heaving fallen trees, dirt and boulders around, I had very few male friends I could talk deeply with, male ego and competitiveness, the "my-penis/life-is-bigger-than-your's-syndrome" always estranging you, but Nory, through his spiritual practice, was long past all that. After our physical labors, we'd cook-up some loaded earth-food from the garden; then sit at the table for hours, sipping wine and talking on the deepest, most intimate levels. Of all the men I know he is the most complete and balanced, and a personification of the African adage: "The lion, sure of his strength, is therefore very gentle." (One time, when he decided to both quit smoking cold turkey and to bottom-out his inherited high cholesterol by taking an experimental drug laced with hidden steroids, Nory's male side emerged exclusively. It was a shocking transformation, as if Yoda had morphed into the "Incredible Hulk!" Almost overnight he developed an Ari Onassis barrel chest sprouting wiry silver hairs and displayed it over skimpy, Speedo-like shorts even in the depths of winter. Usually soft-spoken, he bellowed now in loud, opinionated rants, punctuating his harangues with hammer-like bangs of both fists on the table. He insisted on arm-wrestling to see who would wash the dishes. The shy pterodactyl—now alpha ape!)

The next weekend visit, with Nory over and apologetic for his 'roid-rage and back to normal, at midnight, we went for a hike to the top of Mt. Vision. As we climbed, with the trail illuminated by a full moon, fog poured in from the ocean, filling in all the Pt. Reyes valleys and isolating the highest ridges into celestial "islands" from Chinese scroll paintings. We heard a Zen *satori* rustling sound as the streaming fog brushed against dry pine needles and chaparral leaves. "This is how they drink," Nory said, cupping a bristly cluster. "Not much rainfall here, only about 11 inches, so the rest of their moisture comes from the fog."

Up on the summit of Mt. Vision, I said that I knew I was in Pt. Reyes, yet this night it looked to be a completely different place, with the fog lathering away all but the high ridge-tops and the tiny summit we were standing on. That night we started a discussion that continues to the present day. Seeing Pt. Reyes from a totally new perspective, we talked about the perception of reality. "What happens to you is solely because of you," Nory stated enigmatically.

"What do you mean?"

"You think reality is outside, separate to your existence. Rather it's just the opposite—it is created from within. Frame by frame, you are both the director and the projector of the Movie you call 'Life.'"

"So, you're saying that nothing is random or accidental?"

"Precisely."

"That's hard to accept!"

"It shouldn't be. Try it and you will see your life change dramatically. When I was your age, I didn't believe it either. But then after hearing our Swami say these same things, I decided to put them to the test. First, I got myself into a place where I was 'In the Light'—glowing with positive energy and seeing myself and everyone else as the divine gods that we are. Then I went about my daily business, at work, at the magazine, with the same people I had judged harshly, disliked or did battle with, but now those barriers absolutely melted because of what I truly projected these people to be and they responded in kind, for they had no choice but to react in the roles that I saw them as. For nine blissful days, by totally shifting my reality, I created 'Heaven' on earth! The challenge is to live that way all the time."

Total conversion didn't happen overnight. It was an ongoing discourse. I called Nory from the airport, just back Africa. "I saw kids starving to death. Did they project that from within—or is abject poverty totally circumstantial?"

"While unborn, they chose their parents and are now working-off their karma. As hard as it is to accept . . . . "

"How can you say that—with flies buzzing around their eyes!" I hung-up frustrated at his unflinching resolve and constant equanimity.

I called from Hollywood, about a far more trivial matter. "They didn't buy the movie Treatment . . . the fourth studio to turn it down. Maybe I just can't write for the screen."

"You explained why you were rejected right there."

"What?"

"It's not the material. *You* are stopping the sale. Get over your doubt. Unless you first believe 100% in the project, no one else will. As the Swami said: 'The wind is always blowing. All you have to do is raise the sail'—get your belief up."

Many times I growled in frustration. Nory always turned it back on me, to my own failing within.

Another time, while hiking along the surf-plowed Limantour Beach, Nory pointed to a tall rock, a sea-stack with a hole, an open 'window' cut clean through the center. He told me that as surely as fluid water carves through solid rock— so, too, do our thoughts shape our beings and the very reality around us; that our thoughts are not intangible and ethereal. Rather, they are the most powerful force in the Universe, creating solid effects. Nory made it very clear, as clear as the hole in the rock, that we are not the victims of circumstance, but with our daily thoughts—the very architects of our own lives.

I'm so blessed to have Nory and Jacquetta as spiritual parents. (And I wasn't the only one to sense such a relationship. Just before a public slide show I gave after returning from China, a woman in the audience turned to Nory, whom she didn't know at all, and said, "*You* must be Michael's *father!*") I always felt totally humbled and awed in their presence. They are so highly evolved that if reincarnation means returning to this plane again and again until you get it right, then N and J are on their final go-around.

Like most loving parents, at times, they practiced "tough love." During one visit, I was the deserved subject of an Intervention. After another delicious dinner of homemade lentil soup, coarse brown bread, a crisp California chardonnay, Nory glanced at Jacquetta for assurance, then spoke: "Michael, we have something to say to you, but we're taking a big risk. You may walk out of here and hate us forever, but it's a chance we have to take. Knowing you now for seven years, we've seen a pattern with you and women that you must break . . . . " They then ran through, female by female, many of whom I had brought up to meet them, how and why the pre-Cosmo relationships ended.

Sitting there listening to my stinging litany of defeats, I squirmed, felt angry—then the blinders finally fell from my eyes and I saw the pattern I had repeated over and over: always dating a woman who needed my "help," who was deficient in some way: *She was abused by an alcoholic father and now suffers deep-rooted psychological problems including repetitive alcoholism? No problem! I'll marry her and my love will solve it all!! . . . . She has Epstein-Barr disease and has spent the last year in bed? No problem! I'll put her on vitamin and exercise therapy; and if that doesn't work I have enough energy for us both!!*

"Michael, what you've done is admirable—if you were a trained psychologist or qualified physician and they were your patients. But not for a personal relationship. We've never seen you with someone on your own level," Jacquetta said.

"O.K., so just how do I find Ms. Right? " I snapped out defensively.

"You create her," Nory said.

"What?" I said incredulously. "Don't tell me that we materialize a mate from within!"

"Yes, precisely," Nory said, giving his best Yoda grin.

"Forget that b.s. about Cupid's Arrows," Jacquetta chimed in. "Or just sitting back and letting Fate be the 'Hunter'—that's all romantic balderdash that only happens in the movies. It's all about 'mirroring'—what we have inside, what level of growth we are on, that's the person, the 'Other' we create. We draw a mate to us, by first sketching them in our soul with our own thoughts and actions."

"Michael, it's time for you to change your M.O., break away from your repetitious pattern. Stop trying to dominate, which is what you are really doing, which creates an imbalance that always ends in defeat. Just like in tennis, if you want to really learn how to play the game, choose a partner on your own level, or better yet, someone who runs and stretches you all over the court!"

My anger and tense defensiveness eased. Deep down, I knew they were right. The session ended in comforting hugs and grateful tears.

Than a few days after the Intervention I read from one of the most sagacious souls on the planet, Marianne Williamson in *A Woman's Worth*: "The lover is who appears before us as we emerge from the shadows of our own delusions . . . . Love is not something that comes from someone else; it is an extension of our own minds, reverberating back to us."

The love and wisdom from Nory and Jacquetta and then reading that statement—it all came together in a "Bingo!" moment. From then on I worked on making those inner changes, and sure enough, Famke soon appeared: for the first time returning a love as effortless as breathing; and in the process elevated my game to new levels as with: "When the student is ready, the teacher will appear." It's both wonderful and frightening to realize that we totally shape our lives with our thoughts and actions: wonderful—for we really are in control; frightening—for there's no wiggle room: no excuses, blaming of others, being a victim when we are the very architects of our own lives.

So, with all the past good memories and transformative energy, I knew Pt. Reyes was the place for the spring solstice celebration. And while driving back from the latest visit with Nory and Jacquetta, I found the precise spot.

Famke then arrived, stepping out of the Air Porter van with a man wearing a three piece suit! "Michael—Bob; Bob—Michael!" I glanced over their shoulders, half-expecting the van to then explode as the warlock burst forth—but "Bob" was 'It.'

After a brief visit, Famke said she was starving and would whip-up some dinner and why don't we go off and do something together for awhile . . . . Catching the clear hint, I asked Bob if he wanted to go for a run? We changed clothes and were on our way up into Tilden Park, talking every step of the way.

I cracked him up with my preconceived expectations of what he would be like. Bob then told me his story. "I live and work in New York City, high on the corporate ladder. My office is in the Empire State building. I have a wife and children, and, yes, I am trying to be *wicca* as Famke told you. So is she and from what I've read, so are you. I read your book, *Inside Passage*. Any man that lived on a wilderness island for two years and related to nature the way you did, is *wicca* all the way! The trouble is, Hollywood and organized religion have really done a job against the true concept of 'witch.' An ancient Anglo-Saxon word, it really means 'wise one.' *Wicca* is a gentle, earth-oriented religion centered on reverence for the creative forces of Nature. It doesn't view God as distant, separate from ourselves, but that the Goddess and God are within and manifested in all of nature. Our temples are the forests, beaches, deserts, flowering meadows. And we don't cast spells on people, we only do rituals to gain power over the self and to honor the Divine."

"But how on earth did *you*—excuse the expression: a corporate 'suit' become a witch?"

"That's O.K. Programmed like most men, I was driven to be a 'Success.' And I did well at it: the corporate job, big house, fancy car. But when I had it

'All' I then realized that I really had nothing, for, in the process, I had lost the most important thing in the world: my soul. Deep down there was an unfulfilled part of me that was starving amidst the riches—knowing that there had to be far more to life than what I was experiencing. I then started to simplify my life, pare-down, getting rid of some of the trappings; taking vacations alone to sacred places like Machu Picchu and Stonehenge and reading book after book on spirituality, one leading to another, and that's how I came upon *Wicca*, and then met Famke and so many other incredible people who are practicing."

"What a transformation!"

"Well, it's still going on. I still wear suits and sit closed-up in an office, but in a desk drawer I keep my cauldron, tarot deck and pentagrams! The air freshener hanging from my car's mirror is a pine sprig I pick every weekend up in the Catskills. There's a peregrine falcon nesting on the ledge of a skyscraper across from my office. Some days, right from my desk, I look up from spreadsheets to watch him nail pigeons at over a hundred miles an hour! I'm working toward evolving a life where I am practicing full-time. My dream is to start a healing and education center somewhere deep in nature."

"Why are you so different from what I thought you'd be? I mean what is it exactly, behind the fact, that when people hear the word 'witch,' the knee-jerk reaction is 'batten-down-the-hatches-and-hide-your-daughters-here-comes-the-Devil?'"

"The practice of paganism predates Christianity and Judaism by thousands of years. It's really based on shamanism, the very first religion that recognized and worshipped Spirit in everything. Then Christianity came along and in an effort to gain control they basically did a smear campaign to eliminate the pagan world. They turned the great god Pan, since he already had horns, into the Devil and the world of nature spirits into evil fiends. In the 1500's the Church accused all of nature's caretakers: the witches, gypsies, alchemists of being Satanists, and that's when the blanket cover-up and persecutions began. The Devil never existed until Christianity invented him to gain the upper hand!"

"Wow! Never knew that . . . . You know, as I think about it now—what the church did in Europe; they did with missionaries around the world, and that same attitude was sent over here to America. 'Only to the white man was nature a "wilderness" and only to him was the land "infested" with "wild" animals and "savage" people. To us it was tame. Earth was bountiful and we were surrounded with the blessings of the Great Mystery.' One of my favorite quotes, by Luther Standing Bear."

"That's it precisely. And so effective was the smear campaign that's why, when you hear the word 'Pagan' or 'Witch,' to this day, you subconsciously associate it with dark, demonic forces—when, in reality, the very opposite is true! Luther Standing Bear knew. He and his people lived powerfully and nobly with the Great Mystery out in nature, not 'wilderness.' The word 'wilderness' occurs about 300 times in the Bible, and each time with a derogatory meaning, so no wonder the Europeans who first colonized America were brainwashed to that way of thinking. Who were the pagans, the witches, the gypsies, the alchemists in the New World? The Native Americans! And what the Church did originally was launch a 'dual campaign.' . . . There's a famous statue, I'm sure you've seen her: 'The Venus of Willendorf?'"

"Ah, 'Big-Mama'—with the large breasts and wide fertile thighs!"

"Yes, that stone figurine, only a few inches tall is thought to be the oldest art object in existence, and evidence of the Great Prehistoric Goddess going back to somewhere between 30,000 and 70,000 B.C. From then and leading up to Christianity there were thousands of cultures worldwide, not just in Europe, worshipping a Mother Goddess and for tens of thousands of years. It's only been in the last two millenniums, that male-dominated religions have taken hold, but look at the damage, the havoc they wrecked. Not only did the Judeo-Christian ethic try to squash Nature: but to topple the Goddess, subjugate women, as well. It's why we are in the mess we are, with the environment ravaged, our ecosystems near collapse. It's imperative that we get back to the Source; to throw off this brainwashing, these man-made religious constrictions and controls. I don't know about you, but I only hold two things in life sacred: nature and women, and I view them both as being one-and-the-same. "

I was stunned. I was learning more from this "evil witch" in a half-hour than in years at a university. Bob was amplifying, affirming so much of what I had recently been thinking and struggling with. Now I knew why there was such excitement in Famke's voice. She knew I needed balancing, to experience Spirit in a male vessel. He was a total stranger who helped introduce me to my true self.

"When I lived in the Inside Passage of British Columbia," I responded, "I learned that many of the native peoples are matriarchal. The women own the land and run the show. I quickly learned there's reasons for that. Out there on that island, in those powerful, capricious forces I quickly discovered that 'male ego' has no place. If you try those old male attitudes of 'Conquering the Mountain' and 'Defeating Nature' you, yourself, will be defeated. Rather to survive, a man must learn the feminine principles of *harmonizing* with the world; *blending* with the natural forces; *nurturing* inner and outer resources. Many reasons why it's called 'Mother' Nature. And no coincidence that the Environmental and Feminist movements started at the very same time. As a journalist I've seen in many countries worldwide that men tend to treat Women as they do the Earth. It goes hand-in-hand. In central Brazil, where it's *muy macho,* the rain forest is being raped wholesale and women are treated like third-class citizens. In Scandinavia, where men revere nature, women are elected to the highest political offices in the land. In parts of rural Africa, women are laborious beasts-of-burden while men sleep the day away, getting up to poach elephant ivory. I've seen the correlation in place after place. It's *impossible* for men to both honor women and, at the same time, disrespect the Earth."

"Yes! That's so right on. But, you know, there's hope. The tide is starting to turn. Even the physicists, when they go all the way back to the beginning, to examine the 'Big Bang' or go deep within the smallest particles like muons or gluons, *'inside'* the inside they find a sort of consciousness there—a spark of Spirit directing the Show. And you'd be surprised how many physicists are becoming *wicca*—because of what they're discovering."

"So, it isn't a childish, overly-simplistic way to view the world that science dismissed for so long—that 'uneducated,' indigenous way of seeing Spirit in everything!"

"No, and the native peoples around the world knew that without ever having to look through an electron microscope. They knew it intuitively because there never was the 'disconnect' created by the Judeo-Christian ethic. They were living in such a manner that Nature, herself, was teaching them directly: 'The Circle Unbroken.' There was a lesson in every cloud. And that 'childish,' pagan, sacred manner is the way to view life if man is to have a future. By taking apart the atom, the building block of life, Science has finally proven to itself—that all matter is really what the 'savages' said it was: Spirit or condensed light. When you recognize Spirit in all things, you can't destroy life, not in the slightest way. There's a story about Oppenheimer, the 'Father of the Atomic Bomb'— who after watching the first one explode in a test at Alamogordo, quoted Hindu scripture, the *Bhagavad Gita:* 'If the radiance of a thousand suns were to burst into the sky, that would be like the splendor of the Mighty One;' then as the enormous mushroom cloud rolled up, darkening the day sky: 'I have become Death, the shatterer of worlds.' He never got over it. I still think of that close-up portrait of his face in Life magazine right before he died, with the bulging, absolutely haunted eyes. There's a story that Oppenheimer was walking in the woods with another scientist and they came across a beautiful painted turtle. Oppenheimer picked it up, thinking he'd take it home for his son, but after walking a few paces, he then turned around and put the turtle back in the same spot he found it, saying something like: 'I have disturbed enough . . . .' It's all about living spiritually attuned now to Nature or we won't be here for much longer if we don't start practicing that reverence in a collective way. Wasn't it Thoreau who said something to the effect, 'What's the use of building a new house, when you don't have a tolerable planet to put it on?'"

Back at the apartment, Famke had a glorious meal waiting: *pasta primavera*, so apropos for our celebration of spring: the angel-hair pasta adorned with sun-dried tomatoes, black olives, and bits of feta cheese, all washed down with a tender Beaujolais Nouveau—perfect fuel for a coven of *wiccas*!

After dinner, Bob and Famke packed a few things for the ceremony while I cleaned up the kitchen. Bob proudly showed me his small black cauldron, about the size of a softball—but very heavy, in many ways. Famke came out of the bedroom wearing a beautiful, full-length white dress, trimmed in lace. She looked like a bride.

We then drove west toward the setting sun and the Pt. Reyes National Seashore. Nearly there, Famke had me stop under a grove of giant redwoods. She and Bob got out and soon returned with a "wand"—a tapered redwood stick and bits of bark that looked more like fur.

The specific site I picked for the solstice ceremony was *Kule Loklo,* the replica of a Miwok Indian village before European contact. The Miwoks were the First Nation along the northern California coast, hunters and gatherers, and kudos to the park system for, at least, preserving a bit of their culture. To get to the abandoned village, inside the refuge, we left the car in a parking lot and walked a quarter mile on a dirt trail through the forest. Famke was barefoot and held up the bottom of her long white dress as she walked. As we moved through the woods without flashlights to give us away our eyes adjusted to the darkness, and accustomed to trail-running at night I was "on point"—leading the way, bounding out along the trail.

Famke giggled. "Michael, in a past life you had to be an Indian, a scout!"

"Yes!" Bob replied. "The way you move over a trail is really something to see! It's like you're going 'Home.'"

I shrugged. "There's something about a trail . . . it just takes me over—tugs me along!"

We emerged out of the woods into a clearing with different examples of restored, coastal Miwok buildings.

"Wow! What a place!! You can feel their vibe still here," Bob said.

We headed for a wickup: a large tee-pee-like structure made of bark-covered boards, and respectfully entered through an open doorway.

"Perfect!" Famke said. "And look at *this*! Just what we need!!"

Off in the corner was an old stone bowl, an original Miwok mortar with a heavy pestle resting inside. They got to work: Famke grinding herbs in the mortar then transferring them to Bob's small black cauldron; Bob setting out candles on a low stone altar. The lodge was open at the top; a fire-pit behind us in the center. We looked up at the stars and then the moon appeared, momentarily flooding the lodge with silver light. Famke then sprinkled pinches of the ground herbs from the cauldron, along with bits of redwood bark at the sides of the lodge, and Bob waved a smoldering, sweet-scented sage bundle around—to cleanse away any evil or dark influences. With the redwood stick Famke then drew a circle around us in the dirt floor. She turned to face me; took my hands and opened-up her heart, telling me of her personal feelings. In spontaneous response, I then did the same. She turned to Bob and verbalized a sisterly love. His response seemed a bit strained, as if caught off-guard.

Famke then began the formal ceremony, saying aloud:

"The presence of the noble Goddess
extends everywhere
Throughout the many strange,
magical,
And beautiful worlds
To all places of wilderness,
enchantment, and freedom.

(Bob lit a candle and placed it on the circle's edge, NORTH.)

"The Lady is awesome.
The powers of death bow before Her.

(Bob lit another candle and placed it, EAST.)

"Our Goddess is a Lady of Joy.
The winds are Her servants."

(A lit candle, SOUTH.)

"Our Goddess is a Goddess of Love.
At Her blessing and desire
The sun brings forth life anew.

(A lit candle, WEST.)

"The seas are the domains of our Serene Lady
The mysteries of the depths are Hers alone."

(Famke ceremoniously waved her "wand" from North, clockwise around to North again.)

"The circle is sealed and all herein
Are totally and completely apart
From the outside world,
That we may glorify the Lady whom we adore.
Blessed Be!"

(We all repeated):

"Blessed Be!"

(And recited together):

"As above, so below

As the Universe, so the soul.

As without, so within

Blessed and gracious one,

On this day do we consecrate to you

Our bodies,

Our minds,

And our spirits.

Blessed Be."

Then we meditated silently for a few minutes. *The power of those ancient words!* I felt them resonate, rev-up my vibratory levels; send the chakra wheels spinning!! Famke then finished the last four lines of the Invocation:

"Our rite draws to its end.

O lovely and gracious Goddess

Be with each of us as we depart

The circle is broken!"

We then gathered our things and walked in silence out into the night. Nothing dramatic had happened. The magic was subtle, yet powerful. Striding alone with our thoughts through the forest, I felt like I didn't end at my skin; that I continued on into everything. The ego was gone; the slate wiped clean during spring renewal.

"Congratulations!" Bob said to me as we then walked side-by-side, with Famke up ahead.

"For what?"

"I've been in love with Famke ever since I met her, but hid it behind being her 'Best Bud.' I know her Heart, and most of the reason I came out here was to see this Michael she was raving about. I'm very protective of her. But I see the love she has for you and you for her. I envy you, but now know that you two are meant to be One."

As evolved and involved as my relationship with Famke was, it soon ended. Another Cosmo correspondent entered my life and six months later was my wife! *This* I never, ever expected. Just as Famke and I were making lifelong plans, at the "eleventh hour," Paula appeared. It wasn't as if something different caught my attention. Paula could have been Famke's twin sister: they worked for the very same airline; both of Swedish-descent, identical statuesque figures, white-blond hair, ice-blue eyes! Paula was also a mega-woman: a model; TV & Movie

Actress (a reoccurring role in "Miami Vice" and screen-time in Tom Cruise's "Risky Business"); Playboy Bunny (appearing in the magazine); graduate of chef schools, including the Cordon Bleu in Paris; a chef on corporate yachts cruising the Caribbean; "Flight Attendant of The Year."

She lived in Phoenix and, since I was going to be there visiting family over the Christmas Holidays, we agreed to meet for a drink at a "Friday's" bar and restaurant. My brother, Scott, drove me to the rendezvous and stayed until Paula arrived to help steady my nerves, for these ultimate blind dates never got any easier. We arrived before Paula, and I ordered a stiff drink. Ever-gregarious, Scott told the bartender what was about to transpire. The barkeep (a transplanted New Yorker) responded: "Ah, *fagettaboutit* —blind dates nevah work out!" Paula then walked in . . . . The bartender gave a low-whistle.

She was even more beautiful than her picture. *Ohmygod—we'll probably be able to talk, hold a conversation for no more than ten minutes!* (Other than Famke, my past experiences with drop-dead gorgeous models was that all their "prospecting" had stayed on the surface, with very little ore mined within. And a friend in L.A. had just broken up with a major model [a tick down from 'super']. "The only thing we had in common," Ted said, "was we *both* were in love with her!") After Scott chatted with Paula about the modeling business, he took-off, but not before delivering a parting elbow to my ribs and whispered brotherly encouragement: "Don't blow it!"

OK—it's going to be all about Her, I resigned myself, swiveling on the stool to endure the self-centered monologue.

Instead, it was mostly about Camus, Sartre, De Beauvoir, Rimbaud, Chekhov, Tolstoy, Hemingway, Pat Conroy, Paul Theroux, Updike, Roth, Fay Weldon, Ralph Ellison, Anais Nin, Henry Miller, M.F.K. Fisher and more . . . . Five hours flew by and we barely scratched the surface. Paula Louise Grecco had read rings around me; was a junior high Ohio Spelling Bee Champ (bowing out on "o-x-y-m-o-r-o-n " in the finals in Washington D.C.); speaks 'culinary French' (which is most of the language); and has yet to lose at Scrabble. "Had to deal with it all my life," she said. "It's the 'Marilyn Monroe Syndrome'—not that I'm anywhere near even approaching her league, but men just can't see past the outer package to what's inside. Marilyn got caught in that web, fatally. Lee Strasberg, the acting coach of many stars, said that, of all his pupils, Marilyn Monroe had the most talent. Too bad that gift never got a chance to free itself of the outer wrapping."

When Paula got up to go to the Ladies Room, the bartender leaned-over: "Man, you lied—if that's a 'blind date' then I'm a Cherokee Indian!"

"Bye, 'Chief,'" I grinned, sliding off the stool and walking out with Paula.

Then totally bewildered by her sudden appearance, I tried to push Paula away: Actually telling Famke on the phone, while in Paula's presence, that I loved her! . . Asked to borrow money from Paula; then flew off to Toronto, Canada to do a national TV show and have sex with a Cosmo Girl/Host in the back of a limo and all over town: the condensed version of "Man Behaving Badly"—but Paula wouldn't go away. No matter how horribly I acted, she was somehow on a "Mission." As with most females, she foresaw long before what the male didn't, but later learned to be right and true.

And her offers were irresistible. "Want to go to Aruba for lunch?"

"Where? Aruba . . . Pennsylvania?"

"No, dummy—Aruba . . . as in Caribbean paradise island. There will be a Buddy Pass waiting for you at SFO's 'willcall' window . . . . "

It was outrageous: Feeling like I was playing hooky from life, itself, my bare feet were soon in the sand of Aruba, as I sipped a coconut concoction—with Flight Attendant Grecco, sans uniform, sauntering slo-mo across the beach like Bo Derek!

"How about Paris for the weekend?" And Rome and Madrid and Rio . . . we went, and fell in love. Paula flew, not just for the money, but to quench her hunger to see the world. Many flight attendants are nicknamed "slam-clickers," for no matter how exotic the locale and how long the layover, once off the plane they slam their hotel door and click the lock, only to emerge 20 hours later to re-board the plane. Not F.A. Grecco. Despite being up all night, caring for 300 passengers on a 747, once her feet touched the ground she was off-and-running, and, like two commandos raiding foreign cities with backpacks full of guidebooks, foreign dictionaries and maps, we plotted our course as we went along, filling every minute with adventures. (With Paula bubbling over with enthusiasm about wanting to visit Moscow, another flight attendant turned to her and said, "What's the big deal? That place is so *old!*" "It's called 'history,' hun!" Paula replied.)

As serious and studious as she was, I had never been with a woman who made me laugh so much! From her close observations of the full range of human experiences in the "Friendly Skies," she could have easily been a professional, standup comedian. She had both the material and the delivery. Two samples: "I was working the Inaugural flight from Houston to Tokyo, the very first one for our airline. I was stationed up in First Class—full of Japanese. They are the absolute best passengers, so well-mannered and polite. The meal service went very well and then I walked around with the small dessert menu. Well, everything was written in Japanese, and if you get one 'arm' on one of the calligraphy-like characters wrong, disaster may ensue. And that it did. Upon looking at the menu, everyone, male and female, covered their faces with their hands, shrieking in loud voices: 'Ohhhhh *NOOOOOOO!!!*' Everyone—with the same horrified reaction! The main entrees, like Sushi, were well received and we even did their traditional tea service; the passengers were so impressed—so how could the desserts, just the listing, be *that* bad?! Finally, I went back into Coach and showed the menu to our Japanese Translator. All the blood fell out of her face. Dumb struck—with one hand, she pointed to a word on the menu; then her other hand pointed to her crotch . . . .

" 'NO!' " I said.

"She bobbed her head up and down, too shocked to even speak.

"Sure enough, it turned out that because a few errant characters in Japanese had slipped by the proofreader: 'peach cobbler' took on a whole new meaning!

"To make matters worse, there were more flights to Tokyo on the way—with the very same menus aboard, so I had to alert Operations back in Houston immediately. Once we landed in Tokyo, I ran off the plane; finally figured out how to use the phone system and got the International Supervisor on the other end. I knew him; we had flown together in the past, and as with some males who are flight attendants, he was gay. I'm then frantically telling him that he has to tear-up, shred all the dessert menus; and have them reprinted correctly, immediately because—because . . . then I just suddenly got tongue-tied.

"'*What*, Paula? What does "peach cobbler," the way we have it, mean? Just spit it out!'

"'It means . . . PUSSY!'

"There was dead-silence on the other end of the line, then he said: 'I don't know anything about it!'

"'Yes—maybe that's part of the problem!'

"They got the menus corrected and despite that terrible first-impression, after that, the flights to Japan were all full. Men being men, those inaugural male passengers probably went back to their corporate travel planners and said, 'Switch our account to this airline! You won't *believe* what they serve for dessert!!!'

"Then another time, in First Class, I was serving a black family. Their skin tone was the darkest I had ever seen. Just as I was wondering where they might be from, I noticed that the man's wine glass was empty, so I went back to the galley and picked up a bottle of wine in each hand and walked over to him near the front of First. 'Sir,' I said holding out the bottles, 'would you like white or black?'

"I almost *died!* Everyone stopped talking and eating—their forks frozen in midair. It was like all the air went out of the pressurized cabin and out of me. I was *so embarrassed*—I wanted to disarm the door and jump!

"But, thankfully, the man had a sense of humor and knew it was just a slip of the tongue. He laughed and then everyone else did . . . . I apologized over and over and then once I knew he was O.K. with it, I told him it was 'a blond moment' and he patted my hand and told me they were from Nigeria; and then all throughout the flight he kept teasing me, asking for some more of that 'black' wine; and that he was going to open a winery specializing only in that color; that maybe I was on to something! He was a good sport about it. I don't have a racist bone in my body, but in this day and age of everyone being so sensitive and quick to litigate, that could have been the end of me and the airline."

Putting growing emotion aside, from a practical point of view, I felt the choice came down to this: If I stayed with Famke, I feared that as great as the spiritual experiences would be, that we would simply float-off into the ether, both of us wanting to do nothing else but constantly "go there," with no one grounded in the material plane (which I then really needed to dig into: at a crucial turning point in my precarious career as a freelance writer and public speaker). If I chose Paula, with her intelligence, scintillating personality and marketing skills: a public relations genius (whom I called "P.T. Barnum in a skirt!") I felt certain that my career would zoom, but the paranormal experiences would likely stop. I felt totally overwhelmed, unworthy to be drowning in such riches when I was still so impoverished inside and out, and such confusion caused me to think in a drastic, simplistic manner: narrowing it down to a choice between one extreme or the other.

I finally chose Paula, and tried to be worthy of her (and worthy of the opportunity to even have a choice at all). Now focused, I went all-out to make-up for the shaky start, putting into practice all I had learned about pleasing a woman from the "Cosmo-School-of-Correspondence." With a mutual commitment, our love rapidly grew and deepened: but only after a deserved period of being put on trial—demonstrating that I was really ready to settle down, give-up all the widespread feminine attention, which I really wasn't comfortable with from the get-go. But even then, I failed miserably, though not my fault. During the week or so between Paula's visits, the phone would never ring once, but then the day she arrived, even if only to stay a few short hours on a layover, it was as if her mere arrival launched a long-distance satellite into space and calls started pouring in from past paramours one-after-another, nonstop all evening!? Paula answered the phone crossly, again and again, with me shaking my head in utter disbelief stammering: "I swear— it's just not like this all the time!" But she remained unconvinced. Searching desperately for a solution, I then suggested that we change the message on my answering machine, with her voice and recording of finality then putting an end to that chapter of my life—

(now expanding into my first novel, *Men Don't Understand*, but could just as accurately be entitled *Heart Attack!*)

Success in real estate may depend on 'Location, Location, Location!' but, as the Cosmo Girls taught me, in matters of the heart, it's 'Romance! Romance!! Romance!!!' Early on with the mail pouring in, a male friend, a total techno-geek, who made his living as a computer programmer, setup a database of all vital statistics, including region of the country the correspondents were from. I wasn't interested in age, measurements, and hair color, but was intrigued as to where the most mail was coming from?

Gary clicked a few computer keys, then announced: "The South—by a margin of 4-to-1!"

Curious, I picked up a letter and called Robbi from Atlanta, asking for her take on the geographic discrepancy. "Michael, that's easy! We all grew up on *Gone With The Wind* and we're look'n for Rhett—a man who's very romantic and a tad bit reckless to come sweep us off our feet. But, today, he's an endangered species. A woman is far more likely to meet 'Bigfoot' than Rhett Butler! Men use romance, at first, to hook us, but then after a few months that well runs dry. Just remember, sweetheart, foreplay is what a man does all day!"

I paid attention and got busy—making romance a top-priority, "Job 1," and in the process discovered that it wasn't work at all, a total joy and downright fun to please a woman, to be the reason for that increasing love light in her shining eyes! In Paula's own words, in a letter to Redbook Magazine: "Here's why my husband, Michael Modzelewski, should be included in your upcoming 'Sexiest Husbands in America' feature: With my journalist husband, I've discovered that 'Wedded Bliss' is not an oxymoron. Being a flight attendant, I'm able to flex my schedule to join Michael on his wild assignments all over the world—and he always makes time for us, in the most surprising and romantic of ways.

"We've made love in the Amazon jungle under Angels Falls; and in a sleeping bag filled with wild flowers that he had picked all day while training for a marathon in the California mountains. When apart, he keeps up a steady stream of erotic e-mail and faxes, and more than once, when I check into a lonely hotel room after a hard flight, I'm soon beaming over a 'Treasure Hunt'—Michael, previous to my arrival, fills the room with hidden notes and romantic gifts, one leading to another . . . culminating with him waiting in a bubble bath, two glasses of chilled champagne in hand! His marriage proposal really won me over. It was a total surprise. He had secretly made a 40 foot banner (on the backside of butcher freezer paper) with 'P.G. WILL U MARRY ME?' painted across in big red letters, and then covered the rest of the paper with pictures he cut out of magazines and other things pertinent to our life. Dressed in a tuxedo, he flew ahead to an airport he knew I was arriving at for a layover. In the gate area, he had the passengers, waiting to board, hold up the long banner and then as I walked off the plane, he got down in front on bended knee. I walked right by him and the sign, for I had taken my contact lenses out just before landing! Another flight attendant pulled me back and with my nose nearly touching the scroll, I read the message; then burst into tears, and all the passengers applauded . . . . And now by our very existence, I'm becoming the person I've always dreamed of being: a lady with no limits, who can go from High Heels—to Hiking Boots, often in the same day!"

Invited to appear on Oprah, "How Couples Meet In Unusual Ways!" we flew to Iowa, of all places, to do a live-show in the shadow of a covered bridge in Madison County. At that time, Robert James Waller's novel *The Bridges of Madison County* was all the rage. Waller and his wife (the real-life "Francesca") were the centerpieces of the show, with six other ancillary couples from all across the country with real-life stories to tell. Oprah did the lead-in, (as, under our names and faces on the TV screen flashed: *She Calls Him 'World's Most Romantic Man!'*) Oprah then asked in her inimitable way: "O.K. Michael, of all those letters, how didcha pick Paula?" There had been no rehearsal; we were 'Live.' *Mygawd, how to answer in a twenty-second sound-byte?* "Because she didn't really need me. I don't know if it's because girls are brought up on fairy tales of being helpless in a tower, waiting for their white knight to appear—and a lot of the mail was like that: 'come rescue me', without bringing much to the table themselves, but Paula was so successful in her own right that it was more like 'Strength meeting Strength!'"

The audience applauded; Paula kissed me, Oprah sighed, then gave me a thumbs-up as we cut to a commercial. But most of all, I walked off the set full of silent thanks—to Nory and Jacquetta who loved me enough to dare do that Intervention, showing me the error of my ways—opening the door to present happiness.

As it turned-out, my hunch was right: Paula did take my career to new heights; I was successful financially beyond what I thought possible, and the tradeoff (for awhile) proved to be that we didn't share any of the paranormal experiences. I was convinced that Famke was the key; the required catalyst; and that I couldn't experience that world now by myself or with Paula . . . which was soon proved wrong. Again, the limits were my beliefs.

Acting now as my full-time Manager and Agent, Paula landed me a gig aboard a cruise ship as the Naturalist, with repeated summer sailings through the Inside Passage to Alaska, the home of my deepest being. I have to go to the wisdom of the Chinese to describe the place. It is the total *Tao*, a dynamic equilibrium created by the harmony of opposites: female *yin* (the fluid ocean) and male *yang* (stalwart mountains). Some places have mountains, but being landlocked don't have ocean; other places like the Caribbean have ocean but no (major) mountains. But the Inside Passage has it all—a world in complete balance for it combines all the dramatic geographical elements: towering 15,000 foot mountains, massive glaciers 50 miles long, fiord-deep ocean—all counterpointed by islands, hundreds of forested islands, arranged like varied-shaped thoughts in a stream of consciousness.

I gave four lectures per cruise to hundreds of passengers from all over the world on the scenery, glaciers, wildlife, Native Americans. How wonderful to speak about a place with the very topics looming into view right outside the windows! But it was no longer enough to spout scientific statistics: "The Killer Whale is 20 feet long and weighs 12 tons, blah, blah, blah." Statistics and dry facts only snag us on the surface; barriers to an animal's deeper meanings. On stage, I went out on a limb, trying to move past the superficial to include intuitive and spiritual perspectives; and in doing so, the presentations became infused with Heart-Energy. While talking for a full-hour, I was taken over: as if I was a conduit, a channel that nature flowed through. It came *through*; not from me. My job was to keep out of the way, keep the stream free of obstructions such as ego and pride. My voice changed; and I often heard myself say things that I didn't know that I previously knew! The effect on the audiences was dramatic. As they rushed up immediately afterwards, there were hugs and tears and amazement that I would dare talk on such a level. But there was no choice . . . not when, in Antarctica, the retinas in the eyes of penguins have been burned-out from the hole in the ozone; not when, after the "Exxon Valdez" spilled twelve million gallons of oil into Alaska's pristine Prince William Sound, there were screams from dying sea otters—their silky coats clotted with crude oil, my dreams haunted by those chorusing screams, by our insensitivity to all of God's Children.

Each successive program went deeper, wider. The last program on the Native Americans and their spiritual connection to the magnificent coastline of British Columbia and Alaska really soared. Knowing, ahead of time, the content and reaction of the audiences from weeks/cruises past, one week, the night before giving the final talk, I was in that totally relaxed Alpha/Eureka! state in bed, hovering between wakefulness and sleep, subconsciously conscious, when I flashed-out an invitation: *I've been feeling your presence close by, so tomorrow why don't you ('They') join us in the theater, when our collective vibrations are raised up to your speed?* It was not a wish, but a telegramed Invitation—flashed outward like a pulse of thought-lightning. (Famke had told me that spirits want to interact with us; and will—if we increase our vibration level and simply invite them in!) I then fell into a deep sleep, feeling warm-honey happiness pervading every pore.

The next morning, before the program, I thought nothing more of it. And then as the hour progressed, "It" was especially 'On'—juicing outward through the speaker far more than normal. Afterwards, I sat totally emptied, yet so full at a small table alongside Paula and we conversed and hugged people and signed books. A long line of passengers . . . tears flowing . . . hearts open: the vibration level definitely sped-up and sky-high. I saw the end of the line of people, but no, missed one . . . . A woman approached and instead of standing across the table for a book—she sat down in a theater chair directly alongside me. As she leaned forward very close to sit down, I suddenly felt dizzy, that pressure again pushing at my temples. As her blouse swung toward me, it was the most amazing shade of purple, amethyst that somehow wasn't "limited" to the tunic. The color was oscillating; not at all bound by the cloth, but somehow shimmering outward in tight, undulating waves. She then spoke: *"I can't believe I find you here—on the ship. You are touching human hearts; opening minds—it's wonderful what you are doing!"*

At that, Paula looked up from doing paperwork and her mouth fell open. To say the woman had spiritual presence was an understatement, to say the least. It was as if she was nearly "All Spirit." I couldn't find her eyes. When I tried to bring them into focus, they just weren't clearly defined (very liquid/limpid). Other things seemed strange: her complexion wasn't just pale or white, it was callow—like a waxen candle. And her hair was on crooked, somewhat askew. It was a thick mane, a wild tangle of tresses, but the front hairline seemed slanted. She then stood-up to walk away, saying more about the program. "And you too," I responded. "You keep doing it too, with your life—for I see it around you!" I said, making a swirling hand gesture as if sensing her aura. At this, her head snapped back a bit, startled that I "recognized" her. Then, incredibly, we both did the very same gesture at the exact same time: placing our hands together in the upright prayer/respect/honoring you position and bowed with our heads as our hands dipped . . . only, since she was standing, her dip of the hands lasted longer and turned into a wavelike flow and curtsy from the waist that raised the hair all over my body and thrilled my soul. It was an ancient Dance, a thousand years old, from the depths of India or straight off the temple wall of Angkor Wat. Then, she was gone.

Paula, previously skeptical of all things outside the norm, was up on her feet saying "WOW! WOW!! . . . Who was THAT?! She was certainly *Woo-Woo!!*"

(Her word for spiritual/paranormal things not understood or experienced, firsthand, herself.) But for the very first time, there was nothing the least bit cynical or derogatory in her tone. I was too stunned to reply . . . .

From the moment I saw the oscilating amethyst, reality seemed to shift, open into a new dimension. Just like Sabrina, she seemed to have 'slipped in from the side,' as if normal reality was happening, but she was there, somehow, in addition to it. Paula and I said no more about it, for we then got caught up in many things the rest of the day.

Then that night, after both of us were in solid-sleep for a few hours, we woke up simultaneously at 2:00 a.m.—wide awake—and talked about the "Visitor" for three hours straight. It was as if our subconscious minds needed the time to assimilate the experience, but now, in the middle of the night, the fountain flowed forth. Before I said anything, so as not to color Paula's impressions, I first asked her what she saw. She spoke excitedly, in a tone I had never heard before, like an awed child, and her description of the woman, of her not being quite "all there," finished or fully actualized matched exactly what I saw and even more so, for women discern details; can deconstruct the physical appearance of other females far better than men. We just keep talking and talking about it, deeply awake.

"Awhh, maybe we're getting carried away," I then said. "Maybe she's really on the ship."

"Michael, does it matter if she's on the Passenger Manifest or not? Whether she's from another world or this one . . . Spirits walk among us, *are* us!"

That shocked me. The tables had totally turned: I was now the Skeptic; Paula the Believer! (And since the passengers were all due to disembark in just a few hours, my only way to check would be to stand at the gangplank and stare at everyone getting off.)

I sent out accounts of the experience to close friends, asking for their interpretations. Sonia Sierra-Wolf (now married to physicist and metaphysical author, FredWolf), wrote: "Remember it's not really about reliving the experience or making sense out of something we may not have the constructs for. What is important is the indelible mark it leaves on the psyche and that the message may not be immediately apparent . . . My take is that you have come face to face with the lunar twin archetype of your being. That part of you that is not the creative impulse, but that part of you which takes that impulse and gives it form. On another level you, or the ship passed through what may be called a tear in the fabric of our reality and for a brief moment in time you were able to discern the 'angelic' beings that coexist with us. Remember the Kabbalists taught that there are two angels for every blade of grass telling it to grow. Energy must assume a form we can understand if it is to teach us .... Remember Spirit needs us in order to experience, as we need spirit in order to not forget what we are made of ...."

One day, at home, I was organizing some papers when I found the message from Sabrina. I decided then and there to try the same thing, the "automatic writing" to see if the Visitor would answer as directly. I picked up a pen and held it over a blank sheet of paper. I slowed my breathing, concentrating on emptying the mind, relaxing deeply. I returned to that feeling of melted-honey happiness, the night before the final speech on the ship, when I first flashed-out the invitation. Once I was centered inside that emotion of unlimited love, and rapturous unification, the pen began moving—only this time words were not forthcoming, but circles: small globes covered the paper, orbs all touching; that when looked at together, all-of-a-piece, formed a larger circle. Thinking it was just a warm-up doodle, I got out another piece of paper and tried again .... Again, no words, just circles.

After Sabrina's precisely worded message, I felt disappointed and impatient, as if expecting the automatic writing to always be automatic! This time it wasn't—or was it?

A few nights later, a strong sea breeze was puffing through the house in Floirda. The reason I love living close to the tropical ocean is *plein air*: having the windows open all winter for the trade winds to blow through. Under a window there were tall vertical stacks of books waiting to be shelved. A book atop one of the towers suddenly blew open—the pages flapping like sails. I walked over and picked up a long-forgotten tome of essays by Nietzsche. Two sentences jumped-off the opened page: *"One should have more respect for the bashfulness with which nature has hidden behind riddles and iridescent uncertainties. Perhaps truth is a woman who has reasons for not letting us see her reasons."*

Two phrases resonated in my mind as I went back to bed: *"... truth is a woman who has reasons for not letting us see her reasons"* and *"iridescent uncertainties."* Unable to sleep, I got out of bed; snapped on the light above my desk and pulled out the drawing of the circles. The word *"Iridescent,"* now seemed like a descriptive clue .... As I examined the drawing, suddenly, as if seeing it for the very first time—the small orbs were pearls, a continuous necklace of lustrous, iridescent pearls. I sensed that they were, indeed, a *"riddle"* of sorts: Unlike Sabrina who came through in 'plain English,' could it be that the Visitor communicated in the more ancient language of symbolism?

I began to think "sideways": *What is a pearl but a form of Alchemy ... Nature turning a basal sand particle into a gem?* And there on the page, I interpreted the strung-together-pearls as the attempt at writing words. It showed the process of creation, itself: The Visitor saying that I should use my own transformative powers and tell this story—no longer bury it inside, but fling open the closed shell and offer it to the outer world.

It was the answer, the sign, the reassurance I had long been seeking and because of the Visitor's message this book is now in your hands.

Previously, I shared the paranormal experiences with just a few trustworthy friends, not daring to write them down for publication because of one reason: *Fear*. Fear, not of the experiences, themselves (rapturous all!) but fear of being thought crazy: fear of no longer being taken seriously by a disbelieving public from whom I earn my living by writing and speaking. Even though my senses had clearly perceived the experiences and there were witnesses (Famke and Paula) to the majority—I hesitated, avoided, even, at times went into complete denial about them, falling back on the more familiar security of my rational side that smirked: *This-is-the-way-it-is-and-the-only-way-it'll-ever-be: the-low-down-dirty-and-never-ever-get-any-better-daily-world-around-you.*

However, staring at those 'pearls,' I now felt emboldened. Since I knew this New Territory to be real and true, I could no longer hide its existence. And once you discover *Terra Magnifica*, you want to visit often and then definitely move in; live there! I knew I was on the right path, for I always felt that Ultimate Reality was best described by Henry David Thoreau: "Our truest life is when we are in our dreams awake."

I don't consider myself a psychic or gifted with any special clairvoyant powers. I am a normal human being who merely stumbled upon birthrights given to us all. As we are entering a new Millennium, it is time for what Sabrina called "The Changes": time for man to make that quantum leap in consciousness; maximize our potential; and in doing so, manifest our full destiny.

Guided by (and living for) the appearance of the directional glow-sticks, we pass more aid stations—not chancing a stop now; lifting trembling water cups on the run, forcing the liquid down, so sick-and-tired of the very act of drinking, but knowing full-well that if we don't stay hydrated, our blood will thicken to sludge; and one leg cramp could end it all.

My body is leaden, numb; synchronicity—long gone. That effortless, circular flow of energy between Scott and me is now all one-sided. I'm staying five yards behind my brother only because he is 'towing' me. He's somehow summoned fresh energy on his own, and like a famished cannibal I greedily feed off of it, allowing his life-force to tug me along—but then even that bond breaks and I fall behind . . . farther back until, for the first time, Scott is out of sight. Strangely, I am happy. My attitude going into today was like climbing Everest—the entire expedition is considered successful if only one member makes it to the summit and I'm now certain that Scott has the strength to finish.

Then at that very moment of resignation, as I'm coming to a dead-stop—I hear Scott shout: "A ROAD! WE'RE ALMOST THERE!!"

I punch it; pouring out of the woods onto hard pavement—soothingly flat and even. The blistered bottoms of my feet now strike the surface all-of-a-piece. "Where?" I ask, peering down the road, expecting to see the Rose Bowl on the near-horizon—lit-up and shining like an edifice out of Oz.

"Dunno . . . . " Scott says. "*Damn*—should be seeing it by *now!* That chalk arrow back there, coming out of the woods pointed left . . . . " The way he glances at his watch now requires an act of bravery.

It's a surreal shock being back in civilization. Suddenly dropping out of the wild mountains down into Pasadena proper—everything appears so controlled; grid-like, and overly illuminated under street lights. It feels like we have been away a year instead of a single day. We come up on people, like phantoms in the streets: early risers out walking dogs.

We startle a middle-aged woman leashed to a growling schnauzer. We slow to a crawl. "Rose Bowl?" I mumble, chopping my words, for it even hurts to talk.

"You guys in that crazy race?"

When we nod, she relaxes. "Read about it in the papers. You've really run all the way from Wrightwood? Go for it—the Rose Bowl's just around the corner, less than a mile away!"

We speedup in anticipation; then soon fade, with precious energy lost to anger. More than a mile later, frantic, we ask/demand the distance from another man with a dog.

"Oh—hmmm . . . I'd say a good three miles yet . . . . "

It is our fault for not recognizing the "Threshold Guardian(s)." One of the most important stages of any Quest is having to get by the monster who guards the final gateway to your goal. Threshold Guardians are not always monstrous in appearance. They appear in many forms (often seductive) with the most dangerous existing on the psychological level. Just as with everything this day (this life) the final Chimeras to overcome are of our own making, and it's our fault for openly inviting them in. We should know better than be obsessed with the exact, remaining distance. But in our weakened state, we desperately need something tangible and final to latch on to.

I continue searching the skyline . . . nothing. Then, "What's that?" I ask. We read a distant sign: JET PROPULSION LAB. "Sure wish we had some of that," Scott sighed. Then a chalk arrow on the road to the right. We follow it under a culvert and then uphill to another road, every 'anthill' feeling like Annapurna. Finally topping the rise, we nearly slam into a parked van—with Dad and Joanne inside.

"THANK GOD!" Joanne exclaims, looking both shocked and overjoyed. Dad leans across her: "I just said, 'If they're going to make it they have to get here within the next two minutes' . . . *YESSS!!*"

Joanne's face then looks worried. "But you gotta go. You got to run like never before!"

"WHERE'S THE DAMN ROSE BOWL!!" I bellow.

"Just follow!!"

We then face an ultra marathon runner's absolute worst nightmare. After running 99 miles, and feeling totally whacked, we now have to *sprint* the last mile to buckle! We try to increase our pace, but it's like going back to the bank for money when you already know you're overdrawn . . . . We watch the van zoom away, away, away . . . *stop, dammit, stop!!* Then finally: a tiny speck, anchored in the distance.

I sense Scott is hurting. I pull up alongside his right shoulder. *My turn!* I have absolutely nothing left in my legs, and my feet are raw hamburger, so I run with the only thing left: my arms—pumping them like pistons faster and faster, dragging my legs along; eyes locked onto the van that never seems to get closer—as if we are stuck running in place. Scott "hooks" onto my shoulder and we gulp great chunks of air now from the night, our lungs laboring like forceful bellows. Even though I'm straining with every fiber of my being, a part of me still has that buoyant body-smile: marveling at *how many times our lungs have contracted during this day! How they miraculously convert air into energy!!* But are they still frothy pink balloons or besotted now with all the flotsam and jetsam of the day: frost, dust, and free-radicals—the byproducts of oxygen intake that 'rust' the cells like a sliced apple exposed to air? My breath rattles on the way out, as if sliding over obstructions. The ancient Greeks thought that the lungs, not the heart, were the center of *pneuma* or life-force; the region of the *thymos*, the blood-soul, the very essence of the self. As our breath whooshes out over and over again into the night, it's as if we are no longer bodies, but solely *that breath*, itself, swinging in-and-out, back and forth—the seesaw rhythm pushing us down the road.

Suddenly—Dad, standing, waiting; his feet moving up-and-down. Then facing us, he windmills his arms—motioning us to make a turn. We do and glance ahead: 100 yards away is a glorious sight—the finish line banner fronting the fabled Rose Bowl.

Then-and-finally-*There!*, with The End in sight, perception comes in slow-motion . . . . Across a grassy expanse, 30 years removed from the NFL, Ed "Big Mo" Modzelewski sprints through time, a fullback high-stepping over the open-field, leading his sons to the "goal-line": a One Hundred Mile Touchdown. At the same moment, unplanned—Scott and I fling our arms across each other's shoulders and speed side-by-side under the arching banner, the digital clock flashing **23:47:20**. We cross the finish line in a grateful delirium, arriving more dead than alive.

Dad engulfs us in his arms and we slump over together into a huddle, holding each other in utter disbelief and relief: 13 minutes away from an exact day from when we started running, and now, finally . . . motionless. Our bodies are in shock, all systems struggling to downshift to a sudden and complete stop. Bent-over, in a hoarse whisper, Scott announces: "That was the *toughest* thing I've ever done!" A race official leans-in: "17th out of 160 runners. Congratulations!"

As Scott and I are led away to the medical tent for monitoring, Dad faces the media. "This is my Super Bowl! Seeing my sons put forth such Superhuman effort—I couldn't feel any prouder than I am right now!!"

Our 'vitals' are identical: blood-pressures: 108/75; resting pulses an even 50 beats-a-minute; weight 170 (down only 4 pounds from the start). Now, for the first time in 24 hours, I am separated from Scott. A nurse leads me away . . . . Lying back on a canvas army cot, I watch a doctor's face grimace as he removes my shoes and then with a scalpel, gingerly proceeds to slice crimson socks out of deep blister craters. I finally let go: turn my head to the side and cry—not from the pain but from a sudden flood of feelings—way out beyond the confines of words.

* * *

Just as there is no sleeping the night before you run 100 miles, there's no sleeping the night after. You would think that after such an all-consuming effort, you'd immediately pass out into a catatonic state at the mere sight of a mattress, but the body, exhausted as it is, can not switch-off twenty-four hours of constant movement all at once. Just like if you drive a car across the country, pushing the pace, averaging hundreds of miles a day, when you stop at night, lying anchored in a motel bed trying to sleep, you feel instead as if you are in continuous motion . . . . But if you are both the "car" and the driver, it's doubly difficult to shut off the engine, for the fuel, your blood, is now a raging stew of robust endorphins, high-test testosterone, spent hemoglobin, and rushing-to-the-battlefield white platelets that produces an amphetamine-like effect. You certainly don't want to do any more running, but now the analytical mind starts racing. You announce to everyone within earshot as you are led away from the Finish Line on wobbly legs to the car: *"I'll never do this again . . . . Please, if you ever hear me say I'm going to run 100 miles—shoot me!"* But of course, you will run another and another and another marathon after that, just as women will keep having children, for hardwired into the human psyche is an 'amnesiac erasure' that scrubs away lingering memories of pain so that we might fulfill Faulkner's axiom that "man will not merely endure, he will prevail."

Then finally, in bed, hopefully after the amalgamation of re-heated sweat, trail dust, day-old urine, sweet-and-oh-so-sour spilled Gatorade, rejuvenating Flex-All muscle salve smelling-now-like-centuries-old-embalming-fluid, and god-only-knows-what toxins and unidentified isotopes from the deep-mines of the gut—jarred loose and poured out through the racing pores—are all washed away by a gloriously long hot shower or bath. (If the pitch-black bath water of an ultra marathon runner was analyzed under a microscope, nuclear contamination might be declared!) Then adjusting to the blissful reversal: smelling as fresh as a newborn babe, you ease into bed—to then freeze with *rigor mortis* into the first horizontal position you assume as your body suddenly relaxes, totally lets-go. In complete repose, what you've accomplished now has a chance to fully sink-in. Great tides of emotion swell and break over you, creating the deepest sense of satisfaction. But first you have to overcome sheer disbelief: that you are, indeed, actually down in Pasadena, in the shadow of the Rose Bowl! The start, the little mountain hamlet of Wrightwood seems an entire lifetime away and a country distant. Intense satisfaction keeps washing over you in emotional waves, both in your mind and over your body, raising fields of goose bumps on your skin. You feel as if you've been turned inside-out, your emotions laid bare for all to see. And with two of you, your brother doubling the effect, your crew, your family feels it too. There's no need for words: what you've all gone through together today has made feelings telepathic in the small motel room. There's a golden glow, a solar-like-happiness filling the depths of this night. And you try to slow, stay the moment, for you sense that nothing again will ever feel this satisfying: not sex, a promotion, winning the lottery—for the satisfaction is alive and glowing inside of every single cell. It's animal; all-pervasive, totally quenching, and most valuable. For one of the few times in your life, you've paid for something that can't be bought.

Finally, sleep beckons and, once again, you respond with a full-body smile (the 'widest' of them all!) and *"Wagh!"* the sweetest surrender. If you sleep with a mate, the next morning she or he will tell you that even though you crossed the Finish Line the race wasn't completed, for all through the night your legs continued striding by themselves under the sheet; your breath coming in ragged gasps. And when your legs did stop, lying still—it was as if your body was then being electrocuted—spasms quaking outward from your back and legs, flinging you all over the bed. Medical studies have shown that running 100 continuous, mountain miles causes muscle necrosis (death) in the thigh and hip muscles; renal or kidney damage; tendinitis of the ankle muscles (all conditions temporary for the injured tissues regenerate back to normal within a week or two). Even though the body suffers, you gladly exchange pounds of flesh for what fills the spirit. As the old Siberian proverb states: "The wolf is kept fed by his feet."

The day is successful not because we are physically in shape: honed by 30-40 mile runs, high-altitude trained, rolfed for ten sessions (Scott), and carbo-loaded all week. Those factors count, but they are merely the outer "spokes"—not the central hub or vital essence that propelled us. We really ran on Love, the springboard from which human beings fulfill their highest potential, the transcendent state of elevated vibration that unifies us with a Higher Source; and in that unlimited state we can achieve the Impossible. How does the petite woman pickup the massive car to save the life of her child? How does the doctor leap over an eight-foot wall to save car accident victims? How do loaves become fishes; water—wine? How are Miracles accomplished? With Unconditional Love, emanating full-blast from a radiant heart.

On a smaller scale, *Love* covered 100 continuous miles; *Love* overcame fear, bone-deep doubt, paralyzing lactic acid and blowtorch blisters. Love literally moved mountains (an Everestic 19,000 feet of cumulative uphill and 24,000 feet of down). And the Love this day is of the strongest degree: *Familial.* The course of the 24 hours was really determined in seconds, when just before the start, two brothers wrapped hands, dedicating the day to their father; and that triangular connection empowered us to finish—even if we had to run out of our skins.

We are so fortunate to have grown up with a father who showed us life can be lived without limits. Even though in constant demand by the public, he always made time for us and never once pressured his boys to follow in his footsteps. He demanded only one thing: that we strive to be the absolute best in whatever we did. As the very personification of "The American Dream," going from a Polish-speaking boyhood in a tiny Pennsylvania coal-mining town—to being invited to the Eisenhower White House as a college football all-American, Dad told us repeatedly that the four letter word that bothered him the most; the word he would never ever tolerate in his house was: *can't.* We could do absolutely anything in life if we just put our minds to it and go all-out.

(And the special connection with my father continues . . . . Dad recently was outside on his patio rereading my first book, *Inside Passage*, and during the scene of an eagle feather falling from the sky and his son catching it—just then another feather floated down and landed on that page . . . alighting on the open book. The odds of that happening once were incredible, but then to have it happen again, at the moment Dad was reading that very same passage is soul-shaking! After getting over the shock—he snapped the book shut, preserving the magic.)

Joanne, our step-mom, diminutive in size, but colossal of spirit, we now call Coach after her motivating "speech" with a mile-to-go that infused us with a surge of energy when we were totally depleted.

And I discovered that I now have a brother—in the truest sense of the word.

In a single day, the wilderness of Angeles Crest took us through all the peaks and valleys of human nature, and in the process bonded us forever. Scott and I now live thousands of miles apart, but when we want to be together, all we have to do is put on running shoes, seek out the nearest trail and connect: dialed-in by long-distance.

As for the malarial Fever Dreams, Sabrina, Three Tones, Blue Whorls and the Visitor—"this just in": "Scientists have succeeded in making a frog float in midair, according to the magazine New Scientist. The team from Britain's University of Nottingham and the University of Njimegen in the Netherlands also made plants, grasshoppers and fish float and see no reason why they cannot do the same thing with a human. The levitation works by using a giant magnetic field which slightly distorts the orbits of electrons in the frog's atoms." —Roland Sweet, XS Magazine.

And if you have had similar experiences, beyond the "norm," fear not about now coming forth and speaking out, for as the great poet, Rilke wrote: "That is at bottom the only courage that is demanded of us: to have courage for the most strange, the most singular and the most inexplicable that we may encounter. That mankind has in this sense been cowardly has done life endless harm; the experiences that are called visions, the whole so-called spirit-world, death, all those things that are so closely akin to us, have by daily parrying been so crowded out of life that the senses with which we could have grasped them are atrophied. To say nothing of God."

"The land is within. At the end of the open road we come to ourselves."

—Louis Simpson

*"The sweat that had drenched their shirts had dried again.
They did not talk much. They were happy with that
inordinate happiness that comes of exhaustion
and achievement, and which nothing else
in life– no joy of either the body or the
mind–is even able to be compared."*
–George Orwell
Burmese Days

"The mountain, I become part of it...
The herbs, the fir tree,
I become part of it.
The morning mists,
The clouds, the gathering waters,
I become part of it.
The sun that sweeps across the earth,
I become part of it.
The wilderness, the dew drops, the pollen...
I become part of it."
—Navajo Chant

"Whosoever would understand the book of nature must walk its pages with his feet."
—Paracelsus,
Swiss Alchemist

ACKNOWLEGEMENTS

I've been absolutely blessed by the people in my life. *Angeles Crest* would not have been possible without the help and suport of the following: Doug Latimer who taught me how to run 100 miles; my sister Nancy and brother Bruce, the best crew an ultra runner could have; Ken Hamada, Founder and Director of The Angeles Crest 100 Mile Endurance Run; Mom for encouraging me to read; Nory & Jacquetta Nisbet for practising "tough love"; Leigh Roth who suggested to "Cosmopolitan" magazine that I was Bachelor of The Month material; Helen Gurly Brown for totally changing my life with the riches of women; Oprah Winfrey, Faith Daniels, Bill Cosby and Dini Petty for having me on their shows; Susie Carter of "AlaskaMen" magazine for creating a centerfold at a time when I felt anything but that bold; John Swift Turtle who always spoke the right words at the right time; Carol Powers, travel editor at The Los Angeles Times for publishing my early work; Peter Englehart at Outdoor Life TV who sent us to Patagonia; Enrique "El Puma" Gallego, the finest videographer on Earth; Karen Wheeler for her dazzling art and design; Lance Salkind, Cyber-Wizard Supreme; Bruce Palmer at Nike for sending shoes; Tony Grecco, whom at a most appropriate time uttered a line from the movie "Braveheart": "Every man dies, but not every man really lives."; Pete and Ted for holding down the fort at AdventureM, Inc.; Mary Lou Brown, our Angel-on-Earth.

And my deepest gratitude to the many souls and organizations that were instrumental in the development of both author and man: Cynthia Cooper, Ronna Nelson, Rebecca & Fred Latimer, Joseph Query, Fred & Evangeline LeFever, Bill & Pat Dodd, Ann Grady, Karen Craun at RR Donnelley & Sons, Jack Sokoloff, Rich Carp, Elizabeth Pomada, Michael Larsen, HarperCollins Publishers, Dan Bial, Dessa Brashear, Tom & Priscilla Wruebel, Susita Methvin, Steve Parker, Pamela Sihvola, Tony Farrel, Galen Rowell, Yvon Chouinard, Gaia Books, Moe's Books, Black Oak Books, The Grizzly Discovery Center in Montana, The Jackson County Library in Jackson Hole, Wyoming, The Aspen Insitute for Humanistic Studies, Ben B. Franklin, Yvon Fraunfelder, Keith Rosenthal, Paul De La Garza, German Del Sol, LanChile Airline, UltraRunning Magazine, Charlotte Swazey, Colleen Baldwin, Penny Johns, Rob Huebel, Louise Neff, Beverly Pell, Gail Lang, Nonnie & Chris Lewis, Norm & Helen Kline, David Brower, Jim Brandenburg, Keiko Nelson, Robert Carr-Hartley, The Jane Goodall Institute; George Dyson, M.F.K.

Fisher, U'mista Cultural Center, Yvonne Fern, John de Graaf, Peter Hogan, Natalie Henley, Daphne Hougard, Shireen Jonti, Linda B. Kiehle, Dottie Walters, Gerhard Kiesel, Leigh Keller, Leigh Wells, Doug Keister, Royal Caribbean and Princess Cruises, Will Nordby, Paul Spong, Joe Oakes, Luanne Scarbrough, Riki Rafner, Lenore Tuttle, Bob Lewis, Dom Corso, Kay Alderton, The North Face, David & Kathleen Stone, Fred Agree, Norman Vaughn, Joselle McDowell, Rhonda Berman, Kristin Piljay, Tiffany Coleman, James Schwabacher, Dave Horning, Sonia and Fred Wolf, Bill Moose, Jennifer Carter, Joel Hirshhorn, Richard Retterer, Bob & Diane Craig, Bill Gutbrod, John Storey, Will Malloff, Genevieve "GiGi" Lemarchand, Janet Baird, Peggy Merlin and Jim Martin.

And, finally, I would like to thank the following artists for the songs I played over and over while both living and writing *Angeles Crest*. Their rhythms (and sometimes blues) greatly influenced the work: The Rolling Stones *"Start Me Up"* and *"Some Girls"*; EmmyLou Harris *"Born to Run"* and *"Boulder to Birmingham"*; John Denver *"Rocky Mountain High"*; U2 *"The Joshua Tree"* (entire album); Neil Young *"After The Gold Rush"*; Grofe *"The Grand Canyon Suite"*; John Coltraine *"Giant* Steps*"*; Charlie Parker *"April in* Paris*"*; Miles Davis *"Sketches of Spain"*; Enya *"Watermark"* (entire album); Peter Gabriel *"Sledgehammer"*; Bach *"Brandenburgh Concerto No. 4"*; Elvis Presley *"The Wonder of You"*; Louis Armstrong *"What A Wonderful World"*; Billie Holiday *"All of Me"*; Prince *"Kiss"*; ZZ Top *"Legs"* and *"Planet of Women"*; Tom Jones *"You Can Leave Your Hat On"*; Young MC *"Bust A* Move*"*; George Michael *"Faith"* and *"I Want Your Sex;"* Tone Loc *"Wild Thing;"* James Brown *"It's a Man's Man's Man's World"*; BB King *"Nobody Loves Me But My Mother (And She Could Be Jivin' Too)"*; Willie Nelson *"Red Headed Stranger"* (entire album); Dire Straits *"Ride Across The River"*; Wagner *"The Ride of The* Valkyries*"*; Bill Conti & Carol Connors *"Gonna Fly Now"* (the Rocky theme); R. Kelly *"I Believe I Can Fly"*; Steve Winwood *"Higher* Love*"*; Huey Lewis & The News *"The Power of Love"*; Freddie Fender *"Wild Side of Life"* and *"Wasted Days and Wasted Nights"*; Frank Sinatra *"Summer* Wind*"*; Nat Cole *"A Stranger In Paradise"*; Vivaldi *"Four Seasons"*; Jimi Hendrix *"Fire"* and *"All Along The Watchtower"*; Beethovan *"Pastoral, Symphony No. 5"*; Lynryd Skynyrd *"Gimme Three Steps"* and *"Free Bird"*; Bob Seger *"Night Moves,"* *"Against The Wind"* and *"Like A Rock"*; Gustav Mahler *"Songs of A Wayfarer"* and *"Third Symphony"*; Stevie Ray Vaughn *"Pride And Joy"* and *"The Sky Is Crying"*; John Cougar *"Hurts So Good"*; Joe Walsh *"Life's Been Good"*; Ted Nugent *"Great White Buffalo"*; Sonny Rollins *"Cabin In The Sky"*; R.E.M. *"Losing My Religion";* Pink Floyd *"Learning To Fly."*

And, most of all, thank you Paula. You are the Song in my Heart and the Light of my Life!